Fraud Risk Assessment Guide

Measure your nonprofit's ability to detect and prevent fraud with this new online resource.

How prepared is your organization against the threat of fraud?

Designed as a companion to *Fraud and Abuse in Nonprofit Organizations*, the checklists in the *Fraud Risk Assessment Guide* identify many of the most important financial controls and non-financial policies and procedures that aid in the prevention, detection, and deterrence of fraud and abuse—both from within the organization and from external sources.

By using this electronic product, you will be able to:

- Identify key areas of fraud control where organizational policies and procedures can be improved.

- Spot weaknesses in the organization's defenses against fraud and abuse.

- Access a series of 10 reusable checklists to measure fraud detection and prevention success.

Do not delay, start the process of performing a fraud assessment on your organization—and safeguard its resources—today!

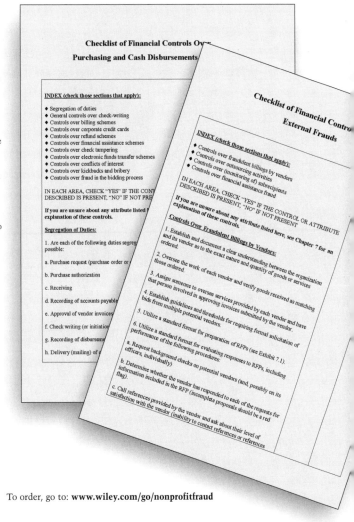

Checklist of Financial Controls Over Purchasing and Cash Disbursements

INDEX (check those sections that apply):

- Segregation of duties
- General controls over check-writing
- Controls over billing schemes
- Controls over corporate credit cards
- Controls over refund schemes
- Controls over financial assistance schemes
- Controls over check tampering
- Controls over electronic funds transfer schemes
- Controls over conflicts of interest
- Controls over kickbacks and bribery
- Controls over fraud in the bidding process

IN EACH AREA, CHECK "YES" IF THE CONT... DESCRIBED IS PRESENT, "NO" IF NOT PRE...

If you are unsure about any attribute listed... explanation of these controls.

Segregation of Duties:

1. Are each of the following duties segreg... possible:

a. Purchase request (purchase order or...

b. Purchase authorization

c. Receiving

d. Recording of accounts payable

e. Approval of vendor invoices

f. Check writing (or initiation...

g. Recording of disbursem...

h. Delivery (mailing) of...

Checklist of Financial Contro... External Frauds

INDEX (check those sections that apply):

- Controls over fraudulent billings by vendors
- Controls over outsourcing activities
- Controls over (monitoring of) subrecipients
- Controls over financial assistance fraud

IN EACH AREA, CHECK "YES" IF THE CONTROL OR ATTRIBUTE DESCRIBED IS PRESENT, "NO" IF NOT PRESENT

If you are unsure about any attribute listed here, see Chapter 7 for an explanation of these controls.

Controls Over Fraudulent Billings by Vendors:

1. Establish and document a clear understanding between the organization and its vendor as to the exact nature and quantity of goods or services ordered.

2. Oversee the work of each vendor and verify goods received as matching those ordered.

3. Assign someone to oversee services provided by each vendor and have that person involved in approving invoices submitted by the vendor.

4. Establish guidelines and thresholds for requiring formal solicitation of bids from multiple potential vendors.

5. Utilize a standard format for preparation of RFPs (see Exhibit 7.1).

6. Utilize a standard format for evaluating responses to RFPs, including performance of the following procedures:

a. Request background checks on potential vendors (and, possibly on its officers, individually)

b. Determine whether the vendor has responded to each of the requests for information included in the RFP (incomplete proposals should be a red flag)

c. Call references provided by the vendor and ask about their level of satisfaction with the vendor (inability to contact references or references

Fraud and Abuse in Nonprofit Organizations

A Guide to Prevention and Detection

Fraud and Abuse in Nonprofit Organizations

A Guide to Prevention and Detection

Gerard M. Zack

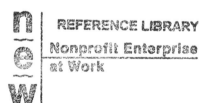
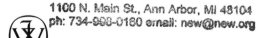

WILEY

John Wiley & Sons, Inc.

Published by John Wiley & Sons, Inc., Hoboken, New Jersey
Published simultaneously in Canada

For general information on our other products and services, or technical support, please
contact our Customer Care Department within the United States at 800-762-2974, outside
the United States at 317-572-3993 or fax 317-572-4002.

Wiley also publishes its books in a variety of electronic formats. Some content that appears
in print may not be available in electronic books.

For more information about Wiley products, visit our web site at www.wiley.com.

Library of Congress Cataloging-in-Publication Data:

Zack, Gerard M.
   Fraud and abuse in nonprofit organizations : a guide to prevention and
detection / Gerard M. Zack.
      p. cm.
Published simultaneously in Canada.
Includes bibliographical references.
   ISBN 0-471-44615-7 (cloth/website : alk. paper)
   1. Fraud—Prevention. 2. Nonprofit organizations—Management. I.
Title.
   HV6691.Z3 2003
   658.4'73—dc21
                           2003002599

Printed in the United States of America

10 9 8 7 6 5 4 3 2 1

This book is for my parents.
To my mother, Marie L. Zack, who is such a remarkable woman.
I could not have asked for a more loving and supportive environment, thanks to your incredible devotion to family.
What an amazing example you set!

To my father, William P. Zack. With an IRS examiner in the house, how could I not develop a desire to thwart the bad guys. Thank you for holding true to the principles of detection of wrongdoing and enforcement of the rules.

Acknowledgments

I want to thank my wife Nikki for so many things that contributed to this book and to my life. In addition to being so supportive and patient, thank you for being my research assistant and a valuable reviewer of the manuscript. It would take more pages than what they'll allow to properly express my appreciation for all that you have done for me.

Two highly respected colleagues also made important contributions during the writing of this book. I'd like to thank Eric Arnold, chief financial officer of Editorial Projects in Education, and Karla Snellings, deputy director of the National White Collar Crime Center, for reviewing significant portions of the manuscript and providing me with extremely helpful feedback. I value and respect your knowledge and judgment.

Of course, so many experiences over the course of one's life also aid in the writing of a book like this that I could think of dozens of people to whom I'd like to express my gratitude. I've had the good fortune to work with and learn from many talented individuals. Let me also thank the thousands of people who have attended my seminars over the years. Believe me, the learning has been a two-way street. I've learned plenty from listening to you and discussing the issues we have in common.

I would also like to express my appreciation to Joseph Wells, founder of the Association of Certified Fraud Examiners. While I have never had the chance to get to know Mr. Wells personally, he has from afar been both an inspiration in my pursuit of fraud examination and an invaluable source of knowledge through his association and its resources.

Finally, many thanks to the Wiley team. In particular, I'd like to express my thanks to the editors, Susan McDermott and Sujin Hong, who have been so supportive and helpful along the way.

About the Author

Gerard M. Zack, CPA, CFE, MBA, has provided consulting, audit, training, fraud prevention, and fraud investigation services for nonprofit organizations, commercial businesses, and government agencies since 1981. Based in Maryland, he has worked with organizations of all types and sizes throughout the United States.

Mr. Zack is founder of the Nonprofit Resource Center, which provides training, publications, web-based services, consulting, and other services for nonprofit organizations and their external auditors and advisors. He is also a Director (Partner) with Williams Young, LLC, a Wisconsin-based accounting and consulting firm that serves nonprofits nationwide.

He is a Certified Fraud Examiner and CPA and has focused much of his career on helping nonprofit organizations. He is a frequent lecturer and seminar instructor, and has trained more than 10,000 accountants and auditors. He is the author of three comprehensive textbooks used in his seminars and a monthly newsletter called *The Tax-Exempt Organization Alert!*®

Mr. Zack earned his MBA at Loyola College in Maryland and his BSBA at Shippensburg University of Pennsylvania.

Mr. Zack can be contacted through the Nonprofit Resource Center Web site at www.nonprofitresource.com.

Contents

Introduction   xv

Part I **Introduction to the Prevention and Detection of Fraud
            and Abuse**

1 Fraud in the Nonprofit Sector   **3**

Types of Nonprofit Organizations Affected
    by Fraud and Abuse   4
Who Commits Fraud Against Nonprofit Organizations?   5
Types of Frauds Committed Against Nonprofit Organizations   6
Fraud By, For, and Through a Nonprofit Organization   8
Legal Aspects of Fraud   9
Duration of Fraud and Abuse Schemes   9
The Importance of an Organization-Wide Approach
    to Controlling Fraud and Abuse   10

**2 Overview of a Model for the Prevention and Detection
    of Fraud and Abuse**   **18**

Factors Present in Fraud and Abuse Schemes   19
Risk Management   25
A Comprehensive Model for Controlling Fraud and Abuse   26
How This Book Is Organized   31
Suggested Uses of This Book   32

Part II **Financial Controls Associated with Specific Categories
             of Fraud and Abuse**

3 Revenue and Cash Receipts Schemes   **39**

Financial Controls Over Revenue and Cash Receipts   39
Skimming   41
Lapping Schemes   57

Write-Offs of Accounts Receivable   59
Unauthorized Credits   60
Unrecorded Sales   60
Theft of Donated Merchandise   61

4   Purchasing and Disbursement Schemes   **64**

Internal Controls Over Purchasing and Disbursements   65
Billing Schemes   68
Fraudulent Classification of Personal Expenditures
    as Business Expenses   75
Refund Schemes   77
Financial Assistance Schemes   79
Check Tampering   81
Electronic Funds Transfer Schemes   85
Undisclosed Conflicts of Interest   88
Kickbacks from Vendors   92
Bribery   92
Fraud in the Bidding Process   94

5   Payroll and Expense Reporting Schemes   **97**

Payroll Schemes   98
Employee Expense Reporting Schemes   107

6   Other Asset Misappropriations and Misuse   **115**

Property and Equipment Schemes   115
Personal Use of Organization Assets and Other Resources   118
Inventory Schemes   121

7   External Fraud Schemes   **127**

Fraudulent Billings by Vendors   128
Outsourcing and Service Organizations   134
Fraud and Abuse by Subrecipients   145
Financial Assistance Fraud   153

**Part III   Fraud and Abuse Committed By, For, or Through
            Nonprofit Organizations**

8   Fundraising Fraud and Abuse   **161**

Deceptive Fundraising Practices   162
Noncompliance with Restrictions   172
Ethics in Fundraising   179

9 Fraudulent Reporting   182

Fraudulent Financial Reporting   183
Fraudulent Statements of Compliance with Requirements of
    Funding Sources   206
Charging Unallowable Costs to Government Grants   209
Other False Statements to Government Agencies   211

10 Other Acts Attributable to Nonprofit Organizations   214

False Statements of Program Accomplishments
    or Capabilities   215
Abuse of Privileges Granted to Charitable Organizations   217
Intentional Violations of Other Laws   223
Fraud and Other Illegal Acts Committed
    Through an Organization   227

Part IV   The Roles of Nonfinancial Systems and Controls

11 Human Resource Policies and Procedures   231

Hiring Practices   232
New Employee Orientation   240
Leave Policies   241
Training   243
Performance Evaluation Systems   244
Compensation Adjustment Policies   245
Grievance Policies   246
Counseling and Other Employee Assistance   247
Exit Interviews   247

12 Administrative Systems and Policies   249

Physical Security   249
Security over Donor, Member, and Customer Information   250
Information Technology Systems   252
Hotlines and Communication Systems   261
Insurance   265

Part V   The Role of Management and the Board of Directors

13 Day-to-Day Management Activities   271

Responding to and Supporting the Board of Directors   273
Development of Policies   274
Establishing and Maintaining an Antifraud Culture   277

The Role of Supervisors and Managers   279
Enforcement of Fraud-Related Policies   281
Responding to Identified Weaknesses in Internal Controls   282
Responding to Fraud   284
Organizational Accountability and Transparency   289

14 The Role of the Board of Directors   **293**

A Nonprofit Board Has Many Responsibilities   293
Specific Responsibilities Pertaining to Fraud and Abuse   296
Establishment of Board Committees   297
The Audit Committee   298
The Role of the External Auditor   301
The Internal Audit Function   307
Managing Conflicts of Interest   308
The First Line of Defense Against Fraud
    by Senior Management   308
A Board's Role in Crisis Management
    and Communications   309

15 Financial Oversight and Analysis   **314**

The Budget as a Financial Oversight Tool   314
Financial Analysis   318
Types of Analytical Procedures   319
Ratio Analysis   323
Useful Ratios   324

Appendixes Sample Policies, Checklists, and Other Resources

Appendix A: Sample Audit Committee Charter   333
Appendix B: Sample Code of Conduct   337
Appendix C: Sample Policy on Suspected Misconduct   339
Appendix D: Sample Conflict of Interest Policy   343
Appendix E: Standards for Charitable Accountability from
    the BBB Wise Giving Alliance   346
Appendix F: List of Useful Web Sites Relating
    to Controlling Fraud and Abuse   351

Bibliography   353

Index   355

Introduction

Anyone who has read the newspapers or watched the news on television over the last few years is aware of the fact that reports of fraud and abuse appear virtually every day. We are continually bombarded with reports of one company or another misstating earnings or otherwise painting an artificially rosy picture of a company's financial health.

While news of fraud in publicly traded companies seems to flood the media, reports of fraud in the nonprofit sector sometimes get pushed to the back pages of the newspapers. Yet, closer inspection reveals that reports of fraud in nonprofit organizations also appear to be increasing at an alarming rate.

Although several studies on fraud and abuse have been performed, none have focused exclusively on the nonprofit sector. One thing that has become painfully clear over the last ten to fifteen years, however, is that nonprofit organizations are by no means exempt from fraud and abuse. Far from it. In many respects, nonprofit organizations may be even more vulnerable to fraud and abuse than many for-profit businesses.

The latest reports indicate that fraud in the United States is growing at an astounding rate. In its *2002 Report to the Nation, Occupational Fraud and Abuse*, the Association of Certified Fraud Examiners (ACFE) estimated that occupational fraud and abuse results in losses equal to about 6 percent of revenue. When applied to the U.S. Gross Domestic Product, this means that approximately $600 billion per year is lost to fraud and abuse, a 50 percent increase from ACFE's estimate just six years earlier. This translates into an astonishing $4,500 per employee lost to fraud.

Another study, this one sponsored in 2002 by the accounting firm Ernst & Young, LLP, found that one out of every five American workers is personally aware of fraud in their workplace. This survey of 617 workers also found that almost half felt their employers could do more to reduce fraud.

The 2002 ACFE report is based on an analysis of 663 reported cases of fraud and abuse. In 13.4 percent of those cases, a nonprofit organization was the victim, for a median loss of $40,000 per incident. This median loss is only about one-fourth the median loss reported in frauds perpetrated against publicly traded companies. But that's not much of a consolation. It's still fraud. And it often represents a more serious blow to the fiscal health of a nonprofit than it does to a for-profit enterprise.

The ACFE report does not estimate what percentage of the $600 billion in losses is associated with the nonprofit sector, but this sector is a huge component of the economy in the United States. Recent estimates from Independent Sector, an advocacy group for charitable organizations, are that nonprofit organizations comprise 8.5 percent of the U.S. gross domestic product and spend approximately $800 billion a year. Given this proportion of the economy represented by nonprofit organizations, it could be concluded that fraud involving nonprofits may represent as much as $50 billion of the ACFE's estimated total of $600 billion. However, knowing that frauds in the nonprofit sector resulted in losses averaging only a quarter the amount of losses in publicly traded companies, the total losses in the nonprofit sector are probably closer to $10 billion. But that's still $10 billion a year lost to fraud!

Nonprofit organizations provide jobs to almost 11 million people, or one out of every twelve employees in the country. It is estimated that another 110 million people volunteer their time for nonprofits. Even though the vast majority of people involved with nonprofits have only honest intentions, out of 11 million employees and 110 million volunteers, there are bound to be some dishonest people. Some will go to work or volunteer for a nonprofit organization for the sole purpose of stealing from the organization.

In recent years, we've witnessed several of this country's largest nonprofits being victimized by acts of fraud and abuse. There have been reports of fraud involving Goodwill Industries, American Cancer Society, United Way, American Federation of Teachers, the Episcopal Church, and several others. Each of these large, well-respected organizations has been victimized by fraud and abuse at the national and/or local levels.

Yet, large nonprofit organizations aren't the only ones impacted by fraud and abuse. Read the local newspapers and you'll see reports of fraud in small nonprofits on a daily basis. In certain respects, we're even more disgusted when we hear about a small local charity operating on a shoe-string budget being victimized by fraud than when it happens in a large organization.

But stealing *from* nonprofit organizations is just one part of the problem. Nonprofit organizations themselves have been accused of wrongdoing at an alarming rate in recent years. The Foundation for New Era Philanthropy turned out to be nothing more than a Ponzi scheme (a scheme in which some early investors receive payouts from the perpetrator using funds received from more recent investors in order to give the appearance that a legitimate investment program is being operated). The Baptist Foundation of Arizona was riddled with fraud. Many nonprofit groups have been accused of deceptive fundraising practices, misleading marketing materials, and exaggerating program accomplishments and staff credentials and qualifications.

And that's where we now find ourselves. Nonprofit organizations are every bit as embroiled in this unsavory upward trend in fraud and abuse as any other sector of the economy.

But it's different when nonprofit organizations are involved. It strikes us as an even more despicable act when a nonprofit organization is victimized than when someone embezzles from a multibillion dollar public company. The same feeling hits us when someone carries out a fraud against others through a nonprofit organization, abusing the trust that many people place in nonprofit organizations. In either scenario, money intended for a charitable program is stolen for the personal benefit of a crook.

So it's time for action! Nonprofit organizations *must* take action to prevent fraud and abuse, before the public's trust is lost. It's time for nonprofit boards of directors to take their financial oversight responsibilities more seriously, or else turn the reins over to someone who is willing to devote the time and energy to protecting the organization from fraud. It's time for every employee, from the executive director down to the most recently hired entry-level staff person, to become more aware of the potential for fraud and abuse in their departments and take a stand in the fight against it.

It's also high time for the public accounting profession to revamp its audit methodology to be more realistic about the potential for fraud. Auditing standards, including the new fraud standard, can go only so far in telling us how to exercise professional judgment. They can't spell out every step auditors should take to address fraud. Put the checklists away for a moment and *think*! It's time to go beyond the bare minimum required by the standards and take an individualized approach to assessing the risk of fraud in each audit and developing tailored audit procedures that respond to those risks—before audits become viewed as worthless or limited in value.

These are just a few of the reasons why this book is necessary.

Fraud and Abuse in Nonprofit Organizations

A Guide to Prevention and Detection

PART I

INTRODUCTION TO THE PREVENTION AND DETECTION OF FRAUD AND ABUSE

Fraud and abuse is clearly on the rise. It impacts every type of organization—business, government, and nonprofit organization. The focus of Part I is to explore this trend and to lay the groundwork for a comprehensive, organization-wide effort to combat fraud and abuse.

In Chapter 1, some of the basic aspects of fraud are introduced, followed by an overview of the current legal and regulatory environment. One of the primary objectives of Chapter 1 is to begin the process of breaking the broad concept of fraud down into its many components. This process is essential to understanding how to prevent, detect, and deter fraud and abuse.

Chapter 2 continues this process by explaining the factors that are involved in all fraud schemes. This chapter also introduces each interrelated component of the organization-wide model of fraud deterrence that is the basis for this book. Finally, Chapter 2 describes how this book can best be put to use by each of the various types of readers, from nonprofit executive or chief financial officer to board members and auditors.

1

Fraud in the Nonprofit Sector

What makes a nonprofit organization vulnerable to fraud? Let's not make this out to be more complicated than it really is. In certain respects, many of the same factors that make a for-profit business vulnerable to fraud are also present in nonprofit organizations. Both types of entities may handle large amounts of revenue, disburse funds by writing thousands of checks, and store valuable assets, such as cash, inventory, and equipment, on their premises. Both types of organizations also hire employees from the general public, and some of those employees are bound to be dishonest.

So in several respects, nonprofits and for-profits face similar risk factors in connection with fraud. However, nonprofit organizations sometimes possess certain distinguishing characteristics that make their vulnerability to fraud and abuse different from commercial businesses. Those distinguishing characteristics may include:

- An environment of trust unlike that found in for-profit enterprises
- Excessive control by a founder, executive director, or substantial contributor
- Failure to include individuals with financial oversight expertise on the board of directors
- The existence of nonreciprocal transactions (contributions) that are much easier to steal than other forms of income
- Failure to devote adequate resources to financial management
- Job security (and perhaps compensation) linked to program and financial reporting, especially with respect to government grants

3

TYPES OF NONPROFIT ORGANIZATIONS
AFFECTED BY FRAUD AND ABUSE

Nonprofit organizations come in all shapes and sizes. Much of the attention to fraud and abuse in the nonprofit sector has focused on charitable organizations. There are many reasons for this focus, such as:

- Charities epitomize the "environment of trust" in many ways, from the trust placed in them by the contributing public to the trust the charities themselves place in their employees in the carrying out of charitable programs.
- Charities have to sell themselves to the public in a manner unlike that encountered in any other type of nonprofit organization or for-profit business.
- Some charities, especially small charities operating at the local level, place little attention on accounting, internal controls, and financial oversight, due to their limited resources.

For each of these reasons, it becomes big news when a charity is victimized by fraud or a charity itself is accused of fraudulent actions.

But the term "charitable organization" or "charity" applies to many different kinds of organizations. It can apply to any organization that qualifies for exemption from federal income taxes under Internal Revenue Code section 501(c)(3). IRS records indicate that there are more than 800,000 such organizations in the United States. Charitable organization status can apply to any of the following types of organizations:

- Churches and religious groups
- Soup kitchens and homeless shelters
- Other social service agencies
- Organizations that administer federal grants
- Universities and private schools
- Health care organizations
- Amateur sports groups
- Disaster relief organizations
- Museums, zoos, and planetariums
- Symphony orchestras and other performing arts groups
- Foundations and supporting organizations
- Certain charitable trusts and donor-advised funds

Charities are certainly not the only types of nonprofit organizations that are affected by fraud and abuse. Any organization that qualifies for tax-exempt status under one of the subsections of Internal Revenue Code section 501(c), along with a few other sections, is generally referred to as a nonprofit organization. Section 501(c)(3) is just one of 27 subsections under which an organization may qualify for exemption from income taxes. Some of the most common noncharitable nonprofit organizations that will be considered in this book include:

- Labor unions
- Trade and professional associations
- Social welfare organizations

Certain types of fraud and abuse schemes are universal in nature, meaning that they can be carried out in a nonprofit environment in the same manner as in a for-profit business. Other fraud and abuse schemes, however, are unique to nonprofits, and some of those schemes are unique to one type of organization or another. As different types of frauds are illustrated throughout this book, the nonprofits that are particularly prone to them will be identified.

WHO COMMITS FRAUD AGAINST NONPROFIT ORGANIZATIONS?

Nonprofit organizations may be victims of fraud and abuse at the hands of a variety of perpetrators, including employees; officers and directors; volunteers; fulfillment houses that handle outsourced functions; vendors; subrecipients; donors; members and program participants; and competitors.

One area in which nonprofit organizations are not much different than any other organizational victim of fraud is in the perpetrator. Just as in for-profit businesses, most frauds committed against nonprofit organizations are carried out by the employees, officers, and directors of these organizations.

ACFE's 1996 study on fraud, *Report to the Nation on Occupational Fraud and Abuse*, provides additional insight into the typical perpetrator of occupational fraud. This study, which was based on analysis of data on fraud cases submitted by 2,608 fraud examiners, found that 58 percent of the reported occupational frauds were perpetrated by employees. Another 30 percent was carried out by managers and 12 percent by owners/executives.

However, in looking at the median loss by position, the opposite image results. Median losses from frauds committed by employees were $60,000, while median losses from those perpetrated by management positions were $250,000. The median loss from frauds carried out by owners/executives was $1,000,000.

A linear relationship between a perpetrator's age and the amount of loss also was demonstrated. Median losses from frauds committed by persons under 25 years of age were just $12,000. This continues to rise, with median losses from frauds carried out by 36-to-40-year-olds being $100,000 and losses from 41-to-50-year-olds being $196,000. The median loss from perpetrators between 51 and 60 years of age was $280,000. Finally, the median loss from perpetrators over age 60 was $346,000.

A similar relationship was demonstrated between median losses and education level of the perpetrator. Median losses of those with high school educations were $50,000. Median losses from frauds carried out by college-educated employees were $200,000, while median losses from frauds perpetrated by those with postgraduate degrees were $275,000.

To a certain extent, these statistics simply verify what many people would naturally assume. As an individual is placed in a higher position of trust, the total dollar potential for fraud committed by that person also rises. This is an important factor to keep in mind, because many traditional internal accounting controls focus on prevention of frauds only at the lower echelons of the organization.

TYPES OF FRAUDS COMMITTED AGAINST NONPROFIT ORGANIZATIONS

So far, we've been discussing fraud and abuse without defining each term. And that is by design. We don't really need a technical definition of fraud. Like many things, we know it when we see it.

Fraud occurs any time a person intentionally acts to cause an economic detriment to another party. Fraud can involve any or all of the following:

- Misrepresentation of facts
- Breach of fiduciary responsibilities
- Suppression of truth
- Omission of critical facts

Fraud is such a broad concept that the term "occupational fraud" is sometimes used to categorically describe what most people think of as fraud in general. Occupational fraud is defined by the ACFE as *the use of one's occupation for personal enrichment through deliberate misuse or misapplication of the employing organization's resources or assets.*

Much of what is explained in this book falls within this definition of occupational fraud. However, many types of fraud do not.

Frauds committed against nonprofit organizations can be classified into two broad categories, based on the perpetrator of the fraud: internal fraud and external fraud. As the term suggests, internal frauds are committed by insiders, such as employees, officers, and directors. External frauds are committed by outsiders, such as vendors, subrecipients, grant applicants, program participants, and competitors.

Internal Frauds

Internal fraud and abuse schemes that are carried out against nonprofit organizations generally fall into one of the following categories: asset misappropriations and acts of corruption or abuse.

Asset misappropriations are far and away the most prevalent of the fraud and abuse schemes committed against nonprofits by insiders. More than 80 percent of all reported frauds involve some form of asset misappropriation. And, to no great surprise, the asset most frequently misappropriated is cash.

Asset misappropriations can involve any or all of the following:

- Revenue and cash receipts (collections) schemes
- Purchasing and cash disbursement schemes
- Payroll and employee expense reporting schemes
- Noncash asset misappropriations

Within each of the four areas, there are many different methods of perpetrating fraud. In the first three, an organization's cash is targeted. Skimming of incoming revenue, forging checks, and other acts of embezzlement fall into one of these areas. In the fourth, some other asset, such as equipment or inventory, is stolen.

Throughout this book, the term "abuse" is frequently used in connection with fraud schemes. The term is used to describe other acts that may not fall within a legal definition of fraud, or may not fall within any criminal definition, but that clearly represent an inappropriate act and unacceptable behavior. For instance, theft of an organization's equipment by an employee is clearly a fraudulent act and one that would be a crime. But, occasional use of an organization's equipment for nonbusiness (personal) purposes is probably not a criminal act. Yet, it is certainly not an act that organizations should tolerate.

Corruption occurs when an employee uses his or her influence in a business transaction in an inappropriate manner to benefit himself or herself at the expense of the employing organization. The most common examples of corruption addressed in this book are kickback schemes (involving under the table payments from vendors to employees for any of a variety of acts, such as authorizing the payment of an inflated price by the organization) and undisclosed conflicts of interest (in which someone involved in making or authorizing a purchasing decision, such as a manager or member of the board of directors, has an undisclosed financial interest in a vendor with whom the organization does business).

External Frauds

External frauds are less common than internal frauds, but can be every bit as damaging to an organization. Most external frauds are committed by:

- Vendors, in the form of charging for goods or services not delivered, inflating prices, or other acts;
- Service organizations (contractors to whom an organization outsources key internal functions) that take advantage of their position of trust;

- Subrecipients, in the form of engaging in fraudulent financial or programmatic reporting to a nonprofit organization that has made a sub-award to the subrecipient out of grant funds it has received;
- Program participants, such as students who lie to receive financial aid or others who fraudulently apply for grant funds or other forms of financial assistance.

An organization's risk of external fraud expands based on the quantity of outside parties with whom it deals and the complexity and diversity of the transactions it engages in with those outsiders. The preceding is only a partial list for many nonprofit organizations.

FRAUD BY, FOR, AND THROUGH A NONPROFIT ORGANIZATION

Recent years have also borne witness to an increase in the reports of wrongdoing by nonprofit organizations primarily against outside parties. These frauds can be classified as follows:

- Frauds *by* nonprofits—These are schemes carried out by insiders on behalf of the organization, often involving the collaboration of several individuals within the organization. Examples include the issuance of organization-wide financial statements that improperly classify expenses to make it appear as if the organization devoted more resources to its programs than it really did, or organization-wide intentional violation(s) of Fair Labor Standards Act provisions with the intent of saving the organization overtime payments to employees.
- Frauds *for* nonprofits—Fraudulent or abusive acts carried out by insiders with the intent of benefiting the organization, such as a fundraiser misleading a donor into believing that a greater percentage of the donor's gift is deductible than what would be allowable under the Internal Revenue Code, or a program director misleading a grantor about the capabilities of the organization's staff.
- Frauds *through* nonprofits—These schemes involve insiders abusing their position of trust or using information to which they are privy in order to carry out frauds against outside parties, such as an employee using credit card information obtained from an organization's donors to fraudulently make personal purchases.

Although there may be fine differences among each of these categories of fraud, the fact of the matter is that in each case *it is possible for the fraud to be attributed to the nonprofit*, thereby resulting in the legal or financial liability of the organization. Even in cases where the organization does not incur a financial liability as a result of one of these acts, the organization's reputation can be tarnished. And in the nonprofit sector, reputation and public image of an organization can mean everything.

LEGAL ASPECTS OF FRAUD

Fraud is certainly a wrongdoing. But not all frauds are necessarily illegal acts or crimes. Accordingly, the term "fraud" should be used carefully when addressing acts of wrongdoing, whether by our own employees or by outsiders.

Certain types of fraud are considered criminal acts under a variety of federal laws. Under these laws, an act that falls within the scope of a particular category of fraud is defined and the penalties associated with conviction are explained. Penalties include prison sentences as well as fines. A few examples of the many federal laws that are frequently used in fraud cases include those dealing with:

- Mail fraud (Title 18, U.S. Code, § 1341)–using the mail to perpetrate a fraud can result in prison terms of up to 20 years
- Interstate transportation of stolen property (Title 18, U.S. Code, § 2314)–interstate or foreign transportation of money, goods, and so forth, can result in prison terms of up to 10 years
- Wire fraud (Title 18, U.S. Code, § 1343)–using wire, radio, or television in interstate or foreign commerce to defraud is punishable with prison terms of up to 20 years (wire fraud applies to the use of a variety of communications devices to commit a fraud, including fax machines and e-mails)
- False statements to government agencies (Title 18, U.S. Code, § 1001, et seq.)–prohibits false statements in general, as well as certain specific types of false statements (such as with loan applications) and is punishable with prison terms of up to 30 years

Maximum mail fraud and wire fraud prison terms were limited to 5 years until 2002. The Sarbanes-Oxley Act of 2002 increased these maximums to 20 years.

In addition to being a criminal act, fraud also may be considered a civil wrong. Penalties associated with civil actions typically involve recovery of damages, such as lost revenue or reimbursement of expenses, but may also include punitive awards.

Fraud can also be a breach of contract. In such cases, the recovery may involve rescinding a contract between two parties.

DURATION OF FRAUD AND ABUSE SCHEMES

The 2002 study on occupational fraud and abuse conducted by the ACFE included several critical facts regarding the detection of these schemes. One of the most alarming of these facts was that the median length of time occupational frauds were carried out before being detected was 18 months. More than 13 percent lasted for 5 years or more! Only 3.4 percent of frauds were detected within 1 month.

Equally surprising were the methods that resulted in the detection of the frauds. In the ACFE study, traditional internal controls accounted for just 15.4 percent of the initial detections of occupational frauds. External audits performed by CPA firms were responsible for detecting just 11.5 percent of the frauds studied (this figure actually compares favorably with the results of a 1998 study conducted by CPA firm KPMG, in which only 4 percent of the frauds studied were uncovered by external auditors).

Throughout this book, many strategies for effective detection and shortening the duration of the fraud schemes will be explained. For now, readers should recognize two important facts:

1. The presumption that internal controls and an audit by a CPA firm will catch all frauds couldn't be further from the truth.
2. Without a multifaceted approach to preventing and detecting fraud, schemes can last for quite some time, draining an organization of valuable resources in the process.

THE IMPORTANCE OF AN ORGANIZATION-WIDE APPROACH TO CONTROLLING FRAUD AND ABUSE

What this introductory chapter has hopefully illustrated is that several commonly held beliefs about fraud and abuse are untrue. The exposure that nonprofit organizations have to fraud and abuse is a very real risk and is growing every day. We can learn a great deal from the unfortunate circumstances encountered by businesses and other nonprofits that have been victimized by fraud. We can learn how the abuses were perpetrated, who carried them out, how they were able to do so, how the fraud was detected, and so on. From these facts, we can take more educated steps toward maximizing an organization's ability to protect itself against fraud.

Before attempting to control fraud and abuse, nonprofit organizations must acknowledge six important facts:

1. There is a high probability that some level of fraud and abuse already exists in our organization or will be perpetrated in the future.
2. The real cost to our organization of a reported instance of fraud cannot be measured only in terms of the dollars lost.
3. People and circumstances change over time, and some of those changes may increase our risk of internal fraud.
4. Traditional internal accounting controls play a critical role in deterring fraud, but represent only one facet of fraud prevention and detection.
5. Reliance on an external audit as the primary method of detecting fraud is not enough.
6. Everyone within the organization has a role in the prevention and detection of fraud and abuse.

The key to preventing and detecting fraud and abuse is the implementation of a multifaceted organization-wide model of deterrence. This model, which is introduced in Chapter 2, relies on involvement in fraud deterrence at every level of the organization and within virtually every function of the organization.

This model includes three interrelated components designed to maximize an organization's chances of preventing or detecting fraud and abuse:

- Financial controls
- Nonfinancial systems
- Management oversight and behavior

The importance of an organization-wide model of defense against fraud cannot be overemphasized. The traditional model of fraud deterrence followed by most nonprofit organizations is flawed for several reasons. First, its financial controls rely primarily on policies and procedures designed to *prevent* errors and fraud from occurring, at the expense of not placing adequate emphasis on timely *detection*. Also, it focuses mostly on frauds perpetrated at the lower levels of an organization and not enough on frauds carried out at upper levels, such as by senior members of the management team. Finally, it considers only traditional financial controls, ignoring several important nonfinancial elements of fraud deterrence.

The remainder of this chapter is devoted to an overview of recent developments pertaining to fraud and abuse.

THE STATE OF THE NONPROFIT SECTOR: THE CURRENT ENVIRONMENT REGARDING FRAUD AND ABUSE

The effects of recent cases of fraud and abuse involving nonprofit organizations and for-profit businesses have been many. The current environment is one that includes a heightened awareness of and concern about fraud, as well as an increased level of skepticism toward nonprofits by the public, press, and government. These attitudes have manifested themselves in:

1. Efforts by the federal government to curb abuse
2. Greater demand for accountability
3. Punishment by the general public of nonprofits impacted by fraud
4. Changes in the accounting profession to improve the quality of audits and financial reporting

continued

Efforts by the Federal Government to Curb Abuse

Recent actions by government officials and regulators in an effort to curb fraud have included:

- Passage of the Sarbanes-Oxley Act of 2002
- Issuance of a new auditor independence standard by the General Accounting Office
- Congressional investigations into assertions of wrongdoing involving specific charities
- Increased pressure on the Internal Revenue Service to step up its oversight of the nonprofit sector

The Sarbanes-Oxley Act of 2002 was passed in direct response to recent scandals involving fraudulent financial reporting by publicly traded businesses, such as Enron and WorldCom. The act imposes several new reporting and disclosure requirements on public companies and their officials, as well as new restrictions on the accounting firms that audit public companies. The act also establishes a new regulatory body that will be responsible for overseeing accounting firms that audit publicly traded companies.

Much of the Sarbanes-Oxley Act of 2002 has no direct impact on nonprofit organizations because most of its provisions apply solely to public companies and their auditors. However, some provisions do apply to nonprofits, such as those establishing new penalties for destroying documents in connection with an investigation by any federal agency. In addition, it reflects current regulatory sentiments regarding disclosures and relationships between auditors and the entities they audit. Several of these provisions have the potential for application to nonprofit organizations and their auditors.

The January 2002 issuance of revised standards for auditor independence by the General Accounting Office (GAO) directly affects many nonprofit organizations and their auditors. The new rules apply to organizations and auditors performing audits in accordance with the Single Audit Act and OMB Circular A-133, which govern audits of nonprofit organizations and state and local government agencies that receive federal financial assistance. Despite their January 2002 issuance, the GAO independence standard was not issued in direct response to the recent for-profit financial reporting scandals and, in fact, had been in development for several years before its release.

The new GAO independence rules prohibit or restrict many nonauditing services that, in the past, have been provided by auditors. The new standard is effective for audits of periods beginning on or after

January 1, 2003. Auditors that provide these services are now prohibited from also auditing the same entity. The new rules are designed to accomplish two objectives:

- Limit the potential for auditor judgment to be impaired as a result of a firm's non-audit work that it performs for a client.
- Improve the perceived value of audits (which has been damaged by the recent reporting scandals) in the eyes of the public and other users of audited financial statements.

When an audit firm provides additional non-audit services to a client, some have asserted that the level of skepticism exercised by an audit firm during an audit could be inappropriately influenced by either or both of the following:

- The amount of firm revenue at stake (does a firm risk losing a valuable consulting engagement by bringing up sensitive issues during the audit?); and
- The nature and extent of the non-audit work (which has the potential for making the audit firm overly comfortable with the accuracy of the entity's financial statements).

There have been very few instances in which either of the preceding circumstances has been shown to result in a deficient audit performed by an auditing firm. However, the *appearance* of a lack of auditor independence is every bit as important to users of financial statements as is *actual* independence. One of the key factors adding value to any audit is the assumption on the part of users that an audit firm is truly independent from its client, with no conflicts of interest that could impair its impartiality in assessing the fairness of an entity's financial statement amounts and disclosures. Therefore, it is difficult to argue with most of the stricter new standards.

The concern over fraud and abuse in the nonprofit sector has received greater attention in Congress in recent years. Sen. Charles Grassley, the ranking Republican member of the Senate Finance Committee, has headed inquiries into several allegations of fraud or abuse involving charitable organizations. Among the organizations investigated by Sen. Grassley are the American Red Cross and the United Way of the National Capital Area.

The federal government's concern over nonprofit oversight in recent years has extended well beyond Congress. A 2002 report prepared by the General Accounting Office was critical of the job done by the Internal Revenue Service in monitoring the activities of nonprofit organi-

continued

zations. Examination rates of nonprofit groups by the IRS are down dramatically in recent years, leading some to conclude that the service is doing little to make sure that nonprofits comply with tax laws.

Most nonprofit organizations are required to file an annual information return with the IRS. This return, Form 990, is akin to an annual report, requiring nonprofits to provide detailed financial information as well as answer a series of questions about their operations and provide information about programs. Many states also require that a copy of federal Form 990 be filed with the organization's state return in order to satisfy state reporting requirements. In addition, Form 990 is a public document and must be made available to any member of the public directly from the nonprofit organization that files the return, or on the Internet, on an organization's own Web site or through other services such as www.guidestar.org.

As a result, Form 990 has become one of the most widely available documents used to assess the operations of nonprofit organizations. More and more individual donors, grantors, and other funding sources, as well as prospective employees, volunteers, and program participants, are reviewing these forms prior to their involvement with a nonprofit organization. Currently, much of the information reported on Form 990 that is of interest to these users is of little importance to the IRS. The reason is that very little of this information, if misstated on the form, would result in any tax or penalty under the Internal Revenue Code and underlying regulations if detected upon examination by the IRS. As a result, there is little incentive for the IRS to look very carefully at items other than those that could result in tax or penalty assessments or major violations that could result in revocation of tax exemptions.

Both the GAO and Sen. Grassley have turned up the pressure on the IRS to greatly improve the oversight of nonprofits. The GAO report suggests that the IRS not only improve the design of Form 990 to make it more useful to the general public, but to do more to ensure the accuracy of all information reported therein.

Greater Demand for Accountability

One of the most frequently used words of recent years in discussions regarding the nonprofit sector has been *accountability*. It is used in the board meetings of many nonprofit organizations as they attempt to improve their public image or avoid the problems encountered by other organizations. It is a term that is also being used by governmental agencies and nonprofit regulators, as well as watchdog groups, with respect to nonprofits.

One example of how the concept of accountability has changed is the set of standards used by the BBB Wise Giving Alliance. This organization is one of the watchdog groups that serves the public by evaluating the operations and activities of national charitable organizations. Based on the group's review of each charity, a report is issued, indicating which standards were passed and failed by the charity. These reports are available on the Web site of the BBB Wise Giving Alliance (www.give.org).

Two important changes in the BBB Wise Giving Alliance's charity evaluation program were announced in 2002:

- Revisions to the standards themselves
- An expansion in the number of charities that the group plans to evaluate

The revised standards were issued in final form in March 2003. See Appendix E for a copy of these standards.

The BBB Wise Giving Alliance also plans to evaluate substantially greater numbers of charities in the future. The current pool of approximately 500 national charities that have been evaluated will be expanded to more than 3,000 in the coming years.

Whether or not your organization is one of the charities evaluated by the BBB Wise Giving Alliance, familiarity and compliance with the group's standards can be a helpful aid in making your organization more accountable. A copy of the group's charity evaluation standards also can be found on its Web site.

Punishment by the General Public of Nonprofits Involved in Frauds

When an employee is caught stealing from a for-profit business, it is unlikely that the business' customers will react by ceasing their relationship with the company. In fact, in many instances, even when a for-profit business issues fraudulently prepared financial statements, there is little or no impact on revenue from customers. If anything, perhaps the company's stock is less valuable to investors.

This is not so with nonprofits and fraud. Whether a nonprofit organization is the victim or the culprit in a fraud scheme, the contributing public (customers *and* investors) often punishes the organization with a reduction in support. This is an interesting phenomenon in the nonprofit sector. As an example, when the United Way of America was the victim of fraud perpetrated at the hands of its former president in the early 1990s, the public responded by providing less support to the organization during the ensuing few years. This is typical, even when the nonprofit organization is the *victim*. When a nonprofit organization is perceived as the perpetrator of fraud or abuse, the penalties, of course,

continued

are even greater. The United Way of the National Capital Area (the District of Columbia region) suffered a dramatic drop in support in light of allegations that it padded fundraising efforts in its financial statements and withheld a greater percentage of donor contributions for overhead than it claimed, among other financial improprieties. In January 2003, the group announced that its fall 2002 private sector campaign raised just $13 million through December 31, 2002, down from the $45 million raised at that point a year earlier. This despite significant actions taken by the organization to shore up its financial operations.

One of the villains in recent stories involving fraud and abuse has certainly been the accounting and auditing profession. This profession is represented primarily by two organizations: the American Institute of Certified Public Accountants (AICPA), which promulgates auditing standards to be followed in the performance of financial statement audits, and the Financial Accounting Standards Board (FASB), which issues the accounting standards to which audited financial statements must conform.

Criticisms of these two organizations have mainly involved two common assertions:

- Accounting principles issued by FASB have not kept up to date with current legal and economic trends or are unclear with respect to certain important issues and are in desperate need of updating.
- The audit approach described in current auditing standards issued by AICPA does an extremely poor job of addressing the risk of fraud.

In 2002, responding to these criticisms, two important changes were made by these organizations:

- FASB changed its policies and procedures for issuing new accounting standards in an effort to streamline and improve the process.
- In October 2002, AICPA issued a new auditing standard addressing auditors' responsibilities regarding fraud (explained in Chapter 14).

Of course, with the enactment of the Sarbanes-Oxley Act of 2002, it remains to be seen just how much authority and influence AICPA and FASB will even have. These are certainly just the beginning of a series of regulatory, oversight, and industry changes that we are likely to see over the next few years.

In Chapter 2, the details of this three-part model of fraud deterrence are introduced and explained in greater detail, followed by individual chapters that illustrate the implementation of each component and the application of the model to specific types of fraud and abuse.

2

Overview of a Model for the Prevention and Detection of Fraud and Abuse

It's always dangerous to use the term "prevention" with regard to fraud and abuse. Quite frankly, it's impossible to completely prevent all fraud and abuse from taking place, no matter how many policies and procedures we put in place. Certain policies and procedures can prevent many fraud and abuse schemes from being carried out successfully. But absolute prevention is simply not realistic. Given enough time, perpetrators can usually figure out a method for committing fraud against an organization. And if collusion involving multiple employees and/or outsiders is involved or controls can be overridden or bypassed, fraud and abuse become even more possible.

Even if we could design controls that would prevent all frauds from occurring, what would the cost of those controls be? There must be a reasonable balance between controlling fraud and carrying out our organization's mission and other responsibilities. The problem, of course, is that many organizations don't devote enough of their resources to the prevention and detection of fraud and abuse.

The goal is to *prevent* as many types of fraud and abuse schemes as possible within the reasonable constraints of time and money. Subsequently, organizations should design appropriate follow-up procedures to *detect*, in a timely manner, those frauds that have been carried out successfully in spite of the preventive controls in place.

However, prevention and detection are concepts comprised of numerous components. To understand how those concepts are applied, first it is important to understand a few additional characteristics of fraud and abuse.

FACTORS PRESENT IN FRAUD AND ABUSE SCHEMES

Certain factors have been found to be present in virtually all reported frauds. Those factors are:

- Intent
- Motive to commit the fraud
- Opportunity to commit the fraud
- Concealment of the fraud
- Rationalization of the fraud

An understanding of each of these factors is important to implementing an organization-wide system of fraud deterrence because a comprehensive system includes policies and procedures designed to identify and manage each factor to the maximum extent practical. A good system of fraud deterrence can have a positive impact in all of these areas other than the first—intent.

Intent

Intent is the characteristic that distinguishes fraud from an error or oversight in the accounting and financial reporting processes of an organization. A perpetrator of fraud *intends* to commit the fraud for his or her benefit to the detriment of another party.

While intent may seem an obvious characteristic, it is an important element to prove when pursuing a fraud case in the legal system. In some cases, little evidence is necessary to show intent. The fact that an embezzler used the proceeds of the fraud to fund personal purchases may be all that is necessary to show that that individual intended to harm the organization. In other cases, evidence of premeditated planning of the scheme may be important to prove.

In any case, for the purposes of this book, which is not designed to be a legal text on the attributes necessary to prove fraud in court, suffice it to say that intent is a characteristic intrinsic to fraud and abuse cases.

Motive

Does something compel a person to commit fraud or engage in abusive activities? Or is that person simply dishonest?

In the 1991 book *The Day America Told the Truth,* James Patterson and Peter Kim reported that 91 percent of the 1,000 respondents to a survey indicated that they lied routinely to matters that they considered trivial. And 35 percent lied about important matters. So there certainly seems to be enough dishonesty to go around.

But does dishonesty by itself compel someone to commit fraud? Consider another finding from the research of Patterson and Kim. In response to a question about what people would do for $10 million, 7 percent said they would kill a stranger! 25 percent said they would be willing to abandon their families, while 3 percent said they would put their children up for adoption. Greed can motivate people to do some incredible things.

One final statistic from Patterson and Kim that is of importance with respect to occupational fraud: 90 percent of working people indicated they were dissatisfied with their jobs.

Motive is a critical element of fraud and abuse. We've all heard expressions of surprise from coworkers and supervisors when it was revealed that a long-time trusted employee was caught embezzling from an organization. In fact, it would be cause for concern if we *didn't* hear this from coworkers (implying that they'd known all the while and it was just a matter of time before the perpetrator was caught red-handed).

Why is motive so critical to our understanding of fraud prevention and detection? Because by being aware of what motivates someone to commit fraud, we may be able to place ourselves in a position to do two things that can help control our risk of fraud:

- Reduce or eliminate one or more of those motives (as some motives may be within our control)
- Become more alert to possible warning signals that indicate someone is, or has recently become, a more likely candidate to commit fraud

Every person's particular life circumstances are in a continual state of change, which is an important characteristic of motive to understand. Some people are probably just born crooks. Others were looking to commit fraud when we first hired them. Other employees had no intention to commit fraud when we initially hired them, but are considering it now due to new pressures, financial problems, anger, or other issues in their lives.

A simple pair of questions illustrates this element of change and how it can impact an organization's vulnerability to fraud:

1. Do you contemplate embezzling from your employer within the next 30 days?
2. Would you consider stealing from your employer if your spouse were being held hostage and were threatened with death unless you pay a ransom that you cannot legally afford?

The vast majority of readers would likely answer no to the first question. Fewer could unequivocally answer no to the second question. Faced with such a horrifying decision, many of us would consider embezzlement.

But where would we draw the line between considering embezzlement hypothetically and actually committing a fraud? The answer is different for everybody. Circumstances change in everybody's lives and most people have some point at which, based on their current situation, they believe it is necessary or appropriate to commit fraud. Many of us have never even imagined what those circumstances could be. Others have been there or have witnessed this breaking point in someone to whom they are close.

Motives to commit fraud can be classified as internal or external, depending on the source of the motive. Internal motives are those that emanate from the workplace itself. Some internal motives can be controlled by an organization, while others may not. Examples of internal motives include:

- An employee feeling undercompensated
- A subordinate being subjected to harassment or abuse by a supervisor
- A worker feeling unfairly treated in performance evaluations
- A high volume of work that results in an employee feeling incredible job pressure
- A staff member sensing that promotions are based more on politics than on hard work (Recall the study cited in Chapter 1 that concluded that one-half of U.S. workers feel that one gets ahead based on politics more than on hard work.)

Some of these internal motives may be real, while others may be perceived (an employee feels unfairly treated when, in fact, they have been dealt with in a manner equal to how all employees are treated). Either way, they represent a necessary component to commit fraud. In addition, regardless of whether the motive is real or perceived, there may be something that we can do about it to reduce the risk of it evolving into a fraud.

External motives originate outside the work environment. There is very little an organization can do to eliminate external motives. However, organizations should be aware of external motives that can contribute to an individual's decision to commit fraud. Examples of external motives include:

- A substance abuse problem
- Extreme financial stress
- Health problems (including those of family members)
- Gambling problems
- A feeling of pressure to achieve a certain lifestyle

Once we understand potential fraud motives, the next step is controlling such behavior in the workplace. How we manage the risk of fraud must be clearly articulated by organization policy. Both awareness of fraud risks and management of those risks are integral parts of an effective organization-wide system of controlling fraud and abuse. In our three-component model of fraud deterrence, described a bit later in this chapter, the second component, dealing with nonfinancial systems, is the one most directly involved with identifying and managing fraud motives.

Opportunity

A real or perceived opportunity to commit fraud or engage in abusive activities is what converts a motive into an action. If a person senses that there is no way that he (or she) could get away with the fraud he is contemplating, he is not likely to attempt it.

Opportunities to commit fraud generally depend upon the quality of internal controls in place in an organization. Of the three interrelated components in our fraud deterrence model, the component dealing with financial controls is most directly associated with limiting opportunities to commit fraud through policies and procedures designed to either prevent or detect it.

Real or perceived opportunities to commit fraud can be classified into three broad categories:

- Weaknesses in the design of financial controls
- Weaknesses in the application of financial controls
- Potential for overriding financial controls

Weaknesses in the design of financial controls typically relate to essential policies and procedures that an organization has not instituted. These weaknesses may pertain to preventive or detective control measures. Examples include:

- Failure to require a clerical check of the mathematical and pricing accuracy of vendor invoices prior to approving them for payment
- Failure to require that bank reconciliations be performed by someone who does not have responsibility for preparing, signing, or recording checks

Weaknesses in the application of financial controls refer to an organization's failure to follow its own policies and procedures. These weaknesses can be due to complete oversight of a policy or carelessness in the performance of a duty. In either case, an organization has established policies and procedures, but is not properly following them. Examples include:

- A supervisor providing rubber stamp approvals on the timesheets submitted by employees under her supervision
- An accounts payable clerk failing to verify that a vendor invoice has not already been paid when preparing a payment to that vendor

Overriding financial controls refers to the ability to circumvent established policies and procedures. Of the three categories of opportunities, this one is most closely associated with fraud because the element of intent is automatically present.

Financial controls can be overridden in any of several ways:

- Collusion between two or more employees, in which key financial controls (such as authorization or review) may be rendered worthless because the parties are not cooperating in the fraud
- Fraudulently documenting a control procedure that hasn't actually been performed (such as when an employee forges the authorization of a department head on an employee expense report)
- Senior management override

The final override, carried out by members of the senior management team, could be considered a failure in existing controls. However, these types of breakdowns in financial control systems are classified with other overrides, due to the intentional nature of the actions.

Overrides of financial controls by senior management occur when a manager forces a departure from standard operating procedures. An example is when a manager commands that an accounts payable clerk process a personally submitted vendor invoice while he waits, without the usual supporting documentation and approvals in place. These exceptions from standard financial controls can occur under the supposition by other employees that the manager knows and does what's best for the organization. An underlying factor may also be that an employee is intimidated by a senior manager and is reluctant to refuse his request due to a lack of compliance with standard operating procedures.

An organization-wide system of fraud deterrence must address all three types of potential overrides, as well as weaknesses in the design or operation of financial controls.

A final thought on opportunities to commit fraud pertains to the manner in which an opportunity is discovered by a perpetrator. In some cases, a perpetrator studies an organization over time, searching for weaknesses in the design or application of financial controls (the opportunity) in order to commit fraud. In others, as with overrides, a perpetrator creates a new opportunity.

But in some cases, an opportunity is accidentally uncovered. An employee honestly forgets to carry out a standard procedure. Yet, afterward, the employee realizes that nobody noticed this failure, indicating that perhaps there is no system in place for verifying this aspect of the employee's work. Lazy employees may take advantage of this knowledge by skipping this step in the future in order to cut down on their workload. Perpetrators of fraud store that knowledge and use it to develop a system for committing fraud against their employers.

Concealment

Nobody who is currently committing fraud against a nonprofit organization volunteered to be interviewed for this book. This statement may seem rather obvious. But it symbolizes another critical element of fraud and abuse.

When someone commits fraud, they usually do not wish to get caught. In order to keep from getting caught, the perpetrator will take steps to conceal their actions. Concealment may involve any or all of the following actions:

- Altering documents
- Destroying documents
- Maintaining a duplicate set of accounting records
- Fabricating phony supporting documentation
- Forging a signature
- Lying to coworkers and supervisors (and auditors)
- Maintaining silence
- Bribing coworkers and others to maintain silence
- Forcing account reconciliations
- Recording bogus journal entries to move their fraud from one account to another
- Recording additional entries to establish an unnecessarily complicated trail of activity
- Never taking vacation or sick leave, in order to ensure that nobody ever fills in for them
- Restricting access to files using personal locks, so that nobody can examine affected files when the perpetrator is not present

As Chapters 3 through 7 will demonstrate, certain frauds are easier to conceal than others. The process of concealing some frauds will leave behind a paper trail that, if properly investigated, can lead to discovery of the scheme. Many perpetrators of frauds have relied on the fact that nobody is checking up on the paper trail, which allows their scheme to continue for many years.

Because of the fact that concealment is necessary and because it may leave a trail of evidence, it is sometimes more practical to *detect* a fraud than to attempt to *prevent* it. The classic example of this involves disbursement frauds. There are so many possible methods of fraudulently withdrawing money from an organization's accounts that focusing exclusively on prevention simply isn't practical, or even possible in some instances. Detective measures in the form of immediate reconciliations of bank statements are always essential as a means of finding many of the disbursement frauds that may not be easily prevented. Certainly, a combination of policies and procedures designed to both prevent and detect all types of frauds will provide an organization with the most comprehensive protection.

Rationalization

Rationalization is the element that keeps someone from turning themselves in after they have committed fraud. Rationalization also aids the continuation of the fraud when it goes undetected for some time.

The element of rationalization also brings us full circle, back to the motive that first causes someone to engage in a fraudulent or abusive activity. Some of the factors identified as motives may also serve as rationalization to continue a scheme.

However, rationalization usually involves something else. Examples of rationalizations to continue a scheme (or not voluntarily admit to wrongdoing) include:

- A feeling that one's embezzlement is small in comparison to the overall size of the organization
- A sense of justification (feeling one is entitled to their take, perhaps because they believe their salary is too low or the organization otherwise owes it to them)
- Depersonalization of the victim (a feeling that stealing from the organization does not harm anyone individually)
- Convincing themselves that they will repay the organization later (or they'll stop at some point), because their actions are only temporary in nature, a short-term solution to a short-term problem
- A feeling that others are doing it, so why shouldn't they do it too

Like most other factors present in frauds, there are steps that can be incorporated into our organization-wide model of fraud deterrence that will address rationalization.

RISK MANAGEMENT

Organizations practice risk management with respect to all sorts of risks. This book is really about one form of risk management—that associated with the risks of fraud and abuse.

There are four aspects of risk management as it pertains to fraud and abuse:

- *Assessment.* The identification of an organization's potential risks of fraud and abuse from within and from external sources
- *Reduction.* The establishment of policies and procedures designed to prevent or detect fraud and abuse
- *Transfer.* The use of insurance or other means to transfer the financial risks associated with fraud
- *Acceptance.* The level of financial exposure to fraud that an organization is willing to accept

The final three elements of risk management form a triad that requires a balancing act. Because it is impossible to eliminate all known risks (much less the risks we haven't been able to identify), we must balance the imposition of a reasonable array of policies and procedures designed to prevent or detect frauds with risk transfer and risk acceptance. Our goal is to reduce acceptable risk to a level that is practical and affordable.

As with the factors present in all frauds, each element of risk management must be identified and addressed in an organization-wide system of fraud deterrence.

A COMPREHENSIVE MODEL FOR CONTROLLING FRAUD AND ABUSE

Minimizing an organization's risk of loss due to fraud and abuse entails an organization-wide effort that involves every officer, director, and employee in an organization. This organization-wide model of fraud deterrence involves three interrelated components:

- Financial controls
- Nonfinancial systems
- Management oversight and behavior

Financial Controls

Financial controls involve specific policies and procedures utilized in the processing of or accounting for specific transactions of an organization. As the term is used in this book, *financial controls* differs from the broader term *internal controls* in several respects.

The term "internal controls" is used frequently by auditors and accountants. The concept of internal controls is very broad and concerns all policies, procedures, behaviors, practices, and related elements designed to achieve a variety of objectives, including, but not limited to:

- Timely, accurate financial reporting
- Safeguarding of assets
- Compliance with laws and regulations
- Efficient utilization of organization resources

Included in discussions of internal controls are elements as specific as who is authorized to sign checks and what steps should be done as part of the process of approving a vendor invoice. Also included in internal controls are elements that are more organization-wide in their application (such as hiring practices or carrying of insurance) or characteristics that are difficult to measure (such as management's overall attitude toward ethical behavior).

Given the broadness of this concept of internal control, as well as its many and diverse objectives, for purposes of the fraud deterrence model described in this book, it was decided that financial controls would be broken out separately from all other internal controls. Many auditors would argue that almost every aspect included within each of the three components of this fraud deterrence model falls under the umbrella of internal control. This is all the more reason to break the model down into three separate and distinct components, each with its own objectives and characteristics.

Thus, the term "financial controls" will be used in reference to specific policies and procedures associated with particular transaction cycles, such as:

- Recording revenue
- Collecting payments (from donors, members, customers, etc.)
- Purchasing
- Disbursing funds (to vendors, etc.)
- Processing payroll
- Administering grant-funded programs
- Periodic reconciliations of individual account balances

The term will be applied to all of these specific steps leading up to the preparation of organization-wide financial statements. Analysis of these financial statements is considered under the management systems and behavior component, along with other management functions (many of which are commonly addressed as internal controls).

The objectives of financial controls in the fight against fraud are as follows:

- To minimize the real or perceived opportunities to commit fraud and abuse
- To identify in a timely manner frauds that have been perpetrated (in other words, make it difficult or impossible to conceal a fraud)

Financial controls can be classified into two categories, based on their objectives regarding fraud and abuse:

- Preventive controls
- Detective controls

Preventive and detective controls are also included in the other two interrelated components of the fraud deterrence model. But they are the very essence of financial controls, and every financial control described in Part II of this book is either a preventive or detective control (and in some cases, both).

Financial controls should be designed to address both internal and external frauds. In fact, many financial controls apply equally to the prevention or detection of internal and external frauds. However, there are several important financial controls designed exclusively to address internal frauds.

As the term implies, a preventive control would stop a fraud before it could be successfully carried out. Examples of preventive controls include:

- Locks on filing cabinets
- Use of passwords that prevent access to certain software applications
- Requiring approvals on timesheets before a paycheck is generated

When thinking of preventive controls and fraud, it is important to think of each transaction that an organization processes (and each potential fraud) as a series of small steps. Preventive controls should be contemplated for each step along the way, to the extent practical. The more roadblocks put up, the greater the chances of thwarting the fraud. In some transaction cycles, it is necessary to string together multiple preventive measures, because individually, each has weaknesses. In simpler transaction cycles, a single preventive control is all that is necessary.

Detective controls are designed to catch the frauds (and honest errors) that make their way through the preventive controls. Recall from the discussion earlier in this chapter that there are three possible breakdowns in financial controls that can result in an opportunity to commit fraud. As applied to preventive controls, those breakdowns are as follows:

- Weaknesses in the design of preventive controls
- Failures in the application of preventive controls
- Circumvention of (overriding) the preventive controls

As a result, regardless of how strong we feel our preventive controls might be, it is *always* essential to include detective measures as a part of the financial controls implemented to fight fraud and abuse. Of course, the weaker the preventive measures, the more important it becomes to add stronger detective controls.

Examples of detective financial controls include:

- Performing monthly bank reconciliations
- Reconciling actual results with expected results
- Requiring mandatory vacations, during which another employee performs the tasks of the vacationing employee

Additional detective controls will be explained in each of the second and third components of the fraud deterrence model.

There is yet one final value in detective controls that demonstrates how valuable they can be to an organization. A well-communicated detective control can be one of the strongest deterrents in preventing a fraud from being attempted in the first place. Nothing illustrates the power of a well-communicated detective measure better than the video surveillance camera. The camera is not going to stop someone from taking money out of a cash register, putting it in his pockets, and fleeing. But, when that camera is visible, a potential perpetrator has to consider whether it's working, if anyone is watching, and if a recording is being made. Just putting the camera in plain view can convince the person that their theft may not be worth the risk.

Nonfinancial Systems

Several nonfinancial systems are important in controlling fraud and abuse. Some of the nonfinancial systems that play critical roles are:

- Human resource policies and procedures
- Information technology systems
- Physical security
- Communication systems
- Insurance

Similar to the financial controls that comprised the first component of our model, nonfinancial systems address multiple factors involved in fraud and abuse. Whereas financial controls deal with opportunities to commit fraud and the concealment of a fraud, nonfinancial systems deal with all of the following factors:

- Motives (through HR and communications systems)
- Opportunities (through IT and physical security)
- Concealment (through IT, physical security, and communications systems)
- Rationalization (through HR and communications systems)

In addition, nonfinancial systems consider multiple aspects of risk management. Whereas financial controls focus primarily on reduction of risk, nonfinancial systems aid in all four elements of risk management:

- Assessment of risk (through communications systems)
- Reduction of risk (through IT, physical security, and communications systems)
- Transfer of risk (through insurance)
- Risk acceptance (through HR and communications systems)

Throughout Part IV, the many important roles of these nonfinancial systems in an organization's fraud deterrence model are explained and illustrated.

Management Oversight and Behavior

Management oversight and behavior represent the third and final component in the defense against fraud and abuse. You may have heard the expression "tone at the top" before. Although somewhat overused, it has never been more applicable. The actions of management do indeed have a direct effect on the behavior of the entire organization. If management expects everyone else to abide by a strict standard of ethical behavior and compliance with organization policies while at the same time they ignore the policies themselves, they will be sorely disappointed.

In our model, the "tone at the top" is just one aspect of management oversight and behavior. Other key elements include financial analysis, budgeting, communicating fraud deterrence responsibilities throughout the organization, the role of managers and supervisors in controlling fraud, internal and external audit functions, the role of the board of directors, audit committees, investigative functions, and crisis management.

Nothing demonstrates the interrelatedness of the fraud deterrence model's three components (financial controls, nonfinancial systems, and management oversight) better than financial analysis. Analysis of financial results can be performed at an individual account balance or functional level. This would typically be considered a financial control. However, big picture financial analysis of organization-wide results and studying financial trends over time is a management oversight function. Accordingly, elements of financial analysis will be presented in each of the first and third components of the model.

Each of these three components by itself is critical to an organization's success in controlling fraud and abuse. Yet they are also interrelated. Focusing entirely on one component at the exclusion of another will inevitably have an adverse effect on an organization's ability to defend itself against fraud and abuse. The three components of the model are also interrelated from the standpoint that for the best defense, the model should involve each and every person, function, department, and level within an organization from board members, executive directors, and department heads to managers, supervisors, and entry-level employees.

HOW THIS BOOK IS ORGANIZED

Now that we've gone over the basics, it's time to move on to the specific steps that each and every nonprofit organization can take to reduce the risk of loss due to fraudulent activities.

The remainder of this book is organized in a manner consistent with the three-part model for deterring fraud and abuse.

- Financial controls regarding
    - Frauds committed against nonprofits (Part II)
    - Frauds committed by, for, or through nonprofits (Part III)
- Nonfinancial systems (Part IV)
- Management oversight and behavior (Part V)

Part II

Chapters 3 through 7 focus on specific financial controls that are helpful in either preventing or detecting certain types of fraud and abuse. Chapters 3 through 6 are devoted to internal fraud and abuse—those committed by officers, directors, employees, and volunteers against their own organization. These chapters are organized by category of fraud and abuse scheme:

- Cash receipts and revenue schemes (Chapter 3)
- Purchasing and cash disbursement schemes (Chapter 4)
- Payroll and expense reporting schemes (Chapter 5)
- Other asset misappropriations (Chapter 6)

Chapter 7 deals with external frauds—those committed by vendors, contractors, subrecipients, fundraisers, consultants, investment managers, fulfillment houses, and other parties with which the organization interacts.

In each section of these chapters, several schemes will be explained in detail. Each explanation will be followed by the specific financial and accounting policies and procedures that apply to that scheme.

The focus throughout Part II is exclusively on the financial policies and procedures that could prevent or detect a specific scheme.

Part III

Whereas Chapters 3 through 7 are devoted to fraud and abuse schemes in which the nonprofit organization is the victim, Chapters 8 through 10 reverse the tables by addressing fraud perpetrated *by, for,* or *through* a nonprofit against outsiders (mostly, the public or the government). Fundraising fraud and abuse, financial reporting fraud, noncompliance with donor restrictions, filing false statements, program fraud, and other frauds that can be attributed to a nonprofit organization will be explained in this section.

Of course, people, policies, and procedures are inevitably behind these outward-directed frauds. Accordingly, Chapters 8 through 10 will include descriptions of the specific financial controls that should be in place to prevent or detect each of the types of wrongdoing that could be attributed to a nonprofit organization.

Part IV

Chapters 11 and 12 explain the roles of nonfinancial systems in controlling fraud and abuse. As explained earlier, these nonfinancial systems play integral roles in the battle against fraudulence. They represent the second part of the three interrelated components in the model of organizational defense.

Specifically, Chapter 11 focuses on the critical role that an organization's human resources play in deterring fraud and abuse. Chapter 12 deals with other nonfinancial systems that help in the fight against fraud, such as the information technology systems and functions, physical security, hotlines and communications systems, and insurance coverage. Chapter 11 also addresses the emerging issue of protecting personal information of a nonprofit organization's donors, members, students, and other program participants.

Part V

Chapters 13 through 15 address the third and final component in our model— management oversight and behavior. These systems include budgeting, financial analysis, internal and external audits, fraud-related responsibilities of boards of directors, the proper use of audit committees, and the handling of accusations of fraud and abuse.

Appendix

Included in the appendix are samples of some of the policies mentioned throughout the book. Also included are a sample audit committee charter and other resources that may be useful in developing an organization-wide model of fraud prevention and detection.

SUGGESTED USES OF THIS BOOK

As stated earlier, there is something in this book for everyone employed by or serving on the boards of directors of a nonprofit organization, as well as for a few others, such as auditors. Some suggested applications of this book for each of these users follows.

For Board Members

Knowing all the intricate details of fraud prevention and detection is probably not required reading, but it could certainly be helpful. The most important uses of this book for board members are to:

- Obtain a general understanding of the model of deterrence by reading Chapter 2.
- Read Chapters 13 and 14 to have a solid grasp of the roles and responsibilities of management and the board of directors and to begin developing a plan of action for dealing with fraud and abuse.
- Make sure you understand the scope and limitations of an independent audit by a CPA firm, a topic that is explained in Chapter 14.
- Request a review of the organization's internal controls and other policies for conformity with the practices recommended throughout this book (see below).
- Periodically reassess the organization's vulnerability to fraud, as well as its systems for deterrence.

In addition, members of the organization's audit committee may wish to read applicable sections of Chapters 3 through 15 to obtain a more detailed understanding of the specific controls, policies, and procedures that are helpful in deterring fraud and abuse.

Many board members will ask who should perform the review of organization policies suggested above. *Each functional area should be reviewed by someone independent of the function being reviewed.* Having each department review its own operations works fine—as long as no fraud is taking place. But keep in mind what we're dealing with here! People will conceal fraud, and that concealment will extend to being dishonest about the policies and procedures in place in their department.

So, while we don't inherently want to distrust everybody, now is not the time for blind faith either. *Independent* analysis of your organization's systems, including the review of policies in this book, is important.

You wouldn't ask your internal accountant to perform an audit. Apply the same principle to the fraud risk assessment that can be performed based on the practices recommended in this book. Options available for independent analysis of the organization's policies include:

- Hiring an outside consultant, such as a Certified Fraud Examiner, to interview staff and review policies, procedures, and practices in place in your organization
- Having personnel from each department within the organization review the operations associated with other departments

- Take on the task directly as board members, by allocating a functional area (or chapter of this book) to each board member
- Form a special ad hoc committee of board members and other volunteers
- Form an alliance with another nonprofit organization in town, under which your organization's staff evaluates their operations and their staff evaluates yours

Obviously, there is a greater level of objectivity when the evaluation of an organization's policies and procedures is outsourced to an independent consultant or fraud specialist than if it is done internally. But this will cost money, just as insurance and other steps to safeguard your organization's assets and reputation do. Realistically, some organizations simply cannot or will not hire independent experts to perform this assessment.

There are certain precautions that should be taken if the review of controls and policies suggested is being performed by people that are not experts in the subject matter (if they are not fraud specialists, auditors, or experts in the subject area, such as human resources or information technology). Chief among those precautions is for preparers to take a "show me" approach to their review. Don't have reviewers simply ask whether the suggested practices are in place. This makes it too easy to get into a yes or no routine with no verification of the answers and no means of determining whether the answers even make sense. Have reviewers ask the interviewees to show them how each step is accomplished.

Even with this approach, it is possible for dishonest people to deceive someone. For this reason, it is always best to utilize experts in fraud, auditing, internal controls, and each of the nonfinancial specialties.

For Executive Directors and Senior Management

The entire internal senior management team, from executive director or chief executive officer to the chief operating officer, chief financial officers, and the leaders of each primary department or division, must take an active stance in fraud deterrence. This is best accomplished by taking the following steps:

- Obtain a general understanding of the current risks of fraud and the comprehensive model of fraud deterrence by reading Chapters 1 and 2.
- Read Chapters 13 through 15 to have a solid grasp of the roles and responsibilities of management and the board of directors.
- Become involved in the review of your organization's controls and policies, especially those in your area(s) of responsibility, and review and understand the results, which may entail reading selected sections of other chapters in detail. You will be ultimately responsible for taking follow-up actions to protect your organization from fraud.

For Chief Financial Officers

Of course, much of the model involves policies and procedures that are typically the responsibility of an organization's accounting or finance department. Under the direction of the CFO, this department will have the greatest level of involvement with applying or enforcing many of the financial controls described in this book.

Accordingly, CFOs of nonprofit organizations should be familiar with all aspects of the model, not just those described in the preceding section for other senior members of the management team. There is probably not a chapter in the book that isn't applicable to most CFOs and their departments. As part of the CFO's broad financial oversight responsibilities, the financial ratios described in Chapter 15 are designed to be of direct use to CFOs in analyzing financial and operating results for presentation to the executive management team and the board of directors. This analysis can be particularly useful as a method of detecting fraud at all levels within an organization.

For Managers and Supervisors

All employees with supervisory responsibilities, whether those responsibilities are programmatic functions or supporting service functions, also have a responsibility to instill an antifraud spirit within their department. Their fraud-related responsibilities extend well beyond this, of course. Chapter 13 explains the key role that supervisory employees play in deterring fraud. It is a must for all supervisors. Based on the functional role each has within the organization, other chapters also should be read to gain a fuller understanding of the nature of the schemes to which their division or department is prone.

For Auditors (External and Internal)

External auditors can utilize this book to help in assessing the risk of fraud in an audit of a nonprofit organization. The October 2002 issuance by the AICPA of Statement on Auditing Standards No. 99 ushers in a new era of auditor responsibility pertaining to fraud. Chief among these is a greater expectation to tailor the audit procedures to the auditor's understanding of the specific fraud risks in place in an audited organization.

This book has two applications for auditors to help meet their SAS 99 responsibilities:

1. As a basis for identifying specific fraud threats to their nonprofit clients as part of the pre-audit "brainstorming" session required by the new standard
2. As an aid in designing specific detective audit procedures to address these threats, based on the suggested controls and policies explained throughout this book

External auditors should read Chapters 13 and 14 for more on SAS 99 as it relates to management's expectations.

As for internal auditors, a similar use of this book is recommended. One of the roles of internal auditors is to focus attention on identified risk areas—more in-depth attention in many cases than would be feasible by the external auditor. The discussions of specific fraud threats, and the suggested controls and policies designed to protect against each, are designed to aid in that cause.

PART II

FINANCIAL CONTROLS ASSOCIATED WITH SPECIFIC CATEGORIES OF FRAUD AND ABUSE

The focus of Part II is on financial controls useful in preventing or detecting specific types of frauds committed against nonprofit organizations. The term "financial controls" is used here rather than "internal controls" for an important reason. Internal controls represent a broad array of policies and procedures designed to accomplish several objectives, from the safeguarding of assets to timely and accurate financial reporting and even efficient utilization of organizational resources. Financial controls represent one component of internal controls. Financial controls, as the term is used in this book, are those policies, procedures, and practices applied in specific accounting cycles to ensure the integrity of an organization's accounting records.

Controlling fraud and abuse involves all aspects of internal controls, including financial controls, as well as other policies and procedures that may not even be considered a part of internal controls. Part II focuses exclusively on financial controls. Other elements of internal control and other policies and procedures will be addressed in later sections of the book. These controls are presented in a manner that corresponds to each specific type of fraud that poses a significant threat to most nonprofit organizations.

Chapters 3 through 6 concern fraud and abuse schemes generally carried out by insiders—employees, officers, and directors of nonprofit organizations. Chapter 7 addresses certain frauds and abuses committed against nonprofits by outsiders, such as vendors.

The format used to address each category of fraudulent activity in Chapters 3 through 7 is as follows:

- Provide an overview of general financial controls applicable to each broad accounting cycle.
- Explain how each specific type of fraud and abuse is carried out and which persons are most likely to be in a position to do so.
- Describe the specific financial controls that could prevent each scheme from being committed.
- Describe the specific financial controls that could result in detection of the scheme.

There are certain common themes to the financial controls described throughout Part II. Those themes are:

- Separation of duties that, if performed by a single person, could make it possible to commit and conceal a fraud
- Appropriate levels of review and approval prior to transactions and entries being finalized
- Timely account reconciliations
- Regular account monitoring and financial analysis
- Promoting the awareness of detective controls as a method of deterring would-be perpetrators from even attempting a fraud (the mere existence of strong financial controls and the fact that staff and volunteers are aware of them go a long way toward discouraging fraud)

The specific application of each of these themes varies from one accounting cycle to another and from one type of fraud to another. This will be explained in each chapter throughout Part II.

In each chapter, examples from real-world fraud cases involving nonprofit organizations will be provided to illustrate specific types of frauds. In each case, readers should note which internal controls were missing and how that enabled the perpetrator to commit the fraud. Also notice how the fraud was ultimately uncovered, for this often provides other clues about how to control fraud and abuse.

While few organizations will likely have to deal with all of the issues explained in Part II, it is not unreasonable to expect those people responsible for preventing and detecting fraud to spend some time thinking through the various processes in place in their organization with an eye toward answering the question, "How could this apply to me?" This process will often identify flaws in policies and procedures, allowing improvements to be made in the quality of the controls currently in place.

3

Revenue and Cash Receipts Schemes

Revenue and cash receipts schemes involve any fraud in which resources intended for a nonprofit organization are diverted for the benefit of the perpetrator. Those resources may involve cash, checks, credit card payments, electronic funds transfers, or even food, clothing, equipment, and other assets donated to an organization. The primary categories of revenue and cash receipts fraud explained in this chapter are:

- Skimming
- Lapping schemes
- Write-offs of accounts receivable
- Unauthorized credits
- Unrecorded sales
- Theft of donated merchandise

FINANCIAL CONTROLS OVER REVENUE AND CASH RECEIPTS

Following the explanation of each method of fraud and abuse involving revenue and cash receipts, key financial controls associated with preventing or detecting that particular scheme will be identified and explained. Nonprofit managers should compare these controls with those in place in their own organizations to identify areas where improvements can be made.

Certain financial controls apply equally to multiple categories of revenue and cash receipts frauds. Segregation of duties is one such element. In the areas of revenue and cash receipts, the following duties should be segregated to the maximum extent possible:

- Billing (invoicing customers for goods and services provided by the organization)
- Recording revenue in the accounting records
- Receipt of payments (opening mail, collecting funds, etc.)
- Initial recording of collections
- Preparation of deposits
- Posting of receipts to the accounting records (including the offset against accounts receivable, if applicable)
- Reconciling the bank statement
- Reconciling accounts receivable subledger (the detailed listing of balances owed by customer) with the general ledger balance

Ideally, each of these duties should be performed by a different person. Often this is not possible, especially with smaller organizations. In these cases, the organization should strive to segregate as many duties as possible, especially the recording of revenue, receipt of funds, and maintenance of accounts receivable records. When one person controls all three of these functions, the potential for a cash receipts fraud increases significantly.

Keep in mind that the purpose of segregation of duties is to prevent a person from committing *and concealing* a fraud. If all duties that should ideally be segregated cannot be segregated, focus on segregating the duties associated with committing a fraud from those necessary to conceal the fraud. For example, separate the duties associated with handling receipts and making deposits from duties connected with recording revenue and maintaining accounts receivable records.

Throughout this chapter, specific financial controls associated with particular revenue and cash receipt frauds will be explained. In addition to these specific controls and the principles of segregation, there are certain other general controls applicable to revenue and cash receipts processing that should be in place in every organization. These general controls are not associated with any one type of fraud discussed in this chapter but, instead, apply to all aspects of revenue and cash receipts accounting. These general controls include:

- Immediate restrictive endorsement of checks received, using a stamp that marks the organization's account name and account number on the backs of all checks received (this simple step makes it much more difficult, if not impossible, to subsequently steal the checks and deposit them into another account, as explained later in the skimming section)

- Timely depositing of funds received (not just cash, but checks too), in order to minimize the risk of subsequent theft (in addition to reducing the risk of theft, making deposits daily also makes it easier to reconcile daily postings to deposits later)
- If it is not possible or practical to make deposits every day, locking up undeposited funds in a safe overnight
- If large volumes of cash or checks are handled in public or centralized areas, such as with some retail operations, conferences, and special events, organizations may consider the following additional safeguards:
  - Installation of security cameras
  - Prohibiting employees who handle funds from bringing purses, bags, briefcases, or similar containers into the area in which they will be handling funds
  - Hiring security personnel to observe or pose as customers or donors
- Maintaining a permanent record of the initial intake of all funds received (a cash receipts log or an equivalent) that identifies, by date received, payor names, amounts, form of payment (cash, check, etc.), and a description of what the payment is for (contribution, dues, etc.)
- Periodic reconciliation of the cash receipts log with deposits made to the organization's bank
- Periodic reconciliation of cash receipts logs with revenue recorded on the accounting records

The last three steps from the preceding list do not *prevent* any frauds from taking place. However, they are critical to the subsequent *detection* of most revenue and cash receipts frauds described throughout the rest of this chapter. Creation of a permanent record of funds received upon their initial intake enables someone to later reconcile this record with bank deposits and accounting entries in an organization's revenue and receivables accounts.

SKIMMING

Skimming of cash receipts involves the theft of funds intended for an organization *before* the funds have been recorded on the books. The term "cash receipts" as it is used here is intended to cover not just cash collected, but also checks, credit card payments, and any other form of payment intended for an organization. Typically, skimming is perpetrated by one of the following employees in an organization:

- Someone who either initially collects or opens incoming mail
- The person who initially logs in cash receipts, prepares the deposit, or takes the deposit to the bank
- An employee involved at a point of sale (cashiers, etc.)
- Door-to-door solicitors of charitable contributions

How does the perpetrator of a skimming fraud benefit from their theft? If cash is stolen, the answer is obvious. But many nonprofit organizations naively think that checks made payable to the organization cannot be converted to cash. This couldn't be further from the truth. The only difference between skimming cash and skimming checks is that the perpetrator must wait two or three days for checks to clear before spending the fruits of their labor. The process of converting stolen checks to cash is remarkably easy. The perpetrator simply opens a bank account in the name of the nonprofit organization to whom the checks are written, with the perpetrator as the authorized signer on the account. The account is usually opened at a bank with whom the nonprofit organization has no current relationship. However, there have been instances in which accounts were opened at the very same bank as the one used by the organization, taking advantage of the bank employees' familiarity with the person opening the account as a reason for not scrutinizing the opening of a new account very closely. The perpetrator's home address, or that of a friend or relative, is used as the address to which bank statements are to be mailed. Sometimes a post office box is used for the receipt of bank statements.

Fraudulently opening such an account is not very difficult to do. Generally, a bank may request copies of organizational documents or other items, such as articles of incorporation, a board authorization, or some similar document. Each of these documents is relatively easy to fraudulently create with modern word processing software. Sample forms and documents are available from many office supply and bookstores. For identification purposes, the perpetrator often uses their own driver's license. Alternatively, fake identification is sometimes presented.

The final step in fraudulently opening an account is the employer identification number. Banks will require this number when opening new accounts. Again, this is not a very difficult obstacle for a crook to overcome. Some perpetrators have used either the organization's real identification number or their own personal social security number to open an account. Others have either provided bogus numbers, illegally obtained social security numbers (often of recently deceased persons), or have applied for and received employer identification numbers from the Internal Revenue Service. To minimize the risk associated with supplying an employer identification number, the perpetrator usually will open a non-interest-bearing account.

This way, there is no reporting of interest income to the Internal Revenue Service (or to the organization, if the organization's employer identification number has been used).

Once an account is opened, the perpetrator deposits the skimmed checks into the account, waits for the checks to clear, and then withdraws the funds for personal purposes as needed. Frequently, perpetrators of skimming frauds write checks out of the fraudulently opened account to pay personal bills, as well as to purchase extravagant items. The existence of fraudulently opened accounts is very difficult to detect, especially if they are at financial institutions with whom the organization does not regularly conduct business. Some of these accounts have remained open for many years, without anyone ever suspecting a thing, before they were detected.

Most skimming activities involve the skimming of cash or checks intended for an organization. However, now that more people are using credit cards to make payments (including charitable contribution payments), the prevalence of credit card skimming has also risen. In many cases, all that is necessary to begin skimming credit card payments is the installation of credit card processing software on a home computer. As with the preceding demonstration of check skimming, once an account has been opened in the name of the organization, people making payments by credit card can rarely tell the difference between a fraudulent account and a legitimate account when the charge appears on their credit card bill in the name of the organization.

Charitable Contributions

Of all the categories of skimming fraud described in this chapter, perhaps of all the frauds explained in this entire book, the skimming of charitable contributions intended for a nonprofit organization is the most difficult to detect. The primary reason is because the fraud is entirely off book in nature, meaning that the fraud can be perpetrated without it being necessary to make any entries in the accounting records to conceal the fraud (unless a receivable has previously been recorded in connection with a pledge or promise to give). Because no accounting entries need to be made, concealing the fraud becomes simple or even unnecessary (see Fraud in the Headlines 3.1).

The characteristic that makes skimming of charitable contributions an off-book fraud is the nonreciprocal nature of a contribution. In virtually every other transaction, an organization provides something of value in exchange for income. As such, an outflow of resources is necessary to generate the revenue, and that outflow is generally recorded somewhere in the accounting records. In many cases, this outflow can subsequently be reconciled with recorded revenue (this becomes an important detective control, as explained later in the sections on skimming of other types of revenue).

This is not so with charitable contributions. All a donor anticipates in exchange for her contribution is a thank you. As a result, there is no outflow of resources that can be reconciled to anticipated income.

FRAUD IN THE HEADLINES 3.1

COLLEGE PRESIDENT STOLE $3 MILLION OF CONTRIBUTIONS

There have been many reported cases in which charitable contributions intended for an organization have been skimmed by someone involved in the collection process. One of the more substantial of these cases involved the former president of Mississippi College, who was sued for diverting $3 million in contributions intended for the college over a 15-year period from 1978 to 1993.

The fraud was perpetrated by personally collecting checks made payable to the college and depositing the checks into an account that the president fraudulently opened in the name of the college. Subsequently, funds were transferred from this account into other accounts controlled by the president. To conceal the fraud, all the president had to do was provide donors with fake receipts, which were later discovered in his office.

One of the reasons that the fraud had not been suspected earlier was the manner in which the president spread the skimming out over such a long period, taking a fairly consistent amount from year to year. The president also targeted large gifts. The college reported that the president diverted at least 54 gifts averaging $55,600 each.

The fraud was discovered only when a college fundraiser approached a prospective donor, only to be told that the person had already made a gift and delivered it directly to the president.

Source: Nicklin, Julie L., "Mississippi College Contends Its President Embezzled $3-Million," *Chronicle of Higher Education*, September 1, 1993.

There are few internal controls that can completely prevent skimming of charitable contributions intended for an organization. The following controls, however, can substantially reduce the risk of skimming:

- Use of a bank lockbox service
- Dual control over the initial intake of contributions
- In situations where an organization receives pledges of future support (promises to give) prior to payment, segregating the duties associated with recording the pledge and posting payments against pledges from duties associated with collecting and depositing payments received

Lockbox services are provided by many financial institutions. With a lockbox service, donors are requested to mail their contributions to a post office box or other box number controlled by the financial institution. The collection and initial record-keeping associated with the contribution payments are handled by the bank and subject to the bank's internal controls. The bank periodically provides the organization with a listing of contributions received by date, along with either copies of the checks or a more detailed listing of donor information (name, address, etc.). The frequency of these listings varies from daily to weekly, based upon the volume of activity and the arrangement an organization has with its bank.

Internal controls at banks that have lockbox services can generally be relied upon by nonprofit organizations. While there have been breaches in security reported (such as one case in which a lockbox employee was found to have taken contributions intended for one charity home and discarded them in her trash in order to "catch up" on her work), controls are usually sound (even in this case, the employee's actions were detected very quickly by the bank). The volume of lockbox activity at these financial institutions usually necessitates the involvement of many people in the process and numerous cross-checks in their systems.

Even with a lockbox service, nonprofit organizations still must take certain precautions to prevent skimming activities. The primary risk associated with lockbox services is that donors will not use the lockbox established by the organization. This has been known to happen in the following situations:

- A perpetrator controls the printing of contribution solicitations and has the correct lockbox address printed on *some* solicitations and a fraudulent post office box controlled by the perpetrator on other solicitations.
- A perpetrator controls the printing or insertion of business reply envelopes into charitable contribution solicitations and inserts envelopes with the correct lockbox address in *some* mailings and an envelope with a fraudulent address into other mailings.

Accordingly, the design, printing, and mailing of charitable contribution solicitations should be subject to oversight.

Dual control exists when two or more people are involved in the initial intake of contributions (or other funds). This initial intake involves the receipt of the funds and the creation of an initial listing of all funds received. Once this listing has been established, there is no further need for dual control for the subsequent steps in the accounting process.

Dual control is a frequently misunderstood concept. It is commonly suggested by auditors in their management letters to nonprofits and often criticized as impractical by nonprofit organizations. The underlying principle behind dual control is that the risk of fraud is substantially *reduced* if collusion among two or more employees is *required* in order to carry out the fraud. The risk of fraud is certainly not eliminated, and numerous cases involving collusion have been reported. But, the concept of reducing risk in this manner is a sound one.

Dual control does *not* mean hiring a second employee to watch the first employee (this is where the misunderstanding sometimes originates). It simply means that at the point in time when funds are first received, two people are present to account for all receipts. This can be a temporary situation, lasting only as long as it takes to create the initial cash receipts listing.

If dual controls are to be implemented, it is critical that they be in place at the *first* receipt of funds. Having dual controls in place after someone has already handled the funds by himself is too late. The point at which dual controls should be in place varies depending upon an organization's operations, but may be at any of the following stages:

- The initial receipt or collection of mail containing payments (not just the opening of the mail)
- The door-to-door solicitation and collection of charitable contributions
- The on-site collection of contributions at charity fundraising events
- Any other initial collection of cash, checks, or other forms of payment

Strict dual control involves one person counting cash and logging in all receipts in the presence of a second person, who subsequently recounts and verifies the listing. The two persons then sign off on the listing as a complete and accurate listing of all receipts prior to the preparation of the bank deposit (which may then be performed by one of these same employees or by another employee).

Another key component of dual control is the creation of a log or cash receipts listing that becomes a *permanent* record. The value of this record is that it facilitates the ability to subsequently reconcile amounts received per the record with amounts deposited intact into the organization's bank account (thereby confirming that nobody who handled the receipts after the application of the dual controls skimmed any of the funds prior to deposit). This reconciliation could also be done on an item-by-item (donor-by-donor) basis, checking that each individual gift logged in under dual control was subsequently deposited into the organization's account. Due to the importance of this listing as a permanent record, it should not be prepared in a manner that is easily altered. Manual listings in pencil should be avoided (use pen, if a manual listing is kept). If listings are prepared using spreadsheet or similar software that allows for subsequent alteration of the file, it is important that a paper copy of the original document be printed and signed by the two persons responsible for the initial dual control.

A practical alternative to the strict dual control described in the preceding paragraph is for each person to count and log approximately half of the total collection, but still in close proximity to one another. This allows for the work associated with initially logging in all receipts to be done in less time, but still with some level of internal control. Though weaker than the strict dual control, each person counting and logging collections in the presence of the other makes it difficult for one person to skim receipts without the other person noticing. It should be pointed out, however, that this is certainly not as secure and would only be suggested in limited cases where time available is very limited and so, too, is the potential for large amounts of money being processed.

There are also a handful of internal controls that can *detect* whether charitable contributions have been skimmed. However, they are very limited in application, so organizations should clearly focus on prevention instead. A few examples of detective controls, none of which are foolproof, are:

- Rotation of duties and mandatory vacations for employees involved in processing charitable contributions received (if, while the person[s] who normally processes cash receipts is away, the amount of recorded collections is noticeably higher or lower, it could indicate that that person is skimming)

- Reconciliation of an organization's use of business reply mail envelopes (if one business reply mail permit is used exclusively for receipt of contributions, the total *pieces of mail* processed by the U.S. Postal Service, for which the Service invoices the permit-holder, can be reconciled with the total *number* of charitable contribution transactions recorded and deposited per the deposit slips)

- Periodically mailing statements of donor activity based on recorded contributions and following up on calls or complaints from donors expressing concerns that their statements do not reflect all gifts made (this procedure is most applicable in situations where donors make repeated gifts to the same organization throughout the year, such as with churches)

- Publishing of donor names (organizations can create an expectation on the part of donors that if they make a charitable contribution, their names will be listed in a periodical published by the charity) and following up on calls from donors stating that their names did not appear in the listing

Be advised, publishing of donor names only provides an element of internal control if donors have an expectation of seeing their names in a publication. Even then, the reliability of this control is rather limited. The expectation of seeing their names in this published listing must be strong enough to trigger phone calls or other communication from donors if their names do not appear in print. If a pattern is detected (i.e., many names were omitted from the listing when the donors, in fact, made contributions), then the fraud can be caught. This limited control is likely to be somewhat reliable in situations where there is a limited pool of potential donors, such as members of a university's alumni association or similar group that routinely receives these periodic listings and has come to expect donor listings to be included.

Still, an internal control is only as strong as its application. The mere publication of a donor listing doesn't accomplish anything other than create a dilemma for the perpetrator of a skimming fraud. The perpetrator must make a choice between skimming the contributions and not listing the donor in the publication, thereby risking phone calls from donors who made gifts (see Fraud in the Headlines 3.2); or skimming the contributions but taking steps to list the donors in the publication, thereby satisfying the donors' inherent desire to see their names published.

Accordingly, if donor listings are published, or otherwise made public, the names on the listing should be spot-checked against deposits made to the organization's bank accounts to verify that the funds were deposited intact.

Missing from the preceding list of detective controls is a system of providing receipts or acknowledgments to donors. The absence of this procedure as an internal control to reduce the risk of skimming may surprise some readers. However, donor acknowledgment systems almost never provide any reasonable level of assurance that skimming is not taking place. The reason that these systems rarely provide any reliable control is that donors can almost never differentiate a legitimate receipt from a fraudulent one. Even if receipts and acknowledgement letters are prenumbered and kept under strong physical security, perpetrators of skimming frauds can very easily replicate or oth-

---

FRAUD IN THE HEADLINES 3.2

NEVER UNDERESTIMATE THE VALUE OF A PUBLISHED LIST

A former office manager and bookkeeper for the National Lumber and Building Materials Dealers Association (NLBMDA) took more than $110,000 of contributions from members that were earmarked for the association's fund established to rebuild headquarters destroyed by fire. She deposited checks made payable to "NLBMDA" into a bank account she fraudulently opened in the name of New Life Business Management and Development Association (also "NLBMDA").

She was eventually fired for her inability to produce financial statements in a timely manner. Her fraud was uncovered, however, when a contributor noted that he had not been acknowledged in a thank-you letter printed in NLBMDA's magazine. A review of the donor's canceled check confirmed the diversion of funds.

The bank ultimately bore the financial losses, but the bookkeeper was sentenced to 25 months in prison and ordered to pay $130,000 in restitution.

Source: Schornstein, Sherri L., "Who Do You Trust?" *Association Management,* November 2000.

erwise design authentic-looking receipts or acknowledgment letters to send to donors from whom contributions have been skimmed. Indeed, numerous cases have been reported in which mail clerks, receptionists, bookkeepers, and others handling contributions have mailed fraudulent receipts or thank-you letters to unsuspecting donors. In some cases, this went on for years without anyone suspecting that anything was wrong with their receipts (as we saw in Fraud in the Headlines 3.1).

Late Fees and Similar Charges

After charitable contributions, the next most easily diverted form of income intended for an organization is late fee income and similar charges. As with contribution income, late charges, penalties, and certain other fees are not associated with an organization's delivery of specific goods or services, so there is no outflow of resources that correspond to expected income, a characteristic that makes this form of income vulnerable to skimming before it is deposited and recorded on the books.

Although this might not strike some readers as a potentially lucrative form of fraud, the case described in Fraud in the Headlines 3.3 illustrates how significant it can be when committed over an extended period of time. Financial controls essential to preventing the skimming of late fees and similar charges for which no service is directly rendered by an organization are virtually identical to those described in the preceding section on charitable contribution skimming (i.e., use of a lockbox or a dual control system).

However, an additional measure that is important in controlling the skimming of late fees is segregating the duty of *assessing* late fees from that of *collecting* these fees. Segregating these duties allows for the subsequent recon-

---

FRAUD IN THE HEADLINES 3.3

LIBRARY UNCOVERS STOLEN FINES AND FEES

An audit of the Muncie (IN) Public Library uncovered $124,000 in suspected fraud. Of that total, more than $72,000 was attributed to the theft of fines and fees collected from library branch supervisors but never deposited into the library's bank account. Library officials contacted local police and the State Board of Accounts when they discovered the fraud. An audit conducted by State Board of Accounts auditors alleged that the library's former bookkeeper diverted the fines and fees between August 2000 and April 2002.

Source: "Audit of Muncie Library Finds $124,000 Is Missing," *Associated Press*, August 23, 2002.

ciliation of late fees deposited into an organization's accounts with late fees that should be anticipated, based on the records created when the late fees were assessed (i.e., making sure that late fees assessed were actually deposited into the organization's bank account).

Other forms of income that could be similarly vulnerable to theft include shipping and handling charges, penalties, and most types of service charges.

Membership Dues

Next in line in terms of susceptibility to skimming is membership dues revenue earned by trade and professional associations, labor unions, and other membership groups (see Fraud in the Headlines 3.4 for an example). Dues revenue is most vulnerable to skimming when the benefits that a member receives for joining an organization are limited. Generally, the greater the benefits provided to members, the greater the chances of skimming being detected. This is because each member benefit provided results in an outflow of organizational resources. Each outflow leaves a paper trail that may be used to determine the number of members the organization has. Once this is determined, it is possible to estimate the amount of dues revenue that the organization should expect to receive.

Prevention of dues skimming is best accomplished in the same manner as prevention of contribution skimming (explained earlier). Use of a lockbox service and implementation of a dual control system for collecting dues payments are the two primary methods of prevention. Most other controls focus on early detection of a skimming fraud.

The ease with which dues skimming can be detected varies based on the nature of the benefits provided to members in exchange for their dues payments. For example, if the only benefits received by members in exchange for

FRAUD IN THE HEADLINES 3.4

SKIMMING OF MEMBERSHIP DUES

Two officials of the District of Columbia branch of the American Federation of State, County, and Municipal Employees (AFSCME) admitted to embezzling more than $830,000 from the organization. AFSCME's Secretary-Treasurer was the primary perpetrator and admitted to embezzling more than $761,000. His primary method of stealing from the organization was to skim membership dues payments and deposit the funds into a fraudulently opened bank account in the name of the organization. The funds were then used for personal purposes.

Source: Miller, Bill, *The Washington Post,* July 24, 1998.

paying dues to an organization are access to the organization's programs or facilities (such as with a fitness center) or discounts on other products and services for which the member will pay a separate fee, detection of dues skimming can be difficult. Each member may take advantage of these types of benefits in varying degrees. Some members may not take advantage of them at all. In these cases, the focus should be on preventing the fraud utilizing one of the controls described earlier.

One process that may provide a means of detecting dues skimming in these cases involves the issuance of and accounting for membership numbers and membership cards. Controls here should include:

- Use a membership card that is difficult to replicate or that has security features, such as magnetic coding.
- Issue new membership numbers in sequence, not out of order (or utilize software to assign membership numbers in order or at random, where the software cannot be manipulated by the person receiving membership dues payments).
- Segregate the duty of receiving membership payments from the duty of entering data into and/or maintaining the membership database.

In situations where members receive more tangible benefits in exchange for their dues payments, more reliable detective controls can be applied to provide assurance that dues revenue has not been skimmed. These detective controls, if properly administered, are often reliable since, presumably, members anticipate receiving the benefits that caused them to join the organization in the first place. If members are not provided with the promised benefits, they will complain. If they are provided with the promised benefits, a detective trail is left for management and auditors to use as a basis for testing the completeness of revenue.

This would be the case with most trade and professional associations, labor unions, and many other membership groups. These organizations often provide a wide array of member benefits, several of which are measurable through the outflow of resources from the organization. Any one of these outflows can be used as the basis for a test of reasonableness, which can be a valuable detective control, as shown in Best Practices 3.1.

Reasonableness tests are by no means a substitute for strong preventive controls. Accordingly, duties associated with collecting dues payments and maintaining an organization's member database should always be separated. However, well-designed reasonableness tests can provide a critical safety net to detect skimming frauds that have not been prevented. Most forms of revenue (other than charitable contribution income) lend themselves to one type of reasonableness testing or another.

Another procedure that can be used to detect dues revenue skimming involves the publication of a membership directory or member listing. This

BEST PRACTICES 3.1

REASONABLENESS TESTING OF REVENUE

Trade and professional associations, labor unions, and other membership groups often provide a variety of benefits to members. One of those benefits may be a subscription to the association's periodical, such as a monthly journal. Information provided through the organization's journal operations provides an independent third-party source of data that can be used to verify membership dues revenue, assuring that no material amounts of this revenue have been skimmed. Data used in reasonableness testing is considered to be reliable if it is developed or provided by persons other than those who control the account balance being tested (in this case, someone other than the person who collects dues payments and updates member records). Two of the most likely forms of reliable external data in this example are:

- Invoices for printing services from the external printer of the periodical
- Postage records from the external mailing service or U.S. Postal Service

Invoices from printing vendors tell us exactly how many copies of a periodical were produced. If it is possible to accurately determine the number of extra copies used for distribution to non-dues-paying members (such as for complimentary subscriptions, copies provided to advertisers, promotional giveaways, additions to inventory for future use, etc.), the remaining issues are presumably provided to members.

Likewise, postage records tell us exactly how many periodicals were mailed on a particular day. Again, factoring in complimentary issues, issues provided to advertisers, and other nonmember circulation, we should be able to back into the number of issues sent to dues-paying members (as long as these quantities are not provided by or under the control of the same person who has access to incoming dues payments).

Once a reliable quantity of periodicals provided to dues-paying members has been established using one of these two sources of information (or another reliable source, if available), the amount of dues revenue that the organization should *anticipate* receiving can be calculated. In most instances, this is a simple calculation where the number of members is multiplied by the dues rate paid by those members. In cases where an organization has many different categories of membership, each with a different dues rate, the calculation becomes more complicated. However, an approximate calculation is usually possible.

> The resulting anticipated revenue amount based on this calculation should then be compared to the revenue recorded on the books and deposited into the organization's bank accounts. Any significant difference between anticipated dues revenue and actual revenue (or cash receipts of dues payments) should be investigated.

detective procedure works much like the procedure described earlier with respect to the publication of donor names. In each case, there is a reliance on the inherent control that if people anticipate seeing their names printed in a published listing in connection with making a payment to an organization, they will follow up by contacting the organization if their names are omitted from that publication. At a minimum (and probably more reasonably), if large quantities of names have been omitted, a noticeable percentage of these persons will contact the organization (i.e., this procedure may not detect small amounts of skimming, but has a much stronger reliability for detecting substantial skimming schemes).

Accordingly, the person that skims dues revenue from an organization that publishes a member directory has the same choices to make as the skimmer of contribution income:

- Make sure that the member's name is included in the directory by processing the dues payment (recording it in the membership records as paid) as though it had been deposited properly into the organization's bank account (thereby leaving a detective trail in the form of the directory listing); or
- Omit the member's name from the directory by failing to process the member's payment in the membership system (which will likely result in an irate member, who is upset over the omission of his/her name from the directory).

Accordingly, the following additional detective procedures should be in place when member directories are published:

- Perform a reasonableness test of dues revenue like the one described in Best Practices 3.1, based on the number of members listed in the member directory
- Spot-check specific members listed in the directory by locating their corresponding dues payment in the bank deposit records of the organization (verifying that their dues payment was deposited intact)
- Follow up on all complaints received from members, particularly those dealing with missing member benefits or omissions from the directory

Conference and Meeting Revenue

Thousands of nonprofit organizations generate revenue from conferences, conventions, seminars, trade shows, educational programs, and other forms of meeting activities. If the benefit that a payor receives in exchange for their payment is admission, attendance, or education, there may or may not be an outflow of resources that can be used as the basis for a reasonableness test of revenue (reasonableness testing was introduced in the preceding section and will be explained further in Chapter 15). Accordingly, prevention of a skimming activity is the first line of defense.

The key to preventing skimming of registration revenue is to segregate the duties that would make it possible for one person to both receive payment and admit the registrant to the conference or meeting. This segregation can be achieved through the use of a bank lockbox service, which separates the receipt of payment function by placing it outside the organization, or by separating the internal duties of personnel. (The concept of separating duties already should be well ingrained from having read the preceding sections of this chapter.) For registrants who pay prior to the event, this means segregating the duty of receiving payment (opening mail, etc.) from that of entering the registrant's name and other information into the database (meeting software, a database package, etc.) that will be used to prepare name badges, admission tickets, rosters, and any other documents used to allow someone to gain access to the event. Just like with other forms of income, have one group of employees open and make the initial records of incoming payments, forward the payments on to another person for deposit, and have the recording of payments (including the entry of registrations for conferences and meetings into the database) handled by other employees (who do not have access to the incoming funds themselves).

However, conference and meeting registrations and collections often have one characteristic that the other forms of income discussed so far in this chapter do not. Many organizations permit on-site registration and on-site payment for their educational programs, trade shows, and conferences. On-site payment operations may present an opportunity for someone to skim payments if they are not properly controlled. The organization must establish controls that prevent one person from accepting an on-site payment and allowing the registrant to attend without ever documenting receipt of the funds.

This is best accomplished by separating the collection function from the admission function. Have on-site registrants check in and make payment with one person (or team of persons, to provide the same element of dual controls described in the charitable contributions section), receive an admission ticket (preferably prenumbered, to allow for subsequent reconciliation of tickets issued), and then hand the ticket to a different person, who admits the registrant to the event.

Although this system of financial controls over on-site registrations is explained here in reference to educational events, the same principle can be applied to special fundraising events and other activities involving on-site payments, such as admissions to exhibits and performances.

Conference and meeting activities also may be subject to reliable forms of reasonableness testing, just like the dues revenue example explained in Best Practices 3.1. To formulate a sound reasonableness test for conference and meeting revenue, a reliable source of data that provides the actual number of people attending the conference must be determined. To be reliable, the source must be a person other than the person(s) involved in collecting payments from attendees. If payment and admission functions have been segregated, the ticket-takers may be a reliable source of this data. Ticket-takers should count the number of tickets in their possession and document this accounting.

There also may be other reliable sources of data for determining the number of attendees at an event. Some of these sources are internal and others are external, adding another element of independence to the data. Examples of other potentially reliable sources of data for conference attendance include:

- Invoices from hotels for catering/banquet services, which may indicate how many chairs were set up in a room, how many meals were served, how many coffee services or snacks were provided, or other indications of the number of attendees
- Inventory and shipping records (internal or from external printers) of books, training manuals, or other materials distributed to attendees
- Sign-in sheets distributed by speakers or others involved in the event, as long as the sign-in sheets are not under the control of the person(s) collecting payments (sign-in sheets are particularly reliable when attendees receive continuing professional education toward a license or are otherwise relying on receipt of a certificate of attendance based on signing in and certifying their attendance)

Once a reliable figure is determined for the number of attendees, simply multiply that figure by the registration rate paid per person to arrive at anticipated revenue. Compare anticipated revenue to actual revenue received and deposited. If the amount deposited is less than the anticipated revenue figure, further investigation should be performed—skimming may have occurred.

Other Program Service Revenue

Once the preceding sections on dues revenue and conference and meeting programs have been read, further explanation of other forms of program service revenue earned by nonprofit organizations is fairly redundant. The principles remain the same. Focus on prevention by segregating the duties involved with collecting and making an initial listing of payments received from the duties associated with providing or recording the service.

Then, regardless of how sound the preventive measures appear to be, design reliable reasonableness tests for each category of revenue. The importance of designing and applying reasonableness tests to revenue accounts cannot be overemphasized. Remember, collusion among multiple employees can circumvent many of the preventive controls described in this book. A nonprofit manager's last line of defense against fraud is a system of sound monitoring of recorded results. This process starts with reasonableness testing of revenue.

Retail Sales

Many nonprofit organizations have retail sales operations. These operations may involve gift shops, bookstores, snack bars, and countless other sales activities. Skimming from retail sales takes place when someone (usually a cashier) sells something to a customer, but makes no record of the sale and pockets the customer's payment. There are three primary methods of pocketing a customer's payment:

- If the customer pays in cash, the perpetrator may simply put the cash into his or her pockets, briefcase, purse, etc.
- If the customer pays by check, the person skimming may alter the payee on the check (see check tampering in Chapter 4) or open an account in the name of the organization, as explained earlier.
- If the customer pays by credit card, the perpetrator may establish a fraudulent account into which credit card payments are processed.

The last method is the most complicated, but in some cases may be easier to conceal. That is because in the first two schemes, the perpetrator must boldly stash cash and/or checks and leave the premises with them. With credit card payments, this is not necessary. Accordingly, when credit card payments are accepted, controls should be in place that prevent sales clerks from processing sales transactions to any account other than the proper organization account.

What all three methods have in common, however, is that the perpetrator must somehow conceal the transaction. Cash boxes and unsophisticated cash registers make this concealment possible. For this reason, utilizing a cash register that is difficult to manipulate can provide a great deal of protection if there is a material risk of retail sales skimming. Register skimming has been carried out using a variety of methods to conceal the fraud, such as:

- Removing the carbon from registers that utilize carbons to make the store copies of register tapes
- Jamming the register so that the tape cannot advance
- Removing the register tape

Financial controls that may be useful in detecting retail sales skimming include:

- Reviewing cash register tapes and/or copies of receipts for signs of alterations
- Accounting for the numerical sequence of receipts, if applicable
- Monitoring gross profit margins for fluctuations from period to period and from department to department
- Installing video surveillance cameras in the areas in which retail sales are processed (i.e., around cash registers, etc.)

LAPPING SCHEMES

Lapping of payments received from customers is a common method of concealing skimming frauds, especially those involving the skimming of payments received from customers for which a receivable has been recorded (i.e., when credit is granted to customers who place orders for products from an organization, such as publications and other merchandise). Lapping occurs when the payment from one customer is applied to the account of another customer whose payment has previously been skimmed.

For example, assume an organization has sold 100 items to 100 different customers, numbered chronologically 1 through 100 as the items are sold. The person in charge of collecting and applying customer payments skims the payments received from the first five items sold as the payments from customers 1 through 5 arrive. When the payments from customers 6 through 10 are received, they are applied to the outstanding balances of customers 1 through 5. At this point, the accounts of customers 1 through 5 appear to be up-to-date (meaning that these customers will not be flagged as delinquent in the accounting system). Perhaps the payments received from customers 11 through 15 are applied to the accounts of customers 6 through 10 before payment from customer 16 is skimmed, and so on.

Lapping schemes tend to continually expand over time, with the perpetrator continuing to steal some payments while applying payments that have not been stolen to the oldest accounts first. Lapping schemes can become extremely complicated, with some perpetrators maintaining a complete second set of books in order to keep track of their fraud.

The primary method of preventing lapping schemes is to properly segregate the duties associated with collecting payments (and making deposits) from those involved with the posting of payments to customer accounts in the accounts receivable system and the preparation of customer statements. Just as the creation of a cash receipts log helps to prevent the skimming of charitable contributions, preparation of a listing of payments received by someone who does not have access to the accounts receivable records makes it impossible to conceal the theft of incoming payments. The person with access to the funds cannot hide their theft because they have no access to the accounts receivable records. The cash receipts listings, without the customer checks, which have been deposited intact by the cash receipts clerk, should then be forwarded to the accounts receivable clerk for posting to the accounts of particular customers.

In addition to these preventive measures, the following procedures can help in detecting lapping schemes:

- Monitor the accounts receivable aging (classify balances due based on how long they have been outstanding, such as 1–30 days, 31–60 days, 61–90 days, etc.). This should be done by someone other than the person who receives payments or applies payments to customer accounts (progressive lapping schemes are often characterized by the deterioration of the accounts receivable aging over time).

- In connection with the preceding procedure, all aging reports prepared for review should be generated directly from the accounts receivable system, rather than being independently prepared as a summary report by the accounts receivable clerk (this policy limits the possibility of a completely phony aging report being fabricated and submitted for review, thereby concealing the true aging of receivables in the detailed accounts receivable subledger).

- Cross-check specific customer payments as indicated in the accounts receivable system with specific deposits made to the organization's accounts on a random and sample basis.

- Match daily deposits to accounts receivable postings on a regular or spot-check basis.

- Periodically send out confirmation statements to customers.

- Follow up on complaints received from customers, especially those associated with delays in posting payments or receiving statements for invoices that have already been paid.

- Rotate duties in the customer payment processing function (since lapping schemes often require constant attention on the part of the perpetrator, who needs to continually track which customer payments have been skimmed and which are next in line to be credited with payments of other customers, etc.).

Note that the second procedure from the preceding list presumes that an organization utilizes an automated accounts receivable system. If an organization tracks accounts receivable manually (or with nonintegrated software, such as a stand-alone spreadsheet package), a more detailed review of aging is necessary, as the person preparing the aging report has a greater ability to create a completely phony report.

Monitoring of accounts receivable aging is critical to detecting lapping schemes in systems where appropriate separation of duties is not possible. However, even in settings in which separation of duties is achieved, monitoring of accounts receivable aging is nevertheless an important financial management procedure to gauge an organization's collection efforts. Accordingly, this monitoring should be performed in every organization that does not require prepayment from customers.

WRITE-OFFS OF ACCOUNTS RECEIVABLE

A method of skimming accounts receivable payments that may be less complicated than a lapping scheme is one in which the receivable itself is written off as uncollectible when, in fact, the customer has made or will make payment. The perpetrator converts the payments to cash using the same methods explained under skimming frauds (i.e., establishing a bank account in the name of the payee organization).

Fraudulent write-offs of valid accounts receivable are possible when an employee who can receive payments also has the ability to:

- Make an entry in the accounts receivable system to write off a particular account as uncollectible
- Authorize or instruct another employee to make an entry in the accounts receivable system to write off a particular account as uncollectible
- Make or authorize a journal entry that increases an organization's allowance (reserve) for uncollectible accounts (or the subsequent journal entry that offsets the allowance against specific accounts)

Accordingly, the receipt of payment function must be separated from each of the preceding functions in order to minimize the risk of unauthorized write-offs of valid receivables. Other policies and procedures that are helpful in preventing or detecting unauthorized write-offs include:

- Require that all write-offs be tracked separately by establishing and utilizing a separate general ledger account for bad debts (rather than netting bad debts with revenue)
- Monitor activity in the bad debt account over time and, if possible, by employee
- Require approvals of all write-offs of uncollectible accounts before any proposed write-off is posted to the accounts receivable system

UNAUTHORIZED CREDITS

In some nonprofit organizations, the initial recording of an account receivable is subsequently reduced with the recording of a credit to a customer's account. The credit may be for a variety of reasons, such as:

- Providing a discount to members of the organization (or members of affiliated organizations)
- Price reductions for customers who are dissatisfied with the product or service provided by the organization
- Incentives for future purchases or the application of a credit due to a current, large purchase (volume discounts, etc.)

In these cases, a fraud much like the unauthorized write-offs of accounts receivable can be carried out if a person in a position to receive payments can also record or authorize credits to a customer's account. Prevention of unauthorized credit schemes is best accomplished by:

- Segregating the duties associated with accepting or handling payments from those associated with posting credits to customer accounts
- Requiring proper authorization of credits prior to posting credits to a customer account

Detection is best accomplished through some form of monitoring activity, in which the level of credits issued and posted to customer accounts is monitored over time and/or by employee. Tracking credits separately, rather than netting credits with sales revenue, may facilitate monitoring.

UNRECORDED SALES

Unrecorded sales involve the receipt of a customer order, processing the order (shipping an item to a customer), and skimming the customer payment. The fact that a customer is not present on the premises is the characteristic that distinguishes this type of fraud from the retail sales skimming activity explained earlier. In unrecorded sales schemes, a customer has likely mailed an order with payment by check to an organization. However, unrecorded sales schemes involving fax orders or electronic mail orders may also occur if a perpetrator has established the means for processing credit card orders.

Unrecorded sales tend to be associated with small organizations, because a lack of separation of duties is essential to carrying out these schemes. Typically, one person receives an order, with payment, and processes and ships the order to the customer. Accordingly, the key to prevention of unrecorded sales schemes is to separate the duties associated with receipt, deposit, and recording of payment from those associated with access to inventory and shipping of customer orders.

The best method of detecting unrecorded sales is through timely financial and ratio analysis of inventory, sales, and cost of goods sold accounts. Ratio analysis is explained further in Chapter 15.

THEFT OF DONATED MERCHANDISE

Merchandise donated to a nonprofit organization can be every bit as susceptible to theft as charitable contributions in the form of cash or checks (see Fraud in the Headlines 3.5). The only difference is that stolen merchandise is more difficult for an employee to conceal in a purse or briefcase.

FRAUD IN THE HEADLINES 3.5

GOODWILL THEFT TOTALED $15 MILLION

Several people pled guilty to systematically looting the Goodwill Industries of Santa Clara County (California) out of at least $15 million. Although this case involves a fraud scheme that is much more elaborate and involved than most, it illustrates the extent to which a fraud scheme can expand over time, if it goes undetected.

The scheme began small in the mid-1970s and progressed to its most extensive stages in the mid-1990s. The culprits sold donated items by the barrelful to private dealers, who sometimes wheeled tractor trailers up to the rear of the Goodwill stores to load the merchandise. The Goodwill embezzlers kept the proceeds and the private dealers sold most of the goods in Mexico. The culprits also skimmed cash receipts from Goodwill cash registers.

The scheme became so elaborate that it eventually necessitated the involvement of many people. It was estimated that an underground workforce of as many as 100 people were utilized to carry out the scheme. This workforce was paid up to $30,000 a week by the seven primary culprits.

Goodwill Industries subsequently made major modifications to its internal controls to reduce the risk of a similar scheme taking place in the future.

As astonishing as this fraud is, how the fraud came to the attention of Goodwill Industries is equally amazing. During a bitter divorce and custody battle involving one of the seven primary thieves, the perpetrator's husband disclosed the existence of the scheme to authorities. Not many divorce cases involve factoring one spouse's burglary activities into the couple's division of property, but this one did!

Source: Billitteri, Thomas J., "Goodwill Looting: California Scam Yields Lessons for Charity Managers," *The Chronicle of Philanthropy*, February 12, 1998.

Theft of donated merchandise is discussed here rather than in the explanation of inventory theft in Chapter 6 because theft of donated merchandise is usually committed *before* the merchandise has been included in an organization's inventory (much like skimming of contribution income before it has even been deposited). Because of the similarities to skimming of contribution income, most of the strategies designed to control theft of donated merchandise revolve around the initial collection of the gift. In particular, having two or more people receive and account for the initial receipt of donated merchandise, including the creation of a permanent record of the gift (just like the dual control procedure described under skimming of contributions), is critical to preventing theft. Even with this dual control, theft remains possible. Rotating the employees and mixing up the teams of employees who collect or receive donated merchandise can further reduce the risk of fraud by complicating the opportunities for collusion.

Additional controls may reduce the risk of donated merchandise theft as follows:

- Establish a dual control system for receipt of donated merchandise similar to the dual control system for receipt of mail and contributions (i.e., require two people to be present and have both sign off on a log documenting receipt of all donated items).
- For donations that the organization picks up at a donor's home (clothing and furniture, perhaps), use teams of two people to receive and document the receipt.
- Install video surveillance cameras in the area where donated merchandise is received and logged in.
- Rotate the duties for personnel involved in receipt of donated merchandise.
- In connection with the preceding policy, monitor recorded receipts of donated merchandise on a team-by-team basis, looking for employees or teams that routinely report a smaller volume of donated merchandise.

In addition, use of a formal or automated donor receipt system can provide a sense of control. Because donors may not be aware of the exact nature of the receipts they should receive, this process may not provide much real control. But, having a formal receipting system in place will make employees and/or volunteers more diligent in their record-keeping (and establish the appearance of a preventive control).

With respect to donated merchandise, using a prenumbered or automated receipt system may be a more effective internal control because many of these donations are made in person. Most financial contributions are made by mail. In a gift-by-mail scenario, the donor has no idea how the receipt or acknowledgment process works and is, therefore, usually unable to differentiate between a legitimate receipt and a fraudulently prepared one.

Since contributions of merchandise are more likely to be made in person, a formal receipt system is a better measure of control for the simple reason that the donor is present and watches the receipt being generated (recall that in schemes involving the skimming of contributions received in the mail, a perpetrator could simply go home at night and prepare fraudulent receipts to send to donors, who will not likely recognize the receipt as a fraudulent one).

4

Purchasing and Disbursement Schemes

The purchasing and cash disbursement cycles tend to be the areas most often associated with fraud and abuse. The majority of known fraud cases involve a misappropriation of cash, either in the form of a revenue and cash receipts scheme, as explained in Chapter 3, or, more commonly, a cash disbursements scheme. Closely related to disbursement schemes is corruption in the purchasing function. Accordingly, this chapter will address both broad categories of fraud.

There are many varieties of cash disbursement schemes, but they can generally be classified into the following categories:

- Billing schemes
- Misclassifying personal expenditures as business
- Refund schemes
- Financial assistance schemes
- Check tampering
- Electronic funds transfer schemes

A related form of abuse involves corruption in the purchasing (procurement) cycle. The most common types of procurement abuse involve:

- Undisclosed conflicts of interest
- Kickbacks from vendors
- Bribery
- Fraud in the bidding process

Each of these ten types of fraud and abuse will be explained in the remainder of this chapter. Frequently, one of the categories of fraud will be further classified into several distinct schemes. For each type of fraud and abuse, an explanation of who is most likely to be involved as well as how the scheme is carried out will be provided.

INTERNAL CONTROLS OVER PURCHASING AND DISBURSEMENTS

Following the explanation of each specific type of fraud and abuse, key financial controls associated with preventing and/or detecting that type of scheme will be identified. Certain elements of internal control apply equally to multiple types of purchasing and disbursement schemes. Segregation of duties is one such element. The following duties should be separated to the maximum extent possible:

- Purchase request (purchase order or other form of request)
- Purchase authorization
- Receiving (for supplies and other items delivered to the organization)
- Recording of accounts payable
- Approval of vendor invoices
- Check writing (or initiation of electronic transfer)
- Recording of disbursements and relief of accounts payable
- Delivery (mailing) of checks to vendors
- Reconciliation of accounts payable subledger
- Reconciliation of bank account

Ideally, each of these functions should be performed by a different person. In many instances, this simply isn't possible. In such cases, an organization should strive to segregate as many of these functions as possible. In the discussion of specific types of fraud and abuse that follows, readers should take note of those duties that are particularly important to segregate in order to prevent each type of impropriety. When few of these duties are segregated, the number of different disbursement schemes to which an organization is vulnerable grows considerably. See Fraud in the Headlines 4.1 for an example of how a lack of segregation of duties can expose an organization to multiple fraud schemes.

Keep in mind that the purpose of segregation of duties is to prevent people from carrying out and concealing their fraud. Not every duty needs to be segregated in order to accomplish this objective—only those duties that are critical to that specific fraud.

In addition, while this chapter identifies many steps that should be taken to prevent particular types of frauds from being committed, there are

FRAUD IN THE HEADLINES 4.1

AN EXAMPLE OF HOW PURCHASING AND DISBURSEMENT FRAUD PROGRESSES OVER TIME

Fraud and abuse schemes frequently start out as a simple plan focusing on one particular type of transaction. However, left undetected over time, perpetrators of fraud frequently expand into other areas.

A classic example is found in the 1992 case involving the former chief financial officer of the American Bar Foundation. This person was convicted in 1992 of embezzling $214,000 from the ABF over an eight-year period from 1983 to 1991. While the dollar amount of this fraud is not overly startling in comparison with others that have been in the news more recently, the diverse manner in which the financial officer engaged in his fraud is. The ABF financial officer utilized each of the following methods to embezzle funds from the foundation:

- Creation of a phony corporation, GSR Services Co., which invoiced ABF for services and supplies never rendered
- Applying for and receiving grant funds from the foundation using an alias
- Diverting refund payments intended for lawyers who had signed up for meetings, but later canceled, by allowing the lawyers to assume there was a no-refund policy in effect when, in fact, they were entitled to refunds

In addition, he engaged in a practice of destroying checks that had been made payable to legitimate ABF vendors that were least likely to complain about receiving payment late. He then used separate checks he had printed with the same numerical sequence to pay his own personal bills, forging the signature of an authorized ABF check signer. As a result, the books of ABF reflected check numbers and amounts that matched up with check numbers and amounts listed on ABF's bank statements. Then, when a statement would arrive from the unpaid vendors showing the old amounts still outstanding, plus new charges, the financial officer would generate and mail a check to the vendor.

This comprehensive system of fraud was uncovered only when another ABF employee happened to notice a check payable to American Express on the perpetrator's desk. This struck her as unusual because she did not think that ABF had any accounts with American Express.

While most fraud and abuse cases are not this complex, the ABF case illustrates the importance of a combination of preventive and detective controls, many of which were lacking at the foundation until this case arose. One of the reasons that the pattern of fraud and abuse continued undetected for eight years was the use of numerous methods involving many different accounts into which individually immaterial amounts of fraud could easily be concealed.

Source: Cassen Moss, Debra, "Schemes Revealed, Former ABF Finance Chief Sentenced," *ABA Journal*, February 1993.

certain general safeguards over the check-writing process that should always be in place. Some of the most important basic measures include:

- The use of prenumbered checks in sequential order
- Prohibiting the signing of checks in advance
- Limiting (or prohibiting) the use of signature stamps and keeping such stamps locked up when not in use
- Prohibiting the writing of checks make payable to cash
- Promptly updating the bank's listing of authorized signers when a check signer is no longer authorized (due to retirement, resignation, termination, etc.)
- Maintaining proper physical security over unused checks (i.e., locking them up and limiting access to only those people authorized to prepare checks)
- Requiring appropriate authorization prior to preparing any checks (what is considered appropriate varies based on the type of expenditure and is explained further throughout this chapter)
- Providing employees who have invoice approval responsibilities with appropriate training in the processes of reviewing and approving invoices (see Best Practices 4.2)
- Requiring two signatures on checks in excess of an established dollar threshold
- Mailing all checks promptly after signature
- Locking up overnight all signed checks that are not mailed the same day
- Reconciling the bank statement in a timely manner by someone other than the person who writes and records checks (see Best Practices 4.3)
- Properly voiding checks that have been incorrectly prepared by clearly defacing the checks, tearing off the signature section, etc.
- Writing off as void all checks that have been outstanding for more than an established time period, such as six months
- Maintaining a list of voided checks, as well as physical custody of the defaced checks, for use in preparation of monthly bank reconciliations

Each of these general controls over check-writing should be supplemented with the specific controls associated with each disbursement fraud described in this chapter.

BILLING SCHEMES

Internal billing schemes perpetrated by employees, officers, or directors involve the fraudulent processing of a vendor invoice for payment. External billing schemes (those perpetrated by vendors against an organization) will be explained later. Most internal billing schemes fall into one of two categories:

- Improper payments to legitimate vendors
- Payments to fictitious vendors

The first category, improper payments to legitimate vendors, can be further broken down into three distinct schemes:

- Purchasing items for personal use from legitimate vendors
- Credit card abuse
- Creating duplicate/additional payments to legitimate vendors

Personal Purchases

Purchasing of items for one's personal use from legitimate vendors of an organization is a common, though not usually material, form of fraud. Personnel most often found to commit this type of fraud include those with purchasing authority and/or receiving responsibilities. Vendors most often utilized in these schemes include those selling supplies, food, books, and clothing to an organization. However, cases involving more valuable items, such as computers, office furniture, and equipment, have been reported.

When items purchased from vendors are taken for personal use, the perpetrator is usually relying on one or more common weaknesses in internal controls in hopes of the theft going undetected. These weaknesses include an organization's failure to consistently follow these financial controls:

- Properly inventory the items purchased and reconcile receiving reports with inventory records.
- Segregate the duties of placing orders with vendors, receiving items from vendors, and approving vendor invoices for payment.
- Maintain adequate physical security over supplies, inventory, and assets (i.e., items vulnerable to theft should be stored in a locked, secure area with access limited to essential personnel).

See Chapter 6 for more details on taking physical inventories of assets and related controls.

FRAUD IN THE HEADLINES 4.2

CREDIT CARD ABUSE CAN COST MILLIONS

Anyone looking for a good reason to avoid having corporate credit cards need look no further than the Washington (DC) Teachers' Union (WTU). In response to allegations of financial improprieties, WTU's parent organization, the American Federation of Teachers, arranged for a special audit. The audit disclosed frauds in excess of $5 million perpetrated at the hands of three former WTU officials (the union's president, her assistant, and the treasurer).

Among the audit's many findings were $1.8 million in unauthorized credit card charges on the union's corporate American Express cards by the former president (along with $381,000 in checks written to herself). The president's assistant received $492,000 in unauthorized funds via credit card charges and checks written to herself. The treasurer diverted $537,000 in the same manners. Diverted funds were used to buy furs, art, jewelry, tickets to sports and entertainment events, and custom-made clothing.

Source: Blum, Justin, "Audit Sets D.C. Union Loss at $5 Million," *The Washington Post,* January 17, 2003.

Credit Card Abuse

Credit card abuse has become a huge problem in a wide variety of organizations in the United States. Organizations ranging in size from small local charities to the U.S. government have all reported detecting improper use of corporate credit cards. Credit card abuse usually involves charging personal items to a credit card that is the responsibility of the organization (see Fraud in the Headlines 4.2).

Short of eliminating corporate credit cards (which many nonprofits have done), preventing this type of abuse is very difficult. However, the worst abuse generally results from an organization's failure to abide by the following controls:

- Control the initial issuance of credit cards.
- Perform credit checks on all employees to whom a corporate card is to be issued, and annually update credit checks on cardholders as a condition of continuing to be a cardholder.
- Establish reasonable credit limits for each cardholder, based on the organization's assessment of the business needs of each person.
- When not in use, lock corporate credit cards in the accounting office until needed, rather than allowing employees to hold onto the cards.

- Properly notify cardholders of the rules and responsibilities associated with their corporate credit cards (see Best Practices 4.1).
- Establish appropriate credit limits for each cardholder.
- Promptly review credit card statements as soon as they arrive from the credit card company for purposes of identifying unusual or inappropriate charges.
- Require cardholders to submit supporting charge slips and invoices on a timely basis so that the accounting department has all necessary supporting documentation in its possession by the time the monthly statement arrives from the credit card company.
- Take quick action, including suspension or revocation of a credit card, as soon as credit card abuse is suspected.

In addition, some credit card companies have programs in which responsibility for payment can be shifted from the organization to the individual cardholder (or there is a sharing of responsibility) when the organization identifies nonbusiness charges and notifies the credit card company in a timely manner. This can provide some additional protection against an organization being held liable for large amounts of nonbusiness charges on corporate credit cards.

BEST PRACTICES 4.1

CORPORATE CREDIT CARD POLICIES

Every organization that utilizes corporate credit cards for purchases should document sound policies and procedures with respect to use of the cards. Every cardholder or user should review these policies and sign off on them, indicating their acknowledgment and agreement to abide by the rules.

Some of the factors to cover in a documented corporate credit card policy include:

- Which employees are entitled to be issued a card or permitted to have access to a card
- A statement that individual cardholders are in a position of trust regarding the use of organizational funds
- Whether individual holders of corporate credit cards should be required to submit to a credit check by the organization prior to use of a card, and whether periodic credit reports may be obtained as a condition of continuing to use a card

- An explanation that the card is to be used only for legitimate business purposes and a description, if applicable, of those purposes (such as, to purchase classroom supplies, for out-of-town business travel, etc.)
- A statement that the card shall never be used for personal purposes or to obtain cash advances, even if on behalf of the organization
- The requirement for the cardholder to provide, where applicable, each vendor with a copy of the organization's sales tax exemption certificate
- A statement that individual cardholders are to exercise proper care in maintaining physical custody of the credit card in their possession (secure from loss or theft)
- An explanation of the procedures to be followed if a corporate credit card is lost or stolen (i.e., notify the bank as well as the designated organization officer)
- Specifed expenditure limits on individual cards and/or on certain types of transactions (for example, the card may be used to purchase classroom supplies not to exceed $500)
- An explanation of which types or amounts of expenditures require prior approval before being charged on a corporate credit card, and who is authorized to approve these purchases
- A policy requiring cardholders to review each and every charge on the monthly credit card statements for propriety and to submit all required supporting documentation on a timely basis (in order to allow for the organization's payment of the balance by the stated due date)
- As part of the preceding policy, a requirement that each individual cardholder report disputed transactions as soon as possible
- A description of the procedures, if any, for requesting increases in credit limits
- An acknowledgment that violation of the organization's policies governing use of the corporate credit card constitutes a violation of its code of conduct and represents grounds for revocation of the credit card, as well as termination of employment and, if applicable, criminal prosecution

In addition, key terms of the organization's agreement with the credit card company should be considered for inclusion in the organization's credit card policy statement.

Duplicate Payment Schemes

Duplicate payment schemes involve the fraudulent generation of multiple checks to pay a legitimate vendor invoice. These schemes are often carried out by an employee with purchasing or invoice approval authority. However, duplicate payment schemes have also been perpetrated by accounts payable clerks and other accounting personnel.

There are several methods of perpetrating duplicate payment schemes. In the simplest cases, a photocopy of a legitimate vendor invoice is submitted for payment or an original vendor invoice that has not been canceled after payment is resubmitted. A more sophisticated variation involves the generation of checks to pay legitimate vendor invoices followed by a holding of the checks until a monthly statement is received from the vendor showing two or more outstanding invoices. At that point, the checks in payment of the individual invoices are released and sent to the vendor and the statement (which often appears to be a new original invoice) is submitted for payment of each invoice listed as outstanding.

Vendors that provide services are more susceptible to duplicate payment schemes than are vendors that provide goods, for the simple reason that concealment of the fraud is more easily accomplished as there is no possibility of a reconciliation of purchases and inventory records disclosing a discrepancy. However, inadequate controls over supplies, inventory, and equipment render these vendors equally susceptible to a duplicate payment fraud.

One of the common weaknesses in internal controls present with duplicate payment schemes is a lack of segregation of two critical duties: the submission or approval of the fraudulent supporting documentation for payment and the delivery or mailing of the check. In order for this fraud to work without the collusion of the outside vendor, the person committing the fraud must be in a position to intercept the duplicate payment so that it is not mailed to the vendor. This weakness is common in smaller organizations, as well as in large organizations that allow for the return of signed checks to the requesters of the payments rather than the direct mailing of payments to vendors by the accounts payable department.

The perpetrator of a duplicate payment scheme converts the duplicate vendor payments to cash by either endorsing the check over to themselves or to a phony name in which they have established a bank account, or by fraudulently establishing a bank account in the vendor's name at a different financial institution than the one used by the vendor (which can be determined simply by reviewing an endorsement on the back of a previous check written to the vendor). In either case, the person committing this type of fraud then has a bank account from which funds are drawn and used for personal purposes. Sometimes, the perpetrator may simply convert the duplicate payment to cash by visiting a check-cashing establishment, thereby eliminating the need to fraudulently open a bank account.

The following internal controls would prevent most duplicate payment schemes from being successfully carried out:

- Following a policy whereby checks or electronic payments are processed only in connection with an original vendor invoice (no photocopies, no statements)
- Matching of vendor invoices with receiving reports and/or purchase orders as part of the review and approval process
- Proper utilization of a purchase order system, which involves the matching of descriptions and accumulation of quantities or units of service against total amounts authorized
- Requiring that vendor invoice numbers be input into the accounts payable module (if available), so that duplicate invoice numbers may be identified
- Immediate cancellation of vendor invoices upon payment
- Segregating the duties of invoice approval and mailing of payment (i.e., prohibiting the practice of returning signed checks to the person requesting the check for that person's hand delivery to the vendor)

In addition, there are several detective controls associated with duplicate payment schemes that should be considered, particularly when an environment precludes proper prevention of duplicate payment schemes:

- Periodic reviews of vendor payment histories, looking for obvious duplicate payment amounts or invoice numbers, payments with missing invoice numbers, or other unexplained entries
- Reviewing endorsements on the back of canceled checks returned with the organization's bank statement for unusual endorsements, such as signing the check over to an unidentified party
- Periodic confirmation with vendors of amounts paid
- Monitoring of expense account balances in comparison with budgeted amounts and with prior period amounts (see Chapter 15 for a more detailed discussion of account monitoring)

Fictitious Vendor Schemes

In a fictitious vendor scheme, invoices that appear to be legitimate are submitted for payment. However, the vendor is nonexistent and has been fabricated by the person submitting the invoice and authorizing the expenditure. Most fictitious vendors provide services rather than goods for the same reason cited in the preceding section on duplicate payments: These payments are easier to conceal if there is no inventory or supplies count to reconcile. Creation of a fictitious vendor was one of the fraud schemes carried out by the financial officer described in Fraud in the Headlines 4.1.

Unlike a duplicate payment scheme, there is no need for the perpetrator to intercept or deliver the payment in the fictitious vendor scheme. In most of these frauds, a post office box is used as the vendor's preferred address for payments. In some cases, a street address of a friend, family member, or other accomplice is used on the phony vendor invoice. In rare and particularly bold cases, employees have used their own home address as the address of a phony vendor—relying on the presumption that nobody will look very closely at the address!

One variation on the fictitious vendor scheme is the fraudulent payment to a vendor that was a valid vendor at some point in the past, but that is no longer providing goods or services to the organization. While the vendor itself is not fictitious, the invoice and the goods or services supposedly provided are. In these frauds, the perpetrator uses old invoices from the vendor to create invoices that appear to be legitimate. In this day of high-quality, affordable scanners, it is quite easy to replicate a vendor's logo and standard invoice format. Next, the perpetrator submits these fraudulent invoices for payment, relying on the reviewer's or check signer's recognition of the vendor name as a valid enough reason for processing the payment, without having firsthand knowledge that the vendor is not currently providing goods or services to the organization. In addition, because the vendor remains in the accounts payable master file, the accounts payable clerk is not as likely to recognize anything unusual about the transaction.

Unlike a truly bogus vendor, using a former vendor to commit this fraud requires either intercepting the payment (if the vendor's actual address is still in the accounts payable system and on the phony invoices) or the submission of an address change to the accounts payable system.

The following financial controls are essential to preventing fictitious vendor schemes:

- Requiring that the following information, at a minimum, be obtained from all new vendors (or at least those that will be paid in excess of an established dollar threshold):
  - Complete name
  - Employer identification number
  - Type of entity (i.e., corporation, sole proprietorship, etc.)
  - Street address (even if payments are to be made to a post office box)
  - Phone and fax numbers
  - Contact and/or officer names and phone numbers
- Verify the existence of new vendors to whom payments in excess of a specified dollar threshold are planned or requested (such verification can be done via phone call, public records searches, or other means)
- Segregate the duties of invoice approval and check preparation

- Periodically purge vendors from the accounts payable master files if a vendor has not been utilized for a specified period of time (perhaps once a year)

The following procedures, when performed on a periodic or occasional basis, may be useful in detecting fictitious vendor schemes:

- Reviewing the accounts payable vendor master file for completeness of information regarding each vendor and following up on incomplete records
- Confirming the existence of vendors via phone calls, public records searches, and so forth
- Reviewing vendor payment histories for irregularities (for instance, some fictitious vendor schemes have been uncovered by noting that invoice numbers on phony invoices that had been paid were either numbered consecutively, which would indicate that the victim organization was their only customer, or made no sense whatsoever, because they had entirely different number series or had a different number of digits each time, due to the carelessness of the perpetrator)
- Monitoring of expense account balances in comparison with budgeted amounts and with prior period amounts (see Chapter 15 for a more detailed discussion of account monitoring)

FRAUDULENT CLASSIFICATION OF PERSONAL EXPENDITURES AS BUSINESS EXPENSES

Each of the billing schemes explained in the preceding section involves the concealment of a fraudulent expenditure through the source documentation used to generate the payment (i.e., creating documentation or hiding information to make an expenditure appear legitimate). An even simpler fraud that is sometimes encountered in smaller organizations, or those with poor segregation of duties and oversight, involves the misclassification and reporting of personal expenditures as legitimate business expenses.

In these cases, inappropriate expenditures are incurred and paid for by organization officials. Nothing is done to disguise the payments themselves. However, in the accounting records, the expenditures are classified as legitimate business expenses by falsely coding the expenses to accounts into which normal business expenditures would be posted.

This type of fraudulent activity usually involves an organization in which expenditure authority and accounting record-keeping are both under the control of a single individual or a small group of individuals in collusion with one another (see Fraud in the Headlines 4.3). Preventing this type of fraud is dependent on separating the duties associated with authorizing expenditures, making payments to vendors, and posting (classifying) the expenditures to the

BEST PRACTICES 4.2

REVIEWING AND APPROVING VENDOR INVOICES

It's one thing to have the appropriate person(s) reviewing and approving vendor invoices for payment (i.e., having duties appropriately segregated). It's quite another thing, however, to *properly* review and approve an invoice. The following components are all essential to the invoice approval process:

- Approval by someone with firsthand knowledge that the goods or services described on the invoice were delivered and are legitimate business expenses of the organization
- Matching invoices with receiving reports and bills of lading (for supplies, equipment, and other goods received from vendors)
- For services provided by vendors, verifying the level of effort (hours worked) and milestones or accomplishments claimed on a vendor invoice (which requires that the organization assign someone to properly oversee the work of vendors)
- Reconciling invoices with purchase orders as to descriptions, quantities, and pricing
- Comparing prices charged with contracts, price lists, proposals, etc.
- Checking the mathematical accuracy of the invoice (multiplying quantities by prices, adding up all amounts, etc.)
- Recalculating any additional charges, such as shipping

Not all of these steps need to be performed by the same person. For instance, it is quite common for the clerical accuracy to be checked by an accounts payable clerk, while final approval of the business legitimacy and receipt of the goods or services is performed by someone else. The key is that all of these steps be appropriately assigned and the individuals performing each step understand their responsibilities.

general ledger. If preventive measures are not possible, or collusion is a concern, there are a number of detective measures that can be employed, such as:

- Undergoing an external audit by a CPA firm (but, understand the limitations of an audit, as explained in Chapter 14)
- Utilizing an internal auditor to analyze expenses
- Monitoring of expense account balances over time and against budget
- More extensive expenditure oversight by the board of directors or treasurer (such as by performing a review of supporting documentation for expenses)

FRAUD IN THE HEADLINES 4.3

EXTERNAL CPA ASSISTS IN CONCEALING NONBUSINESS EXPENDITURES

It's hard enough fighting internal fraud and abuse. When an organization's external auditor helps conceal the fraud, it's even harder.

In August 2002, a partner in a large accounting firm pleaded guilty to helping leaders of a labor union hide $1.5 million in entertainment and dining expenses. The International Association of Bridge, Structural, Ornamental, and Reinforcing Iron Workers has approximately 140,000 members. Between 1992 and 1998, union officers and others spent nearly $500,000 of union funds at a Washington, DC restaurant. Another $1 million was paid directly to union officials or other establishments for dining, drinking, golf, and entertainment during that time period.

The external audit partner helped to conceal the fraud by reporting the expenses as education and publicity costs or office and administrative expenses on reports filed with the Department of Labor.

Source: Strope, Leigh, "Man Pleads Guilty in Union Case," *Associated Press,* August 22, 2002.

REFUND SCHEMES

Two types of refund schemes may be encountered, each with its own unique operations and related internal controls:

- Refunds in the form of checks
- Cash register refunds in retail operations

Refunds in the form of checks written to customers, members, students, and other program participants often represent a more material risk, so those will be explained first, followed by a discussion of cash register refund schemes.

Frequently, organizations have much stronger internal controls over the disbursement of funds to vendors for purchases of goods and services than over the refunding of income to customers who have previously paid the organization for a product or service. This common weakness in internal controls creates an opportunity for someone to fraudulently generate refund payments. These schemes are most often found in connection with refunds for:

- Cancellations of conference, seminar, and meeting registrations
- Cancellations of memberships and subscriptions
- Returns of items sold (books, etc.)

Most refund schemes involve the fraudulent generation of a refund payment when a customer has not canceled or returned their order. Occasionally, a refund scheme is perpetrated when an employee falsely informs a customer that they are not entitled to a refund when, in fact, the organization's policy is to provide refunds (see Fraud in the Headlines 4.1 for an example). A refund check is then generated but diverted by the perpetrator.

Similar to billing schemes, phony refund schemes are more common with respect to cancellations of services than with returns of merchandise, for the simple reason that they tend to be easier to conceal.

To generate a refund check to a legitimate customer or member who has not actually canceled or returned an order, some of the same weaknesses in internal controls described in earlier sections are generally present. Most importantly, in order to benefit from this type of transaction, the fraudster must be in a position to receive the refund payment. Once in receipt of the payment, the check is often endorsed to the name of a business or individual (often an alias) in which a bank account has been established.

The following are some of the most important internal controls for preventing refund schemes:

- Segregating the duties of check delivery (mailing) from authorization of refunds (i.e., it should be impossible for one person to initiate or approve a refund and deliver or mail the refund payment)
- Segregating the duties of initiation and approval of refunds from custodianship of the returned goods (or, in the case of canceled memberships, subscriptions, or meeting registrations, segregating custodianship over membership, subscription, or meeting registration databases)

In addition, certain policies and procedures provide for the detection of refund schemes that have been committed:

- Reconciling recorded revenue, net of refunds, with anticipated revenue, using one of the reasonableness tests described in Chapter 3
- Following a policy in which refunds are posted to a separate general ledger account from the revenue (even though the two accounts should likely be combined for external financial reporting purposes, posting refunds to separate accounts makes subsequent monitoring easier)
- Monitoring of refund account balances in comparison with budgeted amounts and with prior year balances (see Chapter 15 for a more detailed discussion of account monitoring)

A different type of refund scheme is possible if an organization has retail operations. Register schemes are rather infrequent and are generally not responsible for large losses. With register schemes, a refund is recorded on the cash register when no return of merchandise has actually been received. The cash in the drawer and the register tape will reconcile, but inventory records will not. Accordingly, utilizing a register and inventory system that is integrated (inventory records are automatically updated when register sales and returns are recorded) can help in the detection of register schemes. Prevention of register refund schemes is accomplished similarly to register skimming, explained in Chapter 3. Installation of video surveillance cameras or clustering registers and personnel together makes register schemes more difficult to carry out without the collusion of multiple employees. Requiring manager authorization for all refunds also can help to minimize the risk of loss through register refund schemes.

If inventory records are not automatically updated from the register, the risk of register refund schemes will be greater, because there will not be a built-in procedure to identify a loss when the physical inventory does not reconcile to the inventory records. Detection based on thorough monitoring of gross profit margins or refunds processed by each employee or on each shift may alert a manager that something is wrong.

Another method of carrying out a register refund scheme is by overstating the amount of a legitimate refund. In this case, a customer returns an item and is refunded the purchase price. But the perpetrator records the refund on the register at a higher dollar amount. In this case, the inventory records would reconcile, since an item was actually returned. If the process for recording of refunds does not match up original purchase amounts with the refund amounts, or controls over pricing are weak, this type of fraud could go undetected.

FINANCIAL ASSISTANCE SCHEMES

Every organization that provides financial assistance to individuals is vulnerable to occasional fraud in the form of ineligible people attempting to improperly collect assistance payments. However, in this chapter the focus is on internally perpetrated financial assistance schemes, which, when carried out, tend to involve much larger losses for nonprofit organizations, as Fraud in the Headlines 4.4 illustrates.

FRAUD IN THE HEADLINES 4.4

N.Y.U. FINANCIAL AID SCHEME NETS $4.1 MILLION

In December 1992, a retired New York University financial aid administrator pleaded guilty to embezzling $4.1 million from the university by collecting tuition assistance checks she issued to nonexistent students. The fraud took place over a ten-year period. More than 1,000 fraudulent checks were involved. Each check was made payable to a different student. The official converted the checks to cash by endorsing the checks over to the name of an alias in whose name she had established a bank account.

Source: Newman, Maria, "N.Y.U. Official Admits $4.1 Million Theft," *New York Times*, December 6, 1992.

Financial assistance schemes perpetrated by insiders often work much like one or more of the cash disbursement schemes explained earlier. These schemes typically involve one of the following:

- Establishing phony applicants for financial assistance
- Generating duplicate payments to persons entitled to financial assistance, then delivering one to the person and converting the other to cash

Establishing a phony grant applicant was one of several fraud schemes in the case explained in Fraud in the Headlines 4.1. However, what is unusual about the financial assistance scheme described in that case is that it was carried out by someone outside the financial assistance or grants department. Most large-scale financial assistance schemes that are perpetrated by insiders are done so by employees responsible for processing grant and financial assistance applications, like the fraud perpetrated in Fraud in the Headlines 4.4.

Important financial controls that prevent financial assistance schemes from being successfully carried out are as follows:

- Segregate the duties of approval and authorization of financial assistance from preparation and delivery of payment (i.e., have check writing and mailing be performed by someone other than the person[s] responsible for processing, approving, and authorizing financial assistance).
- Require original signatures by applicants for financial assistance, as well as other evidence of their identities, such as copies of driver's licenses, as a means of minimizing the chances of entirely phony applicants (i.e., do not process applications that could be generated internally).
- Require independent review and approval of processed applications (perhaps a summary listing supported by applications) prior to the release of financial assistance payments.

In addition, organizations should include certain detective procedures when monitoring financial assistance programs. The following detective controls may be helpful:

- Monitor financial assistance statistics over time, such as the number of applications received, number approved, average amount of financial assistance per person, and so forth.
- Periodically spot-check financial assistance checks for signs of alteration, unusual endorsements, or counter-signatures on the back of the canceled checks.
- Periodically spot-check financial assistance payments with applications or files supporting those payments.
- Cross-check the names of individuals receiving financial assistance with other files of the organization (i.e., when a university cross-checks finan-

cial aid payments with student master files to provide assurance that all recipients are currently enrolled students).

Some of the other general controls mentioned earlier (rotation of duties, etc.) also may be helpful in preventing or detecting financial assistance schemes.

CHECK TAMPERING

Check tampering involves some form of alteration to an organization's checks, usually by an employee who has the responsibility for, or ability to, record or post payments in the accounting records. This ability is essential to concealing this type of fraud. Most check tampering schemes involve one or more of the following:

- Forgery
- Altering payees or amounts
- Creating duplicate or phony checks

Forgery

Forging the signature of an authorized check signer is one of the oldest and most common types of fraud. Almost impossible to completely prevent, the likelihood of its occurring can be substantially limited by controlling access to unused checks. Organizations that leave checkbooks or supplies of unused checks out in the open for anyone to take are inviting this type of fraud. Strong physical security over unused checks is essential to controlling forgery.

Even with limited access to unused checks, there will always be employees, some of whom may be untrustworthy, with access to checks. For this reason, all organizations must establish sound detective controls in this area. Examples of strong detective controls include having someone with no access to checks open and review the monthly bank statement and canceled checks (see Fraud in the Headlines 4.5) and having the bank reconciliation performed by someone other than the person who records the checks in the system.

Altered Payee Schemes

Most altered payee schemes involve the interception of signed checks prior to their delivery (mailing) to vendors, followed by a manual alteration of the payee. Methods of alteration include:

- White-out or correction tape
- Use of erasable ink to prepare checks
- Adding additional characters to payees (for example, changing IBM to I.B.McDonald)
- Use of chemicals to wash the payee name off the check

FRAUD IN THE HEADLINES 4.5

**FORGERY HIDDEN THROUGH LACK
OF SEPARATION OF DUTIES**

One of the keys to concealing check forgery is a lack of separation of duties, enabling the forger to alter records or destroy evidence prior to detection. This is exactly what happened in the case of a former University of Nevada Medical School staff member who embezzled $61,433 and spent the money on gambling.

The embezzler was responsible for the school's life insurance and disability insurance account. From January 1995 to September 1996, the perpetrator forged the signature of authorized signers on 42 checks she converted to cash for her gambling habit. Since she also received the monthly statement directly from the school's bank, she destroyed the forged checks upon their return from the bank.

While a loss of $61,433 is possible in a smaller setting involving someone responsible for just a single program, imagine the potential when the lack of segregation of duties is at a higher staff level. Such was the case with the Capital Area United Way in East Lansing, Michigan. This United Way affiliate was the victim of a $1.9-million embezzlement perpetrated by its former vice president for finance, who stole the funds over a seven-year period by writing checks to herself, forging the names of the required cosigners, and destroying the checks upon their return with the bank statement.

While destroying canceled checks also leaves a trail, in the form of missing documents that could be requested by auditors or other persons, immediate review of the bank statement and canceled checks by someone other than the check writer would discover this type of check tampering sooner, thereby limiting an organization's losses.

Source: Associated Press, "Ex-Medical School Staffer Sentenced for Embezzlement," *Las Vegas Review-Journal*, August 13, 1997, and Prichard, James, "Mich. United Way Official Admits Stealing," *Newsday.com*, February 6, 2003.

In addition to a positive pay system, described in Best Practices 4.3, proper physical security over signed checks and prompt mailing of checks immediately after signature are two controls essential to minimizing the risk of altered payee schemes.

The key to detecting altered payee schemes is for an appropriate person to review the canceled checks returned with the monthly bank statement. Who should that person be? Someone not involved in the preparation, mailing/delivery, or posting of checks should perform this function. As pointed

BEST PRACTICES 4.3

POSITIVE PAY CAN PREVENT CHECK TAMPERING

Throughout this section on check tampering, a variety of schemes and methods of prevention or detection are explained. One of the best methods of preventing check tampering schemes is through the use of a positive pay system.

With a positive pay system, an organization electronically communicates to its financial institution the date, check numbers, and amounts (and sometimes the payees) associated with the authorized checks that have been prepared. Once this information has been transmitted to the bank, only those checks that match these specifications will be honored by the bank. Alterations of payees, changes in amounts, or any duplicate or out-of-sequence checks should be bounced by the bank.

While this system is not foolproof, it can provide a great deal of protection against phony checks and other forms of check tampering.

out in Best Practices 4.4, this person, who may be a member of the board of directors if an organization has limited staff, should carefully review the fronts of canceled checks for signs of altered payees. Additional procedures could include:

- Comparing payees on the canceled checks with payees on the check registers
- Periodically (and on an unannounced basis) requesting mid-month cut-off account statements from the bank (this is particularly useful if it is not possible to have an appropriate person review the bank statement and canceled checks *every* month or if it is possible for the person who prepares and records checks to intercept the normal monthly statement prior to its review)

Phony Check Schemes

Phony check schemes involve the printing of unauthorized checks for the purpose of fraudulently drawing funds on an organization's accounts. With the evolution of word processing software, scanning equipment, and printers, the ease with which an organization's checks can be replicated is astonishing. The best method of preventing phony checks from being honored by a bank is to establish a positive pay system with the bank (see Best Practices 4.3). If a positive pay system is not utilized, prevention of phony check schemes is difficult, but an organization's exposure to such schemes can be limited by implementing the following procedures:

- Draw accounts payable checks on a bank account that is different from the one used to write payroll checks and the one into which deposits of revenue are made.
- Consider sweeping funds out of accounts into which the organization makes its deposits of revenue, transferring the funds into the account from which vendor checks are written, so that a limited balance is maintained in the revenue account. (Note that when checks received by the organization are restrictively endorsed, the payor will be able to identify the organization's bank account number when he receives his canceled check from the bank; if many unknown donors or other payors have access to this information, the odds of someone eventually attempting to perpetrate a phony check scheme based on this information increase.)
- Limit the number of employees who have access to the organization's bank account number on the account from which vendor checks are written.
- If the organization's bank does not impose a strict time period during which it will honor outstanding checks, consider issuing stop payment orders on checks over an established dollar threshold that have been outstanding for more than a certain time period (several internally perpetrated phony check schemes have been carried out by duplicating the check number and amount, but using a different payee, of a check that has been outstanding for some time).

Detection of phony check schemes is accomplished virtually the same way as detecting altered payees. Careful review of bank statements and canceled checks by someone not involved in preparing or recording checks should result in detection of most phony check schemes. In addition, matching of payees, dates, and amounts on canceled checks with information in the check register can detect phony check schemes.

Keep in mind that phony check schemes may be perpetrated by outsiders as well as insiders. Most of this chapter has focused on internal frauds. But, many people outside of an organization may have knowledge of the organization's bank account numbers. Persons who may have this information include all of the organization's vendors (who can determine the organization's account numbers simply by reviewing the checks they receive from the organization) and donors (who can determine the organization's account numbers by reviewing the endorsement on the backs of their canceled checks).

Organizations that receive large volumes of contributions from a wide variety of donors can take an extra degree of precaution against phony check schemes by depositing contribution checks into an account where the balance is promptly swept out into another account on a regular basis, leaving only a minimum balance in the account. By doing so, the account number that is exposed to the general public is kept at a minimal balance, minimizing the risk of financial loss from that account. A similar strategy could be employed by organizations that receive large volumes of payments of any type (not just contributions), such as universities, which receive thousands of tuition payments, or associations receiving thousands of membership dues payments.

ELECTRONIC FUNDS TRANSFER SCHEMES

Electronic funds transfer schemes take place when someone executes an electronic transfer of funds from the organization's account to a personal account or some other unauthorized account. Most of the large electronic funds transfer schemes have been perpetrated by employees who have been authorized to communicate electronic transfers with the organization's bank (see Fraud in the Headlines 4.6). However, unauthorized electronic funds transfers have also been generated by outsiders and unauthorized employees. Remember, plenty of people have the organization's bank account number, from employees to vendors, donors, students, members, and customers. If appropriate security measures are not in place at the organization and its bank, the organization may be vulnerable to electronic funds transfer schemes from insiders and outsiders alike.

FRAUD IN THE HEADLINES 4.6

CHARITY OFFICER EMBEZZLES $6.9 MILLION IN WIRE TRANSFER

The former chief administrative officer for the Ohio chapter of the American Cancer Society admitted to embezzling $6.9 million from the charity. The officer oversaw computer and financial operations for the chapter and was authorized to transfer funds between bank accounts.

In May 2000, the officer faxed a letter to the chapter's bank instructing the bank to wire funds to a law firm in Austria for use in research. Of course there was no research program in Austria. After flying to Austria, the officer then telephoned his wife, informing her of his embezzlement and that he was not returning to the United States. His wife then called the police.

The charity's bank had no comment as to whether it followed all appropriate procedures in processing the wire transfer.

The officer was sentenced to a 13-1/2-year prison term after pleading guilty to bank fraud, mail fraud, money laundering, and unauthorized use of a device.

Source: Roberts, Kate, "Cancer Exec Turns Self In, Wanted on $6.9 Million Embezzlement Charge," *The Associated Press,* June 10, 2000, *The Chronicle of Philanthropy,* September 7, 2000, and *The Beacon Journal,* January 2, 2003.

BEST PRACTICES 4.4

INTERNAL CONTROLS IN SMALL ORGANIZATIONS—
REVIEWING A BANK STATEMENT AND RECONCILIATION

Throughout this section on disbursement frauds, the need for segregating the duties of approval, check preparation, check recording, and reconciling the bank statement has been emphasized. But in smaller organizations, sometimes it is impossible to fully segregate all incompatible duties. In some cases, one person does everything.

In such cases, an organization's last line of defense is to detect fraud through careful review of the bank statement. Always have someone other than the person who controls the check writing and recording receive the monthly bank statement unopened. In some cases, the only way this is possible is to have the statement mailed to the home or office address of a board member.

This person should then open the bank statement and review every page of the statement for the following:

- Unexplained debit or credit memos
- Checks with no check numbers or with numbers from a clearly different numerical sequence
- Duplicate check numbers
- Transfers to unknown accounts
- Any other unexplained transactions

Additionally, the canceled checks that are returned with the bank statement should be reviewed for the following:

- Obvious forgeries of signatures
- Indications of changes made to payees or amounts, through use of erasures, white-out, or fluids that lift ink from the check
- Endorsements on the back of the check that are inconsistent with the payee name, or that involve multiple parties

Once the bank statement has been reviewed, the reconciliation of bank and book balances can be performed. The monthly bank reconciliation should be performed by someone who does not have the ability to record transactions to the cash accounts on the general ledger, particularly cash disbursements.

If it is not feasible to segregate the duties of preparing a bank reconciliation from those of recording cash activity on the books, then it becomes important for someone else to review the completed bank reconciliation.

When reviewing a bank reconciliation, the reviewer should *always* examine the original bank statement. Several disbursement frauds have been concealed for extended periods of time by providing a photocopy of a bank statement to reviewers. Auditors have sometimes made the same mistake of examining copies of bank statements when auditing cash balances. In making these photocopies, the perpetrator of a disbursements fraud cuts out or folds over fraudulent transactions, then makes the copies. The reviewers and auditors then view a month-end balance that reconciles and a photocopied bank statement that appears to have no suspicious activity.

Preventing the unauthorized transmission of electronic funds transfers requires more than just internal controls within an organization. It requires that an organization seek out a financial institution that utilizes sophisticated security measures and that works closely with its clients to ensure maximum protection of their client's funds. The following controls can help in the prevention of unauthorized electronic funds transfers:

- Use office-wide or organization-wide passwords that identify the organization to its bank (and maintain proper security over this password).
- Restrict access to the electronic funds transfer software access code and install the software only on authorized computers (ideally, there should be one computer dedicated to this function and that computer should be used for nothing but electronic funds transfers).
- Use individual passwords, and change those passwords regularly, so that access to the electronic funds transfer software is further restricted.
- Establish a fixed list of "transfer to" account numbers with the organization's bank (for repetitive transfers to known accounts).
- Require the participation of two people on all nonrepetitive transfers.
- Establish dollar limits (per transaction, per day, per employee, etc.) and communicate these limits to the bank.
- Utilize a daily security code formula agreed to or established by the bank (for example, a daily security code may consist of a sum of the digits of the amount of a transaction plus a fixed amount provided by the bank).
- Require second-person authorization after all data has been entered into the system.
- Require confirmation from the bank of each electronic funds transfer processed (this may be in the form of an immediate call-back, a daily report, or some other form of confirmation).

Relying exclusively on passwords and call-backs for protection from unauthorized transfers is inadequate if large sums of money could be transferred. These procedures are also somewhat antiquated and are being replaced with more modern security measures, such as computerized identification cards that automatically change card numbers at fixed intervals. Some organizations even go so far as to hire a team of specialists to attack their system to find out how well it really protects the organization from electronic funds transfer schemes.

In addition, organizations should inquire about the adequacy of any encryption algorithms and authentication procedures that are in place to protect electronic funds transfer messages. Once a funds transfer has been initiated, it must travel over telephone lines to a modem on the other end. Reliable encryption technology translates the electronic funds transfer initiation message into a code that is unreadable by third parties. This prevents unauthorized people from intercepting and reading these messages.

Even with sophisticated preventive controls, an organization will occasionally find itself the victim of a transfer scheme. Accordingly, several internal control policies and procedures are essential to detecting unauthorized electronic funds transfers in a timely manner:

- Timely review of monthly bank statements by someone not involved in the processing of electronic funds transfers
- Periodically requesting and reviewing mid-month cut-off bank statements
- Closely reviewing daily confirmations or reports of transfers received from the organization's bank (by someone who does not authorize or process transfers)

UNDISCLOSED CONFLICTS OF INTEREST

An undisclosed conflict of interest occurs when all three of the following factors are present simultaneously:

- An individual acting on behalf of the organization has a hidden economic or personal interest in the activity in which he/she is involved.
- The hidden economic or personal interest is adverse to the interests of the organization being represented.
- The hidden economic or personal interest is not made known to the organization being represented.

A conflict of interest represents a violation of the old adage about serving two masters. If someone has a conflict of interest with respect to their duties, they should immediately remove themselves from the duty in the best interests of the organization. The most commonly reported instances of undisclosed conflicts of interest involving nonprofit organizations have pertained to board members or top executives with hidden financial interests in vendors with whom their organization is doing business (see Fraud in the Headlines 4.7). In these situations, the insider to the nonprofit organization looks out for the best interests of the vendor in whom he or she has a financial interest. This is accomplished by:

- Arranging for prices that are favorable to the vendor (greater than market or better than what the vendor could obtain elsewhere)
- Including other terms in a contract that are favorable to the vendor (such as certain vendor options, etc.)
- Entering into a contract that results in the nonprofit organization taking excess inventory off the vendor's hands (i.e., inventory that would otherwise become obsolete or spoil) or that absorbs other excess capacity of the vendor
- Arranging for the awarding of the contract to the vendor at the exclusion of other, more qualified competitors (see the section on bid-rigging, later in this chapter)

FRAUD IN THE HEADLINES 4.7

UNDISCLOSED CONFLICT OF INTEREST IS PART OF $9-MILLION FRAUD

The Jewish Community Center of Greater Washington (DC) was victimized by four of its own officials to the tune of nearly $1 million. The four people involved were the organization's executive director, its chief financial officer, the building superintendent, and an accounting clerk. Over a nine-year period, the four used a variety of schemes to defraud their organization. One of those schemes involved an undisclosed ownership in the company contracted to provide cleaning and vending services to the organization.

All four officials were asked to resign by the organization's board after a special audit confirmed the board's suspicions about financial irregularities at the center. The board decided not to pursue criminal charges, instead focusing on recovering the funds from the four individuals. Most of the stolen funds were returned to the organization. However, Montgomery County (MD) officials investigated the matter on their own and filed criminal charges in the case.

Source: Mooar, Brian, "Deal Struck in Jewish Center Theft; Ex-Official to Help Montgomery Probe," *Washington Post*, May 25, 1995; and Subramanya, Manju, "Alleged Misappropriation of JCC Funds Leads to Investigation of Ex-Officials," *The Gazette*, July 14, 1994.

Other less common conflict of interest schemes have involved the awarding of subgrants by one nonprofit organization to another, in which there are overlapping board members. Even less common are conflict of interest schemes in the revenue cycles, in which a board member, manager, department head, or sales representative of a nonprofit organization enters into contracts to provide goods or services to a customer in which that person has a financial or personal interest. The person looks out for their interest in the customer and ignores their duty to the nonprofit organization, by arranging for sales terms that are favorable to the customer, or otherwise better than what the customer could obtain elsewhere.

Specific laws apply to conflicts of interest involving government employees and entities doing business with the government. Beyond that, a conflict of interest in and of itself is not necessarily a prosecutable offense.

In fact, not all conflicts of interest necessarily result in harm to the organization. It is possible for both the nonprofit organization and the entity in which a representative of the nonprofit has an interest to benefit. Or is it?

Take the very real example of a nonprofit organization that leases office space from a partnership. One of the partners happens to be the chair of the nonprofit organization's board of directors. However, the rental rate charged to the nonprofit organization in the lease is below the going market rate for similar office space in the neighborhood.

Is there a conflict of interest? Yes. But, is there anything inappropriate about this conflict of interest? The nonprofit organization appears to be receiving the benefit of a below-market rental rate.

Would your answer change if you were told that there is a 25 percent vacancy rate for office space in the neighborhood? Is the chair of the board receiving an inappropriate benefit by simply having a tenant, even at a below-market rate, in an environment in which many other landlords are receiving no rent payments whatsoever?

These are tough ethical questions. Their difficulty is, of course, the key reason why full disclosure of conflicts of interest is of paramount importance. If the management team is unaware of a conflict of interest, it cannot appropriately consider and discuss all of the facts and circumstances in order to make an educated judgment about the transaction. In addition, if a conflict of interest is not disclosed, odds are that the person with the conflict feels that his outside interest is benefiting at the expense of the nonprofit organization to begin with, regardless of what the rest of the board feels.

Once a conflict of interest is known, an organization should have established policies and procedures for addressing the conflict. First, it must be ascertained whether the conflict violates any known laws or terms of awards (grants or contracts). Next, if the conflict does not violate any laws or award terms, the organization must decide whether to continue with the transaction(s). Possible courses of action include:

- Having the person with the conflict formally abstain from voting on or participating in discussion of the transaction while the remaining members of the board or management team discuss and approve or reject the transaction
- Going one step further and requiring the person with the conflict to resign their position with the organization
- Going outside the organization for a completely independent assessment of the propriety of the proposed transaction
- Automatically rejecting all transactions that involve a conflict of interest, on the grounds that the mere possibility that something inappropriate may occur is cause enough for concern

Conflicts of interest can be one of the most difficult abuses to prevent. Keys to controlling conflicts of interest include the establishment of the following policies and procedures:

- Document a conflict of interest policy in writing (see the sample policy in the appendix) and have each of the following persons agree to comply with the policy by signing a statement upon joining the organization:
  - Members of the board of directors
  - Executive director
  - Department heads and other members of management
  - Purchasing agents and representatives

- Periodically (once a year) produce a current list of vendors and contractors with whom the organization engages in business; provide the list to each of the preceding persons and have them sign an updated statement asserting that they have no interest in any of the listed companies.
- Include in the conflict of interest policy, or in a separate policy statement, an explanation of the procedures the organization will follow in addressing known conflicts of interest.

With prevention being so difficult, every organization should establish policies and procedures designed to detect undisclosed conflicts of interest. To do this, the following controls can be utilized:

- Periodically cross-check the following data in the vendor (accounts payable) master files with information applicable to board members and employees:
  - Street addresses
  - Phone numbers
  - Employer identification numbers

- Have a policy in which vendor ownership is verified (at least for vendors that will be paid an amount that exceeds an established threshold).
- When exit interviews of departing employees result in disclosures that the employee is leaving the organization to go to work for a company that has been a vendor to the organization, follow up on vendor ownership and review past activity with the vendor. (This procedure begins with instituting a policy that establishes exit interviews. Asking who the employee is going to work for should be part of that interview.)
- Follow up on tips or complaints received from competing vendors.

The most common problems pertaining to undisclosed conflicts of interest involve members of management and the board of directors. Accordingly, see Chapter 14 for more guidance on how a board of directors should manage and deal with conflicts of interest.

KICKBACKS FROM VENDORS

Kickback schemes involve the payment by a vendor to someone with purchasing or invoice approval authority in exchange for that person's approval for payment of vendor invoices that overcharge the organization. These overcharges can be in the form of billing for goods or services never delivered or for charging higher prices than appropriate. Kickback schemes can be almost impossible to prevent and are very difficult even to detect (see Fraud in the Headlines 4.8).

As preventive measures, the following practices are helpful in deterring kickbacks:

- Establishing and communicating a clear policy that the acceptance of kickbacks violates the organization's code of conduct and is punishable by termination
- Involving multiple personnel in the processes of authorizing purchases and reviewing and approving invoices for payment wherever practical

BRIBERY

Bribery takes place when someone gives something of value to another person in order to influence that person in the performance of the person's official duties. Examples of bribes involving nonprofit organizations include:

- A payment from a subrecipient to an organization's representative responsible for subrecipient monitoring, in exchange for the representative ignoring known instances of noncompliance with federal grant requirements applicable to the award

FRAUD IN THE HEADLINES 4.8

KICKBACK SCHEMES CAN INVOLVE MANY VARIETIES

Kickback schemes can involve many different types of vendors and many different circumstances. Some kickbacks may be made in exchange for ensuring that a contract is signed or renewed, while others may be for inflated prices or excessive transactions, as the following examples illustrate.

Construction Contractor Kickback

A father-and-son team was convicted in September 2000 on embezzlement charges associated with a kickback scheme. The father and son perpetrated their fraud against the employee benefit fund of a New Jersey Health Care Workers Union. They were convicted of accepting more than $200,000 in kickbacks from a general contractor who was renovating the union building. The kickbacks were in the form of cash and other items of value, and were paid in order to hold on to the renovation contracts, valued at more than $5 million.

Source: U.S. Department of Labor, Office of Public Affairs News Release, September 29, 2000.

Investment Broker Kickback

Consumers Union, the nonprofit organization that publishes *Consumer Reports* magazine, dismissed its chief financial officer in 1991 after finding evidence of a kickback scheme. The scheme involved the chief financial officer approving the payment of excessive commissions to an outside broker in connection with the broker's purchases of securities backed by mortgages of the Government National Mortgage Association (GNMA). The broker would then share the excess commissions with the chief financial officer. The scheme went on from 1986 through early 1991 and involved several hundred thousand dollars of excess payments.

While mark-ups on GNMA purchases by an institutional buyer were quoted as averaging around 1/16 of a point, the mark-ups on some of the purchases by Consumers Union were as high as six percent. Reports indicated that documents were found that contained a mark-up sharing formula, written in the chief financial officer's handwriting.

Source: Valeriano, Lourdes Lee, "Consumers Union Dismisses Official Over Broker Fees," *The Wall Street Journal*, April 15, 1991.

- A payment from a business to an organization's purchasing representative in exchange for drafting a request for proposals in such a manner that only that particular vendor would be capable of submitting a satisfactory proposal

As with kickbacks, there is very little an organization can do to prevent bribes from occurring, other than clearly informing employees of their duties and responsibilities, including a policy that clearly states that accepting payments or gratuities in exchange for influence over one's decisions or behavior is a violation of organization policy.

FRAUD IN THE BIDDING PROCESS

Nonprofit organizations frequently issue requests for proposals from potential vendors. Several types of fraud and abuse can occur in the process of accepting, reviewing, and evaluating proposals received from vendors. The most common form of abuse in this area involves bid-rigging (see Fraud in the Headlines 4.9).

Bid-rigging occurs when an employee fraudulently aids a vendor in winning a contract. It is most probable in environments in which one employee has a significant level of influence over the selection of vendors from the pool of proposals received by an organization.

Bid-rigging is another variation on the bribery schemes explained in the preceding section. The employee responsible for rigging the bid benefits personally through the receipt of a bribe or kickback from the winning vendor.

Examples of bid-rigging schemes include:

- Drafting the specification requirements of a request for proposal in such a manner that only one vendor could possibly meet the stated criteria
- Creating bogus price quotes or proposals from fictitious suppliers, thereby assuring that the only supplier that actually submitted a bid will win the contract
- Providing advance notice of an upcoming request for proposal to the preferred vendor, then issuing the request for proposal with an unrealistic due date that other vendors would not likely be able to meet
- When an organization's policies require that purchases over a specified dollar amount must be competitively bid, splitting a large purchase into multiple smaller purchases that can be sole-sourced to the preferred vendor
- Allowing the preferred vendor to submit their proposal after all other proposals have been submitted and the pricing included in the other proposals has been disclosed to the preferred vendor

FRAUD IN THE HEADLINES 4.9

BID-RIGGING, KICKBACKS, AND FALSE BILLINGS COMBINE FOR MASSIVE FRAUD

In September 1999, the former director of operations at Odyssey House, a Manhattan nonprofit organization providing substance abuse treatment services, was charged with bid rigging, conspiracy to defraud, and income tax evasion. The charges stemmed from an embezzlement of $2.3 million from the nonprofit over an eight-year period ending in April 1998.

The bid rigging charges stemmed from the director's conspiring with outside vendors to rig bids and allocate contracts awarded by Odyssey House for the supply of food, meat, health and beauty supplies, baby supplies, office supplies, printed materials, janitorial supplies, and medical supplies. The director steered nearly $10 million in contracts to those vendors, neglecting the organization's policies requiring competitive bidding. The conspiracy to defraud charge stems from the director accepting $364,000 in kickbacks from vendors in exchange for his ensuring that portions of the total contracts awarded would be allocated to certain vendors. The kickbacks were in the form of cash, goods, and services.

Because Odyssey House receives significant portions of its funding from federal and state government agencies, it was required to utilize competitive bidding for most of these purchases.

The former director pled guilty to the charges.

In August 2002, Odyssey House's former president and chief executive officer was indicted on conspiracy and tax evasion charges for his alleged role in the same $2.3 million scheme.

Source: U.S. Department of Justice Press Release, "Former Director of Operations at Odyssey House Charged with Bid Rigging, Conspiracy, and Income Tax Evasion," September 16, 1999, and "Ex-Head of N.Y. Nonprofit Indicted," *Associated Press,* August 21, 2002.

Much like kickbacks and bribery, bid-rigging and other forms of fraud in the procurement process are difficult to prevent. Many of the same policies and procedures used to control kickbacks are useful against these types of procurement fraud:

- Establish and communicate a clear policy stating that procurement abuse and corruption violates the organization's code of conduct and is punishable by termination.

- Involve multiple personnel in the processes of purchasing, drafting, and reviewing requests for proposals; evaluating proposals; and selecting vendors, so that one person cannot control the entire process.
- Require the preparation and issuance of formal and comprehensive requests for proposals (RFPs) that clearly explain the exact requirements expected of a vendor (important characteristics that should be included in any request for proposal are explained in Chapter 7, under the discussion of vendor fraud).

5

Payroll and Expense Reporting Schemes

Payroll and expense reporting schemes can involve almost anyone within an organization. This category of fraud applies to any scheme in which the payroll system or the expense reporting and reimbursement system is abused to benefit one or more employees. The most common payroll schemes include:

- Ghost employees
- Overstatement of hours worked
- Overstatement of pay rates
- Commission-based payroll schemes
- Payroll withholding schemes

There are also several types of fraud and abuse involving payroll that result in the organization itself being accused of fraud. These involve misclassifying payroll, fraudulent charging of payroll costs to government grants, and other fraudulent activities in which some outside party other than the nonprofit organization is the victim of the fraud. Those frauds involving mischarging of payroll costs by an organization are explained in Chapter 9. The focus in this chapter will be on the payroll frauds perpetrated by employees against their employer, the nonprofit organization.

Closely related to payroll schemes are employee expense reporting schemes. The most common of these schemes include:

- Fictitious expenditures
- Duplicate payments

- Airfare and travel schemes
- Personal purchases charged to the organization

Employee travel and expense reporting and reimbursement schemes have become one of the most common forms of fraud and abuse in the United States. Some employers have cited rampant abuse among employees in which the per incident loss is inconsequential, but the cumulative effect is quite large.

PAYROLL SCHEMES

Financial Controls Over Payroll

Following the explanation of each type of fraud and abuse, key financial controls associated with preventing and/or detecting that particular activity will be identified. Nonprofit managers and board members should compare these controls with those in place in their organizations to identify areas in which improvements are necessary.

Certain financial controls apply throughout the payroll process. Segregation of duties is one such element. The following payroll functions should be segregated to the maximum extent possible:

- Authorizing pay rates and changes
- Entering master employee data into the payroll system (new hires, terminations, and pay rates)
- Entering timekeeping information (hours worked)
- Authorizing timekeeping information (approving timesheets)
- Processing payroll
- Distributing payroll
- Transferring funds to the payroll bank account(s)
- Reconciling the payroll bank account(s)
- Posting payroll to the general ledger

This is a rather extensive list of duties to separate, and such a level of segregation may not be possible. If this is the case, strive to segregate the duties often associated with the human resources or personnel function (new employee setups, entry of pay rates and withholding information, and removal of terminated employees from payroll) from those often associated with the accounting function (entry of timesheets, processing and distributing payroll, and reconciling the bank accounts). The most substantial payroll frauds are perpetrated when the employees responsible for generating and delivering paychecks or deposits also have the ability to enter employee master data. Employees processing payroll should have read-only access to employee master data. Separating the personnel functions from the payroll processing functions prevents several of the most financially crippling frauds explained in this chapter from occurring.

The second most important element of separation of duties involves the general ledger accounting function. Organizations should strive to separate the duties associated with processing payroll from the accounting functions involved in posting payroll to the general ledger. Separating these duties makes it much more difficult to conceal many of the payroll frauds described in this chapter, thereby making any such fraud easier to detect.

Because payroll is often maintained and processed using one software system, establishing read-only parameters and implementing strong password controls is essential to preventing many payroll frauds.

If an outside payroll processing agency is hired, then certain duties are automatically segregated, which can provide an added element of internal control. However, organizations should not naively assume that reliance on an outside payroll company eliminates the risk of payroll fraud.

Other general financial controls that help to reduce the risks associated with payroll frauds include:

- Maintaining written policies and procedures for timekeeping and payroll processing
- Utilizing a separate bank account for payroll
- Use of prenumbered checks in sequence
- Maintaining proper physical security over unused payroll checks (i.e., restricting access to only those employees responsible for processing payroll)
- Holding unclaimed payroll checks (or confirmations of direct deposits)
- Maintaining a detailed payroll register that lists every paycheck, along with total gross pay, all payroll withholdings, and net pay
- Use of a timekeeping system, such as timesheets or timecards
- Review and approval of payroll tax returns, as well as year-end tax summaries (Forms W-2, W-3, and 1099)
- Review of the posting of payroll from the payroll register (journal) to the organization's general ledger
- Authorization in writing of all salaries and wage rates by a designated organization official

The specific attributes of several of these controls will be highlighted throughout this chapter.

Ghost Employees

As the term implies, a ghost employee is a fictitious employee that is on the payroll of the organization. Of the various types of payroll fraud discussed in this chapter, ghost employee schemes are the least frequently encountered.

Where they have been caught, however, ghost employee schemes are usually the most costly of this chapter's payroll-related frauds.

Although ghost employee schemes are most commonly associated with larger organizations, where the people involved in processing payroll or overseeing the organization are not personally familiar with many of the employees on the payroll, they have been known to occur even in small organizations in which payroll is tightly controlled by a single individual.

In order to carry out a ghost employee scheme, the perpetrator must have the ability to do one of the following:

• Add a new employee to the payroll system
• Keep a terminated employee on the payroll system (and execute an address change and/or direct deposit bank account change)

Even with these abilities, a perpetrator also must be able to generate and intercept a paycheck for the ghost employee. For hourly employees, this means preparing and inserting a timesheet. As stated in the introduction, separating the duties associated with entering employee additions and deletions from those duties associated with generating and distributing paychecks is the key to preventing ghost employee schemes from occurring. Specifically, having paychecks distributed to employees by someone other than the department head or the person who prepares the payroll is particularly helpful in preventing ghost employee schemes. See Best Practices 5.1 for additional preventive controls.

There are also several procedures that can be used to detect ghost employee schemes. Detective procedures are critical in organizations where the preventive measures explained thus far cannot or have not been implemented. However, even in an environment with apparently strong preventive controls, periodically executing certain detective procedures is advisable. Some of the procedures that may detect a ghost employee scheme include:

• Requiring identification to pick up paychecks (or pay stubs for direct deposits)
• Comparing rosters of authorized employees with payroll reports
• Comparing employee identification numbers (if the organization assigns numbers other than each employee's social security number) for out-of-sequence, duplicate, or unusual numbers
• Analyzing employee payroll deductions, taking a closer look at employees with minimal withholdings (ghosts rarely need insurance and usually opt for the minimum income tax withholdings—while legitimate em-

BEST PRACTICES 5.1

MANY GHOSTS ARE FORMER EMPLOYEES

So much emphasis can be put on tight controls over additions to the payroll records that it can be easy to forget about controls pertaining to deletions from payroll. In fact, a significant number of ghost employee schemes have been carried out by fraudulently keeping a terminated employee on the payroll. Because a master record of this employee's data is already on file, all that is needed to carry out such a fraud is to change the employee address, or change the direct deposit information associated with the employee.

Organizations should consider the following policies and procedures to help prevent this type of ghost employee scheme from being perpetrated:

- Segregate all duties associated with deleting employees from the payroll master file from duties involving processing of payroll and generating paychecks. (Ideally, give a separate personnel or human resources department the authority to add or remove employees and input pay rates, but do not allow that department to generate payroll payments. An accounting or payroll processing function should input timesheets and generate paychecks, but should not add or remove employees or input pay rates.)

- Require written authorization, signed by employees and approved by human resources personnel, for all address changes and changes to direct deposit banking information.

- Utilize a payroll system that requires the printout and authorization of all changes to payroll master file information prior to processing any payrolls using the updated information (or software that requires a second person to release postings of changes to master file data).

- Request that all employees who voluntarily leave employment state their intentions to quit in writing and submit their letters of resignation to the appropriate supervisory personnel (someone other than the person[s] responsible for processing payroll).

- Have payroll distributed by someone other than department heads or supervisors who approve timesheets or payroll clerks who process payroll.

ployees may also have these characteristics, it can't hurt to periodically verify that they are, indeed, legitimate workers)

- Comparing the net payroll expense as summarized on reports prepared for management with funds actually issued (i.e., total disbursements from the payroll account), as amounts paid to ghost employees may not have been included on the management report
- Verifying that all employees on the payroll register are supported with employee personnel files (ghosts often do not have personnel files)
- Analyzing payroll master file data for duplicate
  - Employee addresses
  - Social security numbers
  - Direct deposit bank account numbers
- Periodically having someone completely independent of the payroll and human resources functions receive and distribute paychecks (if there is an internal auditor, this is a perfect role for that person)
- Periodically requiring positive identification (such as a driver's license) when hand-delivering paychecks to employees
- Comparing a list of terminated employees with the payroll register (see Best Practices 5.1)
- Timely reconciliation of the monthly payroll account bank statement by someone not involved in any of the following steps:
  - Preparing payroll
  - Signing payroll checks
  - Distributing paychecks
- Reviewing endorsements on the backs of canceled payroll checks returned with the monthly bank statement for anything unusual (such as multiple paychecks being endorsed over to the same payee or two-party endorsements, which could indicate that checks are being issued in the names of departed employees, then being signed over to the perpetrator)
- Reconciling payroll registers with general ledger control accounts
- Looking into other possible indicators of ghost employees, such as "employees" with the following characteristics:
  - No annual or sick leave taken for extended periods of time
  - No changes in pay rates or promotions for unusually long periods of time

As with many of the other fraud schemes explained in this book, careful monitoring of variations between budgeted and actual expenses can be another method of detecting ghost employee schemes. See Chapter 15 for more on variance analysis and budgeting.

Overstatement of Hours Worked

Overstating the number of hours worked is the most common type of payroll fraud. The losses resulting from overstatement of hours schemes are usually among the smallest losses caused by fraud and abuse. However, cases of rampant falsification of hours worked by many employees have been known to accumulate large losses. A 2002 survey sponsored by the accounting firm Ernst & Young, LLP, found that 16 percent of the 617 workers surveyed reported witnessing the claiming of extra hours worked by other employees. If this statistic were applied to the 11 million workers employed by nonprofit organizations, it would mean that 1.76 million employees of nonprofit organizations have *witnessed* this type of fraud. What this means in terms of how many are committing this fraud is anybody's guess—but it would seem to be a significant problem.

There are several methods of falsifying the number of hours worked. If manual timecards or timesheets are used to record hours worked, the following schemes can be used to falsify the record:

- Forging a supervisor's signature of approval on a timesheet
- Making changes to timesheets by intercepting timesheets after they have been approved by a supervisor
- Taking advantage of a supervisor's rubber stamp of approval by overstating hours worked and counting on the fact that the supervisor will not review time records carefully enough to notice

Accordingly, the most important controls for curtailing the overstatement of hours worked in manual timekeeping systems involve:

- Careful review of timesheets by supervisors with firsthand knowledge of the employees under their supervision
- Physical control of the timesheets after they have been reviewed and approved by supervisors
- Direct and timely submission of approved timesheets by supervisors to the payroll department
- Having a formal process for making legitimate corrections to timesheets that requires documentation of the change by both the worker and supervisor

If an automated timekeeping system such as a time clock is utilized, one common scheme involves one employee punching in or out for an absent employee. Having a supervisor present at the beginning and end of shifts is one method of preventing this. Installing a surveillance camera in the area of the time clock is another.

More and more organizations now utilize electronic timesheets. These systems provide for numerous efficiencies with respect to processing payroll and recording and allocating salaries and wages to programs and activities. However, without appropriate controls, electronic timekeeping systems can also create a huge potential for fraud and abuse. Among the key elements to control with electronic timesheets:

- Use of passwords and/or other mechanisms (fingerprints, etc.) to prevent unauthorized preparation or submission of timesheets, as well as to protect against unauthorized changes to previously submitted timesheets
- Use of additional passwords and/or other security measures to restrict electronic approvals of timesheets to specific department heads to prevent unauthorized approvals of timesheets
- Protection of passwords from unauthorized users
- Requiring periodic changes in passwords, or using a system that automatically changes passwords at certain time intervals (see Chapter 12 for more on internal controls pertaining to an organization's software and information technology systems)

Overstatement of Pay Rates

To overstate pay rates, someone must have the ability to access and change master payroll data. These schemes, therefore, tend to be more sophisticated or involve higher-level employees than do schemes involving overstatement of hours worked. The key to preventing pay rate schemes is a series of controls over payroll master file data, such as:

- Segregating the duties of pay rate authorization from entry of pay rates into the payroll master files
- Segregating the duties associated with entry of pay rates into the payroll master file from duties involved with generating individual paychecks (i.e., entry of timesheets and other functions involved in payroll processing from week to week)
- Restricting access to the payroll master files (to prevent unauthorized employees from making changes to pay rates) via appropriate use of passwords and/or physical security measures
- Requiring the use of forms signed by employees and/or appropriate supervisors (depending on the nature of the change) to document all requested changes to payroll master file data (for instance, all changes in pay rates should be supported by an approval documented in each employee's personnel file)

Procedures useful in detecting pay rate schemes include:

- Careful review and approval of payroll registers prior to the distribution of paychecks
- Periodically testing year-to-date wages by multiplying total hours worked by approved pay rates as documented in the personnel files and comparing the result with the year-to-date wages in the payroll register
- Periodically verifying pay rates used in the payroll processing function with authorized pay rates in personnel files

Commission-Based Payroll Schemes

Though not very common in the nonprofit sector, some organizations compensate employees involved in sales activities on a commission basis. Whenever commissions are involved, another type of payroll-related fraud is possible.

Commission-based payroll schemes usually involve one of two possible approaches: overstating sales or overstating a commission rate. To overstate sales, an employee may create a record of fictitious sales, change the pricing listed on sales that have been made, or claim sales that have actually been made by other employees. Internal controls that should be in place to prevent and/or detect falsification of sales schemes are similar to those associated with hours worked schemes explained earlier, except that the controls revolve around a sales report rather than a timesheet.

Prevention of sales commission schemes is best accomplished by integrating the calculation of sales commissions with the sales and customer invoicing systems (i.e., commissions are calculated based on the same records as those used to bill customers). With this type of system, the only way for an employee to overstate sales is for the employee to overcharge a customer. This provides for a built-in control in the form of a customer's review of the sales invoice.

If this type of integrated system is not in place, then prevention of a false sales scheme becomes more difficult. The organization may need to rely more on procedures designed to detect the scheme. Some of these detective controls include:

- Careful review of sales reports by supervisors with firsthand knowledge of an employee's responsibilities and activities
- Cross-checking sales reports used for calculating commissions with actual sales documents and/or accounts receivable and billing reports
- Comparing sales commission from employee to employee and over time, looking for inordinately high commissions paid to one employee

Overstating a commission rate usually requires that an employee gain access to the payroll master files or have an accomplice that has this access. Financial controls designed to prevent or detect unauthorized changes in commission rates are similar to those described earlier for controlling changes to wage rates and salaries:

- Segregate the duties of commission rate authorization from entry of commission rates into the payroll master files.
- Segregate the duties associated with entry of commission rates into payroll master files from processing of individual commission checks.
- Document all approved commission rates in personnel files.
- Restrict access to the payroll master files (to prevent unauthorized employees from making changes to commission rates) via appropriate use of passwords and/or physical security measures.
- Carefully review and approve commission reports and payroll registers prior to the distribution of paychecks.
- Periodically test year-to-date commissions by multiplying total sales per employee by approved commission rates as documented in the personnel files and compare the result with the year-to-date commissions in the payroll register and/or commission reports.
- Compare commissions by employee and over time, looking for unusual amounts or trends.

Payroll Withholding Schemes

Payroll withholding schemes are not very common. However, some of these schemes are rather sophisticated. In one case, an employee responsible for processing payroll withheld very little taxes from her own paycheck. Yet, when payroll taxes were remitted to the government, more taxes were remitted than were actually withheld. The additional amount remitted was then credited to her in the payroll records and reflected as taxes withheld on her annual Form W-2, which made it appear that her taxes were over-withheld. Consequently, the employee received a large tax refund from the government for taxes she never actually paid.

In this case, the organization was the victim of the fraud. In other payroll withholding schemes, fellow employees may be victimized. In these cases, an employee in charge of payroll withholdings credits small portions of the withholdings from other employees to his own withholdings. The net effect is similar—the employee receives a refund on his income tax return due to what appears to be over-withholding of taxes. Numerous other employees end up slightly under-withheld. The same type of withholding scheme can be applied to nontax withholdings as well, such as contributions to retirement plans, contribution deductions, and so forth.

The difference between these two schemes highlights the need for internal control for preventing or detecting payroll withholding schemes. In the first scheme, the total amount remitted to the taxing authorities is greater than the sum of the actual amounts withheld from all employees. In the second case, the total amount remitted agrees with the sum of all withholdings, but the individual allocation among employees has been altered. The following controls should be in place to protect against payroll withholding schemes:

- Maintain documentation (signed by the employees) for all withholdings in separate files for each employee and separate the function of maintaining this documentation from the function of processing payroll.
- Require authorization and approval for remittances of payroll withholdings to taxing authorities and others.
- Review the mathematical accuracy of payroll registers (i.e., make sure the sum of all the individual withholdings agrees with the total on the report).
- Reconcile total withholdings from the payroll register with subsequent remittances of taxes and other withholdings.
- On a test basis, check that withholdings on the payroll register are consistent with the supporting documentation for withholdings in employee files.
- Test some of the year-end tax reports (W-2 forms) for agreement with payroll registers.

Use of an outside payroll processing company can significantly reduce the risk of payroll withholding schemes. With an outside payroll processing company, much of the mathematical testing and cross-checking is either not necessary or can be significantly curtailed.

EMPLOYEE EXPENSE REPORTING SCHEMES

Financial Controls Over Employee Expense Reporting

Just as it was important in the payroll cycle, segregation of duties is essential in the employee expense reporting cycle as well. No single employee should have the ability to prepare and submit an expense report, approve the report, and cause a reimbursement check to be generated. Accordingly, the review and approval of expense reports and supporting documentation must be performed by someone other than the employee requesting reimbursement. Likewise, employees requesting reimbursement of expenses should not have access to the cash disbursements (accounts payable) system.

Abuse in the expense reporting cycle can be particularly difficult to control if it is carried out by upper-level managers. These individuals are frequently in a position of control over their department's travel budget and their own expense reports may not even be subject to review and approval. The expense reports of department heads should be reviewed and approved by the executive director or chief financial officer. Even the expense report of the top staff person, the executive director, should be subject to review and approval. Perhaps this review can be in the form of a periodic review by the board of directors, the internal auditor, or even as part of the annual audit by an external audit firm. If it is not practical to review and approve expense reports of upper-level management prior to making reimbursements, a review of expense reports after-the-fact should be performed.

Other elements of financial controls associated with employee expense reporting should adhere to the following:

- Use an expense reporting system that requires a detailed itemization of expenses claimed by employees on a day-by-day basis.
- Institute a policy that clearly articulates all dollar limitations on spending for employees, so that expenditures in excess of stated thresholds must be preapproved by an employee's immediate supervisor in order to be claimed for reimbursement. (These limitations may address the maximum allowable per day, per employee, per meal, etc.)
- Document a policy that clearly identifies the nature of expenses that are allowable or unallowable (for example, first-class airfare, suites in hotels, luxury rental cars, etc.).
- Establish and monitor travel and entertainment budgets for each department and employee.
- Incorporate a policy requiring employees to submit expense reports in a timely manner (for example, within 30 days of incurring a claimed business expense).
- Include a statement on each expense report attesting that the expenses claimed are legitimate business expenses and require a signature by the employee affirming this statement.
- Require that each of the following elements be documented for every meal or entertainment expense claimed:
    - Names and organizational affiliations of each person involved
    - Business purpose of the activity or nature of the business discussed
- Implement a policy requiring that supporting documentation in the form of original vendor receipts (not copies) accompany the expense report for all lodging, transportation (airfare, etc.), and other expenses, with the exception of expenditures less than a specific small dollar threshold and meals, for which a credit card receipt will suffice.

- Require review and approval of expense reports by an appropriate designated official (a supervisor who is familiar with the travel and other business requirements and/or schedule of the employee).

- Require a detailed review of expense reports, matching expenses with travel dates and timesheets of employees, as well as cross-checking expense reports between employees.

- For organizations receiving federal funds, use an expense report that requires the segregation of expenditures for alcoholic beverages, entertainment, and any other cost that may not be charged directly or indirectly to federal awards.

Fictitious Expenditures

Submission of fictitious expenditures for reimbursement has become quite simple with the evolution of sophisticated desktop publishing. The effort involved in creating a legitimate appearing, but bogus, receipt for an expenditure can be rather minimal. Another method of submitting fictitious expenditures is to obtain blank copies of receipts from legitimate vendors or suppliers.

Procedures that are useful in catching fictitious expenditure schemes include the following:

- Have a supervisor, who has firsthand knowledge of an employee's travel schedule and business needs, review expense reports.

- Carefully review supporting documentation submitted with expense reports as substantiation for expenditures claimed on the report (look for indications that the supporting receipt is phony).

- As part of the review, examine dates and times on supporting documentation for consistency and agreement with an employee's travel schedule and timesheet.

- As part of the review of supporting documentation, check the customer name and the delivery address, if applicable, on the vendor receipt.

- Match receipts for supplies or equipment purchased with receiving reports, fixed asset listings, or inventory records.

- Establish and monitor budgets for travel, entertainment, and other business expenditures likely to be reported on employee expense reports.

Another type of fictitious expenditure reporting involves out-of-town travel. Some employees will report expenses for the same trip on multiple expense reports. On one report they will claim reimbursement for airfare. On another report the employee will claim reimbursement for mileage (business use of one's car). Which did they do, fly or drive? Because this type of expense reporting scheme is similar to duplicate expense reporting and travel schemes, internal controls associated with it will be discussed in the next section.

Duplicate Reimbursements

Duplicate reimbursement schemes involve an employee, officer, or director engaging in one of the following:

- Submitting the same expenditure for reimbursement twice
- Submitting an expenditure for reimbursement that has previously been directly paid by the organization (such as items directly billed to the organization or charged to an organization's corporate credit card)
- Submitting an expenditure for reimbursement that has already been paid for by another organization
- Submitting two different forms of transportation-related expenses for the same trip (as mentioned previously, requesting reimbursement of business mileage on one report and airfare on a second report, but for the same trip)

Submitting the same expenditure for reimbursement twice involves either making extra copies of the required supporting documentation or submitting different versions of support for the same item. An example of the latter is when an employee submits a vendor receipt or invoice as documentation for an expenditure, then separately submits a credit card receipt for the same item.

Organizations that pay certain expenses directly or that utilize corporate credit cards must be particularly careful not to mistakenly reimburse employees for the same expenditures that have already been directly paid.

Another variation on the duplicate payment scheme involves two employees each submitting the same expenditure for reimbursement, when only one employee actually paid for the expense. One common manner in which this occurs is that two employees have a business meal together, perhaps with someone from another organization. One of the employees charges the meal on a credit card. Upon their return to the office, one employee uses the credit card receipt as documentation for a request for reimbursement while the other employee submits the restaurant receipt, or tear-off stub, as documentation for an identical request for reimbursement.

Yet another duplicate payment scheme occurs when a request for reimbursement is submitted regarding an expense that has been paid by another entity. This type of scheme is most often associated with members of an organization's board of directors who may have received reimbursement from their employer. It can also happen in connection with joint activities involving multiple organizations. For example, two nonprofit organizations team up on a joint conference. An employee of Nonprofit A travels to the conference. His airfare has already been paid for by Nonprofit B. But when the employee returns from the conference, he submits to Nonprofit A the receipt he obtained at check-in as support for a fraudulent reimbursement of the airfare.

In addition to requiring that employee expense reports be reviewed and approved by a supervisor with firsthand knowledge of an employee's travel schedule and job responsibilities, some additional internal controls are helpful in preventing or detecting duplicate payment schemes:

- Cross-check expense reports between employees, being alert for the same item claimed by two different employees.
- Compare multiple, sequential expense reports from the same employee, looking for obvious duplication and making sure claims for mileage reimbursements are consistent with claims for other out-of-town travel expenditures. (For example, make sure that airfare and mileage weren't claimed for the same trip.)
- Require employees to submit claims for reimbursement within a certain time period (such as 30 days) in order to receive reimbursement. (This procedure reduces the amount of cross-checking necessary to detect duplicate reimbursement requests.)
- Use the names of coworkers reported as being present at a business meal on an employee claim, pull the expense reports of the coworkers that traveled or dined together, and review them for consistency in times, dates, and types of expenditures as well as lack of duplication (i.e., multiple employees did not submit claims for the same expenditure).
- Cross-check expenditures with the organization's own accounts payable or cash disbursement journals to look for items paid directly by the organization.
- As part of the review of supporting documentation submitted with an employee expense report, check the customer name and the delivery address, if applicable, on the vendor receipt. (This is helpful in determining whether the item may have already been paid by another organization.)

Airfare and Travel Schemes

There are several methods of committing fraud against an organization through an airfare or other travel-related scheme. Some of the most common include:

- Receiving reimbursements for travel never taken
- Switching tickets
- Submitting tickets for companions or other travelers

See Fraud in the Headlines 5.1 for an example of how one of these travel schemes can be carried out.

The key to preventing most airfare and other travel schemes from being carried out is the establishment and enforcement of the following policies and procedures:

- Require approval in advance for all out-of-town travel. (The approval should be documented by an appropriate supervisor familiar with the business plans and travel needs of a department.)
- Require submission of proof that a trip was taken in order to receive reimbursement for the travel-related expenditures. This proof should be in the form of a receipt for the ticket and boarding pass for the flight. (Do not accept itineraries from travel agents, airlines, or Web sites as documentation.)

FRAUD IN THE HEADLINES 5.1

ANATOMY OF A TICKET-SWITCHING SCHEME

One of the classic airfare schemes involves the switching of tickets for the personal benefit of the traveler. An employee, officer, or director with an upcoming legitimate business trip on behalf of the organization purchases an advance ticket from an airline one month before the trip for $225. By making the reservation that far in advance, the lowest possible airfare is obtained. Ten days before the trip, a second ticket using the same itinerary is purchased, only this ticket is at a much higher fare ($750), as it has been booked at the last minute.

A few days before the trip, the traveler cancels the higher-priced reservation, taking credit for a future trip, less a $75 change fee charged by the airline. The employee travels using the lower-priced ticket, maintaining a $675 credit for future travel with the airline.

Upon the traveler's return, the itinerary (and/or receipt) for the higher-priced ticket is submitted to the organization for reimbursement, perhaps with boarding passes from the same flight numbers (but from the lower-priced ticket) submitted as substantiation that the trip was actually taken.

The traveler has now paid a total of $1,050 for the two tickets and a change fee. The traveler has been reimbursed $750 from the organization. However, the traveler still has a $675 credit for future travel with the airline. This credit will be used for personal trips or refunded. The employee has profited by $375 through this scheme. Multiply this scheme by several trips and the employee can eventually receive free personal air travel, as well as cash in the form of excess reimbursements.

This is just one example of airfare and travel schemes. There are many others.

The key to detection of airfare and other travel schemes is careful review of the documents submitted by each employee. Specific elements of this review should include:

- Cross-checking ticket numbers from itineraries, receipts, and boarding passes
- Reconciling the name of the traveler on the submitted supporting receipt with the name of the employee and the name on the boarding passes/ itinerary, if applicable
- Cross-checking dates of travel from submitted airfare documentation with dates reported on hotel invoices, timesheets, and other documents

Personal Purchases

Sometimes an employee will submit an expense report requesting reimbursement for a purchase that is entirely personal in nature. This can occur in any of the following ways:

- There is a lack of segregation of duties, resulting in an employee's ability to generate a reimbursement for an otherwise obviously personal item.
- An employee takes advantage of a careless review process, counting on the rubber stamp approval by a supervisor who is not carefully reviewing expense reports prior to signing them.
- An employee has altered the supporting documentation or otherwise fabricated an explanation of a personal purchase as being business-related.

A personal purchase reported as a business expenditure is one type of fraud that is easier to prevent than to detect. Requiring that all business-related purchases be preapproved by a supervisor or manager or utilizing a purchase order system significantly limits the potential for personal items to be included on expense reports or charged to corporate credit cards. However, this may not always be practical, particularly when employees are away from the office carrying out legitimate business activities, as they will often incur expenses other than lodging and transportation.

Accordingly, an organization that deals with this type of expenditure should perform procedures to detect personal items claimed on a business expense report. If carried out as part of the initial review of supporting documentation, the following procedures often can detect personal purchases included on the report:

- Require submission of original vendor invoices or receipts. (Accepting photocopies of invoices or credit card receipts as a basis for reimbursing an employee should not be permitted.)

- Question the legitimacy of expenditures supported by vendor receipts that are generic or vague regarding the nature of the goods or services provided.
- Check the customer name and the delivery address on vendor receipts or invoices. (This is helpful in determining whether an item has been delivered to a home or other nonbusiness address.)
- Match dates on vendor invoices (date of invoice as well as dates of delivery or date service was provided) with other supporting documentation (for instance, did the expenditure occur on one of the known business travel dates?).
- For all business meal and entertainment expenditures, require that the employee document the name and organizational affiliation of every person entertained or present for the meal, as well as the general business purpose of the meal or entertainment (for instance, require that the nature of the business discussion be documented).
- Be on the lookout for charges associated with additional, unexplained individuals included on an invoice or receipt for a group (i.e., the employee's report lists names and business affiliations of 10 people, but 13 meals are itemized on the restaurant bill, indicating that spouses or other personal friends of the employee may have been present).
- Be on the lookout for unexplained additional charges tacked onto an invoice that involves legitimate charges (for instance, a single receipt from a country club that includes both charges for a legitimate business entertainment golf outing and nonbusiness clothing purchased at the club's retail shop).
- Review all charges individually for propriety and business purpose.

One of the keys to controlling fraud and abuse in employee travel and expense reporting is diligence on the part of the individuals responsible for reviewing and processing expense reports. Many nonprofits claim to have most or all of the policies discussed in this chapter in place in their organization. Yet some of these organizations fail to catch fraudulent expense reporting, while others have a firm grasp on it. The difference is usually in the people charged with reviewing and processing the expense reports. Those who pay careful attention to the details of their job, or that work in an environment that encourages attention to detail, tend to do a much better job of controlling expense report fraud and abuse.

6

Other Asset Misappropriations and Misuse

This chapter is devoted to the final category of fraud and abuse committed by insiders against their own organizations. Whereas Chapters 3 through 5 focused on various methods of embezzling cash from an organization, this chapter is devoted to other valuable resources of nonprofit organizations that are often prone to theft or misuse by employees, officers, or directors. These include:

- Property and equipment
- Inventories of items held for sale
- Supplies
- Personnel

When we think of fraud, we usually think of cash being skimmed or embezzled. But a 2002 survey sponsored by the accounting firm Ernst & Young, LLP, reported that theft of office items was the most common fraud of which employees were aware. An astonishing 37 percent of the 617 employees surveyed reported witnessing this type of fraud. Accordingly, organizations should be aware of the theft and misuse of assets other than cash, and adopt policies and procedures to control such schemes.

PROPERTY AND EQUIPMENT SCHEMES

In property and equipment schemes, a perpetrator takes an asset for their personal use. Unless the theft involves the skimming of assets donated to the organization prior to their being recorded on the books (described in Chapter 3), theft of property and equipment inevitably leaves some trail or other evidence. This trail can be utilized to detect the fraud because at some point it was recorded on the books as an asset or is otherwise being tracked and accounted for as a purchase. Theft of an organization's property and equipment usually occurs in one of the following ways:

- Stealing part or all of a newly arrived shipment of property or equipment from a supplier (for example, shorting an order by removing one of the ten personal computers received from a computer vendor)
- Outright theft of an asset (usually after hours)
- Unauthorized write-offs of property and equipment as missing, obsolete, or damaged

As has been the case with most of the other frauds explained in this book, separation of duties is one of the key components of preventing property and equipment theft. The following duties associated with property and equipment should be performed by different personnel:

- Budgeting for asset additions
- Purchasing of property and equipment
- Receipt of new property and equipment
- Maintenance of property and equipment inventory records
- Write-offs of property and equipment that are fully depreciated, obsolete, or unused
- Physical inventories of property and equipment

If it is impossible for all of these duties to be performed by different individuals, organizations should strive to segregate the duties associated with custody of assets (receiving and custody) from those associated with record-keeping and with physical counting.

In addition to segregation of duties, some of the most important general financial controls relating to property and equipment include:

- Establishing an organization-wide and departmental budget (approved by the board) for additions of property and equipment
- Maintaining proper physical security over the organization's premises and buildings, including:
  - Issuance of keys or passes only to personnel who are authorized for after-hours access
  - Use of time-sensitive passwords or security cards, limiting the times that most personnel may access the building or suite to ordinary business hours

- — Use of an alarm system that sounds (and notifies police) when unauthorized entry is attempted
- — Surveillance cameras in the receiving area
- — Possible use of security guards
- Use of a purchase order system for purchases of new property and equipment (see Chapter 4 for further explanation of financial controls over purchasing)
- Establishing appropriate capitalization thresholds for additions of property and equipment (i.e., unit cost thresholds over which an item will be capitalized and tracked as an asset, otherwise the item is expensed as supplies)
- Using prenumbered identification tags on all newly acquired property and equipment
- Creating a property and equipment listing that includes the following information:
  - — The identification number from the inventory tag
  - — Specific description of the asset, including the manufacturer and model number
  - — The serial number on the asset
  - — The physical location of the asset (i.e., a particular office or employee's cubicle)
  - — Date of acquisition
  - — Cost or other basis (i.e., market value for donated assets)
- Indication of whether the asset was:
  - — Purchased with the organization's unrestricted funds
  - — Purchased with donor-restricted funds
  - — Purchased with federal funds
  - — Donated to the organization
  - — Donated to the organization in fulfillment of a federal cost-sharing or cost-matching requirement
- Periodically taking physical inventories of property and equipment and reconciling the physical inventory with the property and equipment listing, investigating any discrepancies
- Utilization of a disposal form to document requests and approvals for writing off property and equipment that is no longer used
- Maintaining appropriate levels of insurance over theft of and damage to property and equipment

Somewhere between the property and equipment schemes described in this section and the personal use of organization assets described in the next section lies one additional common problem. Personal use of office supplies may sound like an immaterial issue hardly worth noting. But in some organizations, theft of office supplies has become so rampant that the organization has instituted tight controls over office supplies, such as:

- Use of a formal requisition system for the issuance of supplies
- Establishing personal or departmental budgets for office supplies that roll up into the organization-wide budget
- Periodically taking physical inventories of supplies (see the discussion of physical inventories later in this chapter; whether an organization maintains a perpetual inventory of supplies that is reconciled to the physical inventory, or simply uses the physical inventory as a method of assessing the reasonableness of supplies on hand is a matter of judgment, based on materiality of supplies use and other controls and security measures in place)
- Monitoring requisitions and use of supplies by person and/or by department
- Limiting the volume of supplies issued to a person at any one time (to prevent stockpiling of supplies by individual employees or departments)
- Keeping supplies under lock and key, controlled by a limited number of authorized personnel
- Maintaining perpetual supplies inventory records (described later in this chapter for inventories of merchandise held for resale)
- Performing a financial analysis of supplies use over time by comparing supplies expenditures from year to year and calculating and comparing supplies expense per employee

Whether any or all of these measures are necessary depends on the circumstances. But organizations should not automatically assume that a rising cost of office supplies is always due to increasing prices and increased business use.

PERSONAL USE OF ORGANIZATION ASSETS AND OTHER RESOURCES

More difficult to detect than outright theft of property belonging to an organization is the misuse of organizational resources for the personal purposes of individuals involved with the organization. The personal use of organizational resources for nonbusiness purposes is one of the most widespread issues of abuse throughout organizations of all types. Most people would not say that such acts represent fraud. However, most would agree that personal use of organizational resources is a form of abuse. (Some view this as neither fraud nor abuse.) Nonetheless, the potential cost to organizations is huge. Examples of this type of abuse include:

- Use of an organization's computers, software, and printers for personal projects
- Making long-distance personal telephone calls on the organization's lines
- Utilizing the organization's Internet access and electronic mail system for personal purposes
- Using an organization-owned vehicle to run personal errands
- Processing personal mail on the organization's postage meter (this results in a direct cash loss to the organization, because the postage has been prepaid)
- Photocopying personal documents on the organization's copy machine
- Utilizing the organization's fax machine to send and receive personal transmissions

In today's environment of laptop computers and other portable equipment, some of the abusive practices cited above may also take place outside the work area when employees take equipment home to use for personal purposes after hours.

But physical assets are not the only resources that can be abused for personal purposes. Use of personnel for nonbusiness projects is an equally abusive act. Whether it's asking an administrative assistant to research airfares for a director's family vacation or having the senior accountant keep the books for a side business of another employee, the result is the theft of a resource that belongs to, and is paid for by, the organization.

Some of the controls that are helpful in preventing or detecting misuse of organizational assets and personnel for nonbusiness purposes include the following:

- Establish and document clear policies prohibiting the use of organizational assets or personnel for any purpose other than the business of the organization and require each employee to acknowledge receipt of this policy in writing.
- Wherever practical, maintain usage logs for certain equipment, such as photocopiers, postage meters, and vehicles, in which each use is tracked. (This can also be an excellent procedure to aid in allocating the costs associated with each of these assets to the various programs and functions of the organization.)
- Monitor long-distance telephone calls by workstation by reviewing reports of calls made or requiring that employees assign a function code each time a long-distance call is made.
- Require that all employees prepare timesheets and instruct employees to include accurate descriptions of their activities when completing timesheets. (This policy is known to have revealed that one executive director was requiring his assistant to run personal errands and work on

personal projects for him. This became apparent to the chief financial officer when he reviewed the assistant's timesheets, and pressed for more thorough explanations of the vague or incomplete descriptions contained therein.)

- Monitor Internet usage, including sites visited and e-mail activity (see Best Practices 6.1).

In addition, some of the nonfinancial systems described in Part IV, such as hotlines, can be helpful in deterring nonbusiness use of organizational resources.

BEST PRACTICES 6.1

MONITORING EMPLOYEE COMMUNICATIONS

While the introduction of e-mail has created many valuable efficiencies, it has also made it much more possible for employees to engage in nonbusiness activities during working hours—or has it? The American Management Association estimated in 2000 that 45 percent of large U.S. companies monitor e-mail and voice mail communications.

Many employees falsely assume that personal e-mails sent from work are protected from their employer's scrutiny under privacy laws. The Electronic Communications Privacy Act of 1986 (ECPA) prohibits the interception or accession of electronic communications. But, one of the three exceptions to ECPA, known as the "system provider" exception, has been held by the courts to apply to employers who provide e-mail capabilities to their employees. It is unclear whether the provider exception would apply to e-mail services paid for by employers but provided by third-party service providers, since in these cases the employer is not directly providing the service.

Under one of the other exceptions from ECPA, the "ordinary course of business" exception, employers may be permitted to monitor employee communications if there is a legitimate business justification for the monitoring. For instance, the courts have recognized the need to balance an employee's expectation of privacy with an organization's legitimate business needs, such as those that arise when allegations of misconduct result in the need to perform an investigation.

The final exception to ECPA is known as the "consent" exception. As its name implies, when prior consent is given, monitoring of electronic communications is permitted. An appropriately crafted policy regarding an employer's rights to access or intercept employee communications that is acknowledged by each employee can provide a great deal of protection to employers under this exception.

As employers balance efficiency and risk management with employee privacy issues, many have elected to document and distribute monitoring policies to all employees. Before doing so, employers should consult applicable state laws, which may be more restrictive than ECPA.

Some state courts have held that once an employer identifies a communication as personal, monitoring of that communication would be an invasion of privacy. But, there is nothing wrong with monitoring limited to identifying the fact that a nonbusiness communication is taking place. An alternative to personal monitoring of e-mails is the use of monitoring software, which utilizes specified criteria (such as size of messages or attachments, destination addresses, searches for certain words in messages, etc.) to screen and flag e-mail messages that may violate company policies. But before establishing any policies or engaging in any practices involving the monitoring of employee e-mails or phone calls, consult an attorney who is experienced in privacy matters.

INVENTORY SCHEMES

In Chapter 3, skimming of retail sales revenue was explained. In Chapter 4, fraudulent refunds from retail cash registers were described. The next type of retail scheme to be addressed is the theft of merchandise itself. Inventory theft is usually carried out in one or more of the following manners:

- Simply stealing an asset with no attempt to cover it up
- Shorting a customer shipment
- Phony shipments
- Shorting a receipt from a supplier
- Supposedly scrapping an item as damaged, obsolete, or otherwise unusable

Most inventory schemes are not very complicated. They tend to involve one of two groups of personnel: warehouse employees or retail sales personnel and cashiers.

Many of the reported inventory thefts have involved an employee simply walking off with inventory. This is the most basic and involves virtually no attempt on the part of the perpetrator to cover up the theft (other than the obvious aspect of hiding the stolen item[s]).

Other schemes involve more sophisticated methods of concealing a theft. Shorting a customer shipment involves shipping less than the quantity ordered and billed for. For example, if a customer orders ten shirts, the perpetrator ships nine but documents that the order of ten has been filled, resulting in a packing slip and sales invoice for ten shirts. This results in a complaint from the customer. But if there is no proper follow-up, this type of scheme can go on for years.

An entirely phony shipment can be carried out when there is inadequate separation of duties and no reconciliation is performed among shipments, sales orders, and invoices. With a phony shipment, inventory is packaged as though it were being shipped to a legitimate customer. However, the name of the customer may be fictitious and the address is the perpetrator's address or that of someone known to the perpetrator. Phony shipments are not supported by legitimate sales orders and other sales documents that would generate an invoice or account receivable. Because there is no customer, there is no risk of a customer complaint, so this scheme may be easier to conceal than shorting a customer shipment. And it is possible to carry out without detection if prenumbered shipping documents (supported by sales orders) are not required and reviewed as part of every shipment and subsequently matched with sales invoices.

Shorting a supplier shipment works in a similar manner to shorting a customer shipment. An employee in the receiving department opens a box of 100 shirts to be sold by the organization in its retail store and removes 5 shirts for personal use. A receiving report is completed indicating that only 95 of the 100 shirts ordered have arrived. This may or may not result in a complaint communicated to the supplier, depending on how the duties are established at the organization.

Scrapping inventory as being unusable occurs when someone has the authority to initiate and authorize the write-off of inventory and that person also has custody over the inventory. By having the control and authority associated with all of these functions, it becomes possible to carry out and conceal the scheme. Like many other frauds described here, a lack of separation of duties is the factor that makes this fraud possible.

Similar to controlling other fraud schemes, controlling inventory schemes involves a two-pronged approach, emphasizing both prevention and detection. Prevention is accomplished by segregating duties, thereby preventing one person from stealing inventory and covering it up. Appropriate separation of duties is achieved by having each of the following duties performed by different personnel:

- Purchasing (ordering) of inventory
- Receiving inventory
- Shipping or disbursing of inventory
- Receipt of revenue from sales (including proceeds from disposal of scrap and obsolete inventory)
- Periodic physical counts of inventory

Another important element of prevention involves physical security over inventory. The following physical controls designed to prevent inventory theft should be considered:

- Restrict access to inventory (through appropriate use of locks, etc.).
- Use surveillance cameras to observe areas in which inventory is received, stored, or shipped from.
- Follow policies that limit the ability of employees to bring large handbags or similar containers into the inventory area (especially if the organization maintains an inventory of small but valuable items).
- Employ security guards.
- In retail settings, employ security personnel disguised as shoppers.

Of course, one of the most important controls that is helpful in both preventing and detecting inventory theft is the taking of physical inventories and reconciling the counts of merchandise on hand with inventory records. See Best Practices 6.2 for details on the proper way to conduct a periodic physical count of inventory. There are two basic methods used to track inventory:

- Recording additions to inventory in a purchases account and sales from inventory to a sales account, while not making any entries to the inventory asset account, which is periodically adjusted to whatever the physical count determines inventory on hand to be.
- Utilizing a perpetual inventory method, in which purchases are recorded as additions to inventory and sales as reductions in inventory, with the remaining balance representing an amount that should agree (within a range of tolerable difference) with the results of the periodic physical count.

The second method, involving the use of a perpetual inventory system, is preferable to the first. The first method results in all inventory adjustments being recorded through the cost of goods sold or purchases account. This method would fail to distinguish a theft of inventory from a legitimate sale. Many small organizations use this method, but it should be avoided if inventory is a material asset of an organization.

Perpetual inventory records enable an organization to track inventory levels for each item by keeping a record of purchases and sales on a product-by-product basis. Sophisticated and expensive software is available for perpetual inventory tracking. Less sophisticated, even manual, systems can accomplish the same purpose in smaller environments.

One of the advantages of a perpetual inventory system (aside from the ability to compare inventory levels from the perpetual inventory records with actual physical counts on a product-by-product basis) is that it leaves a trail of

BEST PRACTICES 6.2

PHYSICAL INVENTORIES

There is a right way and a wrong way to perform physical counts of an organization's inventory. Whether the inventory is of a warehouse area or a retail shop, certain standard controls and procedures apply. The following are some of the key considerations in taking physical counts:

- Prepare detailed written instructions for all personnel involved in the count.
- Have a meeting prior to the count, during which all instructions are reviewed to make sure everyone clearly understands their responsibilities and expectations.
- Use prenumbered inventory tags and maintain a record of tag numbers used.
- Provide a clear description of the item either on the count tags themselves or on a separate listing that references the tag numbers.
- Suspend all shipping and receiving activities during the physical counting process, and establish procedures for including or excluding items from inventory in the process of being shipped or received.
- Form count teams of two people to perform the physical count.
- Have counters be employees who do not have responsibility for physical custody of the assets they are counting (this may be accomplished via rotation of workers, with workers responsible for one department or area performing the physical counts of items in another department or area).
- Establish procedures for documenting items that the counters feel may be obsolete or damaged, including procedures for review and approval by the inventory supervisor.
- Establish procedures for coordinating the counting of identical inventory items located in different areas or sites.
- Record counts directly on the prenumbered inventory tags, but leave the tags in place until the "all clear" has been given by the inventory supervisor.
- Have test counts performed (or recount all items) by persons other than those involved in the initial count.
- Have counters and test counters initial the inventory tags or the inventory sheet onto which quantities from the tags are transferred.
- Have supervisors perform spot checks, focusing on more valuable items and those easily stolen.

- If more than a limited number of errors are detected in the test counts of a particular area, require that the entire area be recounted.
- After an area has been approved by the inventory supervisor (indicating the results of test counts are satisfactory), pull the inventory tags and put them in numerical order, according to their numerical sequence.
- Transfer counts from the inventory tags onto summary inventory count sheets that will be used to tabulate the final inventory.

transactions for each product stored in inventory. Each and every posting to a particular inventory item is able to be traced and reconciled to a receiving report and vendor invoice (for additions to inventory) or sales record. The only other entries to the perpetual inventory records should be for items taken out of inventory for other legitimate reasons, such as promotional giveaways, obsolete and damaged items, and the like.

In addition to segregation of duties, physical security, and perpetual inventory records, other important general controls with respect to inventory should be established:

- Monitor and follow up on customer complaints. (For example, does the organization frequently receive complaints that their shipment contained slightly less than the quantity they ordered?)
- Using electronic security measures or other methods, limit the times that authorized personnel may access inventory. (Many inventory schemes are carried out by people who are authorized to have access to the inventory, but who perpetrate their scheme after hours.)
- Utilize prenumbered documents for each of the following:
  - Purchases (or purchase orders)
  - Receiving reports
  - Shipping (disbursing) records
  - Sales invoices
- Prepare receiving reports for all additions to inventory.

Detection of inventory theft involves a combination of physical controls and after-the-fact reconciliations and financial analysis. Physical controls include the same policies as preventive controls (use of video surveillance cameras, etc.). The most important after-the-fact reconciliation is between the physical counts and the perpetual inventory records of the organization. Differences in excess of an established, tolerable level should be investigated.

Financial analysis is yet another strong detective measure, and one that has been mentioned in each of the preceding chapters. Financial analysis is helpful in detecting inventory thefts, but is particularly essential if an organization does not maintain perpetual inventory records. As mentioned earlier, without perpetual inventory records, the physical count itself will not detect any inventory shortages. See Chapter 15 for details on financial analysis.

7

External Fraud Schemes

In Chapters 3 through 6, the focus was on fraud and abuse committed by insiders—the employees, officers, and directors of a nonprofit organization. Now, let's turn our attention to frauds committed against nonprofit organizations by external parties. Though not as common as internal fraud, external frauds can be every bit as damaging.

The external frauds explained in this chapter focus on schemes carried out by vendors and other outside parties without any assistance from employees of the victim organization. When external frauds are perpetrated with collusion involving employees, the fraud can be more difficult to prevent or detect. However, in order for there to be any incentive for an employee to participate, the employee generally requires a kickback or some other benefit. Since kickback schemes involve employees, methods of deterring such schemes were explained in Chapter 4, along with other internal fraud schemes.

Most frauds committed by external parties against nonprofit organizations fall into one of four categories:

- Fraudulent billings by vendors
- Fraud committed by service organizations
- Fraud and abuse by subrecipients
- Financial assistance fraud

There are certainly other types of frauds that can be committed by outsiders, such as credit fraud and hacking into the computer systems of nonprofit organizations. But these four categories of fraud tend to be the most common and most material in damages to nonprofit organizations, so in this chapter the focus will be on these types of schemes.

Fraudulent billings by vendors can involve charging inflated prices, billing for goods or services not delivered, duplicate billings, or substituting lower-quality goods than what was agreed upon.

Fraud committed by service organizations involves any type of embezzlement, skimming, theft, or other fraud perpetrated by a vendor as a result of the vendor performing a critical activity on behalf of a nonprofit organization. These frauds can be committed when an activity ordinarily carried out by employees is outsourced to an unrelated third party. The third party may take advantage of this relationship by committing fraud against its nonprofit organization client. Often, vendors to whom an activity has been outsourced have access to valuable organizational assets or data, making certain types of frauds possible.

Fraud and abuse by subrecipients can take place when a nonprofit organization receives grant funds and, out of those funds, makes subawards to other organizations to carry out specific elements of the program funded by the grantor. Particularly if the grantor is a federal agency, the organization receiving the funding initially takes full responsibility for all aspects of the program, including those portions of the program carried out by subrecipients. Accordingly, fraud and abuse at the subrecipient level can have a direct effect on the initial recipient.

Financial assistance fraud occurs when a nonprofit organization is deceived into approving and processing a fraudulent application for financial assistance (or a fraudulent application for a grant, fellowship, scholarship, etc.).

Each of these categories of fraud will be further explained in the remaining sections of this chapter.

FRAUDULENT BILLINGS BY VENDORS

As stated earlier, fraudulent billings by vendors can involve any or all of the following:

- Charging inflated prices
- Billing for goods or services not delivered
- Duplicate billings (which are similar to the preceding fraud)
- Substituting lower-quality goods than what was agreed upon

Controlling any of these fraud schemes is dependent upon an organization's ability to establish and follow procedures designed to:

- Establish and document a clear understanding between the organization and its vendor as to the exact nature and quantity of goods or services ordered.

- Oversee the work of each vendor and verify goods received as matching those ordered.
- Carefully review each vendor invoice and require appropriate supporting documentation prior to authorizing payment to a vendor.

Many of the steps used to control vendor fraud are similar to those used in preventing or detecting disbursement and purchasing schemes attempted by a nonprofit's own employees (particularly in the second and third categories of controls listed above).

One element of controlling vendor fraud that differs somewhat from controlling internal fraud involves the first step from the preceding list—establishing and documenting what is being requested from a vendor. The importance of this step as an element of protection from fraud should not be underestimated. Protection against vendor fraud starts in the procurement process.

With some purchases, an individual employee may have the authority to simply place an order with a vendor without being required to consider alternative vendors. For larger purchases, however, organizations should consider multiple vendors before making a decision. The best method of establishing a clear understanding with a vendor is by formally requesting the submission of proposals (bids) and agreeing to purchase terms in a written contract. Best Practices 7.1 provides information that should be requested from vendors whenever an organization is using a Request for Proposal (RFP) process to make major purchasing decisions.

In purchasing situations not involving a formal request for proposal, an organization should nonetheless consider requesting some of the same information from potential suppliers as that described in Best Practices 7.1

When requesting proposals from vendors, the next step after preparing and issuing an RFP is the collection and evaluation of the proposals submitted by vendors. During this phase, an organization may be able to detect vendors prone to committing fraud against their customers by doing the following:

- Request background checks on the vendor (and, possibly on its officers, individually) using the company information provided in the proposal. (See Chapter 11 for more on background checks—many of the same firms that conduct checks on prospective employees can also perform background checks on potential vendors.)
- Determine whether the vendor has responded to each of the requests for information included in the RFP (incomplete proposals should be a red flag).
- Contact the references provided by the vendor and ask about their level of satisfaction (inability to contact references or references that are vague and unwilling to provide specific information also should be a red flag).

BEST PRACTICES 7.1

REQUESTS FOR PROPOSALS (RFPs)

When purchasing decisions involve a formal solicitation of quotations or requests for proposals (RFPs), this is an organization's opportunity to obtain more than just a clear understanding of the goods or services required of the vendor. It is also an opportunity to gather a lot of information about each potential vendor. This information may be useful in screening out potentially fraudulent vendors. The information may also be useful in proving fraud in court if a vendor fraud is ever committed against your organization.

The RFP should require that each and every potential vendor submitting a proposal make certain representations to the organization in writing. Information requested of each vendor in the RFP should include:

- Exact specifications of goods to be supplied
- Precise description of services requested
- Brand names of goods or supplies delivered or used, if applicable, and provisions regarding substitution of equivalent-quality items
- Delivery dates of goods or services requested, including milestone dates for contracts that will be performed over extended periods of time
- Prices for each item or service (for example, billing rates for each category of labor)
- Quantities of goods requested (and units of service, if measurable, such as hours of service provided)
- Exact legal name of vendor (and all affiliates involved in any way in the proposed transaction)
- Federal employer identification numbers of each vendor (and affiliates)
- Street addresses of vendors (and affiliates)
- Names of principal owners/officers of vendors
- If subcontractors are to be used, the same information for each subcontractor
- Information regarding the vendor's business history (years in business, etc.)
- Information regarding financial stability of the vendor (have they declared bankruptcy in the past, etc.)

- Vendor experience in providing the requested goods or services for other nonprofit organizations
- References of other customers, preferably other nonprofit organizations, that you may contact
- Qualifications and education of vendor personnel who will provide services under the proposed contract
- Certifications and licenses of the business and key personnel providing services under the proposed contract
- Detailed descriptions of the proposed methodology of providing services (applicable only when requesting certain technical or professional services, such as computer programming, consulting, legal, accounting, etc.)

- Check with the local Better Business Bureau using information provided in the proposal.
- Evaluate the degree to which the vendor has provided precise details regarding the goods or services they will provide (vague responses are yet another red flag).

Establishing a fair basis for comparing alternative vendors is the next key element in selecting a vendor. While this may not be a key step in protecting against external vendor fraud, it can help in selecting the best vendor. An example of a format that can be used to evaluate potential vendors responding to a request for proposal is provided in Exhibit 7.1. This form identifies all of the criteria on which vendors should be evaluated. It then assigns a numerical score to each of the criteria, signifying the relative importance of each. The sum of the highest possible scores is 100. Each vendor's response (their proposals) can be scored using this system, which results in a more objective vendor selection process. Another benefit of establishing and using a scoring system like the one illustrated in Exhibit 7.1 is that it helps to deter certain bribe and kickback schemes (explained in Chapter 4), which may involve biased purchasing decisions, as well as purchases involving undisclosed conflicts of interest.

The next phase in controlling vendor fraud involves the proper oversight of the delivery of goods or services from a vendor. For delivery of goods, this entails a strong receiving department within the organization. As goods are delivered, they should be immediately inspected to determine:

- Whether the nature of the items enclosed matches the item descriptions on the bill of lading and/or invoice from the vendor included in the shipment

Exhibit 7.1 Sample Vendor Evaluation Form

	Criteria	Max. Score	Vendor No. 1 Score	Vendor No. 2 Score	Vendor No. 3 Score
	Goods or services being purchased:				
	Proposal due date:				
	Selection date:				
	Evaluated by:				
	Approved by:				
1	Adequacy of proposed methodology:				
2	Skill and expertise of key personnel:				
3	Demonstrated company experience:				
4	Technical specifications (list):				
	a.				
	b.				
	c.				
	d.				
5	Compliance with administrative requirements of request for proposal:				
6	Vendor's financial stability:				
7	Commitment to nonprofit sector:				
8	Results of communication with references:				
9	Ability/commitment to meet time deadlines:				
10	Cost:				
11	Other criteria (list):				
	a.				
	b.				
	c.				
	d.				
	Total Score	100			

- Whether quantities enclosed agree with bills of lading and/or vendor invoices
- Whether the condition of the goods enclosed is acceptable (i.e., make sure there are no damaged goods)

To the maximum extent possible, this inspection should be done immediately upon delivery, so that damaged goods and incorrect shipments can be refused. If this cannot be done, or it can only be performed in a cursory manner (such as by eyeballing the descriptions and quantities listed on the outsides of boxes if there isn't adequate time to open and inspect boxes), a more detailed inspection should be performed as soon afterward as is practical. Obviously, the timeliness and thoroughness of this step correlates to the nature and cost of the items purchased. Performing this inspection immediately is certainly more important for a shipment of new personal computers than it is for a shipment of photocopier paper.

Responsible oversight of vendors providing services means assigning an employee (usually the person who has ordered the service) the responsibility of monitoring the performance of the vendor. The employee should have an adequate level of familiarity with the nature and requirements of the services being provided by the vendor. This person should be in a position to assess the quality of the services provided and whether the apparent qualifications and skill level of the individual(s) providing those services are consistent with what was promised to the organization in the contract and/or proposal. If the organization is being charged for services at an hourly rate, scrutinizing the hours worked by each vendor representative is important. This employee should periodically check on workers to make sure they are working, not taking another break. This employee should keep a record and compare it to subsequent invoices received from the vendor. This enables the organization to be in a position to detect the billing of inflated hours worked.

The final phase in preventing and detecting vendor fraud involves the evaluation of vendor invoices prior to payment. Most of the controls applicable here are identical to those explained in Chapter 4 with respect to prevention and detection of fictitious vendor schemes and certain other disbursement schemes perpetrated by employees. Some of the most important of these financial controls involve performing the following procedures prior to issuing payment to a vendor:

- Compare descriptions, quantities, and prices with purchase orders, contracts, vendor proposals, catalogs, or price lists for agreement.
- Check the clerical accuracy of vendor invoices.
- Match goods on vendor invoices with receiving reports and bills of lading.
- Check to make sure the invoice has not already been paid (using any of several methods, such as looking up a vendor payment history, compar-

ing current invoice numbers and amounts with previously paid invoices, etc.).

- If applicable (for certain service contracts), verify the level of effort claimed by the vendor (i.e., determine whether the number of hours claimed on an invoice appears reasonable, or that the completion of tasks asserted in a progress billing is accurate, based on your ongoing oversight of the work performed).

- Record all items from an approved vendor invoice against the purchase order (especially important when one purchase order is used to support multiple individual purchases and invoices from a vendor).

- Cancel vendor invoices to prevent accidental duplicate payments.

When procuring goods or services that will be utilized in performing services under a federally funded program, additional considerations enter into each procurement decision. Each federal agency has adopted its own set of guidelines regarding procurements made by nonprofit organizations and nonprofits must be familiar with the provisions applicable to each grant. The reference to applicable procurement standards will be listed somewhere in each grant. It can be found in the form of a citation in the *Code of Federal Regulations,* which is available via the Internet. Although procurement standards can vary from one federal agency to another, most of the regulations are similar, and are based on the Office of Management and Budget's (OMB) Circular A-110, *Uniform Administrative Requirements for Grants and Other Agreements with Institutions of Higher Education, Hospitals, and Other Non-Profit Organizations* (available from the OMB Web site, located at www.omb.gov). The procurement standards described in Circular A-110 address such topics as:

- Documentation requirements
- Consideration of minority-owned firms
- Provisions that must be included in all vendor contracts and certifications that must be obtained from each vendor

The importance of understanding the applicable procurement standards relevant to each federal grant is not limited to simply complying with the terms agreed to by a nonprofit organization. Nonprofit organizations must take reasonable steps to ensure that they request all necessary information from prospective vendors and that the information and certifications submitted by vendors are carefully reviewed for signs of fraud.

OUTSOURCING AND SERVICE ORGANIZATIONS

They are referred to by many different names, from service bureaus and service organizations to vendors and contractors. By any name, the use of an outside vendor to perform a critical function(s) of the nonprofit organization is a common strategy employed by many organizations.

This outsourcing is nothing new. Organizations of all types have been using payroll service bureaus and accounting service bureaus to process payroll and general ledgers for many years. However, there has been a steady rise in the use of outside vendors to perform other functions, including many of the most critical daily operations of the organization. In the nonprofit community, specialized vendors are often utilized to fulfill many programmatic and supporting functions. Thus, the term "service organization" will be used throughout this chapter to refer to all of these vendors.

Outsourced Functions

Examples of functions that are often outsourced to third parties by nonprofit organizations include:

Meeting and Conference Planning

Services performed by meeting planners may include the design and printing of promotional literature for the meeting; the arrangement of facilities, catering, and entertainment; collection and processing of registrations and cash receipts; and the on-site management of the meeting. Marketing and administration of exhibit space at trade shows and conferences is also frequently outsourced to third-party vendors.

Fundraising

Vendors of this type may be involved in the design and mailing of solicitation letters as well as the collection and processing of contributions received by mail. Fundraisers may also perform telephone solicitations of potential donors. Another fundraising function that may be contracted out is the planning and coordination of special fundraising events, from large annual galas or concerts to casino nights, silent auctions, and golf outings.

Membership Dues Billing and Collection

Membership organizations, such as trade and professional associations and labor unions, often turn the member dues billing and collection process over to an outside vendor. In these cases, on a regular basis the vendor reports collections and membership statistics to the organization. A duty that is commonly added is the solicitation of new members. This process may include the design and mailing of solicitations in addition to the cash collection and accounting functions.

Storage and Sales of Publications and Promotional Merchandise

In addition to the basic storage and safekeeping of publications and other merchandise sold by a tax-exempt organization, service organizations are often utilized to design and print the promotional literature and order forms; handle cash receipts and process accounts receivable; process and ship orders; and even restock and/or print or produce the publications and merchandise.

Insurance Providers

Many membership organizations offer group insurance benefits for their members at rates better than the individual members might obtain on their own. When this benefit is offered, the outside agent may handle all aspects of the insurance plans, from marketing to enrollment, to collection of premiums and claims processing. Often, the only function of the nonprofit organization is to provide a database of member names and addresses to the insurance company.

Travel Planning

Travel services are another benefit commonly offered to large organizations as a service to their members. Travel planners offer discounted trips and cruises to members of an organization, and the organization receives a fee in return. The only function typically performed by the organization is, again, providing mailing lists to the travel planner.

The outsourced functions highlighted above represent merely a partial listing. Almost every imaginable function of a nonprofit organization may be contracted to an outside vendor. However, as one can see from the preceding list, these vendors handle much more than data processing. They often have direct contact with members or supporters of an organization, and may even process cash and checks remitted by those members and supporters.

Why Nonprofits Use Service Organizations

There are a number of good reasons for a nonprofit organization to utilize a service organization. The mere size of a nonprofit organization is often a determining factor in the decision to outsource. Particularly when organizations are in a growth period or are just starting out, it may be unreasonable for them to hire full-time staff members for each necessary or desired function. If an organization wants to sponsor just one annual convention and doesn't have a staff member on board that is familiar with the process of planning one, perhaps it makes sense to hire a service organization that specializes in this area.

The same theory may hold true simply for internal control reasons. A small charitable organization with limited potential for proper segregation of duties may wish to use a service organization, or more simply, a bank lockbox, for its collection of mail-in charitable contributions.

The economies of scale obtained by retaining service organizations are another good reason for considering their use. A vendor whose sole operation is the performance of one specialized task is more likely to be able to accomplish that task at a lower per unit cost than an organization that performs that task to a much more limited extent. Data processors are a good example. Also, some positions just may be too specialized for an organization to efficiently perform that function, as in the case of a travel planner.

A final reason for using service organizations may be related to the theory of management employed by a nonprofit organization. A charitable educational organization may consider it too distracting or inefficient to attempt to master the functions of data processing or meeting planning. Some organizations prefer to remain lean and only perform the functions that the organization was originally set up to do, leaving the remaining activities to outside vendors.

Operating Risks Involved with Service Organizations

The risk that an organization takes when using service organizations centers around loss of control. When a function is outsourced, an organization opens itself up to a possible compromise in product quality (quality of service) or financial loss (due to poor management or fraud).

Everybody is familiar with the old expression, "If you want something done right, you'd better do it yourself." To a certain extent, the same theory has been known to apply when dealing with service organizations. Certainly, nobody understands and appreciates the importance of an organization's functions more than the management and employees of the organization. Membership organizations understand that providing the highest quality of service to their members is critical to maintaining or growing membership levels, thereby staying in existence. Charitable organizations appreciate the importance of performing their charitable functions in relation to the organization's public image and reputation.

But, can an outside vendor, with profit-minded goals and objectives, ever appreciate the importance of these considerations? Will a service organization ever perform these critical functions as conscientiously and diligently as the nonprofit organization itself? The answer to these questions is yes—sometimes.

There are many very good service organizations that will treat these functions as though they were their own. The quality service organizations do this because they know that their own reputation and profitability depend upon it. There always will be those, however, that will attempt to cut corners or otherwise minimize their effort, which is why it is very important to properly screen and monitor any service organization that is being utilized. Many organizations have suffered damage to their reputation as a result of an outside vendor providing a poor-quality product or service.

The focus of this book, however, is on fraud. And many of the same principles applicable to product quality also hold true in the area of controlling financial losses that can occur when an activity is outsourced.

Nonprofit organizations often go to great lengths to establish and maintain a strong system of internal controls and to carefully screen their new employee selections. Organizations employing service organizations should not assume that the service organization has exercised the same care simply because it has a license to do business.

Many of the same financial risks are encountered whether a function is handled internally (by employees) or by an outside vendor. However, when these functions are outsourced, the nonprofit organization has far less control. As a result, a nonprofit organization must ask many of the same questions it would ask if the function were being handled internally:

- Are the assets of the organization (especially those held by the service organization for the nonprofit) properly safeguarded?
- Is the organization receiving all of the support and revenue from the service organization that it is entitled to?
- Is the service organization properly handling and accounting for postage, supplies, and other directly reimbursable costs incurred on behalf of the organization?
- Are there adequate controls in place at the service organization to prevent their employees from theft of the nonprofit's funds or assets?
- Is the data processing function of the service organization subject to adequate controls to ensure reliable reporting of information to the nonprofit organization, including proper segregation of one customer's data from another?
- Does the service organization carry adequate insurance against loss or theft of the nonprofit's assets?

These are a few of the important questions that an organization should consider before entering into an agreement with a service organization.

The Service Organization's System Is Your System

When a nonprofit organization hires a service organization, it is relying on the policies and procedures in place at the service organization. As such, these policies and procedures represent a component of the nonprofit organization's system of internal controls. This is a critical factor for both the management of the nonprofit and external auditor to assess.

The significance of a service organization's controls depends on two factors concerning the services it provides, primarily:

- The nature and materiality of the transactions it processes for the nonprofit (the inherent risks involved or the sheer magnitude of revenue or expense involved)
- The degree of interaction between the activities (including internal controls) of the nonprofit organization and the activities (including internal controls) of the service organization (the checks and balances that may be in place as a result of the manner in which business is transacted)

The responses to the questions raised by these two factors will indicate the overall risk an organization bears with respect to its service provider (i.e., high materiality and low interaction mean higher risk).

Methods of Reducing Risk

There are a number of ways to reduce the risks identified in the preceding section. These methods fall into two general categories:

- Procedures that should be employed *prior* to entering into an agreement with a service organization (in the discussion and negotiation stages)
- Procedures that should be employed *throughout* the term of the contract with the service organization

Other procedures should be performed both prior to entering into an agreement *and* during the term of the agreement in order to minimize risk. Five important steps to reducing the risks of dealing with service organizations are:

- Proper negotiation of the contract
- On-site visitation
- Reference checks
- Third-party reviews
- Financial analysis (monitoring of results)

Contract Negotiation

One of the most important, yet often overlooked, aspects of dealing with service organizations is the contract negotiation process. Service organizations will almost always attempt to have the nonprofit organization sign their standard agreement, one that is often very limited in terms of defining the responsibilities of the service organization. However, these agreements are almost always negotiable, and are often surprisingly flexible. In addition to negotiating the best price, nonprofit organizations should be very careful to have all responsibilities properly spelled out in the contract.

Some important issues that are often improperly negotiated or left out of contracts entirely include:

- *Shipping methods and pricing.* When a service organization is being used to process and ship orders for publications or promotional merchandise, the contract often addresses the inventory itself, and nothing more. The exact methods of shipping and carriers should be agreed upon, as well as how customers or the organization will be charged for shipping and postage.
- *Insurance.* Responsibility for and required levels of insurance covering acts of the service organization should be thoroughly covered in the agreement. Insurance should cover all forms of accidents, theft, loss, damaged goods, personal liability, and bonding of the vendor's key employees.

- *Reporting.* This section of the agreement should give precise details of the types of information that the service organization is responsible for providing to the nonprofit organization. Reporting should cover performance statistics (numbers of donors, customers, etc.) as well as financial data. Required frequency of reports should also be spelled out. Inadequate reporting by outside vendors is an oft mentioned complaint regarding outsourcing.

- *Handling of returns and customer complaints.* When an outside vendor will be responsible for a function that involves contact with the customers of a nonprofit organization (i.e., members, donors, students, program participants, the general public, etc.), a clear method of handling complaints and returns should be established. The organization may want to handle all complaints and returns itself, rather than let the vendor perform that function. Once again, it boils down to the issue of treatment of customers. If this is a sensitive area, the organization should control it directly. Otherwise, it can be handled by the service organization. However, if handled by the service, there should be some feedback mechanism regarding the vendor's performance.

- *Goals and objectives.* Contracting for services is not enough. If a nonprofit organization wants to get the most out of its service organization, it should establish clear and measurable goals and objectives and include them in the contract. Including financial incentives for extraordinary accomplishments, as well as penalties for failures, provides greater assurance that the service organization will be diligent in its efforts.

- *Right to audit.* One of the most important provisions that must be included in every outsourcing contract is a right to audit clause. This clause grants the nonprofit organization the right to inspect all applicable books and records of the outside vendor (usually for a specified time period and with limits on the frequency). This becomes a critical provision if fraud is ever suspected. The right to audit clause usually will state that the cost of the audit shall be paid for by the nonprofit organization, unless certain specified problems, liabilities, or deficiencies are discovered upon audit. In these cases, the liability of the audit may revert to the vendor.

- *Designation as agent, if applicable.* The concept of an agent relationship between a nonprofit organization and an outside party is explained in Chapter 8 in the context of fundraising activities. But the agency issue extends well beyond fundraising, to include many other situations in which an outside party is acting on behalf of an organization. When an agency relationship is established, the principal (nonprofit organization) is responsible for the actions of the agent. This is desirable in some instances and undesirable in others. If an agency relationship is desired, this raises numerous liability and insurance issues that must be addressed in the contract. See Chapter 8 for more on this issue. Then consult an attorney to ensure that all the necessary terms are included in the contract to protect the organization.

Certain topics are difficult to clearly address in a contract. For example, when a service organization is utilized to plan and handle all aspects of a nonprofit's annual convention, confusion and disputes can arise over things such as acceptance of exhibitors, assignment of exhibitor and attendee space, how cancellations are to be handled, handling of attendance guarantees, handling of on-site registration, adequacy of facilities, and so forth. Nonprofits contemplating the use of any type of service organization should prepare a checklist of all of these areas of responsibility and be sure that they are adequately addressed in the agreement before proceeding further.

Site Visits

One of the best methods for getting a feel for the efficiency (or inefficiency) of a service organization is by performing a site visit. Observing the vendor at work for other customers can tell a lot about the adequacy of the procedures in place.

However, there is a right way and a wrong way to perform a site visit. To maximize the benefits of performing a site visit, the organization should consider the following:

- Unannounced site visits are best, although they are sometimes impossible to get. However, it can't hurt to ask if an unannounced site visit is allowable.
- Perform the visit during work hours. Don't allow the vendor to give the organization a tour of the facilities over a lunch hour or after hours. It is important to be able to watch the vendor at work.
- Walk through an entire transaction cycle, observing the controls and procedures in place. For example, at a service organization processing orders for publications, ask to trace documentation for an individual transaction through the entire system—from receipt of an order, through the pulling and shipping of the order, to the billing and collection of the receivable.
- Ask critical questions about internal controls. For example, at a service organization responsible for collecting and processing charitable contributions or member dues, ask for a detailed description of the controls in place that prevent employees from diverting funds intended for the nonprofit organization.
- Observe the neatness of the facility. Does it meet the standards that would be imposed if the function were being done internally?
- Meet with employees that would be in direct contact with customers of the nonprofit organization (i.e., its members, donors, the general pub-

lic, etc.). It is particularly important to meet anyone that would be handling customer complaints. Talk to these individuals to see if they have an acceptable attitude and demeanor for the organization.

It may also be important to take plenty of notes during these site visits, particularly when several vendors are being compared. Use of a checklist or scoring system may also facilitate the comparison of several vendors competing for the same job. In addition, if the function being considered for outsourcing is financially significant or risky to the nonprofit, it would be prudent to have the organization's external auditor present during the visit.

Site visits are also useful as a means of monitoring the service organization during the term of the contract, in addition to their value during the selection process.

Reference Checks

All potential oursourcing vendors should provide a list of references in their proposals. Obtaining names and telephone numbers of contacts at organizations of similar size and operations can be a helpful step in evaluating potential vendors. When following up on references, it is important to phrase questions properly in order to obtain truly valuable information. Asking the reference to merely rate the performance of the vendor rarely results in any valuable feedback. It will usually produce a generic, useless response. Asking more specific questions can provide much more useful results. An example might be to ask the reference to describe how the vendor handled a specific problem (i.e., for a data processing service organization, ask how the vendor handled computer breakdowns).

Third-Party Reviews

A third-party review is an impartial analysis of a service organization's policies and procedures for handling customer transactions. Third-party reviews are usually performed by accounting or consulting firms. They are most common with businesses that provide data processing services and those that handle cash collections (in the form of contributions, sales, etc.) for other organizations. The resulting report usually includes an overall assessment of the adequacy of the vendor's work, as well as a discussion of any deficiencies found, along with recommendations for improvements.

When evaluating potential service organizations, a copy of the most recent third-party review should be requested. Sometimes a service organization may say that a third-party review hasn't been done, but that the service organization itself has had an independent audit performed. Organizations should be aware that an audit of the service's financial statements is *not adequate*. A financial statement audit in accordance with the AICPA's generally accepted auditing standards covers the financial statements of the service organization, not its operations. Just as the audit of an automobile manufacturer does not evaluate the quality of the autos being produced, a financial audit of a service organization does not address all of the risks and controls of the daily operations. Nonprofits should be particularly cautious of contracting with a vendor that does not have a record of a third-party review of its operations.

When a third-party review is available, it should be read thoroughly. Someone familiar with accounting and operational controls should be responsible for reading the review, in order to properly assess the systems. Again, an external auditor or consultant can be helpful here.

There are two types of third-party review reports:

- *Type 1 Report*—A report on internal controls placed in operation
- *Type 2 Report*—A report on controls placed in operation and tests of operating effectiveness

Type 1 reports may enable a nonprofit organization and its external auditor to gain an understanding of policies and procedures in place at the vendor. But they are not intended to provide a basis for the reliability of those policies and procedures, as these types of reviews do not entail any testing of the vendor's compliance with its stated policies and procedures.

Because Type 2 reports do indicate the effectiveness of the vendor's stated controls, based on testing of those policies and procedures, they provide nonprofit organizations and their external auditors with a much higher degree of comfort. Auditors of a nonprofit organization may even rely on Type 2 reports as a basis for reducing the amount of audit test work necessary at the organization.

Both types of reports generally include a description of controls in place at the service organization, a description of specified control objectives, an auditor's opinion on whether the description presents fairly the relevant aspects of those controls, and an auditor's opinion on whether those controls are suitably designed to provide reasonable assurance that specified control objectives will be achieved if the vendor complies with those controls. In addition, a Type 2 report would include an auditor's opinion as to whether the controls that were tested operated effectively and the specified control objectives were achieved.

Financial Analysis (Monitoring of Results)

There are two aspects of financial analysis that are important in reducing the risks involved with service organizations:

- Precontract analysis
- Analysis during the period of performance

The precontract analysis involves the comparison of costs of each potential vendor and of performing the function internally (do we really even want to outsource this function?). In determining the cost to perform the function internally, all incremental costs, including any increase in overhead, should be considered. This calculation should then be compared with the proposals received from several vendors to determine the lowest cost alternative. Then, a decision must be made as to whether the lowest cost alternative is indeed the most desirable.

Another important aspect of financial analysis pertaining to service organizations is the ongoing analysis of the reports it generates and of the final results of its performance. This analysis should usually be in the form of some analytical review techniques, including some ratio analysis. The goal here, in addition to locating any obvious mathematical errors, is to spot trends or unusual fluctuations that could indicate inadequate performance or lack of internal controls on the part of the service organization. Additionally, questions regarding performance fluctuations and trends should be brought to the vendor's attention. If nothing else, this gives the service organization an indication that its employer is concerned and is monitoring its performance.

Other possible financial oversight procedures that an organization should consider performing with respect to its service organization vendors include:

- Test compliance with the financial terms of the contract between the organization and the service organization. Often, the terms of payment are complicated, and are based on several variables. It is important to continually recalculate the proper amount of revenue that the organization should have received, based on the terms of the contract. If variances between expected and actual results arise, they should immediately be investigated.

- Calculate and track year-by-year performance statistics and ratios in order to detect trends and unusual variances. Significant variances and negative trends should be investigated.

- Attempt to corroborate reports from the service organization with other documentation, either maintained by the nonprofit organization or from some other source. For example, if a convention planner's reports show that a certain number of people attended a convention, and the revenue earned by the organization is based on this number, the organization should attempt to verify the reasonableness of this number. There are several possible ways of doing this. If any meals were served as part of the convention, the catering service or hotel used by the service organization probably keeps records of the quantity of meals served. This would give some indication of the number of people attending the convention. If the organization itself maintained any attendance reports or headcounts, they could be used to verify the service organization's report.

- Reconcile all reports received from the service organization to the general ledger of the organization on a regular and timely basis.

- Consider confirming certain important data with the service organization or with customers as of year end or other cutoff dates.
- Observe the physical counting of inventory or other assets of the organization held by the service organization at year end.

Following these guidelines will greatly reduce the risks of poor product/service quality and potential financial loss that an organization can incur when contracting important functions out to service organizations.

FRAUD AND ABUSE BY SUBRECIPIENTS

When a nonprofit organization receives grants or other financial assistance from a federal agency, it is responsible for compliance with all financial and program terms of the award. If the nonprofit organization turns around and makes subawards to other organizations out of those federal funds, its responsibility for compliance for the program as a whole does not change. The same concept of oversight often also applies to grants and contracts received from state and local government agencies, as well as private foundations or other charities.

In such situations, the nonprofit organization that initially receives the grant is referred to as a pass-through entity, meaning that the organization passes through a part or all of the financial assistance to one or more subrecipients. Pass-through entities are required to monitor all subrecipients. This requirement is established by federal regulations and through the following documents:

- Office of Management and Budget (OMB) Circular A-110, *Uniform Administrative Requirements for Grants and Agreements with Institutions of Higher Education, Hospitals, and Other Nonprofit Organizations*
- OMB's grants management common rule, *Uniform Administrative Requirements for Grants and Cooperative Agreements to State and Local Governments*
- OMB Circular A-133, *Audits of States, Local Government, and Nonprofit Organizations*
- OMB Circular A-133, *Compliance Supplement* (updated annually)

Each of these documents refers to a pass-through entity's requirement to monitor compliance with laws and regulations, including financial and program performance, of subrecipients to whom the organization has provided funds. The requirement to monitor stems from the fact that a pass-through entity is ultimately responsible for all aspects of performance of a federal grant. This responsibility extends to actions taken by subrecipients. The mere fact that a pass-through entity has passed funds through to another entity does not mean that responsibility for compliance and performance is delegated as well.

Indeed, acts of fraud and abuse at the subrecipient level can be cause for any of a number of actions against the pass-through entity, including:

- Cost disallowance (resulting in the requirement that the organization return funds to the federal government)
- Withholding of funds pending resolution of the matter (in which the organization is required to bankroll the program itself while the government investigates the matter)
- Suspension or debarment (being put on a list of entities that are prohibited from receiving future federal funds for a period of time)
- Cancellation of grants and agreements (perhaps not involving any return of funds already received, but with immediate cessation of funding)
- Nonrenewal of grants when the current funding period expires (perhaps the least punitive, as the organization is at least permitted to finish out any grants and contracts that have already been signed, but with the understanding that the awards will not be renewed)

Subrecipient Monitoring

Monitoring of subrecipients will become even more important over the next few years. The Office of Management and Budget plans to increase the threshold for undergoing an audit of federal awards in accordance with the provisions of OMB Circular A-133 from $300,000 in federal expenditures to $500,000. This change is likely to take effect in 2004. The impact of the change will be that approximately 6,000 organizations that receive some form of federal funding that currently undergo one of these specialized compliance audits will no longer be subjected to such an audit beginning in 2004.

Many of these 6,000 audits are audits of subrecipients, not the organizations that receive funding directly from federal agencies. That's 6,000 more possibilities for noncompliance with provisions of awards. And 6,000 more possibilities for fraud and abuse involving federal money.

In response, the federal government will expect greater monitoring of subrecipients by pass-through entities. Nonprofit organizations should be planning a stepped-up level of monitoring in anticipation of the increased audit threshold.

Accordingly, nonprofit organizations that make subawards out of federal awards (and likely out of nonfederal grants as well) should establish a formal subrecipient monitoring system. Key components of this subrecipient monitoring system should include:

- Risk assessments
- Preaward policies and procedures

- Notification and documentation of subrecipient responsibilities
- Desk reviews of subrecipient reports and documents
- Site visits to subrecipients
- Review of subrecipient audits
- Final (closeout) review at conclusion of the subaward

In each of these phases of monitoring, a pass-through entity should consider the financial, compliance, and performance aspects of the subaward.

Of course, the focus of this book is on fraud and abuse, not general noncompliance with terms of grants and contracts. So the explanation of subrecipient monitoring included in this chapter will be more limited than a comprehensive discussion of monitoring in general. But not that much more limited. A variety of acts at the subrecipient level can fall under the broad definitions of fraud or abuse. The most common of these are:

- Intentional charging of unallowable costs to the award
- Fraudulent reporting of levels of effort (quantities of persons served or units of service provided)
- Reporting of inaccurate performance statistics and data

Each of these acts of fraudulent reporting also may be carried out by pass-through entities themselves, a topic addressed in Chapter 9 along with other misrepresentations made directly by nonprofit organizations. But the focus in this chapter is on frauds carried out by outside parties. Accordingly, nonprofit organizations acting as pass-through entities should consider the possibilities of fraud and abuse at the subrecipient levels in each of the stages of the monitoring process:

Risk Assessments

Much like an external audit firm performs a risk assessment at the beginning of each audit, pass-through entities should perform a risk assessment prior to and during subaward periods. The purpose of the risk assessment is to determine the risk of fraud and abuse, noncompliance with laws and regulations, or inadequate performance by a subrecipient. Some of the factors that should be considered in a risk assessment include:

- The complexity of the work and compliance requirements that are involved in the subrecipient's role in the program
- The results of prior audits of the subrecipient (whether the nature of findings reported in those audits reveals weaknesses in the subrecipient's system of internal controls and ability to comply with terms of awards)
- The pass-through entity's satisfaction with prior performance (if applicable) of the subrecipient

- The materiality of the subaward in relation to the total program budget
- The apparent level of knowledge and skill of subrecipient personnel who will be responsible for performing or administering and accounting for the subaward (including their familiarity with the program requirements and applicable laws and regulations)
- The potential effects of known changes in a subrecipient's personnel or systems (accounting, information, etc.), such as the departure of an experienced program manager whose inexperienced replacement has little knowledge of the program
- The level of sophistication and capabilities of the subrecipient's accounting and information systems
- The results of any other preaward procedures (explained in the next section)

Risk assessments of subrecipients should be performed by someone with firsthand knowledge of the program and its requirements. In some organizations, this is a program manager at the pass-through entity. However, due to the financial and internal control ramifications associated with many aspects of the risk assessment, some organizations prefer that an auditor or someone from the finance office perform the risk assessment. The best choice is, of course, an individual or team that combines both programmatic and financial expertise.

Because risk assessments of subrecipients are a required element of a pass-through entity's monitoring activities, they should be documented and retained as part of the pass-through entity's grant and program files. Methods of documentation vary from memos to checklists. Whichever method is utilized to document the performance of a risk assessment, it should clearly outline each consideration that went into the assessment and the results of each aspect of the assessment.

Preaward Policies and Procedures

In addition to performing a risk assessment based on the nature of the subaward and documentation available regarding a subrecipient's prior performance, a pass-through entity should consider performing additional preaward procedures as a condition of making an award to a recipient. The purpose of performing any additional preaward review procedures is to enable the pass-through entity to make a more informed determination about a particular subrecipient's ability to administer and adequately perform under a subaward.

Preaward procedures focus on obtaining a more detailed understanding of a potential subrecipient's:

- Internal controls
- Accounting and information systems

- Capabilities
- Processes

These procedures may be carried out by requesting documentation from subrecipients in each of the preceding areas. For instance, it may suffice to obtain and review a subrecipient's:

- Accounting policies and procedures
- Code of conduct and fraud policy
- Grant administration policies and procedures
- Personnel policies and procedures
- Record retention policies
- Procurement policies and procedures
- Cost allocation plans
- Property management policies and procedures

Performing an on-site review is often necessary to gain an adequate understanding in each of the four areas. Some pass-through entities utilize outside CPA firms that perform preaward audits of potential subrecipients.

These more extensive preaward procedures are certainly not necessary in all subaward scenarios. When considering making a large subaward involving complex activities to a subrecipient with which a pass-through entity has no prior experience, however, extensive preaward procedures are highly recommended.

Notification and Documentation of Subrecipient Responsibilities

The next element of monitoring involves thorough notification and documentation of each subrecipient's responsibilities and expectations in the written contract or agreement. If a subaward involves federal money, notification should consist of:

- The fact that federal money is being passed through
- The complete identifying data associated with the federal program (the Catalog of Federal Domestic Assistance number, program title, etc.)
- Notification that the subrecipient is required to undergo a Single Audit in accordance with OMB Circular A-133 if the total federal financial assistance expended by the subrecipient (including this subaward plus any other sources of federal funding) exceeds $300,000 (or $500,000, likely beginning in 2004)

The remaining notification and documentation requirements simply involve being clear in the subaward as to the subrecipient's responsibilities with respect to:

- Financial performance (allowability of costs, billing terms, cost sharing, documentation requirements, etc.)
- Program performance (level of effort, participant eligibility, range of allowable activities, etc.)
- Reporting (frequency and nature of financial and program-related reports)
- Compliance with laws and regulations (identification of specific applicable laws and program regulations)
- Abstention from fraud, abuse, and illegal acts (i.e., require that the subrecipient notify the pass-through entity immediately upon discovery of suspected fraud, abuse, or illegal acts involving the subaward)

Each of these factors should be addressed explicitly in each subaward document. As a final check, prior to presenting a subaward to a subrecipient for signature, the draft subaward document should be reviewed carefully by someone not involved in its initial preparation.

Documenting each of these considerations does not absolve a pass-through entity of its ongoing obligation to monitor the subrecipient's compliance with the terms of the subaward (see next section).

Desk Reviews of Subrecipient Reports and Documents

Throughout the subaward period, the subrecipient is (hopefully) submitting regular and timely reports to the pass-through entity. An employee (or multiple employees) of the pass-through entity should be charged with reviewing all subrecipient reports. The person(s) charged with this responsibility should be someone that has a firm understanding of the terms and requirements of the subaward. The person should carefully review each report, paying particular attention to:

- Clerical accuracy (do the numbers add up?)
- Completeness of the reports (are any required pieces of information missing?)
- Consistency in reporting (from period to period, as well as from one type of report to another)
- Comparison of grant-to-date actual results with budgeted figures (for level of effort as well as financial data, such as costs incurred)
- Classification of costs (i.e., does it appear that the charging of costs is inconsistent with the budget, or are there any other inconsistencies or indications that unallowable costs may have been charged to the subaward?)

From the perspective of fraud deterrence, a desk reviewer should be looking for anything unusual about the reports. Often, little things like indications of numerous corrections to a report are the first signs of fraud.

Site Visits to Subrecipients

In some cases, desk reviews of subrecipient reports may be all that is necessary to properly monitor a subrecipient during the period of performance. In other cases, the only way to gain comfort with the performance of a subrecipient is by seeing it with your own eyes.

Site visits are the best way to get a feel for a subrecipient's operations. Site visits may involve any or all of the following procedures:

- Perform a walk around of the subrecipient's facilities to observe program activities (for safety standards, compliance with program requirements, etc.).
- Review program participant files for eligibility and completeness (i.e., have all required forms been completed, documents and signatures obtained?).
- Review timesheets and activity reports prepared by subrecipient staff assigned to the subaward.
- Review vendor invoices for allowability of items purchased and charged to the subaward.
- Review supporting documentation for performance and level of effort (to verify that the subrecipient served the number of people they claim to have served, or provided the number of units of service claimed).
- Test internal controls associated with compliance with laws and regulations or allowability of costs.

Review of Subrecipient Audits

If a subrecipient is required to undergo an audit in accordance with OMB Circular A-133, the pass-through entity can expect to receive a copy of the audit reports within nine months of the subrecipient's year end. Therein lies the problem with relying too heavily on subrecipient audit reports as a method of monitoring. Subrecipient audit reports may be submitted too late for them to be of any value in monitoring.

For example, if a pass-through entity has a fiscal year of January 1 through December 31, and a subrecipient has a fiscal year of July 1 through June 30, the pass-through entity may not receive an audit report from the subrecipient for as long as 15 months after year end, and this will be considered on time under current guidelines! Let's say the pass-through entity is developing its monitoring plan for 2003. The second half of 2003 falls under the subrecipient's year beginning July 1, 2003 and ending June 30, 2004. The subrecipient's audit for the year ending June 30, 2004 is not required to be completed until March 31, 2005, a full 15 months after the pass-through entity's year. Without question, this report is completely worthless as a monitoring tool for the pass-through entity.

Clearly, if there is an audit requirement that applies to a subrecipient, a pass-through entity should follow up to make sure the subrecipient is obtaining an audit. Failure to obtain the audit would constitute a violation of the subaward (if properly included in the subaward) and would be grounds for terminating the subrecipient and locating a new one.

If a subrecipient provides a copy of its audit reports to a pass-through entity, the pass-through entity should review the reports carefully for anything concerning its particular subaward. Pass-through entities must keep one additional factor in mind: Just because a subrecipient undergoes an audit does not mean that *the subaward in question* was subjected to any audit procedures. Which programs of a particular entity get audited and to what extent is partially a matter of regulation (based on the requirements described in OMB Circular A-133 for selecting major programs, which are the programs that must be audited). However, it is also partially a matter of professional judgment by the subrecipient's external auditor. It is quite possible that your particular subaward was not considered a major program to the subrecipient and, therefore, was not audited, even though the subrecipient as a whole underwent an A-133 audit.

Conversely, just because a subrecipient may not be required to undergo an A-133 audit (because of being beneath the audit threshold) does not mean that a pass-through entity cannot require an audit of the subaward. Two methods of obtaining an audit of the subaward are possible:

1. Include a provision in the subaward requiring the subrecipient to obtain a program compliance audit even if the subrecipient overall is not required to undergo an A-133 audit. (Keep in mind, however, that the cost of such an audit, because it goes beyond the federal requirements, is an unallowable cost, so having a clear understanding of who will pay for this audit is important.)
2. Arrange for a limited-scope audit of the subaward by an external CPA firm to be paid for by the pass-through entity as part of its monitoring efforts.

The second option is generally preferable. Under the first option, the cost of the audit becomes unallowable. Under the second, instead of its being an audit cost, it becomes a monitoring cost, which is allowable, if paid for by the pass-through entity as part of its monitoring activities. Another advantage of the second option is that the pass-through entity has greater control over the nature and timing of the audit procedures, as both aspects are negotiable with the external audit firm that performs the limited-scope program audit.

Final (Closeout) Review at Conclusion of the Subaward

The final step in a pass-through entity's monitoring of its subrecipients involves the closeout of the subaward at the conclusion of the subaward period.

The objective of the final closeout process is to reach resolution on any outstanding issues, such as funds owed to/from the subrecipient, completion and submission of open reports and audits, and so forth. If any instances of suspected fraud or abuse at the subrecipient level have been identified, they should be fully resolved to the satisfaction of the pass-through entity prior to closing out a subaward.

The final closeout process may also be a collaborative process between a pass-through entity and its subrecipient. The two parties should work together to assure that the objectives and requirements of the program have been met. This should not be an adversarial relationship, but a cooperative one. In fact, a combative attitude on the part of a subrecipient should be yet another red flag that perhaps some as yet undiscovered fraud or abuse is lurking.

FINANCIAL ASSISTANCE FRAUD

Fraud in the application process can occur with respect to any type of financial assistance, such as applications or requests for:

- Grants and scholarships
- Student financial aid
- Loans
- Housing assistance
- Medical assistance
- Disaster and emergency aid

While we don't like to think that dishonest people would attempt to steal from funds reserved for people with real financial needs, the fact of the matter is that fraud happens in financial assistance programs with surprising frequency (see Fraud in the Headlines 7.1 for an example).

Controls useful in preventing or detecting financial assistance schemes include:

- Require a completed application that includes all necessary personal information (an incomplete application is a common characteristic of financial assistance schemes).
- Require documentation supporting an applicant's eligibility for assistance, based on the applicable criteria, such as:
  - Birth certificate for age criteria
  - Documentation of public assistance for income criteria
  - Certification from medical professionals for health-related criteria
- Verify the applicant's identity, either by using an outside service, such as those described in the Chapter 11 discussion of employment practices,

FRAUD IN THE HEADLINES 7.1

FRAUDULENTLY RECEIVED DISASTER AID DETECTED FOLLOWING TERRORIST ATTACKS

In its September 2002 report to Sen. Charles E. Grassley, ranking Republican member of the Senate finance committee, the General Accounting Office (GAO) reported that "relatively few" cases of fraud had been identified in connection with the disaster aid programs established to help survivors of the September 11, 2001 terrorist attacks in the United States. The GAO reported that the New York County District Attorney's Office had arrested at least 20 people for fraud as of August 2002, and that those schemes resulted in the fraudulent receipt of approximately $1 million in aid from several charities. The office also reported that it was still investigating about 50 additional cases of potentially fraudulent receipt of aid. New York State reported that it was investigating 20 cases of fraud involving individuals.

One million dollars sounds like a lot of fraud. But to put it in perspective, as of July 31, 2002, the 34 largest charities involved in September 11 assistance programs had collected about $2.4 billion in contributions for their programs. Nonetheless, the report indicates that even in a situation as serious as the terrorist attacks, dishonest people will continue to attempt to take advantage of nonprofits, which must balance charity with reasonable steps to protect organizational interests and contributed resources.

Source: General Accounting Office, *September 11: Interim Report on the Response of Charities,* September 2002.

or requiring original documentation of positive identification (see Best Practices 7.2).

- Independently review and approve all applications subsequent to initial screening.
- Follow a policy whereby financial assistance checks are made payable to businesses providing needed goods or services to the subject of the assistance, rather than paying the subject directly. (This is also helpful in assuring that the subject uses the assistance for the appropriate purpose, such as food, medical assistance, and so on, rather than for another, perhaps illicit purpose.)

BEST PRACTICES 7.2

HOW TO ID A PHONY ID

If all your organization does to verify someone's identity is examine a driver's license, you should be aware of some of the warning signals of a phony or altered license. Look for the following:

- Confirm that the size, thickness, and color of the card are appropriate for your state.
- Check to see that the state seal is accurate.
- Carefully examine the photo, including the background, for consistency with standard state photos.
- Be on the lookout for blurry or darkened images.
- Look to see whether any numbers have been scratched out, bleached, or cut out and reinserted.
- Compare the thickness of the card to a known authentic license to determine whether it has been laminated over. (A common ploy with stolen driver's licenses is to insert a new photo and laminate the card over, making it thicker than normal.)
- In states that utilize a driver's birth date as part of the driver's license number, make sure that these numbers match.
- Check for numbers that don't line up or that overlap, signs that the laminate has been peeled back and replaced.
- Compare height, weight, eye color, and any other physical characteristics listed on the license with those of the person standing before you.
- Obtain a signature and compare it with the one on the license or other ID card.

PART III

FRAUD AND ABUSE COMMITTED BY, FOR, OR THROUGH NONPROFIT ORGANIZATIONS

Part II focused on fraud and abuse schemes in which a nonprofit organization is victimized by people within the organization (Chapters 3 through 6) or outside parties (Chapter 7). In Part III, we turn our attention to fraud and abuse carried out by, for, or through a nonprofit organization against external parties.

When outside parties are harmed by actions of a nonprofit organization, its employees, or representatives, the wrongdoing generally results from one of the following:

- Fraudulent or deceptive fundraising practices
- Noncompliance with restrictions and other donor intentions
- Fraudulent financial statements issued to the public or filed with oversight agencies
- Making false statements to the federal government regarding compliance or performance associated with federally funded programs
- False or deceptive statements about an organization's program accomplishments, capabilities, or qualifications of program staff
- Specific acts of fraud and abuse carried out by employees, made possible by the position of trust they have been accorded by the organization

- Abusing one of the benefits granted to the organization as a result of its nonprofit status
- Other intentional violations of federal, state, or local laws

The motives behind each of these fradulent acts are not always the same. From an organizational perspective, there may be an obvious need for funds that compels someone to act inappropriately in a desperate attempt to help the organization succeed. But from a personal perspective (and let's keep in mind that *people* commit these acts, not organizations) there can be many motives. In some cases, there is a direct financial reward for the fundraiser, program manager, or executive that may compel the individual to engage in one of the activities described in this part.

More often, however, the acts described in this part are motivated less by opportunity and more by pressures or other incentives. Strong performance evaluations, promotions, and recognition within an organization are all factors that may motivate someone to push for greater return on their fundraising activities, or report stronger program or financial results, regardless of how appropriate or inappropriate their methods.

Occasionally, misleading fundraising activities or other inappropriate actions are unintentional. In the past, these acts were often viewed as innocent mistakes of organizations that are already overburdened with regulations and desperate to keep their cash-strapped programs operating. However, the public (and often the government) seems to have grown tired of this line of reasoning (which is looking more like an excuse every day), and so should we. It's getting more and more difficult to discern unintentional oversights from fraudulent practices. Nonprofit organizations committed to achieving their mission in an environment of compliance and ethical behavior cannot afford even the unintentional oversight. If nothing else, it makes them look bad. Worse yet, it may even make them look guilty.

The discussion of these diverse acts of wrongdoing in Part III is organized as follows:

- Chapter 8 addresses acts of fraud and abuse relating to fundraising practices of charitable organizations.
- Chapter 9 deals with fraudulent financial reporting and other false statements, including false statements to funding sources and government agencies.
- Chapter 10 concerns false or deceptive statements regarding an organization's programs and accomplishments, as well as abuses of exemptions and privileges granted to nonprofit organizations, violations of certain laws, and acts committed against outside parties by organizational employees (acts committed through the organization).

In each case, the actions described in these three chapters can result in substantial damage to an organization in the form of:

- Financial liability resulting from avoided payments, penalties, interest, and punitive damages
- Loss of public support (financial and nonfinancial) due to a tarnished reputation and loss of trust

Along with the financial ramifications of fraud, there is a nonfinancial impact resulting from loss of volunteers and board members as well as the difficulty of recruiting new employees.

One final point to consider while reading these three chapters (especially, if you are a board member or auditor) is the nature of the perpetrators of the frauds described here. Unlike the schemes explained in Part II, which are often attempted by lower staff levels, the frauds described in Part III are typically carried out at managerial and executive levels. Accordingly, there are fewer levels of oversight above these individuals. As a result, board members and auditors should pay particular attention to the risks of these frauds in their organizations.

8

Fundraising Fraud and Abuse

Over the past ten years, the number of nonprofit organizations in the news for engaging in some form of deceptive fundraising practice has seemingly skyrocketed. In some of these cases, it is clear that a nonprofit organization was up to no good. In others, poor communication, rather than intentional acts of deception, appears to have been the culprit.

The two primary categories of fundraising fraud and abuse that are considered in this chapter are:

- Fundraising practices that are deceptive with respect to:
  - What portion of the proceeds will be used in an organization's charitable programs
  - The extent of a charitable contribution deduction that a supporter is entitled to
- Failure to comply with donor-imposed restrictions pertaining to the use of a gift

Noncompliance with donor restrictions is not technically a wrongdoing associated with fundraising, because compliance with restrictions occurs after the funds have been raised. However, as accusations of wrongdoing in this area tend to revolve around the manner in which the funds were first raised, this issue is considered in this chapter.

A related type of wrongdoing that is not considered in this chapter concerns fraudulent financial statements. Frequently, fraudulent financial statements are used in a fundraising capacity as a means of making an organization appear more attractive to potential donors. However, because fraudulent financial statements can be used for any of several purposes, with fundraising being just one of those uses, the topic of fraudulent financial statements is dealt with in Chapter 9, where fraudulent statements are covered.

DECEPTIVE FUNDRAISING PRACTICES

When a nonprofit organization is accused of deceptive fundraising practices, the accusation usually revolves around one or more of the following issues:

- The portion of the proceeds that will ultimately be used in furtherance of the charity's mission
- The deductibility of a donor's payment
- The extent to which the charity has flexibility in how it utilizes the proceeds from a fundraising activity

The final issue from this list relates to whether or not there are restrictions associated with a charity's use of fundraising proceeds. This issue is considered as a topic by itself, and is addressed in the next section of this chapter.

Portion of Proceeds Used for Charitable Purposes

Misleading the public regarding the portion of the proceeds from a fundraising activity that will be used in furtherance of the charity's tax-exempt mission is one of the most commonly cited instances of wrongdoing by charitable organizations (see Fraud in the Headlines 8.1). These accusations seem to arise whether the funds are solicited via telephone, direct mail, or during special fundraising events.

With telephone solicitations, employees, volunteers, or outside contractors contact potential donors by phone in an attempt to solicit donations. If volunteers conduct the fundraising campaign, there may be little or no cost to the effort. However, if employees or outside contractors are involved, there is typically a cost to the activity. And therein lies the first problem.

Is it acceptable to make the statement, "100 percent of the proceeds will be used in charitable programs" if the proceeds will *first* be used to offset the cost of the fundraising activity itself (i.e., to pay the employees for their time or to pay the outside fundraising firm their fee)? The answer is a resounding NO.

The general public (as well as many state regulators) expects to be informed, and has a right to be informed, about what percentage of the gross proceeds will actually be spent on an organization's charitable programs. If any portion of the proceeds of a fundraising activity is to be used to offset any of the costs of the activity or used for any nonprogrammatic purpose, an organization should not state *or imply* that all proceeds will be used for charitable purposes.

FRAUD IN THE HEADLINES 8.1

CHARITIES CITED FOR SPENDING LITTLE ON THEIR MISSION

A 2001 article in *USA Today* profiled several wish-granting charities that came under fire for spending very little of their resources on their mission of fulfilling the wishes of terminally ill children. Two of the charities cited in the article were accused of spending 1 percent or less of their funds on their mission:

- Fondest Wish Foundation, a Michigan organization that in 1999 raised $1.1 million, but spent only $7,374 on fulfilling children's wishes
- Wishing Well Foundation USA, a Louisiana charity whose contract with an outside telemarketing firm allows the contractor to keep 90 percent of the contributions it raises in the name of the charity

Part of the issue involved in these reports is how an organization accounts for its activities and allocates costs to its various programs and activities, a topic that is addressed in Chapter 9. But when a charity intentionally hides the fact that it spends little on its programs, or tells donors that it spends more on programs than it really does, that is when accusations of fundraising fraud arise, as is further illustrated in Fraud in the Headlines 8.3.

Source: McCoy, Kevin, "Some Wish-Granting Charities Take But Don't Give," *USA Today,* June 19, 2001.

The same principle applies to direct mail activities and special fundraising events. In each case, there are costs of conducting the activity:

- For direct mail, there are the costs of printing, postage, etc.
- For special events, there are the costs of prizes, facilities, personnel, etc. (However, in some cases, all or some of these costs are contributed without charge to the charity by hosts and other donors.)

Charities must carefully draft and review fundraising materials, as well as scripts used by fundraisers during telephone campaigns, to eliminate any potentially misleading statements regarding the percentage of the proceeds from the campaign that will either go to the charity (if an outside fundraising firm is involved) or be used in the charity's programs. In some cases, it may be appropriate to refer to a charity's use of the net proceeds from a campaign or to go even further and describe the nature of the costs that will be offset against the gross proceeds.

Deductibility of Contributions

In general, people are quite generous. When presented with a worthwhile cause, the public often responds with financial support. That fact became more apparent than ever in the months following the September 11, 2001 terrorist attacks, when the outpouring of public support was overwhelming. One year later, charities involved in providing assistance in connection with the attacks reported receiving more than $2 billion from donors for their assistance programs.

Examining the charitable sector in a broader context reveals results that are even more staggering. Americans contribute more than $200 billion to charities each year. Charitable contributions have risen at a fairly steady pace for years.

However, despite these statistics, one fact cannot be overlooked. The likelihood of success in soliciting a gift from the general public is certainly increased when the donor is entitled to take a tax deduction for their support. Organizations and fundraisers know this, of course. A handful of unethical fundraisers and managers of charities mislead donors into thinking that their gift is deductible when it is not, or they exaggerate the portion of their payment that is deductible.

The tax rules regarding deductibility of contributions are fairly simple. Donors who itemize deductions on their income tax returns are eligible for a charitable contribution deduction to the extent that the amount of their gift exceeds the fair market value of any goods or services the donors receive from the charity in connection with their gift. The idea of permitting individuals who do not itemize deductions on their income tax returns to claim a limited deduction for charitable contributions has gained in popularity in Congress in recent years. This could become law in the near future, causing the number of people potentially misled by unscrupulous fundraisers and charities to be even greater.

When a noncash gift of property is made, the tax-deductible amount of the gift is generally equal to the fair market value of the item(s) donated. However, there are several exceptions from this treatment, and donors should always be advised by charities to consult their personal tax advisor before drawing any conclusions. Government statistics indicate that U.S. taxpayers deduct approximately $14 billion for gifts of property to charities. Commonly reported noncash gifts include donations of art, land, clothing, household goods, automobiles, and stock in for-profit businesses.

Two types of misleading statements can result in the donor claiming a greater deduction than what is permitted under the income tax rules:

- Exaggerating the fair market value of the item given by the donor to the charity
- Underestimating the fair market value of any goods or services provided by the charity to a donor in connection with the donor's gift

Fair Market Values of Donated Assets

Under income tax laws and regulations, establishing the market value of a noncash gift is the responsibility of the donor, not the charity. A charity is under no obligation to provide market value information to donors. When a charity provides a receipt for a noncash gift to a donor, the receipt should provide:

- The date of the gift
- The donor's name
- A description of the item(s) donated
- A statement that no goods or services were provided to the donor in connection with the contribution, if applicable

Of course, for its own financial reporting purposes, a charity needs to establish a market value. But receipts to donors should be limited to the information here. Donors may ask the charity its opinion about a fair market value, and there is nothing wrong with a charity stating the value it will assign the item. But donors should always be advised that they are responsible for their own valuation for tax deduction purposes. (See Fraud in the Headlines 8.2 for a discussion of how nonprofits may mislead donors regarding market values.)

If a nonprofit organization utilizes an outside contractor to solicit and receive donations of noncash assets, it is critical that the contractor comply with the standards applicable to the nonprofit. In most cases, outside contractors who solicit or collect donated assets on behalf of a charitable organization are considered to be acting as agents of the charity. If this is the case, it means that the actions of the contractor are binding on and attributable to the charity. Accordingly, if a contractor fails to provide a proper receipt, overstates the estimated deduction to which a donor is entitled, or makes other false statements to donors in the solicitation process, the charity may be responsible for any penalties associated with such noncompliance. This is exactly what happened in the Multiple Sclerosis Association of America case described in Fraud in the Headlines 8.3.

FRAUD IN THE HEADLINES 8.2

DONATED CARS FREQUENTLY OVERVALUED

Federal and state lawmakers and regulators have become particularly concerned about one specific type of charitable contribution transaction that seems to be prone to abuse. Donations of used automobiles to charitable organizations have become big business in some areas of the United States. Along with that growth has come abuse, and not all of that abuse is solely attributable to donors.

Many of these programs are operated by for-profit businesses that are unrelated to the charities they represent. These businesses act as agents for their charity clients in promoting and operating auto donation programs.

Where fraud and abuse enters the picture is in the misleading advertisements and other promotional materials asking people to consider donating their used cars. Advertisements for these programs sometimes suggest that donors may deduct the "full Blue Book value" for their donated cars, regardless of the condition of the vehicle.

The "Blue Book" that is being referred to is the *Kelley Blue Book*, which provides estimated current fair market values for many different models and makes of cars. For each model and make, numerous market values are provided. The applicable value is the one that matches the various options available for that vehicle, its mileage, and self-assessment of the vehicle's condition.

Some advertisements have been so bold as to suggest that donors can deduct the full Blue Book value, even if the vehicle needs to be towed from the donor's home!

These misleading statements can be considered a violation of income tax rules. The IRS position on use of the *Kelley Blue Book* or other published guidelines for assessing market value is that the values provided in these guides will generally be accepted if the donor's vehicle matches the descriptions provided in the guides. These descriptions involve the make, model, year, and specific options or characteristics of a vehicle, as well as the condition of the car in various respects. It is suggested that donors take several photos of their vehicle prior to donating it if they plan to use one of these published guides to value their car. Otherwise, a formal appraisal is suggested.

In 1999, the Internal Revenue Service announced that it was beginning to take a much closer look at many of these programs. The service planned to determine whether donors were being told that they could deduct more than what they were entitled to, as well as the nature of the relationship between the charities and the third-party operators. If these relationships are not structured properly from an income tax perspective, there could be tax implications for the charities, or even loss of their tax-exempt status. Between 1999 and 2002, the IRS did, in fact, begin evaluating more of these programs and continues to stress that some of them are not being run properly, resulting in misleading information to donors, among other violations.

Another reason for much of the controversy surrounding donated vehicle programs involves the sharing of the proceeds from the sales of donated vehicles. In many cases, the for-profit operators of the programs retain the vast majority of the proceeds, leaving very little for the charity that supposedly was the reason for the donation in the first place.

Sources: Greene, Stephen G. and Grant Williams, "Donated Cars: A License for Abuse?" *The Chronicle of Philanthropy*, March 26, 1998, and Seeley, Ray, Michael Seto, Debra Kawecki, and David Jones, "T. Fund-Raising Issues: Part I—Car Donation Programs," *Exempt Organizations Continuing Professional Education Technical Instruction Program for FY 2000*, Internal Revenue Service, 1999.

See Best Practices 8.1 for details on how the IRS determines whether an agency relationship exists between a nonprofit organization and an outside contractor.

Valuing Items Provided to Donors

If goods or services are provided by a charity to a donor in connection with the donor's contribution, tax regulations *require* that the organization provide the donor with a good faith estimate of the fair market value of the goods or services. There are two primary exceptions to this requirement:

- Goods with a de minimis cost or value (there are three separate and specific applications of this general rule, each including dollar thresholds that are adjusted annually for inflation by the IRS)
- Intangible religious benefits provided by churches and other religious groups

Ignoring (i.e., not stating that they have been provided with the receipt provided to donors) or underestimating the value of benefits that do not meet one of the preceding exceptions constitutes a violation of the Internal Revenue Code and is punishable with penalties.

For example, if a charity holds a fundraising dinner, charging $100 to each person who attends, the charity must provide attendees with a good-faith estimate of the fair market value (not the cost to the charity) of the meal that has been provided. If the meal has a fair market value of $35, each donor who pays the $100 charge is eligible to deduct $65 as a charitable contribution deduction. If the charity fails to provide this information to each attendee, it is subject to penalties under the Internal Revenue Code.

FRAUD IN THE HEADLINES 8.3

TELEMARKETER'S ACTIONS RESULT IN PENALTY TO CHARITY

In 2001, the Multiple Sclerosis Association of America (MSAA) reached a settlement with the State of New Jersey in connection with a lawsuit brought by the state over a variety of wrongdoings by MSAA and its senior management. MSAA is not related to the better-known National Multiple Sclerosis Society.

One of the actions resulting in liability for MSAA was the filing of fraudulent statements with the state. That issue is explained more fully in Chapter 9.

Most applicable to the fundraising topics described in this chapter is that part of the penalties assessed against the MSAA resulting from actions of the outside telemarketers working under a contract with the association. These telemarketers repeatedly informed potential donors that the entire amount of each donor's check would go to the MSAA. However, the telemarketing firm's contract with the MSAA called for the firm to receive at least 70 percent of the gross proceeds of their fundraising efforts.

The settlement reached in connection with this charge as well as the additional charges described in Chapter 9 was for $225,000. Of that total, $150,000 was paid by the MSAA and $75,000 by the group's now former president and vice president.

The importance of this part of the MSAA case is in the fact that fraudulent or abusive actions of outside parties acting as an agent of a nonprofit organization can be attributed to the organization itself. It is as though the actions were carried out directly by the nonprofit group.

Source: DeMarrais, Kevin G., "Charity Settles Suit with N.J.," *The Record*, April 3, 2001.

Other examples of fundraising events and activities to which this rule may apply include:

- Benefit concerts and performances (even if the performer receives no compensation), in which donors receive the benefit of a performance for which they would ordinarily have to pay an admission fee
- Charity golf outings, in which donors receive golfing privileges for an event
- Raffles, in which donors receive a benefit in the form of a chance to win a valuable prize

One of the exceptions to these disclosure rules involves low cost or value items provided to donors in connection with their gift. In these cases, a non-profit organization is under no obligation to value the items and inform donors of this value. Examples of fundraising activities that often fall within one of these de minimis exceptions include walkathons, races, and other events in which donors receive items such as t-shirts, caps, sodas, and other low-cost items. This exception also applies to certain types of direct mail fundraising solicitations, such as those in which a charity provides postcards, return address labels, or some other low-cost item to potential donors as part of the solicitation of a contribution.

Controls that are helpful in protecting an organization against charges of deceptive fundraising practices include the following:

- Draft and review all fundraising solicitations and drafts of scripts to be read by telephone solicitors, to ensure there are no misleading statements regarding use of proceeds from the solicitation.
- For special fundraising events, determine whether the market value of goods or services provided to donors (whether paid for by the charity or not) exceeds the de minimis threshold currently in effect as established by the IRS.
- If items being provided to donors have market values in excess of IRS-established de minimis thresholds, do not include statements anywhere that indicate donors are entitled to a deduction equal to the amount of their payment.
- If items being provided to donors have market values in excess of IRS-established de minimis thresholds and the amount paid by donors is in excess of $75, provide a good-faith estimate of the items' fair market value to all donors.
- If the organization receives gifts of property and other noncash assets, review all solicitations and receipts to ensure there are no misleading statements regarding the amount of a deduction to which donors are entitled.
- If the charity utilizes an outside firm to solicit cash contributions, include in the contract each of the applicable controls listed in this section and monitor compliance with the contract during the period of performance.
- If the charity utilizes an outside firm to collect noncash contributions of property on its behalf, execute a contract that clearly identifies the firm as an agent of the charity and establishes all of the necessary oversight and accountability provisions referred to in Best Practices 8.1.
- Periodically subject all fundraising materials, forms, and receipts used in connection with charitable contributions to an independent review for compliance with accounting and tax rules, as well as for ethical fundraising practices.

BEST PRACTICES 8.1

WHEN ARE CONTRACTORS AGENTS OF AN ORGANIZATION?

The agency relationship is a complex legal issue that goes far beyond the scope of this book. Legal texts can go on for pages in explaining the characteristics and implications of one party acting as an agent for another.

However, it is critical for nonprofit organizations to understand a few of the basics regarding agents. As should be apparent from this chapter, actions of outside parties acting as agents for a nonprofit organization can be attributed to the organization, resulting in legal liability for the nonprofit. The agency issue is important not only for car donation programs and telemarketing fundraising efforts, but for any arrangement in which an outside party is responsible for raising funds or accepting donated assets on behalf of a charity.

There are many sources of guidance on the agency issue written from legal, tax, and other perspectives. One of the better recent explanations can be found in an Internal Revenue Service publication intended for use by IRS examiners of nonprofit organizations. Agency is defined in this publication as "the fiduciary relation which results from the manifestation of consent by one person (the principal) to another (the agent) that the agent shall act on the principal's behalf and subject to the principal's control, and consent by the agent so to act."

The publication identifies the following as characteristics of an agent:

- The agent is designated as such in a written agreement.
- The agent conducts business in the name of the principal or otherwise makes his agency known to third parties.
- The agent's acts are legally binding on the principal.
- The agent transfers funds received to the principal, or uses them as directed by the principal, rather than using them for his own purposes.
- The income received by the agent is attributable to services and assets of the principal.
- The agent's sole business activity is acting as an agent.
- The agent does not take title to property in his own name (except as nominee).

- All or part of the agent's activity is subject to the principal's right to approve or control.
- The principal actually exercises control or supervision over part or all of the agent's activity.
- The principal rather than the agent bears the risk of loss in the transaction.
- The principal indemnifies and insures the agent in his agency activities.
- The agent is required to financially account to the principal.
- The agent uses the principal's nonprofit mailing rates or sales tax exemptions.
- The agent is otherwise subject to the principal's control under the facts and circumstances (whether the principal exercises control over the agent in reality, not just in the contract, considering all relevant facts).
- Where the agent performs services for others for a fee, the person receiving the services contracts with the principal and looks to the principal rather than the agent for performance, and the agent's services are activities ordinarily engaged in by the principal and fulfill its purposes.
- In charity day situations, the principal conducts the advertising, bears the risk of loss, leases the agent's facilities, provides the liability insurance, provides the employees and management, and handles the proceeds, and the agent is not required to conduct the event as a condition to obtaining its license to conduct noncharity business.

Not all of these factors are required in order for an agency relationship to exist. Rather, each factor should be considered as part of an overall determination of whether such a relationship exists. Certainly, a written agreement or some other formal acknowledgment by the principal is one of the most important factors.

Of course, it is always important to also consider whether applicable state laws and cases could apply a broader or narrower definition of agency to the specific circumstances of an organization.

Source: Thomas, Ward L., and Leonard J. Henzke, Jr., "C. Agency: A Critical Factor in Exempt Organizations and UBIT Issues," *Exempt Organizations Continuing Professional Education Technical Instruction Program for FY 2002*, Internal Revenue Service, 2001.

NONCOMPLIANCE WITH RESTRICTIONS

Compliance with donor-imposed restrictions is a topic that has received a great deal of publicity in recent years. The increased publicity is not due simply to charities getting worse at complying with the wishes of their donors. A significant portion of the increase in accusations of noncompliance with donor restrictions is the direct result of a change in the atmosphere of giving and the type of donor who supports charities in the twenty-first century. Today's donors are much more apt to identify a particular program, not just an organization, that they wish to support. Sometimes, donors restrict their gifts to particular components within a single program.

Either way, the donors of the modern era take action against charities that, in their opinions, fail to comply with donor restrictions on the use of the gift. This propensity to sue charities over the use of gifts is illustrated in Fraud in the Headlines 8.4.

The accounting literature defines a restricted contribution as one that possesses the following attributes:

- It is accompanied by a clearly communicated stipulation from the provider of the gift.
- The stipulation specifies one or both of the following permissible uses of the contributed resource(s):
  - The time period in which the resource(s) may be used by the organization
  - The purpose for which the recipient organization may utilize the resource(s)
- In the case of a purpose stipulation, the intended use of the resource(s) is a purpose that is more restrictive than the overall exempt purpose of the organization.

Legal definitions may differ somewhat from state to state. The accounting definition here is a good starting point in understanding the concept and implications associated with restricted funds. Fundraising solicitations that describe a specific purpose for which the proceeds will be used are considered to be the equivalent of a donor imposing a purpose restriction. For example, if a donor responds to a charity's appeal for funds to construct a new headquarters facility, it is not necessary for the donor to include any form of restrictive language or accompanying correspondence along with the contribution in order for the gift to be considered restricted.

The concept of what is meant by the words *clearly communicated* has caused serious problems for some organizations. In order to be clearly communicated, a restriction does not need to be put in writing by a donor. Verbal stipulations may be considered as binding as if they were in writing. In fact, donors may interpret a variety of facts and circumstances surrounding a charity's fundraising efforts to constitute a restriction.

FRAUD IN THE HEADLINES 8.4

DONOR SUITS OVER USE OF GIFTS ON THE RISE

Something that used to be a rare occurrence is happening with much greater frequency. Donors suing charities for failing to use their gifts in the manner intended by the donors is now an almost everyday item in the news. Three recent cases illustrate this trend:

- One donor sued the University of Southern California over his $1.6 million endowment of a chair in geriatric biology. He asserted that the university used portions of his gift for other purposes, such as payments to scientists ineligible for funds under the donor-imposed terms regarding the gift.
- Family members of a donor waged a legal battle against the Chicago Community Trust regarding control over the $300 million Searle Fund, based on assertions that the Trust has stopped seeking advice from family members on making grants from the fund, in violation of the terms of the fund, as well as the charging of unreasonable administrative fees.
- Family members of a couple who provided $35 million in stock to Princeton University in 1961 (which is now a $560 million endowment) took legal action to regain control over the endowment based on claims that the university has strayed from the couple's initial wishes to restrict the gift to training Princeton graduate students for careers in government service.

Source: Greene, Stephen G., "Seeking Control in Court: Disgruntled Donors Sue Over Use of Their Gifts," *The Chronicle of Philanthropy,* November 28, 2002.

The term "donor-imposed" is a bit misleading as well. A restriction can result from any of the following:

- A written statement provided by a donor in connection with a particular gift
- A verbal discussion with a donor in connection with a gift
- A donor making a contribution in response to a restrictive fundraising solicitation received from a charity

Any of the preceding characteristics generally meet the accounting definition of donor-imposed. The final category is the most common donor-imposed restriction, though some would argue that it is imposed by the charity itself. A clearer way of thinking of a restriction is that it is a stipulation that arises at or prior to the making of a contribution. The source of a restriction (or the initiating party of a restriction) can be either the donor or the charity.

Two of the most common claims made by donors asserting that a charity has not complied with restrictions involve:

- The broadness or narrowness of the description of the purpose of the funds (i.e., the scope of the program or function for which a donor has earmarked his gift)
- The nature of the costs that can be attributed to the purpose (i.e., which costs a donor wishes to fund with his gift)

A recent example of the first issue is the controversy that was generated when the American Red Cross unveiled its initial plans for how it would utilize the funds raised in connection with the September 11, 2001 terrorist attacks on New York City and the Pentagon. At the time the American Red Cross published its plan, the organization had generated more than $500 million in charitable contributions, much of it through its Web site. The initial plan stated that the group would utilize some of the proceeds for direct assistance to victims and families of victims of the attacks. Other portions of the proceeds would be used for a variety of programs aimed at preparedness for future disasters, such as building a supply of blood reserves and other programs.

This proposed plan triggered anger on the part of the general public, the media, members of Congress, and law enforcement authorities. While no one doubted the legitimacy of the programs included in the Red Cross's proposed plan, many people felt that 100 percent of the proceeds of this particular fundraising effort should be earmarked for direct assistance to those affected by the attacks. Allocating *any* portion of the proceeds to any other program, no matter how worthy the program, would not be acceptable.

The plans proposed by the American Red Cross clearly fell within the organization's mission. Further, statements on the organization's Web site made reference to the fact that it is possible for funds raised in connection with any particular disaster to be used for purposes associated with another disaster. Despite these facts, the overwhelming response directed at the organization was that it was expected to use these funds solely for purposes associated with this particular disaster. In response, the American Red Cross changed its plans and stated it would use all proceeds in connection with the September 11 attacks.

Was the American Red Cross guilty of fraud, abuse, or intentionally misleading fundraising practices in connection with its September 11 efforts? There certainly did not appear to be any indication of such wrongdoing. Nonetheless, the controversy demonstrates the importance of complying with the wishes of the contributing public, even when the charity has only the most noble of intentions.

One of the lessons that can be learned from the American Red Cross is that compliance with donor-imposed restrictions involves much more than addressing the explicit statements included in fundraising materials. The events that a fundraising activity is connected with, or the timing of a particular fundraising activity, may *imply* certain restrictions that go beyond the explicitly stated ones.

BEST PRACTICES 8.2

SOME RESTRICTIONS CAN GO TOO FAR

It's okay for donors to restrict their gift for particular purposes or time periods. Purpose restrictions can be quite broad or very narrow. They cannot, however, be so narrow that a donor determines which particular persons or businesses will benefit from their gift to a charity.

Examples of excessive donor control include:

- A gift to a university can be restricted to a particular research program, but should not include a condition that the donor retains control over which specific scientists will be hired to carry out the research, or that the funds be earmarked for a particular curriculum in which the donor gets to select the individual professors whose salaries will be paid with the gift.

- A grant can be given to a museum to fund a particular exhibit, but should not include a stipulation that the donor will select the individual artists.

- A scholarship contribution should not give the donor permission to select individuals who will receive the scholarships.

Depending on whether the donor is an individual or a business, there may be differing reasons for wanting such an extreme level of control. Either way, it is important for donors to understand that the charity must retain final control over the specific persons to whom payments will be made or to whom other benefits may inure in connection with a restricted gift.

Violating this rule, referred to as the private benefit rule in the tax regulations, can cause problems for the donor (in the form of denial of an income tax deduction), the final recipient (in the form of having to pay income tax on a payment that they may have thought was tax-free), and the charity through which the gift was made. The charity can be penalized and could even lose its exemption from income taxes as a result of engaging in private benefit transactions of this sort.

Accordingly, charities must resist the temptation to accept gifts accompanied by restrictions that violate this principle.

Other factors that an organization should consider addressing in fundraising materials include:

- The extent to which proceeds from the fundraising activity will be used to offset the costs of the fundraising activity itself
- The degree to which proceeds from restricted fundraising efforts will be used to offset indirect costs (overhead) associated with the program identified in the fundraising materials
- Whether any portion of the proceeds may be used to reimburse the unrestricted fund of the organization for costs incurred prior to the fundraising activity, but that are associated with the program identified in the fundraising materials
- How the organization will handle excess funds raised, if any, above the stated goal of the restricted fundraising appeal

Each of these considerations involves an issue that potentially can cause significant problems for an organization if not addressed and clarified up front. These problems can range from a few minor calls from donors expressing disappointment in the organization or a feeling of being misled, to accusations of fraud and the initiation of lawsuits aimed at either forcing the organization to comply with its alleged representations to the donors or to return all donated funds.

Offsetting Proceeds Against the Costs of Raising the Funds

Clearly the phrase "proceeds will be used for," followed by the identification of a particular program of an organization, can mean many different things to many different people. To some, it means that 100 percent of the amount collected by the organization will be used directly for the purpose stipulated in the fundraising solicitation. For example, if a solicitation states that an organization needs funds for the construction of a new building, every penny collected should be used for costs directly associated with construction in the minds of many donors.

Using any portion of the proceeds from a fundraising activity to reimburse an organization for the costs incurred in soliciting the contributions is considered inappropriate to some donors. While accountants and managers may presume that the cost of raising the restricted funds is a legitimate cost that can be offset against the proceeds, the contributing public may not see it this way.

Accordingly, unless a nonprofit organization plans to utilize other unrestricted resources (or is one of the few lucky charities that has received grant funds earmarked for fundraising activities), the organization should consider including a statement in its solicitations clarifying that some of the proceeds will be used to offset the costs of raising the funds. Those costs may include postage, printing, staff salaries, outside consultant fees, and many other costs.

If an organization plans to offset proceeds with fundraising costs, it must identify all applicable costs and develop appropriate methods of allocating these costs to the fundraising effort.

Charging Indirect Costs to Programs Funded with Restricted Contributions

Another common problem that arises when restricted fundraising solicitations are not carefully thought out involves the distinction between direct and indirect costs. For example, if an organization's fundraising materials state that it is soliciting support for its scholarship program, what costs can be funded with the proceeds of this solicitation?

Some donors may argue that the only costs that may legitimately be charged against proceeds from such a solicitation are the actual scholarship payments made to students. But what about other necessary and reasonable costs associated with the scholarship programs? Some of these are:

- Salaries of employees involved in collecting and evaluating scholarship applications
- Employee benefit costs of these same employees (such as payroll taxes, contributions to retirement plans, etc.)
- Costs associated with printing forms used for scholarship applications and brochures used to promote the scholarship program
- Overhead costs attributable to the scholarship program (these costs may include allocations of facilities costs, such as rent and utilities, as well as office supplies, telephone, and other charges)

After considering the preceding list (which just scratches the surface of potentially allocable costs), the phrase "funds will be used to make scholarships" becomes less clear. To clarify this, organizations should identify and state the degree to which indirect costs such as these may be allocated to the program (and, therefore, funded with the donors' restricted contributions).

Reimbursement of Presolicitation Costs

Sometimes before a major restricted fundraising campaign begins, an organization has already begun incurring costs. For example, an organization may have already broken ground and incurred certain preliminary construction costs in connection with a new facility before solicitations designed to raise funds for the new building are even mailed.

If these fundraising materials state that proceeds will be used to construct the new facility and certain costs associated with the facility have already been incurred, is it acceptable for the organization to pay for these costs using proceeds from the solicitations? Would the answer change if the organization has not only incurred the costs, but has already paid for the costs using its own unrestricted funds?

Any time an organization is dealing with a broad cross-section of the general public, it's better to be safe than sorry. Accordingly, if it is not possible to defer incurring such charges until after the restricted fundraising effort has begun, the organization should consider addressing the necessary reimbursement within the solicitation materials, clarifying that such use of proceeds is intended.

Use of Proceeds Received in Excess of Stated Goals

Another issue that can arise, especially with large fundraising campaigns, involves stating goals for proceeds of a campaign in the fundraising materials. For instance, an organization may state that it needs $8 million to construct its new building. What if the solicitations result in $8.2 million in proceeds?

To some, this may sound like a pleasant problem to have, but it can be a serious issue if not properly handled during the design of fundraising materials. There are only a handful of potential outcomes when an organization raises more than the target stated in the solicitation:

- Expand the program to the extent that the excess proceeds are used for the same purpose.
- Request permission from donors to retain the excess funds for other purposes.
- Return the excess funds to donors.

Part of the solution lies in the distinction between a need and a goal. Certain goals can be exceeded with no potentially adverse consequences. For instance, if an organization's goal for a fundraising campaign is to provide food, clothing, and shelter to low-income families, excess funds can easily be put to the same use in most instances. However, if a fixed amount is stated, and there is little potential for variance in the amount, the issue of excess funds must be addressed.

One possible solution is to state in the fundraising solicitation an alternative use that is similar to the one on which the solicitation is based. For example, if the organization needs $8 million to construct a new building, the solicitation could state that any funds raised in excess of the $8 million target will be used exclusively for future repairs and replacements associated with the facility. Providing an alternative use that is similar to the primary purpose can provide clarity while minimizing the potential for any negative reactions from stipulating an alternate use.

Controls that are helpful in protecting an organization against accusations of noncompliance with donor restrictions include the following practices:

- As part of the annual planning and budgeting process, determine whether the organization's fundraising practices for the next year will include restricted or unrestricted fundraising efforts.

- Prepare budgets associated with the planned use of proceeds from each restricted fundraising solicitation.
- Identify in each fundraising solicitation (or script, if verbal appeals are made via telephone) the specific program or activity for which proceeds will be used. In so doing, use terminology that coincides with the language used in the organization's financial statements, annual reports, and IRS information returns, so that if donors wish to see how this program is represented, they may do so.
- Carefully review and edit all fundraising materials prior to distribution in order to ensure that they are not misleading to laypeople and are in compliance with the accounting rules described in this chapter.
- Consider including a budget or other information in restricted fundraising solicitations so that donors understand the nature of the costs, not just the name of the program, that they are being asked to fund (or at least disclose whether proceeds will be used to offset the costs of raising the funds and whether indirect costs will be allocated to the restricted program).
- If a goal is stated for total funds needed for a program, address in the fundraising materials what the organization will do with any funds received in excess of the stated goal.
- Establish separate general ledger accounts in the accounting system to track all proceeds from each fundraising event or activity, as well as each component of cost offset against restricted funds.
- In order for any cost to be charged against the accounts established in the preceding step, require approval by someone familiar with the nature of costs allowable under the restriction.
- Monitor actual versus budgeted amounts.
- Consider reporting back to all donors of restricted funds the results of the fundraising appeal and program accomplishments associated with the program they funded.
- If an outside firm engages in fundraising activities on behalf of the organization, address each of the preceding issues, if applicable, in the contract between the organization and the firm and monitor performance of the firm.

ETHICS IN FUNDRAISING

Much of this chapter can be summed up with the phrase "ethics in fundraising." Every nonprofit organization that solicits contributions from the public should keep in mind that it is being given the ultimate degree of trust. People are providing financial support and expecting nothing in return other than your organization's word that you will serve the public.

BEST PRACTICES 8.3

THE DONOR BILL OF RIGHTS

The Donor Bill of Rights was jointly created by the American Association of Fund Raising Counsel, the Association for Healthcare Philanthropy, the Association of Fundraising Professionals, and the Council for Advancement and Support of Education.

Philanthropy is based on voluntary action for the common good. It is a tradition of giving and sharing that is primary to the quality of life. To ensure that philanthropy merits the respect and trust of the general public, and that donors and prospective donors can have full confidence in the nonprofit organizations and causes they are asked to support, we declare that all donors have these rights:

I. To be informed of the organization's mission, of the way the organization intends to use donated resources, and of its capacity to use donations effectively for their intended purposes

II. To be informed of the identity of those serving on the organization's governing board, and to expect the board to exercise prudent judgment in its stewardship responsibilities

III. To have access to the organization's most recent financial statements

IV. To be assured their gifts will be used for the purpose for which they were given

V. To receive appropriate acknowledgment and recognition

VI. To be assured that information about their donation is handled with respect and with confidentiality to the extent provided by law

VII. To expect that all relationships with individuals representing organizations of interest to the donor will be professional in nature

VIII. To be informed whether those seeking donations are volunteers, employees of the organization, or hired solicitors

IX. To have the opportunity for their names to be deleted from mailing lists that an organization may intend to share

X. To feel free to ask questions when making a donation and to receive prompt, truthful, and forthright answers

Source: Copyright 2003. Association of Fundraising Professionals (AFP) and others. All rights reserved. Reprinted with permission.

In living up to the trust that has been placed in charities by the supporting public, many organizations have adopted the Donor Bill of Rights explained in Best Practices 8.3. Much of what is addressed in this document is common sense. But it serves as a healthy reminder to periodically self-assess the degree to which your organization is fulfilling these expectations. Put yourself in the shoes of a donor and you'd probably say, "I'd want to be treated this way, too."

9

Fraudulent Reporting

This chapter is devoted to fraud in the form of preparing and issuing intentionally misleading financial statements and other financial reports, including special reports issued to funding sources. Fraudulent reporting as it is defined in this chapter is intentionally false assertions relating to:

- Financial statements issued by the organization
- Compliance with specific requirements of funding sources
- Charging of unallowable costs to grants
- Other false statements to government agencies

In each case, readers of statements, grantors, or government agencies are misled about some aspect of the organization's activities. Accusations of fraud and abuse relating to these acts generally involve assertions of wrongdoing *by* or *for* (on behalf of) a nonprofit organization. This chapter will explain how and why each of these fraudulent statements occurs, as well as the steps that can be taken to minimize the risk that the organization will be accused of making or filing false statements.

There is one important characteristic that distinguishes the acts of wrongdoing in this chapter from those described in Part II. Frauds carried out against a nonprofit organization are usually done for the direct financial or other personal gain by the perpetrator. The schemes described in this chapter may not have this objective—at least not directly. On the surface it may appear that the act was committed exclusively to benefit the organization. However, personal gain is often still desired. It just may not be as obvious or direct. Some of the possible personal objectives of the schemes described in this chapter include:

- A promotion or positive performance evaluation based on the reporting of good results by an organization or by one of its departments or programs
- A bonus or other incentive for achieving certain performance goals or financial results
- To avoid legal, audit, or public relations problems associated with failures to comply with certain requirements or to achieve certain goals
- To keep one's job by reporting strong performance, both programmatically and financially, to justify continuing a grant or program

However, the objectives behind some schemes may not be personal at all. Some of these schemes are carried out simply to make an organization look good in the eyes of the public. Some representatives of nonprofit organizations want an organization to succeed so desperately that they will engage in unethical behavior to ensure that success.

Regardless of the motive, the schemes described in this chapter are most typically carried out by the top-level executives or senior management of an organization. This is an important distinction for board members and auditors to understand as many of the schemes explained in Chapters 3 through 7 may be attempted by lower-level employees. Since the schemes described in this chapter are perpetrated at higher levels in an organization, there are fewer levels of oversight. Thus, it is appropriate for board members to devote greater attention to these schemes.

In the area of fraudulent financial statements of nonprofit organizations, two broad categories of activities will be addressed:

- Fraudulent reporting of financial statement amounts
- Failures to disclose related party transactions

FRAUDULENT FINANCIAL REPORTING

In recent years, we've been bombarded with news of large corporations issuing financial statements that materially distort the financial position and earnings of the companies. Enron . . . WorldCom . . . the list goes on and on.

Though not on the front pages of newspapers as frequently, the nonprofit sector has had its share of bad press regarding fraudulent financial reporting. Unlike the financial reporting frauds involving for-profit businesses, which center around misrepresenting the financial health or earnings of a company, those involving nonprofit organizations usually deal with other factors.

The single most important difference between nonprofit organizations and for-profit businesses is in their ultimate objectives. While a for-profit business has as its most primary goal the pursuit of profits, a nonprofit organization is charged with the more intangible pursuit of a mission. Profitability and financial health are much easier to communicate and measure in financial terms than the degree to which a nonprofit organization has achieved its mission. In fact, it is often argued that many nonprofit missions cannot be measured in financial terms at all.

But in the areas of accounting and financial reporting, measurements and comparisons are inevitable. As a result, certain standards or expectations of financial performance have been developed for nonprofit organizations. These standards primarily involve percentages of operating expenses (or revenues) devoted to program expenditures.

Nonprofit organizations are expected to prepare financial statements that classify the organization's expenses by function. Two broad categories of functions are presented by most nonprofit organizations: program services and supporting activities.

BEST PRACTICES 9.1

EXPENSE REPORTING REQUIREMENTS VARY BY TYPE OF NONPROFIT

All nonprofit organizations that follow generally accepted accounting principles are required to present three basic financial statements:

- Statement of financial position
- Statement of activities
- Statement of cash flows

It is in the statement of activities that an organization's contributions and revenue, as well as its expenses, are presented.

Nonprofit organizations that qualify as voluntary health and welfare organizations are also required to present a fourth statement—the statement of functional expenses. A voluntary health and welfare organization (VHWO) is a nonprofit organization that performs voluntary services for society and is supported by the public. They generally work on either broad societal health and welfare problems or those of specific individuals. They derive their revenue primarily from voluntary public contributions to be used for general or specific purposes associated with health, welfare, or community services. There isn't an established threshold or percentage test that is applied to determine whether a nonprofit is a VHWO. However, based on this general definition, most voluntary health and welfare organizations report income that is comprised mostly of charitable contributions from the general public. Contributions of this type include not only direct gifts from individuals, but also donations received from private foundations, corporations, and board members, as well as allocations or sharing of contributions from fundraising organizations or affiliates of an organization. Government grants generally are not included within this definition. Accordingly, organizations that rely more heavily on government grants, investment income (interest, dividends, etc.), or on program service revenue (i.e., income received directly from program participants in exchange for goods or services provided by a nonprofit organization, such as admission fees, tuition, membership dues, and other forms of income) are not considered voluntary health and welfare organizations.

A nonprofit organization's classification will determine certain characteristics of its statement of activities. A VHWO will present its statement of activities in a manner that reflects subtotals of expenses by functional category. The statement of activities is supported by the additional statement of functional expenses, which presents expenses on both a natural and functional basis. A natural classification of expenses refers to the objective nature of an expenditure, such as salaries, rent, supplies, and the like.

All other nonprofits, including charities not classified as voluntary health and welfare groups as well as noncharitable organizations, such as trade and professional associations and labor unions, may present a statement of activities that reflects either functional subtotals or natural classifications of expenses. However, presentation of expenses on a functional basis in either the basic statements or in the footnotes is required under generally accepted accounting principles. Therefore, most non-VHWOs present functional subtotals of expenses in the statement of activities. Many will not disclose the natural classification of expenses anywhere in the audited financial statements (but this information will nonetheless be reported on the annual IRS Form 990).

Program services represent the activities that serve as the basis for an organization's exemption from income taxes. Thus, program service expenses are all those expenses associated with the delivery of an organization's programs to its target audience. For charitable nonprofit organizations, examples include:

- Housing
- Emergency assistance
- Education
- Research
- Weatherization
- Substance abuse treatment

For many charitable organizations, a statement of activities and statement of functional expenses may break the preceding programs down further, into individual components of a broad program. For example, an organization may report separate amounts for expenses associated with each geographic location of a program or for each target audience. In the college and university sector, an educational mission may be reflected in a statement of activities as multiple programs consisting of:

- Instruction
- Research
- Student services
- Academic support

For trade and professional associations, examples of programs commonly reported include:

- Seminars and conferences
- Certification
- Publications or periodicals
- Industry promotion

Supporting activities represent all other necessary activities of an organization, but do not directly accomplish the organization's mission. Two common supporting activities reported by many nonprofit organizations are management and general (sometimes called general and administrative) and fundraising.

Membership organizations, such as trade and professional associations and labor unions, often report a membership development function as one of their supporting activities. Membership development is to membership organizations what fundraising is to charities—the costs associated with efforts to attract support (donors or members) to an organization.

In addition, other terminology is frequently used to describe a management and general supporting activity. For instance, in the financial statements of colleges and universities, this function is often identified as institutional support.

Functional presentation of an organization's expenses is often viewed as the closest thing to a financial indicator of how well an organization is achieving its mission, although measuring this exclusively in financial terms is virtually impossible and extremely unfair to the people running the programs. It is one thing to spend money on a program, and that is certainly preferable over spending money unnecessarily or wastefully on nonprogram activities. But, it is something else entirely to *accomplish* something within a program, and this element is inherently absent from a set of financial statements—even those that conform to all of the accounting principles that currently apply to nonprofit organizations.

Charities are often under great pressure to present financial statements that indicate that the organization has devoted a substantial portion of its operating budget to program activities. One of the following ratios is often calculated based on the revenues and expenses reported by a nonprofit organization: program expenses divided by total expenses or program expenses divided by total revenue. In either case, the goal of many organizations is to maximize this ratio, indicating that the organization has devoted a substantial portion of its available resources to programs, rather than to fundraising or administrative costs. Contributing to organizations' drive to meet this goal are several factors:

- Many funding sources, such as government agencies and private foundations, establish specific thresholds (i.e., minimum program expense ratios) or otherwise evaluate charities based on these ratios, often putting charities in competition with one another with respect to these calculations.

- Watchdog groups, such as the BBB Wise Giving Alliance, grade or evaluate charities on a variety of standards, including those relating to these ratios, and issue pass/fail reports to the general public based on their findings (see Best Practices 9.2 and Appendix E).

- Certain state laws require the disclosure to the public of these or similar ratios and percentages.

- In articles about the nonprofit sector appearing in magazines and newspapers, various charities are often compared using these percentages. Frequently, charities are ranked based on which organizations reflect the best ratios in their financial statements or on their information returns (see Best Practices 9.3).

This objective is true not only of charities, but of many other types of nonprofit organizations as well. Associations and other membership groups strive to reflect a high program expense ratio for the simple reason that it is easier to attract members to an organization that does not appear to be wasting its members' money on administration.

What many of these factors have led to is the general public's increased awareness of these ratios. Many potential donors now ask charities for this information and use it to make decisions regarding which charities they will support. Potential members may consider ratios when making decisions regarding joining or renewing a membership in an association or union.

Complicating matters, and frequently frustrating nonprofit organizations, is the fact that allocation of expenses to the various functions of an organization is not an exact science. Far from it. The concepts that nonprofit organizations are expected to follow in accounting for and reporting their

BEST PRACTICES 9.2

CHARITY WATCHDOG GROUPS

There are four groups that are the best known of the so-called watchdogs of the charitable organization sector.

- **The BBB Wise Giving Alliance** (www.give.org). This affiliate of the Council of Better Business Bureaus evaluates more than 500 national charities in terms of whether each charity passes its 20 standards (revised standards took effect in 2003), including standards for how a charity spends its funds. The group posts reports pertaining to each charity on its Web site and also fields complaints on any charity. A copy of their standards can be found in Appendix E.
- **Charity Navigator** (www.charitynavigator.org) assigns zero- to four-star ratings to more than 1,700 charities based, in part, on how the charity spends its funds. The group's Web site includes its ratings as well as a financial analysis of each charity rated.
- **The American Institute of Philanthropy** (www.charitywatch.org) assigns A+ to F grades to more than 400 charities based on each charity's financial reports. The group's Web site provides grades only on the top-rated charities, others are available if you purchase a copy of the group's *Charity Rating Guide*.
- **The Wall Watchers' Ministry Watch** (www.ministrywatch.com) rates more than 400 organizations from one to five stars, based on information from their Form 990 and audited financial statements.

One other resource of note is **GuideStar,** a program run by an organization called Philanthropic Research (www.guidestar.org). This site has information and copies of annual IRS reports (Form 990) for hundreds of thousands of charitable organizations. GuideStar does not rate or evaluate charities. Rather, it serves as the most comprehensive public database of information on specific charities available. It receives Form 990 data directly from the Internal Revenue Service and contacts charities directly for additional information, then posts the tax documents and other information about each organization on its Web site. GuideStar also produces a comprehensive salary study, based on salaries reported by charities on their Form 990s.

Outside of the charitable organization sector, there are no other comprehensive, national watchdog or informational groups providing information on specific nonprofit organizations of other varieties, such as unions or trade and professional associations. However, by law, every nonprofit organization that files a Form 990 information return with the IRS is required to provide copies of its three most recent returns to anyone who requests copies. Alternatively, organizations are permitted to post their returns, in their entirety, on a publicly accessible Web site in fulfillment of this disclosure requirement. The Form 990 is an extremely useful tool in evaluating nonprofit organizations of any type, not just charitable organizations.

expenses are clear, but their application varies greatly from organization to organization and requires significant judgment and estimating.

Most accusations of improper financial reporting in the nonprofit sector have involved one of the following:

- Underreporting fundraising expenses and, therefore, overstating how much was spent on programs (for nonprofit organizations that don't fundraise, an equivalent reporting fraud may be asserted in connection with underreporting expenses associated with any category of supporting activity and overreporting program expenses)
- Overvaluing noncash contributions received and made
- Claiming income for contributions raised on behalf of other organizations

In each of these situations, the effect of the fraudulent reporting is to make a nonprofit organization appear to be spending a greater percentage of its available resources on its programs than it actually is.

Underreporting of Fundraising Expenses

Fundraising costs are defined as the costs of persuading potential donors to make contributions. Expenses are categorized as fundraising regardless of whether a donor is asked to make a gift to the requesting organization or to another organization. For instance, an organization that solicits contributions on behalf of an affiliated charity should reflect the expenditures associated with that effort as a fundraising expense (even though it may not directly receive the resulting contributions).

Examples of activities that are considered fundraising include:

- Direct-mail fundraising campaigns
- Telephone solicitations
- Door-to-door canvassing
- Advertisements in newspapers and other periodicals
- Television and radio announcements

BEST PRACTICES 9.3

HOW THE PRESS RATES CHARITIES

Several magazines attempt to provide a service to their readers by rating charitable organizations. One of the most common measures used is the program expense ratio described in the preceding section.

In its December 2002/January 2003 and December 2001/January 2002 issues, *Worth* magazine published its list of "America's 100 Best Charities." To the magazine's credit, it utilized a variety of factors in developing its list, rather than relying exclusively on the program expense ratio. *Worth* considered a variety of other information, such as the ratings of watchdog groups, and even interviewed representatives of each organization and experts in philanthropy. Most other publications have not gone to this effort to develop their lists of good charities. In fact, some of the "100 Best" reported program expense ratios that wouldn't typically be considered impressive. While the average percentage of revenue spent on fundraising of the 100 organizations reported in 2002/2003 was 5.66 percent, several organizations were included that spent 15 percent or more. However, *Worth* included them and explained that there are often very good reasons why a very well-run charity may reflect lower ratios than others.

However, its 2001/2002 list of "12 to Avoid" and 2002/2003 list of the "10 Worst" indicated there is certainly a lack of trust on the part of the press and watchdog groups in the numbers reported by certain charities. While some were listed due to lawsuits against the organization, admissions of wrongdoing, or reporting spending little on programs, some organizations listed were criticized for reporting portions of their program expenses as being allocated from a joint activity (defined in the next section). No indication was given as to why these expense allocations (which are to be done in accordance with specific accounting standards discussed later in this chapter) were doubted. The charities apparently were listed, at least in part, simply because they allocated expenses of activities that accomplish multiple purposes—something that any nonprofit or for-profit business is required to do.

Whether there was something specific about these allocations that made the watchdog groups or *Worth* suspicious is not stated. But reports like this leave the impression on readers that accounting is simply not to be trusted. This skepticism of expense allocations reported by nonprofit organizations is indicative of the lack of trust that seems to be prevalent in the press these days.

Source: Gossage, Bobbie, "Not Exactly Top 10," *Worth*, December 2002/January 2003, and "12 to Avoid." *Worth*, December 2001/January 2002.

- Personal appeals by volunteers
- Workplace fundraising
- Participation in federated campaigns
- Solicitation of bequests and deferred giving arrangements from individuals
- Distribution of brochures that solicit any type of contribution
- Preparation of proposals for grants from foundations
- Special events, such as dinners, concerts, golf outings, and the like

A solicitation of support is to be treated as fundraising regardless of the nature of a donor's support. For example, it is considered fundraising to solicit any of the following types of support:

- Cash contributions
- Gifts of noncash assets (clothing, equipment, securities, etc.)
- Volunteer labor
- Contributed *use* of an asset (such as use of land or a building)

Solicitations of support other than cash gifts are sometimes misclassified as program expenses due to the fact that the noncash support received is *used* in programs. While the utilization of such support may be properly reported as a program expense, the expenses associated with soliciting the support should always be classified as fundraising.

To further complicate matters, many fundraising activities may be carried on in connection with a program activity. These dual-purpose activities, referred to as joint activities in the accounting standards, can be especially difficult to assign an appropriate cost allocation. In addition to the difficulty in accounting for a joint activity, the very existence of an activity that purports to accomplish both a fundraising and programmatic purpose often raises suspicions (see Best Practices 9.3), suggesting a sentiment on the part of the public that joint activities inherently dilute the value of the program.

The accounting standards governing cost allocations for joint activities were modified in 1998 to require that certain criteria be met in order to report the costs of an activity as anything *other* than fundraising expenses. These rules are explained in the American Institute of Certified Public Accountant's Statement of Position (SOP) 98-2, *Accounting for Costs of Activities of Not-for-Profit Organizations and State and Local Governmental Entities That Include Fund Raising.*

SOP 98-2 is a document with which every charitable organization that receives or plans to receive contributions should become familiar. Thorough explanation of SOP 98-2 is beyond the scope of this book. However, knowledge of its contents is essential to every nonprofit manager's understanding of the risks of financial statement fraud. Executive directors, chief financial officers, directors of fundraising activities, and board members should all be familiar with the impact that SOP 98-2 may have on their organization.

A joint activity is any activity that accomplishes a fundraising purpose concurrently with either a program or management and general purpose. Examples of activities that may be considered joint activities include:

- Direct mail campaigns
- Door-to-door canvassing activities
- Newsletters
- Annual reports
- Telephone communications
- Web sites

Each of these activities, as well as many others, may accomplish a programmatic purpose, while also including a request for financial support (fundraising), hence the term joint activity.

SOP 98-2 requires that all three of the following criteria be met in order to charge the cost of any activity involving a fundraising component to any cost category *other* than as a fundraising expense:

- Purpose
- Audience
- Content

These criteria are applied separately to each activity that may be considered a joint activity. They are not applied to the organization as a whole. Accordingly, some organizations may have dozens of activities that must be individually considered.

The reasoning behind the three criteria is to distinguish legitimate programmatic or management and general activities from those in which materials are utilized in a fundraising capacity. Certain elements of the criteria, particularly in the purpose criterion, are designed to identify program-related information that is used primarily to appeal to potential donors as support for an organization's cause and, therefore, a legitimate object of their financial support.

If an activity fails to meet any one of the three criteria, *all* of the costs associated with the activity must be reported as fundraising expenses. This would include any costs that could otherwise be segregated as educational or some other nonfundraising category. The logic behind this conclusion is that if an educational item is used in a fundraising manner, then the cost of the educational item should be accounted for as a fundraising cost.

In order to meet the purpose criterion, three characteristics must be present:

- The activity must include a call for specific action.

- No one involved in the activity may receive a majority of his/her compensation for that activity based on the amount of contribution income received as a result of the activity.
- Other evidence must exist that a program, management, or general purpose is present in the activity.

The first characteristic applies only if the joint activity purports to accomplish a program purpose in addition to its fundraising purpose. A call for specific action must address specific steps that recipients of the message are encouraged to take. These steps should help to accomplish the organization's mission, other than by simply providing funds for their cause (i.e., asking for financial support is not a call for specific action as the phrase is applied here). Examples provided in SOP 98-2 of calls for specific action that accomplish an organization's mission, rather than simply request support for the mission, include:

- Encouraging parents to counsel their children about the dangers of drug abuse
- Encouraging senior citizens to exercise
- Requesting that people attend a performance
- Encouraging people to recycle
- Encouraging people to mail postcards to legislators urging support for a particular piece of legislation

The second characteristic is fairly straightforward. It is included in the SOP 98-2 primarily to require organizations to report as fundraising expenses all activities involving commission-based fundraising personnel and consultants.

The third characteristic requires the greatest judgment. SOP 98-2 provides one very limited set of circumstances in which the third characteristic is automatically met (carrying on the same program activity without a fundraising component using the same medium and on a similar or larger scale at some other point in time. This indicates that when the fundraising component is added, the activity clearly has two objectives in mind, not merely a fundraising purpose). If this very limited rule is not met, the SOP suggests that all other available information be considered in determining whether a legitimate nonfundraising purpose exists. Examples of some of these other factors are:

- Whether the organization can and does measure the program accomplishments associated with the activity (or is the only measure of performance the amount of contributions raised, indicating that perhaps the only purpose of the activity is to raise funds?)

- The qualifications of the personnel involved in the activity (are they fundraising personnel or program staff, or a combination of both?)
- Minutes of committee, board, and department meetings that discuss the activity as well as internal management memoranda pertaining to the activity
- The organization's stated mission

If the purpose criterion is met, it is time to move on to the second criterion—the audience criterion. The audience criterion includes a rebuttable presumption that it is *not* met if the audience includes prior donors or is otherwise selected based on its ability or likelihood to make a contribution. Since this possibility is almost always present in activities involving a request for contributions, the rebuttable aspect of this presumption becomes the key element of the audience criterion.

The presumption that the audience criterion is failed can be overcome if an audience is *also* selected for any of the following reasons:

- The audience needs to use, or has reasonable potential for use of, the specific action called for by the program component of the activity.
- The audience has the ability to take specific action to assist the organization in meeting the goals of the program component of the activity.
- If the nonfundraising component of the activity involves a management and general function, the organization is required to direct this management and general component to the particular audience or the audience has reasonable potential for use of that component.

The first two reasons are in place to require an organization to appropriately target the individuals who will be requested to take action, which will result in accomplishment of the mission. The mass-marketing approach to accomplishing the mission will always fail the audience criterion because of this rule.

For example, if an organization is working to find a cure for a particular illness that only afflicts people with specific characteristics (such as illnesses unique to one gender, race, age group, etc.), mailing a message to an entire community in hopes of contacting everyone at risk within that community will fail the audience criterion. The logic here is that the only purpose behind mailing the materials to households that are not at risk is to appeal to the household as potential donors by explaining the worthiness of the cause.

The third reason included in the rebuttable presumption applies only in situations involving a management and general component. An example of this situation is mailing donors a receipt for a past gift (the required management and general component) while soliciting another gift.

The content criterion is met if the joint activity supports either a program or management and general function. For program functions, the criterion is met if the specific action required of the recipient will help to accomplish the organization's mission. The action should benefit either the recipient or society in general.

Issuing financial statements or other reports or submitting annual information returns to the IRS or a state that underreport fundraising expenses and overstate program expenses can be the result of either:

- A weakness in financial controls causing one or more of the following:
  - Miscoding of invoices
  - Failure to identify fundraising activities carried out in connection with program or other activities (i.e., failure to properly apply the provisions of SOP 98-2)
  - Failure to properly allocate as fundraising activities overhead and other common costs (i.e., charging only direct costs of fundraising, without burdening the activity with overhead costs)
- An intentional effort to conceal and misclassify known fundraising activities

Whether the cause of underreporting fundraising expenses is an intentional act designed to deceive, or simply a weakness in internal control, can make a huge difference in terms of the assessment of fines or penalties by state agencies. However, from the public's perspective, the cause may not matter at all. Underreporting of fundraising expenses has become as sensitive an issue in the nonprofit sector as overreporting of earnings has been in the for-profit sector. Once the public hears reports of inaccurate financial reporting, that may be all that is necessary to cause significant damage to an organization's reputation (and ability to garner support from the public).

Therefore, every nonprofit organization that engages in any form of fundraising activity should have sound policies and procedures in place to prevent the underreporting of expenses associated with those activities. Preventing such underreporting is dependent on the establishment and adherence to the following financial controls:

- Establish an appropriate chart of accounts (i.e., one that sets up one or more fundraising functions, as well as accounts for all of the underlying costs that may be incurred in any of the organization's fundraising activities).
- Utilize a timekeeping system (such as timesheets) that requires all employees to:
  - Record all time worked (whether it is considered compensated or not)
  - Specifically identify what program or function they worked on each day (use hourly or smaller increments to record time, where appropriate)
  - Obtain the approval of a supervisor who is familiar with the duties assigned to that employee

- Have all vendor invoices coded (for classification in the accounting records) by employees with a detailed knowledge about the organization's activities. (A consulting invoice may not get coded to fundraising if the person coding the invoice doesn't even know that a particular fundraising activity has taken place.)
- Have the coding of invoices reviewed by the chief financial officer or someone other than the person who initially coded the invoice (preferably prior to entry in the accounting system, but even a subsequent review of how expenses have been classified is a valuable control).

FRAUD IN THE HEADLINES 9.1

CHARITY PENALIZED FOR FAILURE
TO DISCLOSE FUNDRAISING FEES

In 2001, the Multiple Sclerosis Association of America (MSAA) reached a settlement with the State of New Jersey in connection with a lawsuit brought by the state over a variety of wrongdoings by the MSAA and its senior management. The MSAA is not related to the better-known National Multiple Sclerosis Society.

One of the accusations in the State's complaint was that MSAA telemarketers misled prospective donors about how proceeds from their contributions would be used. Telemarketers, who worked for an independent outside firm, informed potential donors that the entire amount of each donor's check would go to the MSAA. However, the firm's contract with the MSAA called for the fundraisers to receive at least 70 percent of the proceeds of their telemarketing efforts.

The organization was charged with classifying fundraising fees as program expenditures on reports filed with the State Division of Consumer Affairs, as well as its annual Form 990 filed with the Internal Revenue Service (this practice landed the MSAA on the *Worth* magazine "12 to Avoid" list described in Best Practices 9.3). Additional charges involved use of MSAA funds for personal expenses of association officers and trips to Europe by nonemployees.

The settlement involved payments to the State totaling $225,000. The association paid $150,000, the MSAA's former president paid $40,000, and the former vice-president (who is also the son of the former president) paid $35,000. The State brought its suit in 1999. Since that time, the MSAA has appointed a new president and announced that it has taken actions to improve its operations and internal controls.

Source: DeMarrais, Kevin G., "Charity Settles Suit with N.J.," *The Record*, April 3, 2001.

- Identify all fundraising activities of the organization, including any joint activities that are carried on in conjunction with nonfundraising activities (such as fundraising appeals included in newsletters, etc.).
- For each fundraising activity, identify all resources that were used in that activity (resources may include employees, volunteers, contractors, facilities, desks, equipment, copiers, telephones, office supplies, postage, or any other element that contributes to the activity).
- For each resource listed in the preceding step, identify either:
  - The underlying direct cost that should be charged to fundraising, or
  - The underlying indirect (or joint) cost that needs to be allocated to fundraising (indirect costs are costs that are attributable to multiple functions and activities, such as rent).
- For each indirect/joint cost from the preceding step that must be allocated to a fundraising activity, find an appropriate method for allocating the indirect cost into its fundraising component and any other functions or activities that the cost enables (see Best Practices 9.4).
- For each factor or base that is used to allocate indirect/joint costs identified in the preceding step, establish and follow policies and procedures for measuring utilization of the resource. (For example, once it is identified that the organization's photocopier is used to copy certain fundraising documents, establish a manual log or electronic function codes to track copier usage by function or activity.)
- Utilize an internal audit function to focus on oversight of this area (more on the internal audit function is explained in Chapter 14).
- Undergo an external audit by a CPA firm (and disclose to the firm all fundraising activities at the beginning of the audit, so that the firm can plan to devote appropriate audit resources to an examination of the organization's expense allocation processes).
- Periodically reassess the organization's utilization of resources used in fundraising activities and the factors/bases used to allocate the underlying costs. (For example, do not automatically use the same square footage measurement to allocate rent to each of the functions from year to year; instead, look at how an office setup has changed, whether employees in each section of the office are working on different projects, etc.)
- Prior to issuing financial statements for the year, perform one final review of all charges, looking for any fundraising expenditures that have been misclassified.

One important consideration in performing many of the preceding steps is the involvement of nonfinancial personnel in the process. The accounting/finance department cannot develop reliable allocations of costs

BEST PRACTICES 9.4

FACTORS USED TO ALLOCATE COSTS

Allocating costs to a nonprofit organization's various programs and activities can present several challenges. In addition to identifying the underlying costs that are incurred in any program or activity, appropriate bases or factors for allocating indirect/joint costs or components of overhead must be developed.

Here are some of the more commonly incurred indirect costs and factors/bases that may be useful in allocating these costs among programs and activities:

Cost	Factor or Measure
Accounting	Number of transactions processed
Automobile costs	Mileage
Data processing	System usage
Depreciation of equipment	Actual use/location of equipment
Employee recruiting/hiring	Number of new employees
Facilities (rent, etc.)	Square feet of space occupied
Health insurance	Number of employees
Human resources administration	Number of employees
Local telephone costs	Number of telephones
Long-distance charges	Actual charges by employee
Mailroom costs (other than postage)	Number of pieces handled
Office supplies	Actual usage, if possible (Number of employees, if tracking actual use is not feasible)
Payroll services	Number of employees
Payroll taxes	Salaries
Photocopier	Actual use based on log
Postage/shipping	Actual use based on log
Salaries	Hours charged by employee
Utilities	Square feet of space occupied

without significant participation from program, fundraising, and support staff. Their duties should not be limited to timesheet preparation. Their involvement is critical to identifying fundraising activities, pinpointing the resources used in those activities, and in measuring the utilization of resources in order to properly allocate the underlying costs.

Inflating the Values of Noncash Contributions Received or Made

Another method of artificially making a nonprofit organization appear to be doing more charitable work than it actually does is by inflating the values of noncash contributions received. Reporting artificially high amounts for noncash contributions has the effect of overstating both contribution income and program expenses (because the utilization of these gifts is almost always associated with programs). As a result, an organization's program expense ratio (program expenses divided by either total income or total expenses) appears to be better than it really is.

Charitable organizations may receive any of the following types of noncash gifts:

- Contributed services (i.e., volunteer time)
- Donated use of an asset (such as rent-free use of office space or equipment)
- Contributed assets (donated clothing, food, equipment, supplies, etc.)

Any of these forms of noncash gifts can be fraudulently reported by an unethical individual or nonprofit organization. Accounting standards require that when these types of gifts are recorded on an organization's financial statements, they be reflected at their fair market value at the time of the gift. For example, volunteer time would be accounted for at the fair market value of the service provided (which is not necessarily the same as the work that the volunteer performs in his day job) and donated equipment or other assets at market value on the date of the gift. The same theory applies to donated use of assets (value at the going rental rate for the item whose use is being contributed). The valuation should take into consideration whether the asset is new or used and its current condition.

As with the underreporting of fundraising expenses, whether the issuance of statements that inflate the values of noncash gifts is done intentionally, by accident, or due to weaknesses in internal controls makes little difference to the general public. Either way, the organization looks bad (at a minimum, mismanaged, and at an extreme, criminal). Accordingly, it is important for nonprofit organizations to establish and follow sound policies and

FRAUD IN THE HEADLINES 9.2

**CHARITY CHARGED WITH OVERVALUING IN-KIND
CONTRIBUTIONS**

The Pennsylvania Bureau of Charitable Organizations charged Children's Wish Foundation International with 95 violations of the state's Charitable Solicitations Act. The charges stemmed from in-kind contributions made by the charity to 41 Ronald McDonald Houses. The Foundation valued these grants-in-kind at $1.6 million. After review and investigation, operators of the houses claim the market value of the gifts was no more than $136,500. The state's complaint also alleged that Foundation funds were used to support a lavish personal lifestyle for the organization's officers.

The Georgia-based Foundation was previously the subject of a 1992 charge by Connecticut officials of filing financial documents that overvalued donations made in that state. Children's Wish Foundation International was one of five charities that settled a pool of complaints by paying $206,212 in civil penalities.

Source: McCosh, John, and Ron Martz, "Finances of Children's Wish Questioned. Pennsylvania Accuses Charity of Padding, Misspending, But Group Defends Itself," *The Atlanta Constitution,* October 4, 2000.

procedures for valuing noncash gifts received and made. Some of the most important of these controls include:

- Training on valuation techniques and procedures for all personnel who are involved in the valuation process (i.e., how to classify donated items into standard categories, how to assess the condition of donated assets, etc.)
- Establishment of standard valuation techniques (for example, standard rates for donated items classified into each of several categories, such as a rate per pound for donated food items of a certain type)
- Documentation of all standard policies, procedures, and valuation methods in the form of a brief policy statement or manual that is distributed to all employees involved in the valuation process
- Following a policy of valuing all noncash items received immediately upon receipt (rather than waiting until year-end or some other point to assign values based on listings of items received)
- Requiring supervisory approval for certain types of donated assets or of all donated items in excess of an established dollar threshold (or require spot-checking and approvals by supervisors)

- Using a standard form to document the initial intake of contributed assets, and including the following on the form:
  - Donor name and address
  - Date of gift
  - Complete description of each item contributed
  - Quantities of other units of measure (pounds, etc.)
  - For each item or group of items, an assessment of the condition of the items (if applicable)
  - Assessment of market value (item by item, or by category, whichever is appropriate)
  - Signature of the representative receiving the donated assets
  - Approval of a supervisor (where appropriate)
  - Sign-off by accounting department personnel indicating that the donation has been recorded (or placed in inventory, depending on the nature of the donation and the organization's operations)
- Using separate general ledger accounts to track all noncash gifts received and made separately from cash contributions (and, depending on the circumstances, consider establishing separate accounts for each category of noncash contribution)
- Performing periodic physical counts of donated items received and held by the organization (if applicable) using the same procedures described in Chapter 6 for performing counts
- Monitoring recorded donations of noncash assets over time, looking for unusual trends

Claiming Income for Contributions Raised on Behalf of Others

The third form of fraudulent financial reporting occurs when an organization reports as income and expense contributions it raises on behalf of other charities. When Donor A contributes $1,000 to Charity B, but stipulates that Charity B forward $300 of the gift to Charity C and $300 to Charity D, how much contribution income should Charity B report? $1,000 or $400? If Charity B reports all $1,000 as income and the $600 forwarded on to Charities C and D as program expenses, its program expense ratio will appear stronger than if it simply reflects the net of $400 as contribution income. As a result, Charity B may have an incentive to report all $1,000 as its own income.

Until recently, the accounting standards were not entirely clear on this issue and the resulting financial reporting by nonprofit organizations reflected inconsistency from one group to another. However, in June 1999, the Financial Accounting Standards Board (FASB) issued SFAS No. 136, *Transfers of Assets to a Not-for-Profit Organization or Charitable Trust That Raises or Holds Contributions for Others.* SFAS No. 136 states that whenever a donor explicitly earmarks contributions for one or more specifically named final beneficiaries (other charities) or the fundraising materials of an organization indicate that the proceeds of the fundraising activities or the overall purpose of the organization is to support another identified charity, the initial recipient of the contributions should *not* recognize contribution income unless either of two characteristics are present:

- The donor explicitly grants variance power to the recipient organization (i.e., the donor states that the recipient may redirect the use of the gift so that a charity other than the one named by the donor may benefit from the gift).
- The initial recipient and the final beneficiary organization are financially related, a condition that is considered met if *both* of the following elements are present:
  - One organization has the ability to influence the operating and financial decisions of the other. (For instance, the two are affiliates, there is considerable representation on the other organization's board of directors, or the governing documents of one group limit its activities to those that benefit the other.)
  - One organization has an ongoing economic interest in the net assets of the other (i.e., a residual interest, such that one organization is entitled to a certain percentage of the net assets of the other upon its dissolution).

In most cases in which neither of the two preceding conditions are met, the initial recipient of support is required to reflect a liability to the named final beneficiary on its financial statements rather than treating it as income. Such is the case with many organizations, such as the many United Ways, which raise funds on behalf of numerous other charities.

SFAS No. 136 permits one alternative method of presentation for organizations that are precluded from reporting income as a result of the standard's rules. These organizations may report the gross amounts received, less the amounts received on behalf of others, on the statement of activities, provided both amounts and a final net contribution income figure are all reported in the income section of the statement (rather than reporting the amounts raised on behalf of others as an expense). This way, the organization is permitted to reflect its total activities, yet the net amount that the organization is entitled to keep as its own income is still separately reported on the statement of activities without inappropriately labeling anything as a program expense.

The intentional reporting of this type of activity as income (when the recipient is merely acting as an intermediary between a donor and a final beneficiary) is considered to be fraudulent financial reporting. To maintain control over this, an organization should:

- Carefully review fundraising materials and communications received in connection with contributions in order to identify all instances in which donors have earmarked funds for final beneficiaries and neither of the SFAS No. 136 criteria are met.

- Segregate contributions that are precluded from being recognized as income and account for them as a liability until remitted to the final beneficiary.

- Track total contributions received on behalf of others for disclosure in the financial statements.

Failure to Disclose Related Party Transactions

At the conclusion of every audit of an organization's financial statements, the external auditor requests a signed representation letter from the organization's management. This is typically a letter that is signed by the chief financial officer and the executive director, although others also may be involved.

A management representation letter includes numerous boilerplate representations that auditors are required to obtain under the AICPA's auditing standards. Additional representations may also be requested, based on specific circumstances or unusual transactions that may have occurred in the period under audit.

One of the standard representations included on all of these letters is management's assertion to the auditor that all related party transactions have been disclosed to the auditor. Many executive directors and chief financial officers sign this representation letter without understanding exactly what a related party is (and auditors do a notoriously poor job of explaining this definition to their clients).

With all of the recent controversies in the for-profit sector over undisclosed related party transactions, it should come as no surprise that the sensitivity of these transactions in the nonprofit sector has also risen. Failure to disclose related party transactions, even if the transactions are perfectly legitimate and fair to the organization, can leave the impression of wrongdoing when the failure is made public. Accordingly, every nonprofit organization should have a firm understanding of any and all related party transactions and fully disclose these transactions in their financial statements.

Related party transactions should also be subject to an organization's conflict-of-interest policies, a topic covered in Chapters 4 and 14.

The accounting profession's definition of a related party is found in the Statement of Financial Accounting Standards No. 57, *Related Party Disclosures*. In this standard, related parties are defined as:

- Affiliates of an entity, defined as any party that, directly or indirectly through one or more intermediaries, controls, is controlled by, or is under common control with the reporting entity (for purposes of this rule, control means the possession, direct or indirect, of the power to direct or cause the direction of the management and policies of an entity through ownership, by contract, or otherwise)

- Entities for which investments are accounted for by the equity method of accounting
- Trusts for the benefit of employees, such as pension and profit-sharing trusts that are managed by or under the trusteeship of management
- Principal owners of an entity (owners of record or known beneficial owners of more than 10 percent of the voting interests of an entity)
- Management of an entity, defined as persons responsible for achieving the objectives of the entity and who have the authority to establish policies and make decisions by which those objectives are to be pursued (normally includes members of the board of directors, the chief executive officer, chief operating officers, vice presidents in charge of principal functions, and other persons, regardless of title, who perform similar policymaking functions)
- Members of the immediate families of principal owners of the entity and its management (including family members whom a principal owner or member of management might control or influence or by whom they might be controlled or influenced because of the family relationship)
- Other parties with which the entity may deal if one party controls or can significantly influence the management or operating policies of the other to an extent that one of the transacting parties might be prevented from fully pursuing its own separate interests
- Other parties that can significantly influence the management or operating policies of the transacting parties or that have an ownership interest in one of the transacting parties and can significantly influence the other to the extent that one or more of the transacting parties might be prevented from fully pursuing its own separate interests

It is clear from this definition that the concept of a related party is quite broad. Organizationally, the definition extends both vertically (to parent and subsidiary organizations), as well as horizontally (to organizations under common control). In addition to the commonly recognized members of management (board members and senior management), the definition extends to anyone in charge of a principal function (such as department heads, directors, managers, vice presidents, etc.), as well as to the immediate family members of each of these members of the management team.

Once an organization has identified all of its related parties, it must determine whether there have been any transactions with those parties. If there have been any such transactions, the following information must be disclosed in the organization's financial statements:

- The nature of the relationship(s) involved
- A description of the transactions, including transactions to which no amounts or nominal amounts were ascribed, for each period for which a statement of activities is presented; also such other information deemed necessary to an understanding of the effects of the transactions on the organization's financial statements
- The dollar amounts of transactions for each of the periods for which a statement of activities is presented as well as the effects of any changes in method of establishing terms from that used in the preceding period
- Amounts due from or to related parties as of the date of each statement of financial position presented and, if not otherwise apparent, the terms and manner of settlement of those balances

Transactions with related parties are particularly sensitive, primarily because readers of financial statements may presume that these transactions were negotiated at less than arm's length. Related party transactions of concern may occur between a nonprofit organization and individuals, businesses, or other nonprofit organizations. Examples of related party transactions that may be of concern to readers of a nonprofit organization's financial statements include:

- Transfers between the organization and affiliated organizations
- Leases between the organization and businesses in which board members have a financial interest
- Contracts between the organization and family members of the executive director or members of the board
- Provision of services to other organizations under common control of several of the same board members
- Lending of money to a for-profit business owned by the organization

In each of these cases, the related party transaction may be perfectly acceptable and even result in a good deal for the nonprofit organization. However, the fact that it takes place with a related party makes it vulnerable to abuse and therefore, also vulnerable to skepticism. Failures to disclose related party transactions can have disastrous effects on nonprofit organizations, even if the failure was completely innocent in nature and no inappropriate activity has taken place.

Accordingly, every organization should establish the following controls to ensure that related party transactions are properly disclosed:

- Identify all related parties on an annual basis (this includes obtaining updated information from known related parties, such as board members, regarding names of family members and of businesses in which they hold financial interests).

- Identify all related party transactions (preferably before they occur) and track all activity with related parties separately.
- Require special levels of review and approval of all related party transactions by persons without a conflict with respect to the transaction (coordinate this with your conflict of interest policy described in Chapter 14 and illustrated in the appendix).
- Document all approvals described in the preceding step contemporaneously with the making of the decision.
- Establish appropriate terms with respect to all related party transactions, such as interest rates and due dates of payments (again, this may be coordinated with the conflict of interest policy).
- On an ongoing basis, monitor related party transactions and outstanding balances for compliance with the terms established in the preceding step.
- Prepare a summary listing of all related party transactions for the year and balances due to/from related parties at year end for disclosure to the external auditors and inclusion in the organization's financial statements.

FRAUDULENT STATEMENTS OF COMPLIANCE WITH REQUIREMENTS OF FUNDING SOURCES

Much like the issue of compliance with donor-imposed restrictions explained in Chapter 8, providers of grants to nonprofit organizations often attach a variety of stipulations or expectations to their financial support. This is particularly true if the grantor is a federal, state, or local government agency. These compliance requirements (or goals, objectives, and other expectations) may address a wide variety of issues. Some of the most common compliance requirements established by funding sources involve:

- Eligibility of program participants, such as income levels, age requirements, and so forth
- Service levels, such as a stated number of hours or units of service provided during a grant period
- Achievement levels, as with students earning a certain score or passing grades on a test or in a class
- Allowability of specific activities within a program, as with a private foundation grant that funds the research and writing associated with a series of articles on a particular topic in a journal
- Preparation and issuance of reports concerning activities funded by the grantor
- Matching or cost-sharing requirements, in which an organization must contribute to the costs of a program by locating a second funding source, through in-kind contributions of services or other means

Of course, with government grants, there can be a plethora of additional requirements. Some of these requirements may involve allowability of costs charged to a grant, a topic that will be explained further later in this chapter.

If a nonprofit organization receives financial assistance from a federal agency, the organization may be subject to a Single Audit in accordance with Office of Management and Budget (OMB) Circular A-133. (See Chapter 7's discussion of fraud involving subrecipients for more on this audit requirement.) If an organization undergoes an audit in accordance with OMB Circular A-133, its external audit firm will test the organization's compliance with certain requirements applicable to its federally funded programs.

However, an A-133 audit is by no means a guarantee that a nonprofit organization is in full compliance with all of the federal requirements applicable to its programs. The external audit firm may be only auditing certain federally funded programs, not all of those funded with federal money. In addition, it is always important to keep in mind that an audit involves testing samples of transactions and activities. Not all of the transactions or activities will be tested during an audit.

For this reason alone, it is imperative that every nonprofit organization receiving government support establish and follow a series of policies and procedures governing compliance with funding source requirements. The same can be said for nonprofits that receive other forms of support that have accompanying stipulations or expectations, such as grants from private foundations and corporations. The compliance requirements associated with non-governmental grants and support tend to be far less complicated than those connected with government awards, but compliance with these requirements is every bit as important.

Some of the most crucial compliance policies and procedures that should be established for nonprofit organizations that receive government assistance include:

- Create a separate file for each funding source, in which all documents associated with that particular grant or award are stored (budgets, proposals or applications for the grant, correspondence, the grant document itself, attachments and amendments to the grant).
- Review the grant document and prepare a short written summary of all key requirements cited in the grant.
- For federal grants, obtain copies from the Code of Federal Regulations (available on the Internet at www.access.gpo.gov/nara/cfr/cfr-table-search.html#page1) of key program regulations that are referred to, but not detailed, in the grant document.
- Assign responsibility for compliance and monitoring of compliance to appropriate levels of personnel within the organization.
- Provide appropriate training and background materials for all personnel with responsibilities for compliance.

- Prepare and maintain documentation for compliance with all material funding source requirements.
- Establish internal controls associated with compliance with funding source requirements.

This final point is intentionally stated in broad terms. The nature of the internal controls over compliance will inherently vary depending on the nature of the compliance requirements and the risks involved.

But keep one critical factor in mind. Even though an employee involved in a grant-funded program may not be directly embezzling funds from the organization, it does not mean there isn't a motive for the person to commit other acts of fraud. Because the person's employment with the organization may be directly or indirectly based on the organization's continued receipt of grant funds for that employee's particular program, that alone may be reason enough for some people to falsify documents to make it appear that the organization has complied with a requirement that, in fact, it has not. In other cases, falsely stating compliance with funding source requirements may lead to promotions or performance-based bonuses. See Fraud in the Headlines 9.3 for an example of this motive in action.

Clearly, one of the key elements of internal control over this type of fraud involves a separation of duties, as well as review and approval of reports dealing with compliance. Examples of these controls follow:

- Separate the duties associated with preparing source documents used to substantiate compliance from duties associated with preparing reports that summarize program accomplishments, levels of effort, and so forth. (This prevents the easiest form of report falsification, which occurs when it is not necessary for the person preparing the report to falsify any supporting documentation as part of their scheme.)
- Utilize documents and policies that require recipients of program services to provide a signature acknowledging receipt of the stated service, where appropriate.
- Require independent review and approval of all reports summarizing program accomplishments, levels of effort, matching, and all other key compliance requirements.
- Perform an independent spot-check of data included in reports to funding sources by comparing this data to supporting documentation. (For example, if a report claims that the organization provided services to 125 individuals, review underlying files and documentation for some or all of these individuals to provide assurance that the service was truly rendered.)

FRAUD IN THE HEADLINES 9.3

**FRAUDULENT STATEMENTS OF COMPLIANCE
WITH FEDERAL GRANT REQUIREMENTS**

In April 2000, the director of the School for Careers (a school run by the charity Project Social Care) was arrested and charged with making false claims to the U.S. Department of Education in connection with the receipt of federal Pell grants. These grants are awarded to eligible needy postsecondary school students. The funds are paid directly to the educational institution to cover a student's tuition. Class attendance directly affects a school's authority to request and retain Pell grants.

The former director instructed employees of the school to falsify student attendance records in order to maintain a flow of Pell grant funds. She allegedly directed employees to create phony make-up sheets for students with attendance problems, falsely crediting students with having attended make-up classes that they never attended. Sometimes, hundreds of these phony make-up sheets would be created in a single week. Students were also allegedly told that they would be credited with six hours of attendance if they attended one hour of make-up class. Students were allegedly permitted to read magazines or do anything else they wanted during these make-up classes, as long as they didn't create a disturbance, since no formal instruction was given. In many cases, instructors were not even present.

The director received an annual salary of approximately $175,000. Included in that salary were bonuses based on the number of students enrolled.

Source: "Director of Queens School Charged with Fraud in Connection with Receipt of Federal Pell Grants," Press Release from the U.S. Department of Education, April 26, 2000.

CHARGING UNALLOWABLE COSTS TO GOVERNMENT GRANTS

When a nonprofit organization receives cost-reimbursable grants and certain other financial assistance from federal agencies, it must account for the costs of that grant in accordance with specific guidelines established by the federal government. Those rules are primarily found in two documents issued by the Office of Management and Budget (OMB): OMB Circular A-21, *Cost Principles for Educational Institutions,* and OMB Circular A-122, *Cost Principles for Non-Profit Organizations.*

Other rules apply to other types of entities, such as Circular A-87 for state and local government agencies, and each federal granting agency may have additional regulations unique to grants made by that agency. But the majority of the do's and don'ts regarding billing the federal government for the costs incurred by a nonprofit organization will be found in Circulars A-21 or A-122, depending on the type of organization.

A comprehensive explanation of cost-charging under the OMB circulars is beyond the scope of this book. Also, in the vast majority of cases, if a nonprofit organization *mistakenly* bills the federal government for unallowable costs, the government simply requires the return of the funds.

However, when the government asserts that an organization *intentionally* overcharged for services provided under federal grants, additional punitive damages can be assessed against the organization beyond just returning the funds. Such assertions are not very common and are usually limited to the following situations:

- There is documented evidence of a plan to overbill the government.
- There is a pattern of repeated overcharging.
- The nonprofit fails to take corrective action after cost-charging problems have been pointed out by the government or its auditors.

Included in the OMB cost principles circulars are explanations of the criteria required to charge costs to the government. In addition, the circulars identify:

- Certain costs that are always considered unallowable
- Costs that only may be charged under certain circumstances or with specific authorization from the granting agency

Some of the costs that cannot be charged to federal awards are direct, out-of-pocket expenses. Examples of costs that are always unallowable include alcoholic beverages, entertainment, fines and penalties, and losses from other federal awards. Examples of costs that are only allowable in limited instances or with specific authorization from the awarding agency include advertising, interest, overtime payments, and certain specific elements of compensation and allowances.

Certain costs listed as unallowable are, in essence, unallowable *functions*, to which an appropriate share of indirect costs (overhead) must be applied. Fundraising and lobbying activities are two such categories. Accordingly, if an organization engages in fundraising or lobbying activities, particularly if it utilizes its own employees in doing so, it must allocate an appropriate share of indirect costs to the unallowable function (see the discussion of allocating indirect costs to fundraising earlier in this chapter for details). Failing to allocate a fair share of indirect costs to fundraising or lobbying activities can result in overcharging the federally funded programs with these indirect costs.

Every nonprofit receiving cost-reimbursable federal awards, or other federal awards requiring an accounting for actual costs incurred, should have financial controls in place to provide assurance that unallowable costs are not billed to any federal award. Some of the most important of these financial controls include:

- Establish a chart of accounts that separately breaks out any unallowable activities (such as fundraising or lobbying) and any unallowable costs that are likely to be incurred by the organization (so that there's a place to classify these costs in the general ledger when they're incurred).

- Maintain in the accounting department a budget and summary of every federal grant as a reference regarding the nature of costs that are allowable for each award.

- Make sure that all coding of invoices or other charges to federal awards is done by someone with proper training on cost charging and familiarity with the budget and terms of each award.

- Maintain copies of all current regulations that apply to programs funded by the federal government.

OTHER FALSE STATEMENTS TO GOVERNMENT AGENCIES

As the cases described in Fraud in the Headlines 9.3 and 9.4 illustrate, filing reports with federal, state, or local government agencies that contain information that has been intentionally misstated is generally subject to fines and penalties. Both the organization and/or responsible individuals can be penalized.

The source of many of the penalties assessed for filing intentionally falsified reports with U.S. government agencies is the False Claims Act, summarized in Best Practices 9.5. Given the sensitive nature of reports filed with federal agencies and the risk of monetary penalties for falsifying those reports, organizations should have basic controls in place with respect to any report filed with federal agencies, particularly those related to federal grants:

- Have all information reported to federal agencies supported by reports generated directly from the accounting system (for all financial data) or other information system (for nonfinancial data).

- Require all entries in the accounting system (and other information systems) to be supported by appropriate source documentation. (The nature of this source documentation will vary based on the information reported; for example, when reporting on the number of children served in a program, back it up with a complete file that includes all required applications, forms, and documents for each child served.)

- Independently cross-check data input and included in the information system to appropriate source documentation.

- Segregate the preparation of federal reports from the duties associated with accumulating the data to be included in the reports.
- Independently review and approve all federal reports prior to filing.
- Subject all federal reports to internal audit procedures.
- Correct all errors that are identified during the auditing in a timely fashion.

FRAUD IN THE HEADLINES 9.4

DEFRAUDING U.S. GOVERNMENT RESULTS IN STEEP FINES

In July 2001, a nonprofit community-based organization was indicted on six counts of defrauding two agencies of the U.S. government: the Federal Emergency Management Agency (FEMA) and the Department of Education (DOE). The six counts included:

- Three counts of mail fraud associated with the submission of timesheets to FEMA by individuals who had nothing to do with the counseling or outreach activities that FEMA was funding in response to the Northridge earthquake of 1994
- Three counts of making false statements in the jurisdiction of a federal agency in connection with misrepresenting to the DOE the number of hours students attended classes provided by the nonprofit organization and funded by the DOE, as well as for overstating program expenditures on reports filed with the DOE

From July 1995 to June 1998, the nonprofit received approximately $6.6 million in federal grant funds. Allegedly, the organization spent only half of that amount on program expenditures.

If convicted, the organization could be subject to fines of up to $3 million, plus payment of full restitution.

Source: "Hermandad Legal Center Indicted on Charges of Defrauding Government by Overbilling for Services," Press Release from the U.S. Department of Justice, Central District of California, July 12, 2001.

BEST PRACTICES 9.5

PENALTIES UNDER THE FALSE CLAIMS ACT

The False Claims Act (31 U.S.C. 3729) establishes a system of assessing penalties for submission of false claims to the U.S. government. It is considered a false claim to do any of the following:

- Knowingly present, or cause to be presented, to an officer or employee of the United States government or a member of the Armed Forces of the United States, a false or fraudulent claim for payment or approval
- Knowingly make, use, or cause to be made or used, a false record or statement to get a false or fraudulent claim paid or approved by the government
- Conspire to defraud the government by getting a false or fraudulent claim allowed or paid
- Have possession, custody, or control of property or money that is used or is intended to be used by the government, and intend to defraud the government or willfully conceal the property, or deliver or cause to be delivered less property than the amount for which the person receives a certificate or receipt
- Authorize, make, or deliver a document certifying receipt of property used or to be used by the government and, intending to defraud the government, make or deliver the receipt without completely knowing that the information on the receipt is true
- Knowingly buy or receive as a pledge of an obligation or debt, public property from an officer or employee of the government, or a member of the Armed Forces, who lawfully may not sell or pledge the property
- Knowingly make, use, or cause to be made or used, a false record or statement to conceal, avoid, or decrease an obligation to pay or transmit money or property to the government

Civil penalties imposed under the False Claims Act are a minimum of $5,000 and a maximum of $10,000 (per false claim), plus three times the amount of damages that the government sustains as a result of the act committed by the person. Courts are permitted to reduce the additional penalty to two times the damages if the person fully cooperates with the government and provides all information regarding the act to the government within 30 days of receiving the information.

A claim under the False Claims Act is defined as any request or demand, whether under a contract or otherwise, for money or property which is made to a contractor, grantee, or other recipient if the United States government provides any portion of the money or property that is requested or demanded, or if the government will reimburse such contractor, grantee, or other recipient for any portion of the money or property that is requested or demanded.

In addition, under the False Claims Amendments Act of 1986, persons found to have made false claims to a federal agency, knowing the claim is false, fictitious, or fraudulent, can be imprisoned for up to five years.

10

Other Acts Attributable to Nonprofit Organizations

This chapter is devoted to other fraudulent, abusive, or illegal acts that can be attributed to nonprofit organizations, resulting in liability to the organization. The acts described in this chapter can be attributed to the organization if they are carried out by, for, or through the organization. The acts of wrongdoing addressed in this chapter include:

- Fraudulent or misleading statements of program accomplishments or capabilities
- Abuse of special exemptions and privileges granted to charities
- Intentional noncompliance with other laws and regulations

In each case, readers of statements, grantors of funds, or government agencies are misled about some aspect of the organization's activities. Accusations of fraud and abuse relating to these acts generally involve assertions of wrongdoing *by* or *for* (on behalf of) a nonprofit organization. This chapter will explain how each of these fraudulent statements occurs and why, as well as the steps that can be taken to minimize the risk that the organization will be accused of making or filing false statements. The motives behind these acts are generally similar to those explained in the introduction to Chapter 9 in that employees, officers, or directors usually engage in these activities to benefit the organization, which in turn may or may not indirectly benefit them personally.

Also addressed in this chapter are acts of wrongdoing committed *through* nonprofit organizations. Unlike acts committed by or for organizations, which are designed to benefit the organization, fraud committed through an organization never benefits the organization. In these acts, a person abuses their position in a nonprofit organization to carry out fraud or some other illegal act against third parties.

FALSE STATEMENTS OF PROGRAM ACCOMPLISHMENTS OR CAPABILITIES

Donors, grantors, and others like to become involved with organizations that are known to be providing a valuable service and are effective and efficient in their utilization of resources. Fraudulent financial reporting, described in the preceding chapter, is just one method of misleading people into thinking an organization is doing more than it really is. Overstating nonfinancial statistics pertaining to program accomplishments is another.

Many donors make donation decisions based, at least in part, on an organization's statements of program accomplishments. These accomplishments are reported in an organization's annual reports, newsletters, and fundraising materials, as well as other materials (see Fraud in the Headlines 10.1). Program service accomplishments also must be reported in every nonprofit organization's annual information return filed with the Internal Revenue Service, Form 990.

FRAUD IN THE HEADLINES 10.1

FALSIFYING DOCUMENTS TO SUPPORT OVERSTATEMENT OF PROGRAM ACCOMPLISHMENTS

Remember the school in Fraud in the Headlines 9.3 whose director was charged with falsifying documents in order to receive Pell grants? That same school also allegedly boasted an abnormally high graduation rate. The reason: Few students were *allowed* to fail. The director routinely instructed teachers to change students' failing grades to passing grades. One source claimed that 25 percent of the school's graduating students were unable to be placed in externships due to lack of skills, attributable in part to frequent absenteeism.

Source: "Director of Queens School Charged with Fraud in Connection with Receipt of Federal Pell Grants," Press Release from the U.S. Department of Education, April 26, 2000.

Adding to the potential for program reporting fraud is the fact that a personal motive may exist. Employees responsible for accumulating and reporting statistics regarding program service accomplishments may not exaggerate those numbers purely so that the organization looks better to donors and the public. Exaggeration may serve a personal purpose similar to the motives introduced in Chapter 9:

- A bonus or better-than-deserved salary increase
- A promotion or excellent performance evaluation
- Maintaining funding levels for a program, which results in a person keeping their job

Because of these additional motives, fraudulent reporting of program service accomplishments represents a potentially significant risk in many organizations.

When a program is funded by government support, reports pertaining to program service accomplishments may be subject to audit, as discussed in Chapter 9. But what about accomplishments in programs that are not federally funded? What's to keep those organizations (or their employees) from exaggerating statements of program accomplishments?

Reporting of program service accomplishments either for internal performance evaluation purposes or for external reporting purposes should be subject to controls, just like the reporting of financial results. Some of the controls useful in preventing or detecting program reporting fraud include:

- Segregate the duties associated with establishing and documenting the provision of service (i.e., admitting and serving persons) from duties associated with accumulating, summarizing, and reporting on levels of effort (units of service, quantities of people served, etc.) and other program service accomplishments. (This limits the ability of one person to falsify program reports *and* create fraudulent supporting documents to substantiate the phony service levels.)
- Wherever possible, utilize documents that require signatures of program participants as a means of acknowledging that a service has been rendered.
- Require an independent review of reports that summarize program accomplishments. (This review should include making sure that program service levels are supported by listings of specific individuals served and cross-checking a sample of individuals on that listing with underlying files and supporting documentation to ensure that the service was actually provided.)
- Focus internal audit efforts on the preceding testing of program reporting.
- Perform ratio and other financial analyses of program service levels and monitor these ratios for trends over time. (For example, track reported

service levels in relation to numbers of employees or certain expense accounts for unusual fluctuations, which would indicate unrealistic levels of effort being reported; see Chapter 15 for more on financial and ratio analysis.)

ABUSE OF PRIVILEGES GRANTED
TO CHARITABLE ORGANIZATIONS

A wide variety of other acts carried out by nonprofit organizations, or by their employees and representatives, can be considered fraud or abuse and can result in liability for the organization. In this section, abuse of certain privileges granted to organizations as a result of their nonprofit status will be explored. There are many of these privileges available to nonprofits. Some tend to be more vulnerable to abuse than others, and this abuse can result in loss of the privilege as well as substantial financial liabilities. Those privileges most vulnerable to abuse are:

- An organization's sales tax exemption
- An organization's nonprofit postal mailing rate
- An organization's property tax exemption

Sales Tax Exemptions

Most nonprofit organizations, other than charitable groups, pay sales tax just like anyone else. Charitable organizations, however, may be eligible for two types of benefits relating to state sales taxes:

- Exemption from the requirement to pay sales tax on purchases
- Exemption from the requirement to assess, collect, and remit sales tax on sales to customers made by the organization

In either case, the laws and regulations dealing with these exemptions vary greatly from state to state. Especially with regard to the second issue (assessing sales tax on sales of products), the rules are particularly complicated, and the level of exemption granted to nonprofits varies significantly from one state to another. Some of the factors that may have an impact on whether an organization is required to assess sales tax include:

- The specific category of charitable organization involved (religious, health care, educational, etc.)
- The type of item sold
- The type of customer (i.e., is the item sold to the public, patients, doctors, etc.?)
- The frequency of sales

Organizations should not mistakenly assume that because a category of income is exempt from federal and state income taxes that it is also exempt from a requirement to assess sales taxes. The correlation between the two issues is very limited. Many sources of income that are exempt from the unrelated business income tax and/or state income and franchise taxes are nonetheless subject to sales taxes (i.e., the nonprofit must assess, collect, and then remit sales tax to the state).

Additionally, the final factor may be of importance to organizations that hold special fundraising events and activities that involve sales of products to the public. Many states have exemptions for sales of items that would otherwise require the assessment of sales taxes when the sale is infrequent or associated with occasional fundraising events. However, organizations should become familiar with the specific requirements in their jurisdictions prior to conducting any such fundraisers (even if the fundraising event is being handled by an outside fundraising firm, which will be acting as your agent). Though fraud is rarely asserted in failures to assess sales tax, repeated and willful ignorance of this requirement can result in substantial financial liabilities for nonprofit organizations.

The first sales tax issue is the more likely of the two issues to result in an assertion of intentional abuse and violation of state laws. Exemptions from the requirement to pay sales tax on purchases made by nonprofit organizations tend to be a bit broader than the exemptions from assessing sales tax. Most states provide exemptions for either certain specific categories of charitable organizations (particularly religious and educational) or for most or all charities. Again, noncharitable nonprofit organizations typically must pay sales tax.

To obtain an exemption from sales taxes, an organization generally must apply for an exemption certificate from each state in which it makes purchases. Once an exemption certificate is obtained, an organization must then comply with each state's restrictions on the use of their exemption. This is where the potential for fraud and abuse comes into play.

Though the specific rules vary from state to state, in general, the exemption from paying sales taxes applies only to purchases of items that will be used by the certificate-holding organization for exempt purposes. Accordingly, the two most common types of violations of sales tax exemptions by nonprofit organizations involve one or both of the following:

- Using the exemption to purchase items that will be used by an entity other than the certificate holder, such as a third party, an affiliated organization, or even an officer or employee
- Using the exemption to purchase items that will be used in an unrelated trade or business activity

As stated previously, failure to comply with a requirement to assess sales taxes can easily result from a simple oversight or lack of knowledge of the requirement, but violations of the rules dealing with paying sales taxes on purchases are much more likely to be attributable to *intentional* avoidance. When it is asserted that intentional noncompliance has taken place, penalties against an organization may involve:

- Payment of unpaid sales taxes
- Payment of interest on the unpaid taxes
- Assessment of additional penalties for noncompliance
- Revocation of the sales tax exemption certificate

To avoid such assertions and the resultant penalties, nonprofit organizations should take precautions to protect their sales tax exemptions through the establishment of policies and procedures designed to ensure compliance with applicable state laws and regulations. Some of the most important of these controls include:

- Restrict the issuance of the organization's sales tax exemption certificate (or copies of the certificate) to a limited number of purchasing personnel.
- Establish written policies regarding appropriate and inappropriate uses of sales tax exemption certificates.
- Distribute copies of the policies developed in the preceding step (or copies of the state laws and regulations) to each purchasing representative.
- Periodically update the organization's policies to reflect changes in state laws and regulations. (It is suggested that this review be performed annually, because many states make rather frequent changes to their sales tax rules or the application of those rules to nonprofits.)
- If your organization has affiliations with related organizations (such as other nonprofit organizations that have board members in common with your organization or taxable subsidiaries, joint ventures, and partnerships with other entities, etc.), establish a system that prohibits the organization from making purchases on behalf of those affiliates or that separately tracks all such purchases (and the reimbursement of those purchases) and prohibits the use of the organization's exemption certificate for those purchases.
- Require that all third-party vendors, other than those acting as agents of your organization (such as fundraising firms, in certain situations), make all purchases of items that will be used in serving your organization separately.
- Periodically review purchases charged to nonexempt functions (unrelated business activities, if any, and items purchased on behalf of employees) to determine that the organization did not utilize its sales tax exemption certificate to avoid paying taxes.

More information on sales taxes can be obtained from the Multistate Tax Commission. Their Web site (www.mtc.gov) includes sales tax registration forms for each state, as well as links to the sales tax Web sites of each state.

Nonprofit Mailing Rates

Some nonprofit organizations are eligible for substantially reduced postal rates from the U.S. Postal Service. Most charitable organizations are eligible, as are certain other groups.

Once a nonprofit organization has obtained recognition as a nonprofit mailer from the U.S. Postal Service, its mailings must conform to certain restrictions in order to be eligible for the reduced rates. There are three primary categories of mailings that are not eligible for the nonprofit rate:

- Cooperative mailings
- Announcements for certain travel programs, insurance policies, or credit cards and similar financial products
- Advertisements for products and services that are not substantially related to the organization's tax-exempt mission

The U.S. Postal Service may open samples of mailings prior to accepting and mailing the pieces, if nonprofit mailing rates are being claimed. As such, the service may reject mailings that do not comply with nonprofit mail guidelines. If an organization deceives the postal service in order to get ineligible mail accepted by the service (such as by making it appear that all pieces in a mailing are identical, when the contents differ from one envelope to another), the organization can be penalized and lose its nonprofit mailer permit.

Of particular potential for abuse is the rule prohibiting cooperative mailings. A cooperative mailing is one that a nonprofit permit holder mails on behalf of any unauthorized mailer. Just like the potential for abuse of an organization's sales tax exemption, unauthorized uses here may involve mailings for employees, vendors, other third parties, and affiliated entities.

In order to protect an organization from loss of its nonprofit mail permit, as well as assessments of additional postage for previous ineligible mailings, nonprofits should consider the following controls:

- Utilize an outside mailing vendor who specializes in nonprofit mail and has a current understanding of the nonprofit mailing rules.
- Restrict access to and use of the organization's nonprofit mailing permit to one person or a limited number of persons, all of whom have a current understanding of nonprofit mailing rules.
- Maintain current copies of applicable U.S. Postal Service guidelines (USPS Publication 417, etc.) in the organization's mailroom.
- Establish and circulate to all employees a documented policy statement regarding appropriate and inappropriate uses of the organization's nonprofit mailing permit.

Details on nonprofit mailing rates and qualifications for using these rates can be found in U.S. Postal Service Publication No. 417, *Nonprofit Standard Mail Eligibility*, as well as its *Domestic Mail Manual*. Another resource for nonprofit mailers is the Alliance for Nonprofit Mailers (www.nonprofit mailers.org), which monitors and reports on cases and interpretations of the nonprofit mailing regulations, as well as rate adjustments.

Property Tax Exemption

Much like the exemption from sales taxes, charitable organizations often qualify for exemption from state and local taxes on real property (land, buildings, and improvements) and personal property (auto, equipment, furniture, etc.). Rarely do noncharitable nonprofit groups qualify for these exemptions.

Also similar to the exemption from sales taxes, an organization's property tax exemption is conditional upon certain criteria that may be susceptible to abuse. Most notably, exemption is usually contingent upon a minimum of two factors:

- The real or personal property being titled in the name of the charitable organization eligible for the exemption
- The property being used exclusively for the charitable programs of the eligible organization

Accordingly, the most likely abuses of exemptions from real and personal property taxes are:

- Using the underlying (supposedly exempt) assets on noncharitable activities, especially if the activity is unrelated to the organization's charitable mission
- In cases in which a charity is affiliated with other organizations, claiming exemption for assets owned by affiliates (instead of the eligible charity) or claiming exemption for assets used, at least in part, for programs of the affiliated entities

The second issue has the potential for occurring under several different scenarios, such as when:

- A charity is affiliated with a noncharitable nonprofit organization (such as an educational foundation affiliated with a trade or professional association)
- A charity establishes a taxable subsidiary
- A charity forms a joint venture or partnership with other entities (whether those entities are charitable or not)

The sharing of real and personal property owned by a charity with any of the above listed affiliates can easily result in loss of exemption and a requirement to pay back taxes. In addition, the organization may be assessed interest charges on the unpaid taxes, as well as penalties for failure to properly report taxable property. These assessments can result even if the affiliated organization reimburses the charity a reasonable amount for its use (rental) of the property.

Of course, individual rules vary from jurisdiction to jurisdiction. But every organization with an exemption from real or personal property taxes should take the following measures to protect its exemptions:

- Inventory all personal property owned by the organization and maintain a listing of all inventoried assets (this may be part of the organization's fixed asset depreciation schedules used for accounting purposes, but it must also include fully depreciated assets that are still being used).

- As part of the inventory performed in the preceding step, identify the use of each asset as:

    - Used exclusively in charitable programs
    - Used exclusively in noncharitable programs
    - Mixed use by the organization
    - Shared use with affiliated organizations
    - Exclusive use by affiliated organizations

- Establish documented policies regarding the claiming of exemptions from taxes on personal and real property that conform to state and local laws for the jurisdiction in which the organization is situated (including policies that address multijurisdictional locations when an organization has more than one office).

- Use the preceding listings to prepare the organization's property tax returns.

- Perform a review of property tax returns prior to filing to ensure that only eligible property is claimed for exemption and/or that property not qualifying for exemption is reported as taxable.

- Establish a policy whereby the asset listings described in the preceding steps are reviewed and updated each year to reflect changes in use of assets.

- If assets owned by a charity but used by or shared with affiliates can potentially endanger the overall exemption for the charity (i.e., even the fully charitable-use assets could lose exemption), consider transferring the mixed-use assets to the affiliate and have the affiliate pay property taxes on those assets while the charity maintains exemption for the charitable-use assets.

INTENTIONAL VIOLATIONS OF OTHER LAWS

Nonprofit organizations are expected to comply with a wide variety of federal, state, and local laws. Many of these laws are complex and easy to violate unintentionally. Some are prone to intentional violation for many of the same reasons explained earlier. Of the many laws to which an organization may be subject, two jump out as being especially vulnerable to intentional avoidance: the Fair Labor Standards Act and the Copyright Act. Violations of these laws could result in the possibility of huge financial liabilities for an organization.

Of course, there are many other acts that could be considered as well. The area of employment law is certainly one of the most significant of these areas. However, employment law is simply beyond the scope of this book, so our attention will focus briefly on the Fair Labor Standards Act and Copyright Act violations.

Fair Labor Standards Act

Nonprofit organizations must comply with a variety of employment laws. At the federal level, there are the Americans with Disabilities Act, Civil Rights Act, Age Discrimination in Employment Act, Occupational Safety & Health Act, Family and Medical Leave Act, and several others. In addition, organizations must be familiar with state employment laws, which may differ from or be more stringent than federal laws.

Of all the federal employment laws, the one that is most appropriate to discuss in this book is the Fair Labor Standards Act (FLSA). The reasons are simple. Unlike most other employment laws, which are designed to ensure that employees are treated fairly, FLSA directly impacts compensation paid to employees for their hours worked. Accordingly, any intentional violation of FLSA results from an attempt to avoid a known financial liability, which certainly fits our definition of fraud.

The objectives of FLSA are very straightforward. However, interpretation of its provisions are anything but. The section of FLSA that is most likely to result in accusations of intentional noncompliance is the section dealing with payment of overtime to hourly workers. (Incidentally, FLSA also addresses child labor rules, minimum wages, certain recordkeeping requirements, and other provisions.) In particular, two provisions of FLSA are most likely to be violated:

- The classification of workers as exempt (meaning they are salaried and not subject to overtime pay) or nonexempt (hourly)
- The calculation of hours worked by nonexempt employees

If an employee is nonexempt, the employer is required to pay that worker their regular rate of pay times one and one-half for all overtime (work in excess of 40 hours) during any consecutive seven-day work week. (Nonprofits should be aware that individual state laws also may address overtime and some of those laws are stricter than FLSA, in which case an employer must comply with the stricter of each law's provisions.)

Noncompliance with FLSA can result in three forms of financial liability for an employer:

- Payment of back wages to each affected employee (i.e., compensate employees for hours worked that were previously not counted and/or the 50 percent overtime premium for hours worked in excess of 40)
- Penalties of $1,000 per violation if it is determined that an employer willfully or repeatedly violated FLSA
- Liquidated damages, which generally equal the basic liability for violating FLSA (thus, the organization pays double what its liability would be had it compensated the employees correctly in the first place)

Before going any further, it should be pointed out that most violations of FLSA likely result from *unintentional* noncompliance. Much judgment is required when applying provisions of FLSA to a workforce, especially in the area of classifying workers as exempt or nonexempt. Several exemptions are provided from FLSA, including executive, administrative, and professional employees. But application of the specific descriptions associated with each of these exemptions requires a great deal of judgment. It is probably not an exaggeration to say that most employers have some degree of exposure resulting from the misclassification of nonexempt (hourly) workers as exempt (salaried).

Because the goal of this book is to control liability associated with intentional acts of wrongdoing, emphasis will be placed on policies and procedures designed to prevent and detect willful noncompliance with FLSA. To this end, the following controls should be considered:

- Document and maintain accurate, current job descriptions. (Periodically review job descriptions that have been around for a while.)
- Establish FLSA-compliant policies for classifying employees as exempt or nonexempt.
- Periodically perform an internal audit of exempt vs. nonexempt classifications of employees.
- Document FLSA-compliant policies regarding the determination of work hours (i.e., under what conditions employees should be compensated for travel time, training, lunch periods, etc.).
- Require that employees prepare timesheets that account for all hours worked and that provide an accurate and complete description of the work performed.

FRAUD IN THE HEADLINES 10.2

NONPROFIT AND ITS PRESIDENT PENALIZED FOR WILLFUL VIOLATION OF FLSA

To demonstrate the reality of the application of FLSA to nonprofits and the potential for penalties resulting from intentional violations, organizations need look no further than one recent court decision. In January 2001 a court ruled in favor of the Department of Labor, which sued a nonprofit nursing home *and* the home's president and CEO.

The nursing home and its president were ordered to make payments to compensate employees for unpaid wages and overtime, plus liquidated damages, for violating FLSA. Specific violations cited in the suit included:

- Failure to pay for training time that counts as hours worked under FLSA
- Failure to pay overtime for shifts exceeding 40 hours
- Failure to compensate employees for half of the lunch hour that employees could not take because they were required to perform certain job duties

Liquidated damages equal to the basic liability resulting from each of the preceding violations were also awarded.

One of the important elements illustrated by this case is the fact that the existence of a corporation as an employer does *not* preclude a determination that an individual also constitutes an employer of the same workers for purposes of FLSA. Simply having control over payroll matters or having supervisory responsibility over employees will generally not create this type of personal liability. But, in this case, the court determined that the president had significant ownership interest in the nursing home and personal responsibility for the decisions that led to the conduct which violated FLSA. Generally, FLSA defines an employer to include "any person acting directly or indirectly in the interest of an employer in relation to an employee."

Source: Herman v. Hogar Praderas de Amor, D. PR., Civ. No. 98-1342 (HL), January 25, 2001.

Copyright Act

The Copyright Act, Title 17 of the U.S. Code, provides the owner of a copyright the exclusive rights to reproduce the copyrighted work and to distribute copies of the copyrighted work. A variety of works can be protected under the

Copyright Act, including written materials (articles, books, periodicals, etc.), music, software, and other materials.

Nonprofit organizations must be careful not to violate the Copyright Act by using copyrighted works on their Web sites, in their written materials, or during their fundraising events (such as with unauthorized playing of copyrighted music).

A growing concern in recent years is the piracy of software. Software piracy includes making and distributing counterfeit versions of software, unbundling of software, and renting software without authorization from the copyright holder.

However, the most likely intentional act of piracy in nonprofit organizations that have purchased software involves softloading. Softloading occurs when a purchaser of a single-user software license subsequently loads the software onto multiple computers or servers. The unauthorized computers are most likely to be additional workstations at the office of the organization or personal computers at employees' homes. If a nonprofit organization intends for multiple employees to use a particular software, each computer must have a licensed version of that software.

Softloading constitutes a violation of the Copyright Act. Penalties for violating the act include liability for any damages suffered by the copyright owner plus any profits of the infringer that are attributable to the copying, or statutory damages of up to $100,000 for each work infringed. In addition, unauthorized duplication of software is also a federal crime if it is done "willfully and for purposes of commercial advantage or private financial gain." (Title 18 Section 2319(b).) Criminal penalties include fines of up to $250,000 and up to five years in prison.

The preceding rules and penalties apply equally regardless of whether the software involved is a $25 game or a $10,000 accounting package. The software industry estimates that piracy costs the industry more than $10 billion annually. Each year, millions of dollars in penalties are assessed against businesses for software piracy.

Making unauthorized copies of software can be quite tempting from either a personal standpoint or from the perspective of attempting to save an organization much-needed money. Therefore, every organization should attempt to control software piracy, as well as other copyright violations. The following list presents some of the useful controls to prevent softloading:

- Centralize the purchasing and custody of all software with one person or a limited number of employees.
- Document and distribute to all employees a policy prohibiting the copying of software from one office computer to another or from an office computer to a home computer.

- Periodically test each computer in the office for the existence of unauthorized software (i.e., make sure the software on each computer is a licensed copy).

FRAUD AND OTHER ILLEGAL ACTS COMMITTED THROUGH AN ORGANIZATION

Most of the acts described in this chapter thus far are acts committed by or for a nonprofit organization. Some serve a dual purpose of benefiting someone personally as well as the organization, while a few may serve a purely personal interest.

The final section of this chapter is devoted to a few additional acts that can be carried out through a nonprofit organization for the sole purpose of personal gain by the perpetrator. These acts have no intended benefits for the organization.

The most common of these fraudulent or abusive acts involve:

- Using credit card or bank account information of donors, members, or other program participants to fraudulently make personal purchases
- Taking the preceding fraud one step further, stealing the identities of donors, members, or others based on access to personal information, then incurring large debts in the names of the persons whose identities have been stolen

In other cases, an employee is not seeking financial gain but, instead, some other goal. For instance, some employees are put in a position of trust with respect to vulnerable individuals and then they abuse that trust by mistreating the individuals in their care.

Examples of both types of situations are illustrated in Chapter 11. Also in Chapter 11 is a discussion of the primary methods for preventing such frauds. The most useful of these methods involves performing background checks of all potential new hires who:

- Will have access to financial or personal information of an organization's donors, employees, members, or other program participants
- Will be in a position of trust with respect to vulnerable populations of persons served by the organization, such as children, the elderly, individuals with developmental disabilities, and so forth

See Chapter 11 for details on conducting background checks.

In addition to the preventive measures explained in Chapter 11, an organization should take appropriate detective measures to uncover frauds and abusive actions carried out by its employees against others. Detective measures in this area primarily involve being aware of the warning signals of fraud and abuse. This awareness is enhanced through strong communications systems, such as hotlines and customer complaint systems, as explained in Chapter 12.

Other detective measures that will help protect vulnerable populations include random, on-site inspections of employees and work areas. Unannounced inspections (or use of surveillance cameras, where appropriate), in addition to detecting some of these acts, have the added effect of serving as a preventive measure when they are well-communicated, because the potential perpetrators are aware that they may get caught in the act.

PART IV

THE ROLES OF NONFINANCIAL SYSTEMS AND CONTROLS

Parts II and III focused on the financial controls that are useful in preventing or detecting specific types of fraud and abuse. In Part IV, we turn our attention to the second interrelated component in our model of fraud deterrence. The nonfinancial systems described in Part IV rarely address specific types of fraud and abuse. Rather, certain nonfinancial systems play an integral role in an organization's overall deterrence of fraud and abuse. The most important of these nonfinancial systems are:

- Human resource systems, including hiring, training, performance evaluations, compensation adjustments, grievance policies, and counseling, which are covered in Chapter 11
- Administrative systems, such as security over physical premises and confidential information, information technology systems, insurance and risk assessments, and communications systems, all of which are addressed in Chapter 12.

Administrative systems such as these do not receive nearly enough credit for their role in deterring fraud and abuse. While these systems are not responsible for preventing or detecting many specific acts of fraud or abuse, they nonetheless are a critical element of an organization's efforts to establish and maintain a fraud-free environment.

11

Human Resource Policies and Procedures

Human resource systems play a direct role in deterring fraud and abuse. Unlike financial controls, which concern policies and procedures primarily associated with the processing of transactions, human resource policies and procedures deal with the people processing those transactions.

We've all heard the expression, "Where there's a will, there's a way." Nowhere is that statement truer than with internal fraud. Employees gain an intimate understanding of the financial policies and procedures associated with their functions. If there is a weakness in the financial controls, no one is better suited to identify this fact than the employees themselves. Given enough time to study an organization's processes, employees can often figure out a way to commit fraud.

In order to conceive of the role human resources play in deterring fraud and abuse, refer back to the discussion in Chapter 2 regarding the factors present in all frauds. Recall that a real or perceived opportunity (i.e., a weakness in financial controls) is only one of those factors. The others are a motive to commit fraud and subsequent rationalization of the fraudulent actions.

Here is where human resource systems can become an asset in the fight against fraud and abuse. Many of the policies that will be explained in this chapter can directly or indirectly reduce some of these motives or rationalizations. Others serve to identify personnel that may pose a risk of committing fraud.

The discussion of human resource systems and their role in deterring fraud and abuse in this chapter is organized based on the following functions:

- Hiring practices
- New employee orientation
- Leave policies
- Training
- Performance evaluation systems
- Compensation adjustment policies
- Grievance policies
- Counseling and other employee assistance
- Exit interviews

Each of these human resource functions should be considered an important element of not just managing an organization, but of its organization-wide system of fraud prevention.

HIRING PRACTICES

Much can be done in the hiring process to screen out applicants who pose a greater risk of fraud. Had some simple steps been carried out in the employment screening process, many organizations could have saved themselves the headache and financial loss that comes with employee fraud and abuse.

Five employment screening practices that are most likely to be helpful in deterring fraud are:

- Criminal background checks
- Identity verification
- Other public records searches
- Honesty testing
- Qualification verification

Criminal Background Checks

If a potential employee is being considered for a position of trust and authority within an organization, for example, in the accounting department or as a department head, it is important to consider the risk or likelihood that that person will commit fraud against the organization or engage in other detrimental acts, such as workplace violence, drinking, or substance abuse. One of the considerations in making this assessment should be whether the person has prior convictions for criminal activity.

While some courts have ruled that it is discriminatory to automatically deny employment based on the existence of a criminal record in certain circumstances, it is usually acceptable to consider a past criminal history, along with all other pertinent facts, when making certain types of employment decisions, such as those involving the handling of funds and financial records or those involving employees who will work with vulnerable populations. The employer in Fraud in the Headlines 11.1 certainly would have benefited from knowing that its applicant had a criminal history.

There are a few important things to keep in mind before embarking on a policy of conducting criminal background checks. First, limit inquiries to those positions to which a criminal history could be relevant (e.g., financial positions and certain others). Searching for larceny, burglary, and similar financial offenses is relevant for many financial positions, as well as home care workers. Searching for sexual offenses is relevant (and required in certain instances) for many positions involving work with children, individuals with developmental disabilities, and certain other populations. In addition, if a past criminal record is found, you may want to consider the time of the offense and the individual's age at the time.

Next, consult state laws applicable in your area. State laws vary quite a bit. Some states permit a considerable amount of criminal background checking. Others require that consideration of past convictions be limited to crimes that are relevant to the job or that consideration of criminal histories be limited to specific positions or for specific time periods.

Finally, establish and follow policies regarding who has access to information obtained from criminal background checks, how this information is stored, and how and when it is to be destroyed when it is no longer needed. The sensitivity of the information included in these reports warrants extra care and protection from unnecessary disclosure.

FRAUD IN THE HEADLINES 11.1

FAILURE TO DO BACKGROUND CHECKS RESULTS IN LOSSES

Remember the wire transfer fraud described in Chapter 4, the one involving the Ohio chapter of the American Cancer Society? After the organization's former chief administrative officer admitted to embezzling $6.9 million via a fraudulent wire transfer among other charges, the chapter announced that it was unaware of one major fact when it first hired the officer five years earlier. In 1987 and 1988, he was sentenced to two prison terms in Hawaii for credit card fraud. In 1992, he also admitted taking $20,000 from the Maui Foodbank, where he served as executive director.

Source: The Chronicle of Philanthropy, September 7, 2000, and starbulletin.com (Honolulu Star Bulletin), August 25, 2000.

In addition to identifying persons convicted of crimes prior to making them a job offer, conducting criminal background checks may have two other benefits:

- Some insurance companies offer discounts on premiums to organizations that perform these checks prior to employment.
- Informing applicants of the organization's policy regarding criminal background checks may discourage applicants with something to hide from attempting to apply in the first place.

Determining whether an applicant has a criminal background is not as easy as it sounds. Private employers usually do not have access to government databases of criminal records, and there are more than 10,000 federal and state courthouses and 3,200 jurisdictions in the United States that could be searched. Deciding which of these sources will be checked, and then following up by visiting each source, can be a time-consuming process.

There are, however, many vendors that offer reasonably comprehensive criminal background check services. Typing the words "background checks" into any search engine on the Internet will produce numerous options for this service. Most of these services are quite affordable, ranging from a few dollars to fees in the hundreds of dollars for extensive searches. A few things to keep in mind when using these services:

- Most searches are done by state, county, or other locale, meaning that if someone has been convicted of a crime in a different state than the one you searched, it may not show up in the search.
- There are legal limitations regarding how long these services may report convictions (often seven years), so older convictions may not appear in a search.
- Available records are generally limited to convictions and pending cases, so arrests without conviction will not appear, and there are limits on the reporting of misdemeanors.
- Mistaken identities can occur, resulting in the assumption that an applicant has a criminal background when, in fact, he or she does not. (See the next section on other public records searches and identity verification.)

Also, the organization should be clear as to what types of offenses are being researched. There are three broad categories of criminal offenses:

- Felonies
- Misdemeanors
- Infractions

Felonies are the most serious offense. Some offenses can be classified as either a felony or a misdemeanor. Some very serious offenses can be classified as misdemeanors, such as assaults and certain sexual offenses. In addition, it is not unusual for a felony charge to be plea-bargained down to a misdemeanor. Accordingly, some serious offenses may be overlooked if a search is limited to felonies.

One additional consideration with criminal background checks is that they are covered under the Fair Credit Reporting Act (FCRA) if they are performed by an outside agency. (Internally conducted checks are not subject to FCRA, but can be extremely time-consuming and costly.) They also may be covered under specific state laws. To fully comply with FCRA, an organization should follow certain guidelines before obtaining a criminal background check:

- Certify to the reporting agency that the organization is in compliance with FCRA and that it will not improperly use the information it receives in the report.
- Disclose to the applicant (or employee, if a background check is being performed after someone has already been hired), on a form separate from the employment application, that the organization plans to obtain a background check and that the report will be used exclusively for employment purposes.
- Obtain written authorization from the applicant (or employee).
- Inform the applicant (employee) that he or she has the right to request additional information on the nature of the report or means through which the information will be obtained.
- Inform the applicant (employee) that the report may contain information obtained from personal interviews regarding the person's character, reputation, and personal characteristics.
- Provide the applicant (employee) with a summary of his or her rights under FCRA.

If the organization decides not to offer employment to a particular applicant (or decides to terminate an existing employee) based on information obtained in the background check, the organization must do the following:

- Inform the applicant (employee) of its decision.
- Provide the applicant (employee) with a copy of the report.
- Inform the applicant (employee) that, under FCRA, he or she is entitled to dispute any inaccurate or incomplete data included in the report.

Despite these limits and restrictions, nonprofit organizations should perform criminal background checks, at least with respect to certain positions. The value of performing these searches only becomes apparent when an organization fails to perform them.

Identity Verification

In addition to checking whether an applicant has a history of criminal convictions, there are two other uses for background checks:

- To verify the identity of an applicant
- To determine whether there is any other public information that provides insight into an applicant's character

Identity verification has become an absolute requirement for employers, particularly when hiring individuals for positions of trust, such as chief financial officers, executive directors, and department heads. As Fraud in the Headlines 11.2 illustrates, failing to verify an applicant's identity may have serious or even disastrous consequences.

Similar to criminal background checks, identity verification services are available from a variety of vendors. Typing the words "identity verification" into any search engine on the Internet will identify many vendors, such as:

- InstantID, a Web-based service of LexisNexis located at www.lexisnexis.com/riskwise/instantid/
- Verify Ids, located at www.verifyids.com or by calling (866) 837-4397

Identity verification services rely primarily on the cross-checking among multiple databases for consistency in data provided by an applicant. Inconsistencies in data, such as driver's license number, address, social security number, or other information may indicate a risk of phony or stolen identification.

Some providers of identity verification services also offer criminal background checks and other public records searches useful in assessing an applicant's background.

Other Public Records Searches

In addition to searches for criminal records and identity verification services, other publicly available records that may provide insight into an applicant's character and background include:

- Driving records and traffic cases
- Bankruptcy records
- Credit records
- Civil and domestic suit records
- Sexual offender records

FRAUD IN THE HEADLINES 11.2

THE IMPORTANCE OF VERIFYING IDENTITIES OF NEW HIRES

Even when background checks on new hires are performed, employers may still be subject to the risk that they are not hiring who they think they are.

In August 2002, it came to the attention of the State of Indiana that the chief benefits officer of the state's $11 billion Public Employees' Retirement Fund was a convicted felon. The officer pleaded guilty in 1996 in U.S. District Court for the Southern District of Ohio to two counts of bank and mail fraud after admitting to stealing the identities and Social Security numbers of two people. As chief benefits officer of the state's retirement fund, he had access to more than 200,000 Social Security numbers of working and retired public employees.

So how did this happen, when the State reportedly performed a criminal history check on the officer when he was hired?

The officer graduated from Ohio State University with a law degree in 1993. He went to work for Procter & Gamble Company upon graduation. His resume stated that he stayed with Procter & Gamble until accepting a new position with Cook, Incorporated in January 1997. He then worked for Cook until 2001. In late 2001, he came to work for the State of Indiana. The problem: He served time in prison from November 15, 1996 to January 10, 1997, during which time his resume states that he was still working for Procter & Gamble. Evidently, there were also inconsistencies on his resume as to the nature of the positions he held with his previous employers.

Making matters even more complicated, he used the Social Security number of a different person with the same name when applying for his job with the state. By doing so, he passed his criminal background check.

Whether a more detailed review of his resume would have revealed his lies is difficult to say with certainty. But, unlike the standard employment application form used for most other State jobs in Indiana, the application form used by the Public Employees' Retirement Fund did not specifically ask applicants to answer a question as to whether or not they had ever been convicted of a crime.

Source: McNeil Solida, Michele, "Felon Helped Run State Fund," *The Indianapolis Star*, August 15, 2002.

Searches of driving records may reveal signs of substance abuse problems (if there are driving under the influence citations) or problems controlling stress. Bankruptcy records and credit reports can provide signs of financial stresses, a key motivator to commit fraud. Civil and domestic suit records also may reveal either financial or personal problems.

The final category, sexual offender records, may be included in a criminal background check, but some background checking vendors offer searches of sexual offender records as a separate service. This service, of course, should be utilized (and is likely a condition of government funding) by nonprofit organizations serving children, victims of abuse, and many other populations.

FRAUD IN THE HEADLINES 11.3

SEX OFFENDER MANAGES SHELTER, RESULTING IN SUIT AGAINST NONPROFIT

A registered sex offender managed a nonprofit house for young adult mental health clients for more than two years before finally being terminated amid a growing controversy. The sex offender was hired about one year after being paroled from state prison in 1996, where he served seven years of a 16-year sentence for molesting a boy.

Seven young adults and one parent filed suit against the sex offender in 2000, but also against the nonprofit organization that hired him in 1997. The suit stated that the sex offender engaged in a variety of offenses, such as forcing young women to have sex with people he knew, extortion of money, and threatening to kill or rape residents.

The suit accuses two nonprofit organizations involved of negligence, fraud, physical and emotional abuse, breach of privacy, and false imprisonment. The suit claims that the two nonprofit organizations concealed information about the sex offender. It was unclear whether the agencies checked the background of the sex offender or whether they were aware of his stay in the state prison. However, the suit claimed that one of the nonprofit organizations told clients that the offender was a licensed psychotherapist with 15 years of counseling and therapeutic experience.

As it turns out, the man's 1988 conviction that resulted in his seven-year stay in prison was not his first sexual offense. He was in high school in the 1970s when he was first convicted of molestation, then was convicted again in 1981.

Source: Spears, Larry, and Scott Marshall, "Molester Managed Shelter," CNN.com, June 20, 2000.

Honesty Testing

Another potentially helpful step in the employment screening process is the administration of so-called honesty tests to applicants. As the name suggests, the purpose of honesty testing is to assess an applicant's attitudes toward theft and other acts of wrongdoing as a method of predicting future dishonest behavior by that individual.

Honesty tests attempt to make this determination based on a series of questions that fall into four categories:

- Admission of illegal or unacceptable activities
- Opinions toward illegal or inappropriate activities
- Descriptions of the test taker's own personality or beliefs
- Reactions to theoretical and/or hypothetical situations

The number of employers that utilize honesty tests or some other form of preemployment testing has continued to increase in recent years. A 1999 article published by the Society for Human Resource Management (SHRM) reported that 20 percent of SHRM members used some form of preemployment testing.

Recall from Part I that a 1998 survey found that 36 percent of workers observed coworkers lying on reports or falsifying records, and 45 percent observed lying to supervisors. With so much lying going on, and some of it related to employees attempting to conceal fraud and abuse, wouldn't it be great if we could determine who the dishonest people were prior to hiring them?

Unfortunately, no honesty test is foolproof. But advocates of honesty testing claim that the tests work for one simple reason: Dishonest people tend to rationalize their behavior (much like fraudsters rationalize their actions, as noted in Chapter 2). For instance, less honest people are more likely to indicate a higher tolerance for dishonest behavior, and are more likely to come up with excuses for dishonest behavior. These characteristics can be brought to light in a well-designed and properly administered test. The Association of Personnel Test Publishers Model Guidelines include the following factors that should be considered when selecting a test instrument:

- Select testing programs that are professionally developed and validated.
- Use testing programs only for the purpose for which the tests are designed.
- Administer tests in a proper testing environment.
- Train qualified testing personnel to administer the program and to handle and protect all forms of relevant employment data.
- Select testing programs that are fair to protected subgroups in the population.
- Provide and enforce written guidelines on all matters related to test security and confidentiality.

Verifying Qualifications

Another common employment-related scheme is qualifications fraud, which occurs when an applicant intentionally misstates his or her qualifications or other pertinent background information in a resume or job application. The most common qualifications frauds misstate:

- Educational achievements
- Licenses and certifications
- Prior salaries
- Depth of experience in a particular position

Due to the rapid rise in qualifications fraud, nonprofit employers should establish policies requiring that qualifications be verified as part of the employment screening process. Education, certification, and salary information can usually be verified quite easily by:

- Independent verification (i.e., contacting a university to verify graduation, an association to verify a certification, or a government agency to verify a license)
- Examining documents provided by the applicant (a paystub or W-2 Form to verify prior salaries; a current, valid license (see Best Practices 7.2 for tips on recognizing phony licenses), or certification, etc.)

Failure to verify qualifications of job applicants, particularly those who will be placed in positions of trust or who will be providing services to the public, places an organization in a position of unnecessary risk. Even if people who lie about their qualifications do not directly commit fraud (although a notable number of fraud perpetrators have been known to lie about their qualifications in order to get into the position necessary to commit their fraud), when qualifications fraud becomes public knowledge, the damage to the organization's reputation can be significant. This is particularly true when it is discovered that unqualified persons have been working with the public or vulnerable populations.

NEW EMPLOYEE ORIENTATION

After all of an organization's preemployment screening is completed and a person is hired, the next step in the fight against fraud occurs during the new employee orientation process. An important part of new employee orientation is to establish a tone of intolerance toward fraud and abuse. This can be done by covering each of the following topics in a reasonable amount of depth during the orientation:

- Go over the organization's code of conduct (especially the discussion and definitions of what actions constitute violations of the code of conduct or other unacceptable behavior).
- Explain the organization's physical security measures.
- List the recordkeeping and documentation expectations for every employee (timesheets, expense reports, etc.).
- Inform new employees about the availability of hotlines and other communications systems in place so that they may report suspected fraud and abuse (see Chapter 12).
- Stress the importance of a fraud-free environment to the organization and its reputation.

While most of the employee orientation may be delivered by a human resources representative, the final point may be best delivered by the executive director or other member of the senior management team. There is no better time for senior management to personally communicate the importance of ethical behavior than in the orientation process.

A similar orientation process should be established for new volunteers. Although the volunteer orientation may be a bit less comprehensive than that for employees, many of the fraud-related elements are the same and should be incorporated into this orientation.

LEAVE POLICIES

The term "leave" applies to compensated absences as well as unpaid leaves of absence. Accordingly, organizations should establish leave policies in connection with everything from vacation, sick and personal leave that is compensated, to leave that falls under the Family and Medical Leave Act (FMLA), and other unpaid leaves of absence. Leave policies and practices play two roles in controlling fraud and abuse:

- Satisfactory leave policies result in a more content work force that is less likely to reach a point of discontent that causes employees to respond with acts of fraud or abuse.
- Requiring mandatory use of paid leave provides an opportunity for the detection of fraud during an employee's absence.

The first point reflects a component of an organization's overall attempt to establish and maintain a satisfying work environment for its employees. Though it's impossible to assign any rates, percentages, or probabilities to it, a stressful and ungratifying work environment certainly leads to dissatisfaction among employees, and such dissatisfaction may be one factor that, when combined with other personal factors and motives, prompts an individual to alter his or her behavior. Dissatisfaction and stress can lead otherwise honest people to do some very dishonest things.

Recall from the introduction in Part I that it is rarely one factor that turns someone into a criminal. Being dissatisfied with an employer's leave policy is certainly no justification for committing fraud against that employer. Nor will this dissatisfaction, by itself, be the cause of the fraud. But, as an individual's circumstances change over time, any combination of factors may cause the person to change his or her mind about the acceptability of committing a particular dishonest act. And that is often where a fraud scheme begins.

The second point, enforcing the use of vacation time, is extremely important to fraud detection. Mandatory vacations are often cited, but rarely understood, as a fraud detection method. Many of the fraud schemes explained in this book require that the perpetrator be vigilant in his or her concealment of the scheme. In some cases, sophisticated recordkeeping is required in order to properly conceal a fraud. In addition, the factor that may allow a fraud scheme to be carried out in the first place is a lack of involvement in a transaction cycle by other employees.

For these reasons, it is imperative that organizations require the mandatory use of paid leave by all employees. Simply having a use it or lose it philosophy is not enough. The perpetrator may be making more money through their fraud scheme than the value of their paid vacation!

But there's a right way and a wrong way to handle leave. The wrong way is to allow an employee's work to pile up while they're off on vacation or sick leave. The right way is to have another employee handle the nonworking employee's duties while that person is on leave.

If an employee committing internal fraud against her employer knows that nobody will be filling in for her while she is on leave, it's the equivalent of providing paid leave to a criminal! Some perpetrators have gone to extreme lengths to make sure that nobody does their job while they are away. They often make it impossible for someone to fill in, perhaps claiming that all of their functions are either too complicated or are in some stage of partial completion. Others have gone to the extreme of locking everything up in filing cabinets to which no other employee has access. (I encountered one situation in which the fraudster locked up her files, computer, and office door while she went on vacation, and left strict instructions that nobody disturb her office while she was away—and everybody, her boss included, obeyed her request!) Sometimes a perpetrator will put forth more effort to conceal the fraud scheme than is expected in doing the work he or she was hired to do!

Therefore, it is important that while personnel are on paid leave, some other employee fill in, at least with respect to the routine processing functions. In order to do this effectively and efficiently, the following steps should be followed:

- Maintain current job descriptions for all personnel.
- Prepare and maintain written documentation of all important policies and procedures followed in each employee's job function.

- Formally assign backups for each key function, so that in times of unexpected absences (illness) or planned absences (vacation), there is a clear understanding of who is expected to fill in and how the absent person's tasks are to be divided up.
- Provide appropriate levels of cross-training to all personnel who are expected to serve as backups and fill-ins during absences.

Last, but not least: Make sure that employees serving as fill-ins and backups know that they are expected to report to their supervisor or other appropriate person anything unusual that they notice while filling in for another employee. This may be one of the few opportunities to become aware of warning signals that indicate something inappropriate may be going on. Make sure that it does not go to waste.

TRAINING

Employee training serves two roles as a deterrent to fraud:

1. As a benefit to employees designed to provide a greater degree of self-satisfaction through the achievement of new technical skills and qualifications useful in their jobs; and
2. As a method of increasing awareness of fraud and specific techniques useful in preventing or detecting fraud.

Each of these uses for training is fairly self-explanatory. But their importance should not be underemphasized. Just like many of the other factors that contribute to dissatisfaction in an organization's work force, inadequate job or technical training results in employees feeling unfairly treated. Often, a lack of skills training makes employees feel that they are being asked to perform at a level beyond their skills and with inadequate tools and resources. Resentment and feelings of being undercompensated and unfairly treated inevitably follow.

The second use of training, increasing awareness of fraud and promoting prevention, is more easily recognizable as fraud deterrence. Fraud-related training should be provided to employees in the following manner:

- Provide annual reeducation on the organization's code of conduct and other fraud-related policies and their importance to the organization.
- Require mandatory attendance at fraud awareness training (i.e., how to recognize signs of fraud and the importance of reporting it).
- Stress specific fraud detection skills applicable to particular employees.

The final training category may not necessarily apply to all employees. Rather, an organization should assess which employees are in positions where this type of training might be particularly useful in the organization's fight against fraud and abuse.

PERFORMANCE EVALUATION SYSTEMS

A 1992 research project conducted by James Patterson and Peter Kim concluded that approximately one-half of workers in the United States feel that the way to get ahead at work is through politics and cheating rather than through hard work. This shocking statistic illustrates the importance of fair performance evaluation systems. Clearly, if workers feel that cheating is one of the primary methods to get ahead, then one of the principal motivators of occupational fraud and abuse is already in place.

From a fraud deterrence perspective only, the most important elements of an organization's performance evaluation system are:

- Establishing accurate, current, comprehensive job descriptions
- Establishing and articulating clear performance standards and expectations, particularly requirements for promotion to the next level or to another position
- Designing and requiring training on performance evaluation for all persons who are expected to prepare evaluations (training should be on both the organization's specific criteria and policies, as well as on performance evaluations in general)
- Making the preparation and delivery of proper performance evaluations one of the documented elements of managerial job descriptions for all persons expected to conduct such evaluations (i.e., this should not be something that they are expected to squeeze in during the evenings)
- Establishing a comprehensive and consistent format to be used in the documentation of performance evaluations
- Where applicable, developing methods for soliciting input from multiple supervisors (for employees who interact with multiple departments or who serve multiple bosses)
- Establishing a system for reviews of performance appraisals prepared by supervisors prior to delivery to employees (i.e., require that the supervisor's supervisor review each documented performance evaluation prior to delivery)
- Establishing and following standards for the delivery of performance evaluations to employees (do not allow one supervisor to meet with employees in his office during work hours while another supervisor takes her employees to lunch for their evaluations)
- Establishing systems for direct or anonymous feedback from employees regarding their thoughts on how they have been evaluated and what they think of their immediate supervisor

Many organizations claim to have each of the preceding elements in place, yet they continue to be frustrated by accusations of unfair performance evaluations. This is usually a result of noncompliance with the policies by supervisors or inconsistent application of the policies from one department or supervisor to another.

Accordingly, organizations should establish systems for monitoring compliance with these policies. For organizations large enough to have a separate human resources department, this is a perfect duty. Smaller organizations should nonetheless appoint someone to oversee this process.

COMPENSATION ADJUSTMENT POLICIES

Closely related to an organization's performance evaluation system is its system for adjusting compensation and awarding bonuses or other incentives to employees. Feeling unfairly compensated has been cited on numerous occasions as one of the key factors that led someone to commit fraud against their employer. An effective compensation adjustment system is one that is perceived as treating all employees fairly. (See Best Practices 11.1 for some sources of information on comparing your organization's salaries and benefits with those of others.) An effective system employs some of the same elements as the model for performance evaluation systems explained in the preceding section.

Feeling underpaid for the effort is one thing. Feeling singled out or not given a fair shake in the process is something else entirely. Organizations should strive for compensation adjustment systems that incorporate the following elements:

- Periodic comparisons of salaries and benefits offered by the organization with those of similar organizations, using salary and benefit surveys or direct contact with other nonprofits
- Organization-wide standards or formulas for determining ranges of salary increases or bonuses (for example, high–low salaries for each level of employment, what portion of the salary adjustment will correspond to an employee's performance evaluation versus across-the-board adjustments, etc.)
- Involvement of multiple people in the compensation adjustment process (for example, formation of a compensation committee)
- Review and approval of all salary adjustments and performance bonuses by the executive director, the board, or some person other than the one primarily responsible for initially determining the compensation
- Proper documentation of compensation adjustments and performance bonuses in each employee's personnel file
- Consistent manner of communicating bonuses and compensation adjustments to all employees

BEST PRACTICES 11.1

SALARY AND BENEFIT SURVEYS

Nonprofit organizations can turn to a variety of sources for comparative salary and benefits information. Among these are:

- Local, state, and national associations of nonprofit organizations (many of which are geared toward a specific type of nonprofit, such as associations, hospitals, etc.)
- Personnel recruiting and consulting firms, such as Towers Perrin, that compile and publish salary and benefit data
- Periodicals, such as *The Chronicle of Philanthropy* and *The NonProfit Times*, which publish salary studies each year
- GuideStar, the organization that compiles copies of the annual Form 990s filed by charitable organizations, also studies compensation reported on these returns and publishes the results of this study (www.guidestar.org)

One of the best methods of gathering salary and benefits data from comparable organizations is to simply do it yourself. Identify organizations most like yours and either obtain a copy of their Form 990 information return filed with the IRS (from GuideStar or by contacting the organization directly) or by offering to share data with the organizations that you have identified. In exchange for similar data on your organization, many other organizations may be willing to provide you with valuable data that wouldn't otherwise be discernible from the Form 990.

GRIEVANCE POLICIES

Despite having the most wonderful human resource policies in the world, it is inevitable that there will be dissatisfied employees from time to time. Some grievances may be well justified, while others may seem unreasonable (we've all been around people who just never seem to be happy).

Because unresolved or ignored grievances can become yet another contributing motive toward fraud, it is essential that organizations establish a grievance system that includes some or all of the following:

- A formal and documented policy for airing grievances that is communicated to all employees
- The ability to air a variety of different types of grievances, including those associated with performance evaluations, promotions, compensation, harassment, daily behavior and environment, and so on

- The ability to communicate grievances to someone other than an employee's immediate supervisor
- A formal grievance committee (one that may include representatives from other departments or levels of the organization, board members, or even outsiders)
- The ability to anonymously report grievances

The most important elements of an organization's grievance policies are that the policies provide an opportunity for every employee to air grievances (or, better yet, multiple opportunities) and that, once aired, their grievances are subject to a system that fairly considers and addresses each grievance. Much like performance appraisals and compensation adjustments, if one employee feels singled out as being treated differently than everybody else, trouble will ensue.

COUNSELING AND OTHER EMPLOYEE ASSISTANCE

Certain employee assistance programs also may assist in controlling fraud. In particular, the following are considered to be valuable in this cause:

- Counseling of employees with substance abuse or other problems
- Career coaching services
- Personal development programs

The first program may be of particular benefit. Counseling of employees with substance abuse or other personal problems is helpful because these programs deal directly with factors that are known to contribute to someone's decision to commit fraud. Troubled individuals frequently resort to fraud in the workplace as a means of funding their habits or otherwise getting them out of trouble. Confidential counseling can mitigate this cause.

EXIT INTERVIEWS

The use of exit interviews as a fraud deterrence measure is probably quite obvious. Many employees are reluctant to report fraud and abuse among coworkers and immediate supervisors. These employees may fear retaliation if they report the fraudulent activity, especially if they suspect their own boss of wrongdoing.

When someone leaves employment, whether it is a voluntary departure or a termination, the exit interview represents one last chance for an organization to solicit what may be valuable information from the departing employee. The exit interview should involve someone from outside the department or function in which the person worked. This is another role best served by a human resources representative, if the organization is large enough to have such a position. As part of the exit interview process, departing employees should be asked directly if they are aware of any fraud or abuse involving employees. Depending on what the response to this question is, the human resources representative should take appropriate follow-up action. Any accusations of wrongdoing should be passed along to the proper person or audit committee member.

12

Administrative Systems and Policies

A variety of administrative systems and policies play integral roles in deterring fraud. Some of the most important are explained in this chapter. They are:

- Physical security
- Security over donor, member, and customer information
- Information technology systems
- Hotlines and communication systems
- Insurance

PHYSICAL SECURITY

The first and most basic set of administrative systems and policies pertains to physical security of an organization's premises. Physical security should be addressed with respect to all levels of access to the facilities:

- Parking garages and lots
- Buildings
- Individual floors or suites of a building
- Departments within the building
- Individual offices and rooms
- Filing cabinets and other document storage devices
- Safes in which cash and other valuables are stored

Access to computer programs and electronically stored data is another important element of security, but that topic is addressed later in this chapter, in the section on information technology systems.

Every nonprofit organization should ask the following questions with respect to each of the preceding areas of physical security:

- Which individuals should have access to this aspect of our facility?
- Should the individuals to whom we grant access have restrictions as to the days of the week or hours of the day that such access is permitted?
- What is the most practical method of prohibiting access by unauthorized individuals?

SECURITY OVER DONOR, MEMBER, AND CUSTOMER INFORMATION

Regardless of the type of organization, many nonprofits handle important and confidential information about individuals with whom the organization has some form of relationship. Charities retain confidential information regarding their donors. Universities handle confidential data about applicants, students, and their families. Associations store confidential information about their members. The list goes on and on.

While it is necessary for nonprofit organizations to receive, process, and store a lot of important information about various people, how the organization protects this information from abuse has emerged as a critical issue for nonprofits. In addition to personnel authorized to have access to sensitive information, any number of other individuals may have access unnecessarily:

- Personnel from other departments or functions
- Volunteers
- Program participants
- Repair technicians working on office equipment and computers
- Maintenance workers repairing electrical, plumbing, and other aspects of the organization's facilities
- Couriers and delivery personnel
- Temporary workers hired by outside temporary services firms
- Evening and weekend cleaning personnel hired by the cleaning contractor
- Visitors to the organization's facilities

Most of these individuals would never consider inappropriately using confidential personal data that they have come across. Occasionally, however, one might seize the opportunity. Sometimes, people specifically look for carelessly stored information to carry out a fraud, such as someone who wishes to steal another's identity or someone who wants to fraudulently charge purchases to a stolen credit card number (see Fraud in the Headlines 12.1 for an example).

Although there are other types of fraud and abuse that can be carried out using confidential information obtained from a nonprofit organization, identity theft and unauthorized credit card use are the most common.

To protect against such unauthorized use of personal information, nonprofit organizations should take the following measures with respect to documents containing such information:

- Shred documents with personal information that are no longer needed by the organization.
- Store all necessary documents in locked filing cabinets or in locked rooms and restrict access to keys (or combinations) to necessary personnel only.
- Do not store keys to filing cabinets containing personal information in the lock. (This may sound obvious, but it's amazing how many keys have been observed dangling from their locks during work hours and even overnight!)

FRAUD IN THE HEADLINES 12.1

THEFT OF DONOR IDENTITIES

On July 15, 2002, a janitor for WNYC, New York Public Radio, was arrested and charged with grand larceny and conspiracy by the New York State Attorney General's office. The station immediately began an investigation to track how 198 donor names had been stolen by the janitor. WNYC found out about the theft when State authorities notified the station. Evidently, WNYC was one of numerous targets of identity thieves who accessed donor records of charities.

The arrest was part of a probe than began a year earlier with the arrest of a state worker who allegedly stole identifying information of thousands of people. The case includes other charities as well as government agencies and for-profit businesses, all of whom were used in a similar manner by the identity thieves—as sources of personal information.

WNYC officials would not reveal exactly how the janitor stole the 198 names, but indicated that steps were being taken to improve controls and information security.

Source: Pope, Tom, "WNYC Theft Sparks Questions About Donor Security," *The Nonprofit Times*, September 15, 2002.

- Consider electronic access to rooms in which personal information is stored, using passwords or key cards, which are more effectively controlled than keys and combinations.
- Adopt a policy of assigning numbers other than the person's social security number for purposes of identifying and tracking donors, students, members, or customers. (Never use a person's social security number for internal identification purposes or on membership cards, etc.)
- Limit the number of temporary agencies with which the organization does business and gain an understanding of the policies and procedures in place at the agency for hiring new workers.
- Utilize passwords or access codes on photocopiers (because that is the most common method of stealing personal information).
- Require that all employees working with personal information store any work-in-process in a locked drawer of their desks when leaving the work area for:
  — Breaks
  — Lunch
  — Meetings away from their workstation
  — The end of the workday
  — Vacations
  — Holidays
  — Other leaves of absence
- Train all employees on information security issues.
- Promote staff awareness of information security and information handling procedures.

INFORMATION TECHNOLOGY SYSTEMS

While some small organizations still keep their books manually on ledger sheets, automated accounting systems are used by most organizations. Automated systems are utilized by nonprofit organizations for a variety of purposes though, not just accounting. A wide array of database packages, human resource systems software, membership and donor tracking systems, conference and event management software, admissions and student tracking software, and many other automated systems are now utilized by nonprofits.

Some of these systems are off-the-shelf software that is simply installed on stand-alone personal computers. Others involve off-the-shelf software that is installed on a networked system. Some systems start with off-the-shelf software, but have been modified or include customized add-ons. Others are entirely custom-written by programmers based on the exact specifications of the organization.

Regardless of how simple or complex an organization's information technology systems, a security plan is an important element of controlling fraud and abuse. To adequately protect an organization from fraud, the security plan should address, at a minimum, the following:

- Segregation of duties
- Physical access
- Controls over access to data
- Data transmission controls
- Data input controls
- Software controls
- Protection of hardware
- Disaster recovery
- Documentation standards

The purpose of such a security plan is to minimize an organization's vulnerability to computer fraud and other frauds involving automated systems in one manner or another. Most computer frauds involve one or more of the following:

- Altering data being input into a computer
- Tampering with software that is used to process data
- Unauthorized use of or access to data
- Manipulating data after it has been input into a system
- Theft (or copying) of data or equipment

The remainder of this section will explain the specific aspects of each element of an information technology system security plan designed to protect against these computer frauds.

Segregation of Duties

Similar to its importance with regard to accounting controls, segregation of duties is important to the information systems functions of an organization. In particular, each of the following functions should be performed by different people:

- Programming (if applicable)
- Use (recording transactions, authorizing data to be input, generating reports from the system, etc.)
- Custody of data and software

In some organizations, there may be another function, which also should be performed by a different employee. This function involves a review and reconciliation of input and output. It is with this person that a record of input errors and other observations resulting from the monitoring of work processed through the computer should be maintained.

Physical Access

Depending on the size and complexity of an organization, there may or may not be a separate computer room. If such a room exists, it should be subject to strict security measures designed to restrict access to authorized personnel. The computer room should be locked at all times. Keys or badges allowing access should be issued only to authorized personnel.

Controls Over Access to Data

Access to data should be restricted in a manner that permits each user to carry out only those functions for which that user is authorized:

- Viewing data (read-only access)
- Copying data
- Adding, deleting, or changing data

Logical access controls apply both to external parties (keeping outside parties from accessing your organization's data) as well as to internal personnel (making sure employees only have the appropriate level of data access for their position). Generally, this is done with two levels of controls: one to distinguish an authorized user of the system from an unauthorized one, and another to distinguish which level of data access a particular user may have.

The most common method of accomplishing these control objectives is through use of a password system in connection with a system that requires some form of user identification (an employee number, identification number, etc.). When an authorized identification number and password are properly entered, access is granted.

Password systems are notoriously abused by employees. We've all seen users with their confidential password taped to the corner of their monitor. Some use passwords that are no more complicated than the user's own name.

There is most definitely a correct and an incorrect approach to password systems. A few considerations in establishing and maintaining a strong password system are:

- Randomly assigned passwords seem to work better than user-selected passwords, which can become predictable unless the system requires a certain level of complexity (such as a system that requires each user-selected password to include at least one lowercase letter, one uppercase letter, and one number).
- Use fingerprints, handprints, or other features in conjunction with passwords.

- Require users to keep their passwords confidential. (Posting them anywhere near their work area should be prohibited, and the system itself should not display passwords during the logon process or at any other time.)
- Change passwords on a regular and frequent basis to provide greater assurance that they remain confidential.
- Require all users to log off the system when they are not at their computers and using the system.
- Implement an automatic log-off feature for systems idle for more than a specified time period. (This prevents unauthorized access if a user forgets to log off.)
- Consider restricting system access to specified hours.
- Disconnect and invalidate the identification number of any user who fails to provide a valid password within a specific number of attempts (such as three or five) as a method of preventing unauthorized users from attempting to log on using many different combinations of possible passwords.
- Investigate internal attempts to access the system that have been denied.
- Immediately invalidate the identification numbers of terminated employees.
- Immediately update data access authorizations and restrictions if an employee changes functions or departments.

The final procedure may seem unimportant since it involves an authorized user. However, cases have been reported in which upon an employee's promotion, they were authorized to perform certain new functions on the system, but were not restricted from the functions necessary for their previous position. The result was that two duties that had previously been properly segregated could now be carried out by a single person. In one case, the employee could now initiate *and* authorize certain transactions with no involvement from other employees.

Of course, as technology continues to advance, the level of sophistication of passwords and system access controls also advances. Identification systems that rely on fingerprints, voice recognition, and other personal characteristics are currently available and are being used by more and more organizations every day.

Data Transmission Controls

When the only transmission of data in an organization takes place from one cubicle to another, data transmission controls may not be all that relevant. But when data is being transmitted to or from outside parties, these controls are extremely important. Think of the risks associated when a wire transfer is being transmitted electronically to a bank, or confidential payroll data is transmitted to a payroll service bureau. The purpose of data transmission controls is to minimize the risk of unauthorized parties intercepting important data while it is being transmitted.

Some of the most important data transmission controls were mentioned earlier in Chapter 4, in the section on electronic funds transfer schemes. One of the most important of these controls is data encryption, which translates data into a code that (hopefully) cannot be deciphered by outside parties.

Data Input Controls

Most of the IT controls explained so far have been broad policies and procedures that address an organization's IT system as a whole. Data input controls represent the first in a series of controls often referred to as application controls. Application controls are designed to ensure the reliability of the input, files, programs, and output associated with each application of the IT system. Application controls address each specific application, such as payroll, accounts payable, membership, and so forth.

Data input controls provide assurance regarding the integrity of data that is being entered into a system. Data input controls involve a series of procedures that validate data sources and input of the data. Examples of important data input controls include:

- Verify prenumbered forms sequence, which is useful to detect gaps or duplicate numbers when an organization utilizes prenumbered documents, such as with purchase orders.
- Document cancellation, in which any document that has been input into the system is immediately marked in a manner that indicates that it has been input (to avoid duplicate entries).
- Visually scan documents prior to entry, to identify items that appear unusual.
- Review input files prior to processing. (In certain important functions, two employees key in the same data, after which the two files are compared.)
- Utilize field checks, which determine whether characters entered into a particular field are of the proper type (alphabetical, numerical, number of digits, etc.).
- Institute range and limit checks, in which input is subject to predetermined limits that will not allow input outside that range. (For example, the hours worked field in a payroll system will not allow hours in excess of 50 per week without a manual override by a supervisor.)
- Implement validity checks, which compare identification numbers to a list of preauthorized numbers. (For instance, in order to input a sale of a

publication to an association member at the member discount rate, a member number must be input, which is electronically compared to a list of currently valid membership numbers.)

- Do a data match, similar to a validity check, but require that data be matched before an action can occur (such as requiring that pricing or other information on a vendor invoice must match up with data on a purchase order prior to processing payment).

- Design the software to check the mathematical operation, which will prohibit the entry of negative numbers in fields that should always be positive (such as inventory purchases) and vice versa.

- Require field checks, in which a transaction cannot be processed without certain information being input (such as a street address for a new vendor).

- Compare batch totals calculated during the input process to batch totals generated during the processing of files.

There are many other data input controls. But the preceding controls are some of the most important as they relate to controlling fraud.

Software Controls

The next application control involves an organization's software. If all of the software utilized by an organization is off-the-shelf, it is unlikely that manipulation of the software is a major threat to the organization. Only a highly trained software specialist would have the expertise necessary to modify the software.

However, many organizations utilize a variety of custom-written software for certain applications. The term "custom-written" as it is used here does not apply exclusively to elaborate software applications written in a language that only software specialists understand. It also applies to files that have been created in everyday software programs to meet a particular need of the organization. For example, a nonprofit organization may use the off-the-shelf Microsoft Access program to create a donor or member database, or a Microsoft Excel spreadsheet to calculate a cost allocation.

Many people have heard the reports of frauds in the banking industry in which someone manipulates the bank's software so that hundredths of cents rounding differences associated with interest calculations are transferred into one person's account, resulting in the accrual of thousands of dollars over the course of many months and thousands of transactions. Similar risks are present in nonprofit organizations that utilize custom-written software or that use off-the-shelf packages to create custom applications for specific transactions. (See Fraud in the Headlines 12.2.)

FRAUD IN THE HEADLINES 12.2

SOFTWARE MANIPULATION

Not all frauds involving unauthorized manipulation of software are carried out by expert programmers. Many, in fact, are rather unsophisticated.

In one case, a fraud was perpetrated by the person responsible for generating statements requesting payment from donors who had made pledges. The perpetrator manipulated the software (which was simply a standard word processing package) so that a fraudulent post office box address was printed on some statements, while the correct post office box address was printed on others. The result was that the organization received some, but not all, of the money to which it was entitled. Meanwhile, the perpetrator collected thousands of dollars of money intended for the organization in a skimming fraud similar to those described in Chapter 3.

To protect against unauthorized manipulation of an organization's custom-written software, the following controls should be in place:

- Maintain a documented record of all requested changes in software.
- Require management-level review and authorization of all requested changes to software.
- Follow the segregation of duties criteria described at the beginning of this section.
- Thoroughly document all software modifications made.
- Independently review and test all modifications made to software.
- Update documentation in user manuals to reflect software changes.
- Restrict access to software, as explained earlier.
- Periodically test custom-written software and applications using test data.

Protection of Hardware

Returning to general, system-wide IT controls, another aspect of system protection pertains to the individual pieces of hardware utilized by an organization. Most aspects of hardware protection are unrelated to fraud. Obviously, keeping personal computers protected against theft by securing an organization's offices is an important safeguard. Most other hardware protection measures, however, are designed to preserve the life expectancy of the hardware itself.

In recent years, however, one significant fraud risk associated with hardware has emerged. With the increased capabilities and portability of laptop computers, many applications can now be performed off-site, outside of the controlled headquarters or office environment. The following situations pose the most common risks:

- Allowing employees to work from home using one of the organization's laptop computers
- Transporting a laptop computer to off-site programs and activities, such as seminars and conferences, fundraising events, and trade shows

Due to their small size, laptops are very easily stolen, along with all of the important data and programs stored on the machine. Another risk associated with off-site use of laptops is the ease with which information can be downloaded from the laptop onto a diskette. This method of stealing software and data is less obvious than outright theft of the laptop, and may not ever be noticed. Thus, practicing the same policies and procedures regarding the use of laptops off-site as for on-site computer use is an important aspect of laptop protection. Some of the most important control considerations for laptops are:

- Clearly communicate to employees the risks associated with off-site use of laptops and their responsibility to protect the laptops in their possession.
- Require that data stored on a laptop be backed up prior to embarking on a trip that will involve off-site use of the laptop.
- Communicate a policy to employees stating that laptops shall never be left unattended when used for off-site purposes, and that laptops used in work-at-home situations shall be properly protected in the home environment.
- Store highly confidential or personal data on diskettes rather than on the laptop's hard drive, and maintain physical custody of the diskette (either in the employee's possession or in a locked location).
- Permanently mark laptops as property of the organization (consider engraving the organization's name and phone number directly onto the laptop).

In addition, there are many software and hardware modifications that can be made to laptop computers to further enhance their protection, such as:

- Software that makes it impossible to boot the laptop up without the use of a password
- Software that periodically disables the laptop's sound system and dials a toll-free phone number to check in (this type of software also may per-

mit the laptop to call at fixed intervals if it is reported as stolen, making it easier for police to locate the machine)

- Motion sensors that emit a loud alarm if the laptop is moved
- Data encryption software that makes data stored on the laptop's hard drive unreadable to anyone who has stolen it

Of course, all of these policies are in addition to those described earlier pertaining to unauthorized personal use of laptops, personal computers, and other organization assets.

Disaster Recovery

When the term "disaster recovery" is mentioned, images of fires and floods come to mind. But there are other disasters as well, everything from system crashes, to viruses and intentional corruption of data, software, and systems as part of a fraud and abuse scheme.

Some of the key elements of disaster recovery planning include:

- Identification of the applications that are necessary in order to keep the organization operating
- Storage of program files and software
- Data files backed up on a regular basis
- Off-site storage of data backup files
- Arranging for backup computer processing facilities, perhaps via a reciprocal arrangement with another nonprofit organization
- Insurance coverage for damaged equipment and software

In addition, an organization's disaster recovery plan should be fully documented, with copies distributed to every employee who has a responsibility in the event of a disaster. Copies should also be stored off site. The last thing an organization should have to go through when attempting to recover from a disaster is confusion over who is responsible for which element of the recovery or what steps are required.

Finally, every disaster recovery plan should be reviewed and updated on a regular basis. As applications, configurations, and personnel change, there is likely to be an impact on the disaster recovery plan.

Documentation Standards

The policies and procedures associated with each of the areas addressed in this section on information technology should be documented and centralized. Specifically, each of the following areas should be formalized in writing:

- Physical and data security measures
- User instructions
- Disaster recovery procedures

The importance of keeping up-to-date user/operating manuals cannot be overemphasized. Particularly in larger, multiuser environments, maintaining current procedures is critical to ensuring that all controls that are not built into the software itself are consistently followed.

HOTLINES AND COMMUNICATION SYSTEMS

The Association of Certified Fraud Examiners *2002 Report to the Nation, Occupational Fraud and Abuse* studied how the initial detection of fraud occurred in 532 specific frauds studied. The most frequently cited method of detection was tips from employees, responsible for initial detection in 26.3 percent of all cases. Also on the list of most common initial detection methods were tips from the following sources:

- Customers (8.6 percent)
- Anonymous (6.2 percent)
- Vendors (5.1 percent)

In summing these figures, almost one-half of the frauds studied were initially detected by tips from employees or external parties with whom the organization did business. If there is a lesson to be learned from these statistics, it's that every organization should establish and publicize a variety of methods by which employees and external parties can communicate suspected fraud and abuse or other forms of dissatisfaction.

In addition to those already mentioned, there are other ways that organizations might receive a tip. Some other valuable sources of information include:

- Donors
- The general public
- Other nonprofit organizations
- Subgrantees
- Independent contractors
- Volunteers
- Bankers
- Watchdog groups
- Government agencies and law enforcement
- Former employees, vendors, and the like

Recall that hotlines and communication systems do not *prevent* fraud and abuse from taking place. But providing an easy and practical method of communicating suspected fraud and abuse plays an integral part in *detecting* schemes at the earliest possible stage, minimizing an organization's losses. Remember, the average fraud scheme lasts 18 months before being detected.

When frauds are detected earlier, the likelihood for financial loss is reduced substantially, due to a number of factors, including:

- The perpetrator has had less time to carry out the scheme.
- The perpetrator has had less time to spend any funds that have been embezzled, thereby improving chances for recovery directly from the perpetrator.
- There is less time for records providing evidence of the scheme to be destroyed or altered by the perpetrator or, worse yet, destroyed as part of the organization's own record retention policies.
- There is a much greater likelihood that any documents needed from outside sources, such as banks or vendors, will be available to help in substantiating a claim.
- Recovery from insurance policies can be limited by a number of factors when claims are based on older schemes. (See the discussion of fidelity bonding later in this chapter.)
- Liability on the part of financial institutions for honoring fraudulent checks may be limited to items reported within a specified time period.

Because tips from employees represent such a powerful method of detecting fraud and abuse among fellow employees, it is critical that every organization establish appropriate communication systems to allow workers to report suspected wrongdoing. There are several important aspects to developing and maintaining proper channels of communication for these allegations:

- Managers should have an open door policy with their subordinates and encourage them to report suspected fraud and abuse. (See Chapter 13 for more on management's role in deterring fraud.)
- All employees should be made aware of the identities and phone numbers of audit committee members, as well as the role the audit committee plays in following up on allegations of fraud and abuse. (See Chapter 14 for more on the role of the audit committee.)
- Consider periodic use of anonymous employee surveys to request their input regarding knowledge of fraud and abuse in the workplace, a technique that some organizations have found to be quite successful.
- Provide a method of reporting suspected fraud and abuse in an anonymous manner.

This final technique should not be overlooked. Recall the statistic that was introduced in Chapter 1: A 2002 study sponsored by Ernst & Young, LLP, found that one in five Americans is personally aware of fraud in the workplace. However, the matter is complicated by the fact that many employees who are aware of fraud and abuse among fellow employees are hesitant to communicate their knowledge to supervisors, audit committee members, or anyone else for that matter. The reasons for this hesitancy are many, but some of the most common include:

- Concern that their identity will be revealed to the perpetrator(s), who may then take retaliatory actions against the whistleblower (See Fraud in the Headlines 14.1 and Best Practices 12.1.)
- Knowledge that the party to whom they are expected to report the allegations is actually involved in the fraud scheme (such as with subordinates who become aware that their direct supervisor is engaging in fraudulent activities)
- Uncertainty over the extent of the wrongdoing or who is involved in the scheme(s)
- Uncertainty over whether the actions observed constitute fraud or even a violation of the organization's code of conduct

For these reasons, it is important for nonprofit organizations to establish a confidential reporting mechanism for suspected wrongdoing. A system in which employees submit communications in writing, but without identifying themselves, provides a partial solution. A better system is the implementation of hotlines administered by outside parties.

Hotline services enable employees to confidentially report suspected fraud or abuse and provide details to people who are experts in handling such allegations. This may be done via recorded messages or by speaking directly to someone handling incoming hotline calls. The arrangement between the hotline service provider and the organization typically states that the hotline service assesses incoming messages and determines the appropriate method

---

BEST PRACTICES 12.1

WHISTLEBLOWER PROTECTION

Not only is protection of people who report instances of suspected misconduct a good idea, it's now the law. One of the provisions included in the Sarbanes-Oxley Act of 2002 makes it a crime to knowingly, with intent to retaliate, take any action harmful to any person, including interference with the employment or livelihood of such person, for providing to a law enforcement officer any truthful information relating to the commission or possible commission of any federal offense. Violators are subject to fines and/or imprisonment of up to 10 years. Unlike many other sections of this law, which apply solely to public companies and their auditors, this provision has broad application to any federal offense. It amends Section 1513 of Title 18 of the United States Code.

of communication to the organization, including a determination of who the appropriate person to contact within the organization may be. Hotline services are very affordable, yet they provide one of the most effective methods of detecting fraud and abuse at an early stage.

If hotline services are established, the organization should prominently communicate the phone number of the service to all employees. Providing the hotline number to volunteers and others who are involved with the organization can provide even greater protection.

Hotline services are available from a variety of providers, such as the Association of Certified Fraud Examiners (ACFE), or certain security firms, such as Pinkerton. The service provided by ACFE, known as EthicsLine, is a 24-hour-a-day, 7-day-a-week service that allows employees to anonymously report suspected acts of fraud and abuse. The EthicsLine service consists of the following steps:

- The interview, in which employees are interviewed by experienced multilingual interview specialists
- An incident report, in which all pertinent details are captured in a report that can be used as a basis for taking follow-up action
- Quality assurance, in which each incident report undergoes an automated data integrity check
- Rapid report dissemination, whereby information is communicated to appropriate organization officials
- Scheduled callbacks for follow-up questions

In addition to fraud, EthicsLine can be used to report workplace violence, sexual harassment, substance abuse, release of proprietary information, and violations of government regulations. More information is available on the EthicsLine Web site at www.ethicsline.com or by calling (800) 357-5137.

The Network, a provider of employee feedback services, also offers a hotline service. Recently, EthicsLine and The Network entered into a strategic alliance. For more details on The Network, go to www.tnwinc.com

One final employee reporting service that all nonprofits receiving federal grants and contracts should be aware of is FraudNet, a service of the General Accounting Office (GAO). This service should be used to report allegations of fraud, waste, abuse, and mismanagement of federal funds. Allegations can be reported by telephone, at (202) 512-3086, or via the Internet, by sending an e-mail message to fraudnet@gao.gov. Every nonprofit organization receiving federal financial assistance should post this information or otherwise notify every employee of this reporting service.

As noted earlier, employees are not the only source of tips regarding fraud and abuse. Several external sources, such as vendors, customers, and donors, can also provide valuable information that can help to detect schemes at the earliest stage possible. Accordingly, organizations should take measures to ensure that these outside parties have an open channel to communicate their observations and concerns:

- Include a hotline phone number, or at least the organization's general phone number, on all invoices, statements, and other documents sent to outside parties.
- Consider periodic use of surveys requesting input from select outside parties regarding observations of fraud, abuse, or unethical behavior on the part of the organization's employees. (These surveys can also double as a valuable source of input on other operational issues, such as satisfaction with the organization's service, timeliness of payments, etc.)

INSURANCE

According to statistics compiled by the Association of Certified Fraud Examiners, in almost 40 percent of frauds committed against organizations, the victim was not insured against the loss. That's an astounding statistic that can mean one of two things:

- Organizations feel that fraud insurance is not essential because they operate in a low-risk environment or that the premiums associated don't justify the benefit that the expenditure would provide.
- Organizations think they have insurance that will provide coverage against losses from fraud, only to find that their existing policies do not provide any such coverage.

Insurance against fraud and embezzlement is just one of the many types of insurance coverage a nonprofit organization may need. Many nonprofit organization managers unfortunately believe that the organization's general liability insurance policy provides adequate protection against employee embezzlement. Usually, this is not the case. General liability policies often do not provide any coverage for embezzlement and those that do usually are limited to very small amounts.

Employee dishonesty bonds or fidelity bonds provide the specific type of coverage necessary to protect an organization against losses from employee embezzlement. These bonds provide coverage only against acts by employees (and, in some cases, volunteers, though every nonprofit should check on this with their insurance agent). Coverage against theft or other crimes by outsiders, such as temporary workers, contractors, and vendors, must be addressed in other insurance policies.

Coverage for embezzlement by employees may be purchased as a standalone policy or as part of a commercial insurance package. Coverage can be for specific employee positions or for all positions and employees (blanket coverage).

Nonprofit organizations should be aware of several conditions that apply to coverage under employee dishonesty and fidelity bonds:

- The perpetrator must be an employee or, in certain cases, a volunteer. (Coverage is usually not available for board members under these policies, but may be covered under the organization's directors and officers liability policy.)
- There must be a dishonest act, such as theft, embezzlement, or forgery.
- Many policies require that the organization report the loss to law enforcement officials in order to be covered.
- Coverage will only be provided if the employee intends to (1) cause a loss to the nonprofit organization and (2) confer a financial benefit to himself or a third party.
- The dishonest act must occur and be discovered during the bond period.
- Some policies provide coverage for fidelity claims expenses and some do not. (This is the coverage associated with the cost of investigating a fraud scheme, such as the cost of hiring forensic accountants, a coverage that may make the difference between recovering all of a loss or only a portion of it.)
- Coverage will not be provided if the nonprofit organization makes poor business decisions, fails to follow its own accounting rules, or maintains sloppy accounting records.

The importance of this last point cannot be overemphasized. Having insurance *does not* automatically equate to recovery of losses from fraud. Three of the more common reasons for insurance companies denying claims are:

- The organization did not take reasonable precautions to protect itself against fraud (i.e., it failed to follow its own policies and procedures, making poor business decisions, etc.).
- The organization failed to report losses in a timely manner.
- The organization provided misleading information in the initial application for insurance coverage (or failed to update this information as circumstances changed over time).

There is another important consideration when an organization applies for or renews its coverage for embezzlement. Nonprofit organizations must carefully and honestly reply to all questions on the application for insurance coverage. In an effort to obtain more affordable premiums, organizations may be tempted to minimize the appearance of fraud risk by providing misleading information or omitting key pieces of information. This can backfire if the insurance company later denies a claim for understating the risk of fraud. Insurance applications are no place to paint a rosier picture than reality. Quite a few organizations have discovered this the hard way.

In terms of updating information provided to an insurance company, the insured should always communicate changes of the following nature in a timely manner:

- Changes in the name(s) of the insured (this is particularly important when a nonprofit organization has several affiliated entities that share employees and facilities)
- Changes in material facts and circumstances pertaining to the operations of the insured organization(s), such as changes in internal controls and loss prevention measures

An excellent source of additional information about these and other types of insurance and risk management issues for nonprofit organizations is the Nonprofit Risk Management Center (www.nonprofitrisk.org).

PART V

THE ROLE OF MANAGEMENT AND THE BOARD OF DIRECTORS

The third component in the three-part model for deterring fraud and abuse involves the management team of an organization. Management of a nonprofit organization has several key roles regarding control of fraud. The term "management" is used in Part V to refer to all of the following individuals:

- Members of the governing body (the board of directors)
- Executive management (executive director, chief operating officer, etc.)
- Vice presidents, department heads, and other members of senior management
- Program managers, supervisors, and others with mid-level manager/supervisor responsibilities

The roles that these members of management play in controlling fraud and abuse are varied, but can be classified as follows:

- Day-to-day managerial activities
- Organizational oversight
- Fiscal management

Part V is broken down into three chapters that explain each of these roles:

- Chapter 13 addresses the policies, practices, and behaviors of the day-to-day on-site management team, from the executive director and individual department heads down to certain supervisory employees.
- Chapter 14 takes a look at the oversight role of the board of directors and how it plays a part in deterring fraud.
- Chapter 15 examines the role of budget and financial analysis in the overall fiscal management of a nonprofit organization, especially as these techniques relate to the ability to detect fraud.

13

Day-to-Day Management Activities

Day-to-day management of an organization involves every member of management except the board of directors. On the typical organization chart, this would include all of the following:

- Executive director
- Chief operating officer
- Chief financial officer
- Department heads (directors, managers, etc.)
- Program managers
- Supervisors

Each of these individuals has a wide variety of responsibilities. But in the area of controlling fraud and abuse, their responsibilities typically fall into one or more of the following areas:

- Responding to and supporting the board of directors
- Development of sound policies dealing with internal control and fraud (including the assessment of fraud risks)
- Establishing an antifraud culture throughout the organization
- Enforcement of all fraud-related policies
- Taking corrective action with respect to identified weaknesses in internal controls
- Following up on actions relating to known fraud
- Establishing transparency and accountability

271

Each of these areas relates in one manner or another to identifying and understanding fraud roles and responsibilities. See Best Practices 13.1 for more on this issue. The remainder of this chapter will be devoted to further exploration of each of these areas of responsibility.

BEST PRACTICES 13.1

MANAGEMENT EXPECTED TO UNDERSTAND FRAUD RISKS

It is expected that the senior management team have a thorough grasp of the fraud risks to which their organizations are exposed. This expectation results from top management's role as overseer and protector of the organization's resources.

Under the AICPA's new auditing standard (SAS No. 99) issued in October 2002, external auditors will be testing management's knowledge regarding fraud risks. In addition to inquiring about known or suspected frauds, SAS No. 99 requires that auditors query management about:

- Management's understanding about the risks of fraud in the entity, including any specific fraud risks that the entity has identified or account balances or classes of transactions for which a risk of fraud may be likely to exist
- Programs and controls the entity has established to mitigate specific fraud risks the entity has identified, or that otherwise help to prevent, deter, and detect fraud, and how management monitors those programs and controls
- For an entity with multiple locations, (a) the nature and extent of monitoring of operating locations or business segments, and (b) whether there are particular operating locations or business segments for which a risk of fraud may be more likely to exist
- Whether and how management communicates to employees its views on business practices and ethical behavior

Furthermore, at the conclusion of each audit, external auditors present to management for their signature a representation letter, which signifies that management has provided everything that the auditors have requested, and that they've made auditors aware of all important facts. Typically, this management letter is signed by the top executive (executive director) and top financial person (CFO or controller). Most of the representations included in this letter are standard representations required under auditing standards issued by the AICPA.

The new auditing standard on fraud adds an additional representation to this letter. It reads: "We acknowledge our responsibility for the design and implementation of programs and controls to prevent and detect fraud." Another representation states that "We have no knowledge of any fraud or suspected fraud affecting the entity involving management, employees who have significant roles in internal control, or others where the fraud could have a material effect on the financial statements."

Under previous auditing standards, much of the consideration of fraud in an audit was silent. Auditors assessed the risk of fraud with little or no direct inquiry of management. The new standard brings fraud out into the open, where it belongs, and makes clear two important expectations:

1. Management *had better* have an understanding of fraud risks and develop policies and procedures to mitigate those risks.

2. If management hasn't adequately addressed these risks, auditors *had better* consider this weakness in planning (or expanding) their audit procedures.

In other words, no more pretending that there isn't a risk of fraud. Every organization has this risk, and management should follow the outline provided in the remainder of this chapter, and throughout this book, in proactively addressing these risks.

RESPONDING TO AND SUPPORTING THE BOARD OF DIRECTORS

As Chapter 14 will illustrate, an organization's board of directors has numerous fraud-related responsibilities. However, the board's primary role is one of oversight. Accordingly, much of what the board must do will be carried out through the management and staff of an organization, subject to the board's approval.

However, keep in mind that the board should also oversee the individual actions of management, particularly the top executive (executive director, CEO, etc.). Many of the financial controls described in Part II rely on the activity of one employee being reviewed and approved by the next level up on the organizational chart (i.e., the employee's supervisor). This concept works well up to the top internal position. But what about the actions of the person in the top position? This top executive should *insist* on there being controls over her or his actions as well. Some of these controls may rely on someone beneath the top executive (such as a CFO who must approve the top executive's expense report prior to a reimbursement check being generated). But this scenario can often become awkward or a rubber-stamp form of approval.

A better system is to have transactions involving the top executive subject to review and approval by the board (or a committee of the board). For recurring transactions or those that may be impractical to approve prior to the transaction (such as certain expense reimbursements), an after-the-fact review and approval may suffice, provided it is done in a timely manner. For all other transactions, preapproval should be the norm.

The top executive also must recognize that at some point, he or she may be accused of wrongdoing by someone within the organization. Again, the executive must defer to the board and allow the board (or audit committee) to investigate the allegation in accordance with the guidelines described in Chapter 14. An executive director with nothing to hide should not be offended by a board that makes inquiries about either specific transactions and activities, or about allegations of wrongdoing. People in the top position must recognize that scrutiny over their activities comes with the territory.

DEVELOPMENT OF POLICIES

While a board of directors may take responsibility for developing some policies, the details of most policies are developed by management and approved by the board. This is particularly true with respect to internal control-related policies, which form the cornerstone of much of the organization-wide model of fraud deterrence. But, as we've seen throughout Chapters 3 through 12, fraud deterrence extends beyond traditional financial controls to include policies that traditionally were less directly associated with fraud. Fraud-related policies that must be developed by management address all of the following areas:

- Financial controls
- Physical security
- Behavioral policies (codes of conduct, etc.)
- Human resources
- Information technology
- Administrative
- Programmatic policies

Management must develop policies addressing each of the areas covered in this book. The guidelines explained throughout Chapters 3 through 15 should be used as the roadmap for developing those policies.

Many organizations that have developed policies also have complained that the policies become cumbersome, confusing or, for other reasons, ignored. In many instances, the reason for this is that the policies have not been properly developed in the first place. Though there is no one universally correct approach to developing policies, there are several common characteristics associated with successful policies. Organizations should strive to:

- Involve the people affected by a policy in the development of the policy to the maximum extent practical. (Granted, in some instances management may need to simply lay down the law with little input from others.)
- Keep policies as clear and specific, as well as short, as possible. (Avoid use of vague terms and provide clear definitions of terms used in policy statements.)
- Document all policies in writing. (Obviously, policies not put in writing are always subject to greater misunderstanding.)
- Utilize one consistent format in documenting policy statements.
- Review all draft policy statements carefully before issuing them in final form. (For example, do not hold a group meeting of five people who agree on a policy and then leave it to one of the five to document and distribute the policy without the other four first reviewing the draft, because that version has been prepared exclusively from the one person's memory or notes and is subject to his interpretation.)
- Centralize policies in policy manuals (i.e., one manual for accounting and financial-related policies, another for human resources, etc.), preferably using loose-leaf binders, which are much easier to update as policies change. This makes the manual much more likely to be kept current and useful.
- Distribute all new policies to everyone affected, along with instructions regarding which policy, if any, is being replaced by the new one.
- Consider using policy numbers as a method of identifying and tracking policies.
- Assign effective dates to all newly issued policies and include the date on the printed document.
- Retain old policies that are no longer effective for at least three years, noting the expiration date of the policy's effective period somewhere on the policy statement. (The three-year period should cover most periods subject to audit by grantors, IRS, and others who have the right to audit the organization. These agencies will be interested in the policies in effect during the period being audited, not necessarily the current policies.)
- Periodically review policy statements for accuracy. (Inevitably, almost all organizations experience situations in which informal changes have been made based on day-to-day practices, leaving an inconsistency between a documented policy and common practice, which may be an improvement over the documented policy or an inappropriate shortcut.)
- Provide staff training on the organization's policies (a combination of training involving new employee orientation, introduction of new policies necessitating training, and periodic retraining of all staff).

Of course, development of policies without considering the possible frauds that an organization may be vulnerable to will result in ineffective controls. Accordingly, each member of management, from executive director on down to individual supervisors and managers, should be involved in answering the question "what could go wrong in my area?" or "what type of fraud and abuse are we vulnerable to?" This requires that each member of management think through all of the activities under his or her supervision with an eye toward identifying where opportunities or incentives/motives for fraud exist. Then each manager should develop policies to reduce the opportunities and/or incentives and to establish detective controls. More on this process is explained later in the section on supervisor/manager responsibilities.

There is one additional consideration when developing policies governing the actions of employees. As explained more fully in Best Practices 13.2, organizations can be held accountable for the actions of their employees. If an employee engages in criminal activities, federal guidelines provide for the employer to be assessed penalties and even receive probation. This can occur even if the organization did not know of or approve of the employee's actions. Accordingly, the policies explained in Best Practices 13.2 should be enforced diligently by management.

BEST PRACTICES 13.2

**ESTABLISHING POLICIES TO AVOID
CORPORATE SENTENCING**

Chapter 8 of the U.S. Government's *2002 Federal Sentencing Guidelines* addresses "Sentencing of Organizations." Under these guidelines, which first took effect in 1991, organizations (including nonprofit organizations, trusts, and unions) can be fined for the criminal acts of their employees if the acts are carried out in the course and scope of their employment and for the purpose of benefiting the organization. Base fines range from $5,000 to $72,500,000 based on the level of offense, but can be even higher in certain situations. In addition, a corporation can be placed on probation for up to five years.

Establishing and following a program designed to prevent and detect violations committed by employees is a key element in having these fines reduced substantially or in potentially avoiding them altogether. In his book, *Occupational Fraud and Abuse*, Joseph T. Wells identifies the following seven aspects of due diligence that may result in avoidance or reduction of corporate fines:

- Establish policies that define standards and procedures to be followed by the organization's agents (see Chapter 8 for an explanation of the term "agent") and employees.

- Assign specific high-level personnel who have ultimate responsibility to ensure compliance.

- Use due care not to delegate significant discretionary authority to people whom the organization knew or should have known had a propensity to engage in illegal activities.

- Communicate standards and procedures to all agents and employees and require participation in training programs.

- Take reasonable steps to achieve compliance, such as through the use of monitoring and auditing systems and by having and publicizing a reporting system where employees can report criminal conduct without fear of retribution (hotlines or ombudsman programs, as explained in Chapter 12).

- Consistently enforce standards through appropriate discipline ranging from reprimand to dismissal.

- After detecting an offense, the organization must take all reasonable steps to appropriately respond to this offense and to prevent further similar offenses—including modifying its program and appropriate discipline for the individuals responsible for the offense and those who failed to detect it.

The guidelines utilize a scoring system which involves adding or subtracting points based on aggravating or mitigating factors to arrive at a final score that corresponds to a base fine amount. In addition to the seven due diligence factors cited, the guidelines consider whether there have been previous violations and whether there was knowing participation by high-level management.

Source: 2002 Federal Sentencing Guidelines, United States Sentencing Commission, November 2002, and Wells, Joseph T., *Occupational Fraud and Abuse*, Obsidian Publishing Company, 1997.

ESTABLISHING AND MAINTAINING AN ANTIFRAUD CULTURE

If it is expected that everyone in an organization participate in combating fraud and abuse, senior management must actively cultivate a culture that is intolerant of wrongdoing. This can be done by:

- Serving as a role model for everyone else
- Actively communicating the importance of fraud awareness and intolerance
- Cultivating the involvement of supervisors and managers
- Enforcing fraud and code of conduct policies consistently
- Communicating actions involving enforcement and corrective measures

As mentioned earlier in this book, the expression "tone at the top" may seem overused, but it remains an applicable principle when it comes to fraud deterrence. If the senior management team fails to practice what they preach, they are naive to think that everyone else in the organization will do as they say by regularly following organization policies. This means senior management should exhibit model behavior in terms of complying with corporate policies on a consistent basis (never overriding or circumventing controls) and displaying the utmost in ethical behavior at all times.

Most employees and volunteers look to the organization's executive director, president, or chief executive officer, as well as the senior management team supporting this person, to be the model of behavior for everyone else. Many employees will follow the executive director's lead, for example:

- Adoption of a more casual dress code if senior management dresses informally
- Increased propensity to leave early or goof off and make personal telephone calls if senior management does so

The mirroring of senior management certainly doesn't end with standards of attire or phone calls to Aunt Marge. If senior management, particularly the senior-most employee (executive director, CEO, etc.), doesn't conform to established policies and procedures regarding fraud and abuse, noncompliance will inevitably permeate every level of the organization. Management must be committed to setting the example for everyone else in the organization.

Next, management must help in establishing an organization-wide awareness of fraud risks and the importance of deterring fraud and abuse throughout all levels of an organization. Setting an example is a start, but management also must stress the need for fraud awareness by getting personally involved in the communication of policies and code of conduct to the entire staff. The key will be to involve the supervisors and managers of the organization. Senior management must establish a sense of responsibility for the prevention and detection of fraud within the ranks of the supervisors and managers of the organization.

One of the best ways to do this is to provide fraud awareness training to these individuals. Most of these individuals are not accountants and have little or no training or experience with fraud detection and prevention. As such, it is unrealistic to think that handing the managers a copy of the organization's code of conduct, along with a directive to enforce it, will result in an effective system of fraud prevention and detection. Fraud awareness training for supervisors and managers should not involve fraud investigation skills. Rather, this training should focus on:

- General knowledge about fraud risks
- How to identify fraud risks in their areas

- Knowing what fraud may look like if they encounter it
- Suggestions on how to prevent fraud

Senior management must be committed to providing fraud awareness training to the supervisor/manager group, providing them with the skills necessary to carry out their fraud-related duties, which are explained in the next section. If the ability to provide this training does not exist within the organization, management should consider outside sources of training. Many consulting firms and fraud specialists are capable of providing this training to an organization's supervisor/manager group.

THE ROLE OF SUPERVISORS AND MANAGERS

Although the top few executives in an organization set the tone for organizational behavior, much of the day-to-day follow-up on this tone is demonstrated and carried out by department heads, program managers, and other employees with supervisory responsibilities. Collectively, these individuals will be referred to as supervisors in this section, indicating that these people all have varying levels of supervisory responsibilities over others, but are not part of the senior management team.

Often, supervisors fail to prevent, detect, or take action regarding fraud and abuse simply because these actions are not considered a part of their daily job expectations and routines. Supervisors must understand three important facts about fraud and abuse:

1. Fraud prevention and detection is not the sole responsibility of the accounting/finance functions.
2. Even the strongest systems of internal controls will not prevent and detect many frauds.
3. Supervisors, therefore, play a critical role in assisting the organization in its fight against fraud and abuse.

In many respects, supervisors play a role in fraud deterrence that is every bit as vital as that of senior management, perhaps even more so. And the reason is simple. Supervisors are more likely to have greater contact with more employees, vendors, and program participants than senior management. As a result, supervisors can have an even greater impact on fraud prevention and detection.

Specifically, supervisors should be responsible for taking the following actions to deter fraud:

- Serve as a role model for all persons under their supervision by demonstrating compliance with all applicable organizational policies and procedures as well as highly ethical behavior in all respects.
- Identify the assets and organizational resources for which the supervisor has responsibility (i.e., cash, personal computers, supplies, etc.).

- Continually identify and maintain an awareness of the types of fraud and abuse that could occur (the fraud risks) in their particular area(s) of responsibility. (Formal training may be necessary to acquire this knowledge.)
- Gain an understanding of what indicators may look like for the frauds that may occur in their areas.
- Develop or recommend policies and procedures designed to combat the specific types of fraud and abuse that could occur in their area of responsibility.
- Make recommendations to senior management regarding changes in organization-wide policies based on their day-to-day experiences with respect to those policies.
- Maintain an awareness of changes in the behavior of employees under their supervision, as well as any other signs of fraud.
- Communicate their interest in fraud deterrence, safeguarding of assets, and maintaining a strong system of controls to all employees and other persons under their supervision.
- When fraud or abuse is suspected, immediately communicate that concern to the appropriate persons within the organization.

Awareness of the Indicators of Fraud

One of the responsibilities identified in the preceding list is an awareness of behavioral changes and other warning signals of fraud and abuse. Many supervisors aren't familiar with what is meant by an awareness of fraud's warning signals; they simply don't understand what it is they are supposed to be on the lookout for. Supervisors should receive instruction on two types of fraud indicators:

- Physical indicators
- Behavioral indicators

Physical indicators are the signs of fraud that may appear to a supervisor through the documents, assets, and other physical evidence that are observed or examined on a routine basis. The nature of physical indicators varies depending on the role of the supervisor. The specific nature of these physical indicators can be identified and understood by reviewing the portions of Chapters 3 through 10 that apply to each supervisor's role. For instance, if a supervisor has a responsibility to review and approve vendor invoices, she should be familiar with the signs of tampered or fraudulent invoices as described in Chapters 4 and 7. Examples of physical indicators include:

- Signs of altered timesheets that a supervisor is asked to approve (Chapter 5)
- Signs of corrections or overrides made to inventory count sheets or receiving reports (Chapter 6)

- Indications of photocopies or otherwise suspicious-looking vendor invoices submitted for approval (Chapter 4)
- Signs of nonbusiness expenditures incurred while on a business trip that are being charged to the organization (Chapter 5)

Behavioral indicators are the changes or unusual patterns that a supervisor may become aware of in an employee. Examples include:

- An employee who always seems to stay at work a little bit later than everyone else or always wants to leave after the supervisor leaves
- A formerly outgoing employee who has become very withdrawn, indicating he may be having personal or work-related problems
- An employee showing signs of substance abuse
- An employee who refuses to take any vacation or other time off

Supervisors should be instructed that these behaviors, as well as many others, *may* represent a warning signal. By themselves, changes in behavior do not automatically mean that someone is committing fraud. There are many non-fraud-related reasons that may explain changes in an employee's behavior. However, behavior change may be a precursor to fraud or a response to having already committed fraud. Either way, supervisors must be aware of changes or unusual patterns in employee behavior.

ENFORCEMENT OF FRAUD-RELATED POLICIES

While one key component of the tone at the top involves management setting an example of ethical behavior, another important element involves the enforcement of fraud-related policies at all levels of an organization, which involves three practices:

1. Reward employees who display the model of ethical behavior that is the goal.
2. Take all allegations of fraud and abuse seriously.
3. Discipline employees who violate fraud-related policies.

When we think of enforcement, it is easy to skip to the second and third actions. But, we should not forget that rewarding employees who go above and beyond the call of duty or who otherwise exhibit the type of ethical behavior that we would like everyone to display has the effect of communicating to an entire staff that senior management is aware of employee behavior and has taken notice of a particularly good example of that behavior; and also values the exemplary behavior enough to take the time and effort necessary to reward that individual.

Once it is suspected that fraud and abuse may have occurred within an organization, management's actions must further demonstrate the seriousness with which these allegations are taken. This can only happen when reports of wrongdoing are addressed in a timely fashion and with complete disregard for a perpetrator's (or suspect's) position or length of employment.

The first characteristic is obvious. The more immediate the action, the more speedy the resolution. Granted, immediate action does not mean *uninformed* action. Management must carefully investigate allegations, being careful not to discipline someone without having all of the facts necessary to make such a decision (see Best Practices 13.3).

The second characteristic, the accused's position, if not handled properly, can lead to feelings that there is a discriminatory policy in place. Management must take an allegation made against a 20-year, trusted employee as seriously (and follow the same established procedures) as an allegation levied against someone who has worked for the organization for only 6 months. Remember, we're talking about fraud here—not whether someone was late to arrive for work, where granting the long-term employee with a good history a bit more slack than a new employee may be acceptable. With allegations of fraud and abuse, initially there should be no such thing as giving someone the benefit of the doubt based on their tenure with the organization. Investigate all allegations with the same level of scrutiny.

Of course, it is impossible to treat everyone the same when investigating allegations if the organization has not established clear, documented policies regarding this matter. For this we return to our discussion of an organization's code of conduct. The code of conduct must not only spell out unacceptable behavior, but also enumerate all fraud-related policies and disciplinary policies.

RESPONDING TO IDENTIFIED WEAKNESSES IN INTERNAL CONTROLS

One thing about deterring fraud and abuse is always true—an organization will not adopt all of the necessary policies and procedures at the same time, upon its initial formation. As the organization evolves and changes, it will become aware of weaknesses in its financial controls, nonfinancial systems, and management policies. A system can *always* be made better. Management may become aware of these weaknesses as a result of:

- External audits by CPA firms
- Internal audit procedures
- Audits or investigations by funding sources
- Other audits or investigations by regulatory bodies
- Supervisors or employees calling weaknesses to the attention of management
- New board members' or managers' input, based on their previous experiences
- Known and reported instances of fraud and abuse

BEST PRACTICES 13.3

WHISTLEBLOWERS GAIN PROTECTION

Management has an ethical responsibility to look into accusations of fraud, including allegations made by subordinates against their supervisors. The Sarbanes-Oxley Act of 2002 backs up this ethical responsibility with tough new requirements designed to protect whistleblowers. Best Practices 12.1 explained one such provision that applies to *all* entities, including nonprofits. Other provisions apply solely to public companies, although it would surprise few to see these provisions extended to other entities, such as nonprofits that receive federal funding.

Among the key whistleblower protection provisions of Sarbanes-Oxley that apply only to public companies are those that:

- Require audit committees to establish procedures for hearing whistleblower complaints.
- Make it illegal to discharge, demote, suspend, threaten, harass, or in any manner discriminate against a whistleblower.
- Grant the Department of Labor the authority to order a company to rehire a fired whistleblower with no court hearing.
- Grant whistleblowers the right to a jury trial, which circumvents administrative hearings that could last months or even years.

Though these provisions only affect public companies at this time, this law should illustrate the seriousness with which the government desires to protect those who identify fraud and abuse.

Our discussion of financial controls in Part II focused on two types of controls—preventive and detective. Some textbooks and articles on controls identify a third category—corrective controls. These are the steps that management takes to correct known deficiencies in either the design or execution of the policies and procedures employed by the organization.

In several of the preceding avenues of discovering weaknesses in controls, the initial communication of the weakness may be made to an organization's audit committee or board of directors, not directly to management. Communication of weaknesses in internal controls received from an organization's external CPA firm is one example (see Chapter 14 for an explanation of communications between CPA firms and audit committees). In these cases, the board or audit committee may or may not become directly involved in taking corrective action, depending on the nature of the weakness. But in most cases, the board will direct management to correct the problem and report back to them regarding the status of the corrective action.

How management responds to known weaknesses in its fraud deterrence policies, procedures, and practices sends the same signal to the entire staff that other actions described in this chapter do. If management fails to take action, delays action, or takes shortcuts around the auditors' recommendations, this will communicate a tolerance for systems that do not fully protect the organization from fraud and abuse. Management's corrective actions in response to identified weaknesses should be one of the factors on which their performance is evaluated.

RESPONDING TO FRAUD

The first thing to keep in mind when fraud or abuse is suspected—do not panic! Remain calm, decisive, and firm in all actions and communications that comprise your organization's response to the situation. Responding to suspected fraud and abuse entails four components:

1. Immediate measures to protect the organization's assets
2. Notification of appropriate external parties
3. Formal investigation
4. Activating internal and external communications systems

All four of these steps should commence immediately (and almost simultaneously) upon discovery of suspected wrongdoing. Organizations should not mistakenly believe that the investigation is a phase that takes place at some later point in time. Early stages of the investigation begin immediately upon discovery or allegation of a fraud. The specific actions that should be taken are:

- Immediately stop the bleeding in situations where organizational assets are being lost, or put a stop to abusive behavior, by:
  - Dismissing, placing on leave, or transferring to another position the employee suspected of wrongdoing
  - Putting stop payment orders on outstanding checks suspected of being fraudulently prepared or closing accounts, if deemed necessary
  - Communicating with other parties, if any, who may assist the organization in putting an immediate stop to the wrongdoing (such as credit card companies, vendors, donors, etc.)
- Notify the organization's insurer by telephone as well as in writing, preferably via certified mail with a return receipt requested in order to properly document notification in accordance with terms of the policy. (See Chapter 12 for an explanation of fidelity bonding and other insurance issues associated with fraud.)

- Carefully take steps to preserve documents and other evidence that may help in substantiating the fraud (see Best Practices 13.4).
- Inform the audit committee and/or the board of directors.
- Inform the organization's legal counsel.
- Consider referring the matter to law enforcement (see Fraud in the Headlines 13.1).
- Implement the organization's internal and external crisis communications plan (explained below).
- Plan and coordinate the investigation, including the hiring of forensic accountants and other experts who will make up the investigation team, as well as the appointment and oversight of a leader of the investigation team.

One important point regarding firing or suspending an employee suspected of fraud or abuse. Organizations should resist the temptation to become emotional in these situations. Calm but decisive and firm action always works best. Do not accuse someone of or use the word "fraud" when firing or suspending the person. Remember from Part I that certain frauds are crimes. At this stage of an investigation, many outcomes other than a conviction on criminal charges are still possible. The last thing you want is to set the organization up for a countersuit by the very person who wronged the organization.

Instead, be clear that the organization is terminating or suspending an employee based on their suspected and actual violation of the organization's code of conduct. Even though fraud is one of several acts covered under your code of conduct, termination based on violating the code of conduct is far less likely to result in a countersuit than accusing someone of a crime.

This is why it is so important for every organization to have a comprehensive code of conduct, one that is referred to in the organization's personnel policies as a basis for termination in cases of noncompliance. A sample code of conduct can be found in the Appendix.

The fourth step in an organization's response to fraud involves activation of its internal and external communications systems. The communications system is a vital component of an organization's comprehensive crisis management system. Every organization should establish a policy for internal and external communications in times of organizational crisis. Many organizations have been harshly criticized for their poor communications in times of crisis usually due to poor planning and coordination, particularly of external communications with:

- The press
- Donors and grantors
- Program participants
- Other members of the nonprofit community
- Government oversight agencies
- Watchdog groups

BEST PRACTICES 13.4

PRESERVING THE EVIDENCE

Preserving evidence is a critical step in the initial phases of a fraud investigation. There are several important steps in preserving evidence:

- Suspend, for the time being, all document destruction (shredding) that is currently in process or scheduled for completion.

- Secure all documents that may be used as evidence, including using secure off-site storage if there is any risk of collusion (is it possible, based on the type of fraud perpetrated, that the fired or suspended employee has an unknown partner in crime within the organization?) or re-entry by the fired or suspended employee (would the person consider breaking into the organization's offices to steal and destroy incriminating evidence?).

- In the immediate work area of the alleged perpetrator of fraud, *save everything*, even the trash, which may contain evidence.

- Unplug, remove, and secure, but DO NOT BOOT UP, any personal computers and laptops used by the perpetrator. (Leave the booting up to the professionals, who are more likely to be capable of avoiding programs designed to automatically destroy files and programs if a secret boot-up sequence is not followed; these programs are installed by many criminals who carefully plan their actions.)

- Make backup copies of data and documents that may be needed in the daily operations of the organization, but that also would be possible evidence in a fraud investigation.

- Immediately identify and obtain reports or any other information (whether internal or external) that is only available for a limited time as it may be of use in the investigation. (For example, save the detailed reports printed by fax machines that list the fax numbers to which facsimiles were transmitted. Such data is often stored for limited periods of time in the fax machine or is limited to a certain quantity of stored transmissions, such as the last 50.)

This final step is extremely important: An attempt should be made to identify every possible document or piece of information that could have been used in perpetrating or concealing the fraud. Should any of these items have a limited availability, obtain them as quickly as possible. For example, availability of copies of canceled checks from a bank may be limited to a specific number of years. If the fraudulent activity has gone on for several years, and especially if the perpetrator destroyed the incriminating canceled checks and other bank documents, request these items immediately from the bank.

Different problems have been encountered by organizations that fail to properly communicate information *internally* to employees and volunteers. This failure can have the effect of demoralizing employees and volunteers, and making them feel as if they have been left out of the loop.

Whether these shortcomings are external or internal, they are often the result of an organization's failure to take a few basic steps in anticipation of the possibility of a crisis:

- Appoint one person as the chief external spokesperson for the organization, plus one backup person in case the chief spokesperson is either unavailable or is the target of the crisis.
- Establish a communications policy that prohibits anyone but the appointed chief spokesperson from making statements to the press or other outside parties. (Everyone should be instructed to be polite but refer all questions to the chief spokesperson.)
- Document the crisis communication policy and distribute it to all employees and volunteers.
- Provide training to the appointed spokesperson on crisis communications, so that the person understands the proper methods of delivering information in a manner that reflects a positive approach to dealing with the crisis.
- Cultivate an ongoing relationship with the media before a crisis occurs in order to improve your organization's chances of being given fair treatment when a crisis does occur.

What and how an organization and its chief spokesperson(s) communicate to the media can have a dramatic effect on how the organization is perceived. A few things to keep in mind when addressing the media during crises are:

- Go to the media before the media approaches you (i.e., if there is even the slightest chance that the press can find out about something, they will, so approach them first to announce the news).
- Although it is best to have just one or two spokespeople addressing the media, balance this with granting as much access to information and people as possible in order to satisfy the media's curiosity. (If you don't, it may appear as if the organization is hiding something.)
- Provide as much information as is necessary and legally possible about the activity, as well as about the organization as a whole. (Have a kit ready that provides details about the organization's history, staff, and programs.)
- If there is damaging information to be released publicly, try to do so all at once, rather than gradually releasing negative information over time.

- Avoid no comment responses, which are virtually always interpreted as a confession of guilt.
- If miscommunication occurs or incorrect information is released, acknowledge and correct it as soon as possible.

FRAUD IN THE HEADLINES 13.1

TO CALL THE POLICE OR NOT TO CALL THE POLICE?

As explained in Chapter 12, reporting fraud to the police may, in certain cases, be a requirement in order to collect any amount under fidelity bonding coverage or other insurance policies. In cases where reporting fraud to the police is not required for insurance purposes, however, an organization may face a difficult decision.

One 1997 fraud illustrates the difficulty of this decision. Officials of the Ogden, Utah Chamber of Commerce quietly handled internally the embezzlement of $50,000 by a former manager. Officials decided to focus solely on repayment of the stolen funds rather than pursuit of criminal charges, choosing not to disclose the fraud for nearly a year.

Some of the chamber's board members speculated that the decision not to seek criminal charges was, at least in part, intended to spare the chamber from public embarrassment, a sentiment common in nonprofits that have been victimized by fraud. Members of the chamber's board were told of the embezzlement in a series of confidential, small-group meetings. General members of the chamber were not told of the theft (at least not until it became public knowledge through reports in the press).

The former manager skimmed funds from deposits of membership dues between 1992 and 1995. The skimming went undetected during audits by the external CPA firm. In fact, the embezzlement was undetected until after the perpetrator had left the chamber. The former manager signed a confession of judgment, acknowledging her actions, and borrowed $40,000 from family members to make partial repayment to the chamber before signing the confession. A confession of judgment is a civil matter, and does not result in any form of criminal record.

One chamber official stated what many victims of fraud have said previously—that incarceration of a perpetrator reduces the chances of receiving restitution. That feeling, along with the fear of embarrassment, are two of the most frequently cited reasons for not seeking criminal charges against perpetrators of fraud. Of course, this approach leaves criminals on the street. Another organization that is considering making an offer of employment to this person will find nothing if they perform a criminal background check.

Neither concern over restitution nor fear of embarrassment are particularly valid reasons for failing to seek criminal charges against a perpetrator if the organization has:

- Properly insured itself against embezzlement, which ensures restitution
- Taken actions to correct weaknesses in internal controls that permitted the fraud (which chamber officials claim to have done)
- Communicated these corrective measures in a positive manner, rather than waiting for the fraud to unveil itself publicly, as it did in this case

All in all, things still worked out well for the chamber. It got its money back, and the press reports regarding failing to disclose the embezzlement to members and the public were not overly negative. Nonetheless, the chamber's experience is an excellent illustration of the pros and cons of going public and pursuing criminal charges.

Source: O'Neil, Marina, and Don Baker, "Chamber Settles Embezzlement—Former Manager Agreed to Pay $50,000 Stolen from Member Funds," *Standard-Examiner* via Standard.net, January 25, 1998.

One final consideration in dealing with known fraud involves the reporting of wrongdoing to the Internal Revenue Service. As explained in Fraud in the Headlines 13.2, a 1996 law permits the IRS to penalize upper-level managers and board members of certain nonprofit organizations in cases in which those individuals take advantage of their influence in a manner that benefits them personally, directly, or indirectly through businesses, family members, and so forth. Nonprofit organizations should be aware of this law and take actions to protect innocent managers and directors by properly approving and documenting transactions between them and the nonprofit organization. However, this same law may represent another method of recovering losses resulting from unscrupulous managers and directors embezzling funds from nonprofits or otherwise obtaining inappropriate benefits as a result of their position within the organization.

ORGANIZATIONAL ACCOUNTABILITY AND TRANSPARENCY

One final issue for managers of nonprofit organizations to consider is that of transparency. This term, which is used with ever increasing regularity, refers to a level of accountability that leaves nothing hidden from the outside world—everything about the organization is an open book. Nonprofit organizations of all types, but charitable groups in particular, are expected to be

FRAUD IN THE HEADLINES 13.2

TAX IMPLICATIONS OF FRAUD

A 1996 law, the Taxpayer Bill of Rights 2, established a new tax that can be assessed with respect to excess benefit transactions between section 501(c)(3) charities or section 501(c)(4) social welfare groups and parties considered disqualified persons with respect to those nonprofit organizations. Disqualified persons include all voting members of the board of directors, presidents, chief executive officers, chief financial officers, and others who may exert substantial influence over an organization's affairs. As its name implies, an excess benefit transaction is one in which what the nonprofit receives is less than what it provides in exchange. Examples may include everything from paying too much compensation to an executive in comparison with industry averages or paying above-market rents to an entity controlled by a board member. The IRS published final regulations designed to interpret the law in January 2002, and has begun enforcing the new rules in recent years.

The tax (provided under Internal Revenue Code Section 4958) is assessed on the disqualified person, not the nonprofit organization, as a penalty for, in essence, abusing the influence they hold over an organization for personal gain. Sound like fraud? It may be. And, in fact, some nonprofit organizations have used Section 4958 taxes as one method of recovering funds stolen by upper-level employees or board members. Here's how:

- If an excess benefit transaction is deemed to have occurred, the IRS assesses a first-tier tax equal to 25 percent of the excess benefit.
- Along with the 25 percent tax assessment comes the ultimate warning shot: Return the excess benefit to the nonprofit organization or pay the IRS another 200 percent tax!

The logic behind a 200 percent tax is that, hopefully, nobody would elect to pay such a tax when they could get off with paying half that amount (the excess benefit) back to the nonprofit.

Nonprofit organizations can turn in upper-level managers and board members to the IRS by reporting the existence of excess benefit transactions on their Form 990.

Furthermore, board members who participate in excess benefit transactions knowing the transaction to be a violation may be subject to an *additional* 10 percent penalty tax, up to $10,000 per transaction. So if a board member votes to approve a transaction that amounts to an excess benefit, even if the board member does not personally benefit, he or she could end up with a stiff tax penalty.

open with their supporters, volunteers, program participants, and the general public regarding all aspects of their operations.

Many models of corporate accountability and transparency have been formulated and discussed over the years. The term "accountability" implies an obligation to meet the public's expectations of not merely complying with laws and regulations, but serving a higher authority. In 1991, one organization, Independent Sector, adopted the phrase "Obedience to the Unenforceable" to describe the level of ethical behavior that should be strived for in the nonprofit sector. That phrase continues to be an applicable goal today (and in 2002, Independent Sector issued an updated report, *Obedience to the Unenforceable*, reflecting their continued commitment to this goal). The phrase embodies the spirit of going beyond simple compliance with laws, accounting standards, regulations, and donor expectations by holding the organization to a higher standard of behavior, top to bottom.

But how does an organization establish and implement this approach? One way to begin is by asking two questions:

- Who are we accountable to?
- What are we accountable for?

Initially, the first question seems fairly simple. However, when one starts listing all the people that an organization is accountable to, it can be intimidating. It may include:

- Donors and grantors
- Founders and their heirs
- Members, students, and other program participants
- Employees and volunteers
- Beneficiaries of services
- Partners (other nonprofits, etc.)
- The general public
- The nonprofit sector, especially peers
- Government agencies (IRS, states, etc.)
- Banks and other lenders
- Neighbors

The more difficult question involves identifying what the organization is accountable for. Many nonprofits fail to address this question, simply continuing to carry out their programs. Some of the things your organization may be accountable for include:

- Compliance with laws and regulations
- Meeting the specific requirements imposed by donors and funding sources

- Quality of programs
- Maintaining a consistent focus on the organization's mission
- Appropriate use and allocation of organizational resources
- Safeguarding of resources
- Ethical behavior in all activities
- Full disclosure of information (transparency)

Every nonprofit should take the time to formally consider these two questions. Every organization should establish standards that address each element of accountability and that ensure transparency. One of the possible starting points are the standards developed by the BBB Wise Giving Alliance (an affiliate of the Council of Better Business Bureaus). A list of the standards by which this watchdog group evaluates charities is provided in the appendix.

Ultimately, an organization's standards of accountability and transparency should go beyond the basics to address all of the areas of importance not only to the organization itself, but all to whom it is accountable.

14

The Role of the
Board of Directors

A nonprofit organization's board of directors serves a vital oversight role. This role is comprised of many different responsibilities, several of which have implications on an organization's ability to control fraud and abuse. This chapter will address these responsibilities by explaining each of the following elements of a nonprofit board's role as it relates to fraud:

- An overview of the board's general responsibilities
- Specific board responsibilities relating to fraud and abuse
- Establishing a committee structure
- Audit committees
- The external audit function
- Internal auditing
- Managing conflicts of interest

A NONPROFIT BOARD HAS MANY RESPONSIBILITIES

The board of directors of a nonprofit organization has a fiduciary responsibility to the organization. In fulfilling this general responsibility, the board has many specific responsibilities. Each of these responsibilities falls into one of four broad areas:

- Policy
- Planning

- Fiscal management
- Public liaison

Within each of these areas of responsibility, a board must address a variety of issues. Equally important, elements of fraud risk management can be found in each of these areas.

Policy

The area of policy covers everything from broad and major policy issues, such as the overall mission of the organization and its structure, to lower-level policies such as dress codes, office decorations, parking, and standard daily operating procedures.

Of course, the board is not responsible for establishing policies in each of these areas. Logically, the board's involvement in major policy matters should generally be greater than with lower-level policies. Most policies are likely to be developed by senior and mid-level management, subject to the oversight and review of the board. Obviously, many of these policies have a direct or indirect impact on fraud deterrence. Internal control policies and codes of conduct are two such policy areas.

One area of policy that directly impacts internal controls is organizational structure, or the organization chart. Due to its direct impact on internal controls, the board should pay close attention to this aspect of policy. The organization chart establishes the chain of command, which in turn determines the hierarchy of internal controls (i.e., who will be authorizing and approving the transactions and activities of whom). Whether a particular internal control policy directly affects one person or ten people may depend on how the organization chart is structured. Accordingly, the board must involve itself directly in the formulation and/or modification of the organization chart in relation to the internal control policies in place.

Planning

In the area of planning, the board's role is often focused on long-term and strategic planning. These planning responsibilities may find the board delving into a variety of topics, such as:

- Programmatic strategy
- Funding sources and diversification
- Geographic expansion
- Meeting demand for services
- Overall organizational growth
- Leadership and succession issues
- Changes in legislative or political climates

Just as was the case with policy matters, the board's role with planning is to oversee the process and to assure each of the key aspects of planning is addressed. This may necessitate more detailed involvement in certain aspects of planning than others.

A board's level of involvement in planning is also impacted by the environment and personalities of the parties involved. Nowhere is this more apparent than in strategic planning. In some nonprofit organizations, the board spends significant amounts of time developing a detailed strategic plan. In others, the board establishes broad goals and objectives, then turns the planning process over to senior management and staff. In yet other environments, the staff of the organization develops all aspects of the strategic and implementation plans and submits the plans to the board for approval.

Fiscal Management

Fiscal management is the area that jumps out immediately as a function that directly impacts an organization's management of the risks associated with fraud and abuse. Key elements of a board's responsibilities with respect to fiscal management include:

- Budgeting and financial planning
- Monitoring revenue and expenses in light of the budget
- Assuring adequate cash flow and other resources for the organization's programs
- Safeguarding the organization's resources
- Management of financial risks
- Building appropriate reserves
- Compliance with requirements imposed by funding sources

Public Relations

The final area of board responsibility involves public relations. This is an area that is left out of many discussions on board responsibilities, but it is an increasingly important role and one that boards must recognize. The board may play an indirect as well as a direct role in public relations.

The composition of the board and the standing that board members have in the community clearly can enhance or detract from an organization's public image. Recruiting board members who are highly regarded and who take their roles seriously is an important step toward a positive public image for the organization. If the organization ever has to weather the storm caused by a public scandal or fraud perpetrated by an employee, a well-respected and proactive board can be one of its greatest assets in restoring public confidence.

Accusations of fraud and abuse often put the board in a position in which it becomes the primary link between the organization and the press.

This is particularly true if the accusations involve the executive director or other senior management team members.

SPECIFIC RESPONSIBILITIES PERTAINING TO FRAUD AND ABUSE

As explained earlier, a board's role is one of providing oversight. The term "oversight" can be confusing. It should not be interpreted as a rubber stamp approach to the actions of senior management. However, it should not result in meddling in the daily affairs of management either. Rather, a board must strike a balance by using sound judgment to determine whether limited oversight or more direct involvement is appropriate in various situations.

This balance is particularly important in fulfilling a board's responsibilities regarding fraud and abuse. Some of these responsibilities are best characterized as oversight roles, while others require a board to roll up its sleeves and delve into greater detail, in order to meet what we'll call its direct responsibilities. The following summary of responsibilities illustrates a board's multifaceted role in relation to fraud:

Oversight Responsibilities

In order to properly fulfill its fraud-related oversight responsibilities, a board should:

- Ensure that the organization has adopted adequate fraud prevention and detection and risk management policies.
- Ensure that the organization has taken appropriate steps to identify fraud risks and has adequately protected itself against fraud through insurance and building of reasonable reserves.
- Oversee senior management's follow-up actions in response to findings and recommendations of auditors or investigators.
- Oversee the organization's budgeting, financial reporting, and financial analysis processes.

The final oversight responsibility is one that plays a particularly important role in detecting fraud. Proper budgeting, monitoring of actual results against budget, careful review of financial statements, and ongoing financial analysis are some of the best tools for identifying fraud, if they are performed properly. Because these functions are typically carried out initially by management, it is important that a board of directors (the audit committee in particular) exercise diligent oversight of these four areas. Because these functions require integration between management and the board, monitoring budget versus actual results and monitoring financial results over time are explained in detail in Chapter 15.

Direct Responsibilities

A board's direct responsibilities are to:

- Serve as liaison with external auditors.
- Direct the internal audit process, if there is one.
- Manage conflicts of interest.
- Serve as a direct internal control with respect to actions of the most senior members of management.
- Serve as spokespeople for the organization in addressing assertions of wrongdoing or actions taken in response to known frauds (particularly those involving senior management).

In each of the preceding areas identified as direct responsibilities, a board should not limit its role to simply overseeing the actions of senior management and organization staff. Instead, the board should be expected to actively participate and take direct responsibility for carrying out these tasks. The remainder of this chapter will focus on explaining how a board should best tackle these areas of direct responsibility.

ESTABLISHMENT OF BOARD COMMITTEES

One of the first things that should be apparent from the introduction to this chapter is that a nonprofit board of directors has numerous responsibilities that span a wide variety of functional areas. The question then becomes—how does a board meet these responsibilities in an effective and efficient manner?

The average nonprofit board of directors has between 16 and 20 members. Large, complex organizations may have more. Smaller nonprofit organizations and those with few programs and rather simple operations often have smaller boards, sometimes as few as five board members.

The frequency with which these members meet (either in person or by telephone conference call) ranges widely, from once or twice a year to monthly. The typical scenario involves quarterly meetings. Meetings may be scheduled for full days, but are often planned to last just a couple of hours.

Given the many and diverse responsibilities that nonprofit boards have, along with the constraints on the frequency and duration of their meetings, most boards of directors operate much more effectively and efficiently by creating committees. It is usually unrealistic to expect that the full board of directors will be able to adequately address all of its responsibilities in the time provided for it to meet. Boards that attempt to do this typically end up devoting far too little attention to certain areas of responsibility.

Therefore, board committees are formed. They typically consist of three to five members of the board, and serve the full board by delving into a particular area of responsibility in greater detail than what would be practical or possible for the full board. The committee addresses issues in its area of specialization and brings its recommendations to the full board for approval.

The full board is ultimately responsible for its actions, so it may accept a committee's recommendations with limited discussion, or it may decide that further analysis and debate is necessary. The board may request that the committee return after it has proceeded with this additional discussion and analysis, or it may decide that it is appropriate or necessary for the entire board of directors to confer.

Examples of some of the more commonly established board committees include those focusing on:

- Programs
- Development and fundraising
- Bylaws and governance
- Personnel
- Finance
- Investments
- Audit

Some organizations may need just one or two board-level committees in order to adequately address all responsibilities. Other nonprofit organizations have ten or more standing committees. The number of committees that is best for any particular organization depends on several factors, such as:

- Size of the board
- Frequency and duration of meetings
- Whether meetings are face-to-face or via telephone
- Complexity of the organization's operations
- Size of the organization

In the area of financial management, three examples of standing committees are provided: finance, investments, and audit. Again, perhaps only one committee is needed to cover all financial areas. Some organizations have three or four financially oriented committees. Whichever structure an organization chooses, audit and fraud-related responsibilities should be assigned to a committee and not be left as a general responsibility of the entire board.

THE AUDIT COMMITTEE

The most logical committee to whom audit and fraud-related responsibilities are assigned is the audit committee. An audit committee should be comprised of three to five current members of the board of directors. Some of the traditionally important responsibilities of the audit committee include:

- Select and evaluate the organization's external audit firm.
- Review and evaluate the scope and plan for the external audit.
- Review and approve the annual financial statements audited by the external audit firm.
- Review and approve all reports prepared by the external auditor in connection with its performance of a Single Audit of the organization's federally funded programs in accordance with OMB Circular A-133, if applicable.
- Monitor the adequacy of the organization's internal controls (including the financial controls over specific acts of fraud and abuse identified in Parts II and II of this book, as well as the broad nonfinancial controls and practices identified in Parts IV and V).
- Monitor accounting policies adopted by the organization in the preparation of its financial statements and in the preparation of financial reports of government grants.
- Receive and review all communications from the external audit firm that are required under generally accepted auditing standards and have direct contact with the external auditor, preferably in the form of a face-to-face meeting, at least once a year. (Auditor communications required under auditing standards are explained in the next section on the external audit function.)
- Review and discuss as a committee and with appropriate members of management all findings reported by the external audit firm (internal control findings, noncompliance with laws and regulations, and other findings and observations reported by the auditor).
- Monitor the external auditor's independence in accordance with current auditing standards (including the 2002 changes to *Government Auditing Standards*, which impose stricter limitations on nonaudit services provided by an organization's external CPA firm).
- Review the performance and fee arrangement of the external audit firm.
- Review and discuss with management the findings of any examinations conducted by regulatory agencies or other oversight bodies, including pass-through entities.
- Monitor the organization's internal audit function, if applicable. (The benefits of and the need for an internal audit function are explained later in this chapter.)

In addition to these traditional responsibilities, there are numerous other areas in which an audit committee can and should play an active role. The audit committee should:

- Monitor compliance with the organization's code of conduct and conflict-of-interest policies.
- Monitor the filing of tax and information returns for compliance with IRS, state, and local requirements.
- Direct any special investigations into allegations of fraud and abuse, as well as any other violations of the organization's code of conduct or conflict-of-interest policies.
- Monitor the organization's policies for complying with applicable federal, state, and local laws and regulations.
- Review expenses associated with officers and directors and board meetings.
- Serve as a contact point for any employee or volunteer who desires to report allegations of suspected fraud or abuse within the organization.
- Monitor the reliability of the organization's information technology system, physical security, and other applicable security measures for purposes of protecting the organization from fraud and abuse.
- Review with the organization's general counsel the status of litigation and other legal matters that may have a significant impact on the organization.
- Monitor adequacy of insurance coverage associated with fraud and abuse, as well as noncompliance with laws and regulations.
- Assess the possibility of financial risks to the organization resulting from the current operating environment, changes in legal or regulatory requirements, and any other factors.
- Perform any other oversight functions requested by the board of directors.

In fulfilling these responsibilities, the audit committee should document all of its decisions and periodically report to the full board of directors. As part of this periodic reporting, the audit committee should present its recommendations to the entire board of directors for its approval.

Every audit committee should have clearly defined responsibilities, as well as clear authority to carry out those responsibilities. The best method of establishing these responsibilities and authority in a manner that minimizes the risk of confusion and disagreement is by preparing and ratifying an audit committee charter. An example of an audit committee charter can be found in the Appendix.

Although every board-level committee should have a formal charter, it is absolutely critical that one exist for the audit committee. This committee may be called into action when significant controversies emerge or when the organization is in the midst of a crisis stemming from a fraud. This is no time for confusion and disagreement over what the committee can and cannot do!

Once a charter has been ratified for the audit committee, it's time to select committee members. Based on the significance and complexity of the audit committee's responsibilities, the determination of who should serve is a matter that should not be taken lightly. Nor should assignment to the audit committee be something that "the new guy gets stuck with." Audit committee members should be selected based on their ability to carry out the numerous responsibilities described in this section. Some of the most important characteristics of audit committee members include:

- Independence from management
- Financial literacy
- An inquiring attitude
- Understanding of the organization's programs and activities
- Sound business judgment
- Willingness to challenge management when necessary

The term "financial literacy" does not mean that audit committee members must be CPAs. However, members of the audit committee should possess at least a general understanding of basic nonprofit accounting, financial reporting, and tax issues. They should also be knowledgeable about the organization's budgeting process and methods of accounting. Experience in running a business or exposure to financial and accounting issues of for-profit enterprises (i.e., general business acumen) can be a helpful start, but members of the audit committee must have an *awareness* (even if it is not a complete understanding) of the unique accounting rules applicable to nonprofit organizations. In other words, audit committee members should have enough knowledge of the pertinent issues to know when to ask a question (they also should have the assertiveness that may be necessary to ask these questions). If members of the committee do not have this level of knowledge, the organization should arrange for training on these topics.

THE ROLE OF THE EXTERNAL AUDITOR

The *2002 Report to the Nation: Occupational Fraud and Abuse*, from the Association of Certified Fraud Examiners, reported that only 11 percent of the frauds that were studied had been uncovered as a result of an external audit by a CPA firm. Does this mean that in 89 percent of the cases, the external auditors performed a substandard audit? Hardly. While some audits certainly are poorly planned and performed, the more likely reason for such a small percentage of frauds being detected by the external audit is that an organization's own employees and internal controls are much more likely to catch the fraud first.

In addition, any external audit has inherent limitations in terms of how far one can reasonably expect it to go in an attempt to detect fraud. These limitations are frequently misunderstood by the organizations being audited, as well as the general public. In an effort to close this expectation gap and to improve the quality of audits, the AICPA has issued new guidance on fraud detection for auditors to follow on all financial statement audits. But even with the new audit standard on fraud, there will continue to be limitations on even the best-planned and best-performed audit.

Misstatements

Two sentences in the standard auditor's report on financial statements sum up the extent of an audit and its inherent limitations. In the scope (second) paragraph, the audit firm states that its goal is to "plan and perform the audit to obtain reasonable assurance about whether the financial statements are free of material misstatement." This is followed up in the opinion (third) paragraph with the conclusion that, based on the audit, the financial statements "present fairly, in all material respects," the financial position of the organization and its activities and cash flows for the year. Two things that are important to understand about the limitations of an audit in detecting fraud are:

1. An audit provides *reasonable*, not *absolute*, assurance.
2. The assurance provided by the auditor is that the financial statements are free of *material*, not *all*, misstatements.

Confusion frequently arises over what sort of misstatements an auditor is supposed to look for. The auditing literature identifies four types of misstatements:

1. A difference between the amount, classification, or presentation of a reported financial statement element, amount, or item and the amount, classification, or presentation that should have been reported under generally accepted accounting principles (GAAP)
2. The omission of a financial statement element, account, or item
3. A financial statement disclosure (in the footnotes) that is not presented in accordance with GAAP
4. The omission of information required to be disclosed (in the footnotes) in accordance with GAAP

In general terms, all misstatements can be thought of as *unintentional* (errors) or *intentional* (fraud). Until recently, the auditing standards provided little guidance for auditors regarding how to look for the intentional misstatements.

Materiality

The next issue, and one that is even more confusing than the concept of a misstatement, is the determination of what is material and what is immaterial to the financial statements and footnote disclosures. Most auditors use one or more equations to determine materiality for audit planning purposes. These equations typically consider an organization's size expressed in terms of either total assets, total revenue, or total expenses, or some combination thereof.

However, auditors are also required to consider qualitative characteristics of materiality, not just the numbers. Examples of these qualitative characteristics are:

- Whether a difference, even a small one, would turn a profit into a loss, or vice versa
- Whether a difference would affect bonuses or management compensation based on achieving or failing to achieve certain financial results
- Whether a difference would impact an important financial ratio, such as a loan covenant regarding a current ratio or a funding source's requirement that the organization report a certain percentage of expenses as program expenses
- The sensitivity of a misstatement (such as misstatements resulting from fraud or an illegal act, even if very small in amount)
- The motivation of management, if any, with respect to a misstatement (for example, misstatements of overhead allocations in order to maximize recovery under grants)

Common Misconceptions About Audits

There are several misconceptions among managers and board members when it comes to the scope of financial statement audits. Among the most common of these are:

- That an audit provides assurance regarding an organization's internal controls
- That all, or a significant percentage, of an organization's transactions are tested during an audit
- That an audit will detect all frauds

Regarding the first misconception, pertaining to internal controls, get one thing straight—an audit provides no level of assurance regarding an organization's internal controls. Auditors are required to gain an *understanding* of an organization's internal controls and utilize that understanding in formulating appropriate audit procedures. However, there is no requirement that an auditor must *test* whether the internal controls supposedly in place are operating as intended (one significant exception to this statement pertains to audits of federally funded organizations conducted under OMB Circular A-133 and in accordance with *Government Auditing Standards*, which requires the testing, albeit limited, of an organization's internal controls). In the typical financial statement audit, a CPA firm does little or no testing of internal controls beyond simply gaining an understanding of the organization's primary policies and procedures governing:

- Cash receipts (receiving and depositing money)
- Cash disbursements (purchasing and check writing)
- Payroll (timesheet preparation and preparation of paychecks)

Even in situations where internal controls are tested, only a small sampling of transactions is typically tested in each broad category of transaction. For example, a CPA firm may select between 20 and 40 general disbursement checks and a similar quantity of payroll checks to assess whether the internal controls required under the organization's policies actually operated properly for the selected transactions.

Auditor Responsibilities Pertaining to Fraud

Without a doubt, a significant portion of the public discussion in recent years has been on whether auditors do enough to identify fraud. In response to criticisms directed at auditors and the American Institute of Certified Public Accountants for several high-profile failures to detect fraudulent financial statements, the AICPA spent much of 2002 revamping its guidelines on fraud. In October 2002, a new auditing standard on fraud was released, followed by several new publications and other resources to assist auditors in understanding the new standard and improving their fraud detection skills.

The AICPA's new standard on fraud is Statement on Auditing Standards (SAS) No. 99, *Consideration of Fraud in a Financial Statement Audit*. It is effective for audits of periods beginning on or after December 15, 2002 (i.e., mostly audits of December 31, 2003 year end or later), but the AICPA has encouraged firms to adopt the new standard early.

SAS No. 99 replaces SAS No. 82, which was issued in 1997 with the objective of clearing up the confusion over the auditor's role in catching fraud. SAS No. 82 made a number of changes, such as requiring auditors to separately consider the risk of a misstatement in the financial statements as possibly being due to fraud. In doing so, auditors were expected to identify fraud risk factors associated with the entity being audited. The standard, and its accompanying guidance, identified a variety of possible fraud risk factors that may be present in an entity. Despite the improvements brought about by SAS No. 82, it is generally felt that it did not go far enough in requiring auditors to take specific measures to detect fraud.

What SAS No. 99 does is subtle but important. It is subtle because it does not make substantial changes in the basic requirements associated with an auditor's responsibility to detect fraud. But this is not a flaw in the standard at all. Making substantial changes in the auditing standards to the point of providing auditors with a detailed roadmap to detecting fraud would be virtually impossible. Assessing the risk of fraud requires an auditor to use professional judgment. And the problem with professional judgment is that it is partly a skill (which can be learned) and partly a characteristic (which an auditor either has or doesn't have). An auditing standard can instruct an auditor on what the goals and objectives are, and even on some of the steps necessary or useful in meeting those goals, but it cannot contemplate all of the various possibilities in an audit. It cannot provide detailed instructions as to what questions to ask, what documents to examine, and other specific steps to perform.

Where SAS No. 99 represents a notable improvement over SAS No. 82 is in the guidance it provides auditors for considering the risk of fraud in an audit and in designing appropriate audit procedures in response. Numerous examples of inquiries and audit procedures are provided. In the end, though, auditors must still exercise their own judgment in terms of tailoring inquiries and audit procedures to each individual audit. This means being familiar not only with the requirements of the audit standard, but with the various methods of perpetrating and concealing fraud and the controls that would be necessary to prevent or detect those frauds.

As explained in Chapter 13, the new standard will require auditors to make more extensive and more direct inquiries of management about fraud. These inquiries will be directed toward the senior management team more so than the board or audit committee. But board members should read Chapter 13 to become familiar with the nature of these inquiries and to oversee how management addresses the issues raised in these inquiries.

Auditor–Audit Committee Communications

It is important for audit committees and other board members, as well as management, to understand the nature of the communications between the

---

BEST PRACTICES 14.1

Audit committees should ask their external auditors what specific training their audit team members have received regarding the new fraud auditing standard and fraud detection techniques. The AICPA has requested (but not required) that CPAs devote 10 percent of their continuing professional education to fraud-related topics. If your auditors (the ones in the field doing the work, not just the partners of the firm) have not had training on the new audit standard *and* on fraud risk assessment and detection techniques, it's time to find new auditors.

external CPA firm and the audit committee. For starters, management and boards must understand that an auditor's reporting responsibility is to the audit committee (or the board equivalent thereof), *not* to management. Certain communications with management are necessary to conduct the audit, such as obtaining a written representation letter from them, but the results of an audit must be communicated to the audit committee. (In certain limited situations, an auditor also may be required to report fraud or illegal acts to governmental funding sources if the auditor determines that the organization has not, or will not, inform the funding source itself).

Accordingly, audit committees should anticipate receiving and discussing certain communications from auditors in addition to the basic financial statements. The auditing standards require that certain items be communicated by an auditor to the audit committee. The most important of those required communications are:

- Any fraud, regardless of how small, that was identified during the audit
- Illegal acts uncovered during the audit
- Reportable conditions, defined as weaknesses in the design or operation of an organization's internal controls that could adversely affect an organization's ability to record, process, summarize, or report its financial statements
- Any disagreements with management that arose during the audit
- Difficulties encountered in performing the audit
- Significant audit adjustments that were necessary in order for the organization's financial statements to be fairly stated in all material respects
- Uncorrected misstatements (i.e., differences identified during the audit that were deemed immaterial and, therefore, not adjusted in preparing the organization's financial statements)

Each of these items is important because, in one manner or another, each is reflective of an organization's ability to control fraud. But these communications are not required to be written. Verbal communication is acceptable and is a common practice among many CPA firms, at least for some of the preceding communications. (However, if the audit is done in accordance with OMB Circular A-133, the communication of fraud, illegal acts, and reportable conditions pertaining to internal control must be made in writing.)

If none of the preceding situations or findings arise during an audit, the auditor is not required to communicate the lack of such findings to the audit committee. But if an audit committee does not receive any communication from their CPA firm regarding these matters, the audit committee should nonetheless directly inquire of the auditor as to their existence.

Reportable conditions are of particular importance since they result not only from failures in the operation of an organization's systems, but from weaknesses in their design. Audit committee members should feel free to quiz their auditors regarding the depth of work done to understand the design of the organization's internal controls, particularly whether the key controls necessary to prevent and detect fraud are in place.

Finally, it bears repeating: Any communications pertaining to the preceding matters should come directly from the CPA firm to the audit committee, not through management. If the audit committee has not previously established a direct relationship with its external auditors, it should do so immediately.

THE INTERNAL AUDIT FUNCTION

According to the Association of Certified Fraud Examiners *2002 Report to the Nation, Occupational Fraud and Abuse*, internal audit procedures were responsible for the initial detection of fraud in 18.6 percent of the cases studied. This makes internal auditing more likely than both internal controls (15.4 percent of cases) and external audit (11.5 percent of cases) to detect fraud.

Equally important, the median loss from frauds in which an internal audit function was not present ($153,000) was nearly double that of frauds in which the victim had an internal audit function ($87,500). While an internal audit function doesn't prevent fraud from happening, it clearly results in:

- An increased likelihood of detecting fraud
- Earlier detection of fraud, resulting in a reduction of losses

Remember, a well-communicated detective control has a pronounced preventive effect, as it can deter would-be perpetrators from attempting to commit fraud in the first place.

However, many organizations have some common misconceptions about internal auditing, starting with a misunderstanding of what it really is. The nature of internal auditing procedures can be similar to those performed by external auditors, such as verifying that transactions are supported by legitimate documentation and testing compliance with established internal controls and other policies. Internal auditing also can involve procedures not customarily included in an external audit, such as assessing efficiency of operations and cost savings.

Where the differences between internal and external auditing may be most important, from a fraud detection standpoint, are in the scope and extent of the auditing procedures. External auditors, as explained in the preceding section, design their work to gain assurance that the organization's financial statements are free of material misstatement. As such, the focus is on larger transactions, along with perhaps some random or judgmental sampling of transactions. In some cases, the external auditor may plan to test a certain percentage of transactions in a particular area.

Internal auditing knows no such boundaries to its procedures. If a particularly sensitive or fraud-prone area warrants it, an internal auditor can examine 100 percent of the activity in that area. This is what makes internal auditing so useful as a fraud detection tool. An internal auditor can assess where an organization's greatest vulnerabilities exist, regardless of whether those areas are material to the financial statements taken as a whole, and plunge into those areas to ferret out the fraud.

MANAGING CONFLICTS OF INTEREST

In Chapter 4, the issues associated with conflicts of interest were introduced and explained. In this chapter, the board of director's role regarding conflicts of interest is discussed.

The board's first responsibility in this area is to develop (or oversee the drafting of) a conflict of interest policy statement. The board should make sure that each of the following issues is addressed in this statement:

- Its scope of coverage (which people are covered)
- The nature of the activities covered
- Identification of who is responsible for considering conflicts of interest
- Methods of resolving conflicts (i.e., resignation, corrective actions, etc.)
- Manner of administering the policy (i.e., annual disclosure statements, etc.)
- Penalties for noncompliance, including failures to disclose conflicts

Although a sample conflict of interest policy can be found in the Appendix, organizations should be careful to tailor the policy to their own unique circumstances, considering each of the preceding issues.

One of the more difficult issues to tackle in crafting the policy will be the determination of exactly who will address and resolve individual conflicts and how. Will the entire board do this? A committee? The chair of the board? In most instances, relying on the entire board will become cumbersome. So, assigning this responsibility to the chair or to a committee usually makes the most sense.

Whichever approach the organization takes, it is important that, regardless of who is involved, all members of the board who are not completely independent of the conflict should abstain from voting on any resolution pertaining to the conflict. For example, if a conflict pertains to one board member and a business partner of that board member is also on the board, both parties should abstain. Or, if all conflicts are to be resolved by the chair, but the conflict itself involves the chair, the policy statement should address who the backup person for this function should be.

THE FIRST LINE OF DEFENSE AGAINST
FRAUD BY SENIOR MANAGEMENT

One of the most common weaknesses in internal control, as well as a common deficiency in external auditors' consideration of fraud, is the hierarchical nature of internal controls. The controls put in place in most organizations are generally much more reliable for preventing or detecting fraud committed at low or middle levels of organizations. Frauds committed at the highest level, by senior management, are the most costly. Yet these frauds are often subject to the fewest or weakest internal controls, or those controls can be overridden or circumvented by senior management.

Even the new auditing standard on fraud bases part of its procedures on inquiries of management. This works fine for management's assessment of the risk of fraud at lower levels. But if management itself is engaging in fraud, what should the auditor do to detect it? This is all part of the greater expectation for auditors to assess the risks of all potentially material frauds, including those perpetrated by management.

In many cases, frauds committed at lower levels will be identified and resolved by the senior management team, with little or no involvement by the board. But for frauds perpetrated by senior management (or unethical behavior tolerated by senior management), the board must be prepared to step in and play a more direct role.

The first step in this process is to identify which member(s) of the board is responsible for receiving communications from employees and volunteers regarding allegations of fraud or other unethical behavior by senior management. Someone from the audit committee is perfect for this responsibility. As pointed out in Chapter 12, this board member's contact information must be communicated to all employees and staff, so that they clearly understand who to inform if they do not feel comfortable going through the normal chain of command within the organization.

The next step is for the person (or committee) receiving the allegation to seriously consider it, regardless of the previous level of trust the board has held for the accused. See Fraud in the Headlines 14.1 for an illustration of how *not* to handle allegations of fraud and abuse.

From here on out, the board's role (or audit committee's role) in investigating allegations of fraud on the part of senior management is similar to that described in Chapter 13. The only difference is that the executive director or other senior manager is being investigated. The exact same procedures described for management in Chapter 13 should be followed by the board or audit committee in looking into allegations of wrongdoing by senior management.

There are a few additional considerations when the fraud has allegedly been perpetrated by senior management. Those considerations are addressed in the next section.

A BOARD'S ROLE IN CRISIS MANAGEMENT AND COMMUNICATIONS

When fraud strikes an organization, its board of directors will need to serve one of two roles, depending on the parties involved in the fraud. Frauds carried out below the senior management level should be addressed directly by

FRAUD IN THE HEADLINES 14.1

DON'T SHOOT THE MESSENGER!

A nonprofit organization was ordered by the Supreme Court of Alaska to pay $400,000 in punitive damages, and its president was ordered to pay another $200,000, to a former employee fired over questioning the president's use of organization funds (*Central Bering Sea Fishermen's Association v. Anderson*, No. S-9955, No. 5623, September 6, 2002). The former employee was hired as a temporary controller while the regular controller was absent due to illness. Coworkers advised the temporary worker that the absent controller may have stolen funds from the organization. When the temporary worker informed the president of this, the president refused to look into the matter. Later, the regular bookkeeper informed the temporary controller that the president appeared to have misappropriated funds as well. The temporary controller received the permission of two board members to look into the matter, but the next morning was told by the president to go home.

The president informed the organization's attorney of his intent to fire the temporary controller. The president also informed state funding sources and other state officials of the fired employee's false accusations of misappropriation. The organization's board then held a meeting at which the fired employee was accused of breaking into the organization's offices, illegally accessing its computers, stalking the president, making death threats, and retaliating against the organization.

A few weeks later the board learned that the fired employee's concerns regarding the association's president were indeed valid. At that point, the board offered the fired employee a job in another town, which she turned down and then sued the organization and its president, claiming the job offer was the board's way of just getting rid of her. The Alaska Supreme Court awarded her punitive damages based on several factors, including:

- The association and its president were aware that their conduct would likely cause the fired employee serious harm since they had "effectively shut her out of the career and field that she had chosen."

- The association's and president's conduct was motivated by substantial financial gain or avoidance of financial losses that could have occurred had the state investigated the allegations and reduced the organization's funding.

- When the board arranged for an audit to look into the allegations, it was designed to be as narrow as possible and failed to investigate the broader issues of possible financial misdealing identified by the fired employee.
- Evidence indicates that the board's behavior toward the fired employee did not change after the discovery that her concerns were legitimate.

Source: Kramer, Don, "Board Must Pay Fired Worker Who Questioned Expenditures," *Don Kramer's Nonprofit Issues*, October 2002.

senior management, who should lead the investigation and take appropriate follow-up action, including modifications to internal controls to prevent future occurrences. The board's role with respect to each of these actions on the part of senior management is an oversight function, including approval of any policy revisions recommended by management.

But when fraud on the part of senior management is asserted, the board's role changes from an oversight function to one of much more direct involvement. The board may need to step in and dismiss members of senior management or temporarily suspend them during an investigation. During this period, the board may need to take certain actions:

- Keep the daily activities of the organization moving forward by bringing in interim replacements for senior management, if necessary.
- Lead or coordinate the investigation into the actions of senior management, similar to the manner in which this role was described for senior management in Chapter 13.
- Begin the process of finding permanent replacements for senior management, if necessary.
- Directly address the need for changes in policies and procedures to prevent future frauds of a similar nature.

In many cases, fraud perpetrated by senior management presents an additional problem for an organization. When senior management commits fraud, the public may view an entire organization as untrustworthy. A board of directors that steps in to take control and make improvements may not always alleviate this problem, for two reasons:

- The board may be viewed by the public as not involved enough (why didn't they prevent this in the first place?) or as not having adequate skills or even the time necessary to save the organization.

- The board may be viewed as being closely tied to the senior management team member(s) who committed the fraud; in other words, guilty by association.

In these cases, a board should consider the potential benefits of bringing in a completely independent team of individuals to help guide the organization through its tough times. Several organizations have done this with success. One of the most common methods of accomplishing this is to form a special task force comprised of people who are not currently board members or involved with senior management. Task force members may be persons who have already had involvement with the organization (past officials, representatives of other nonprofits with whom the organization has done business, etc.) or persons who would bring a completely fresh perspective. Next, the board must establish the following:

- Exactly what the board expects the task force to do (make recommendations for policy changes, etc.)
- An appropriate level of authority that is necessary for the task force to do its job

The board must accept the risks that come with using an outside task force. The task force may make recommendations that directly affect the board (see Best Practices 14.2) or that the board does not necessarily agree with, remembering the purpose of the task force is to represent the interests of the public, which, in turn, regains the trust of the public.

BEST PRACTICES 14.2

PLACING AUTHORITY IN TEMPORARY TASK FORCES

In the fall of 2002, the United Way of the National Capital Area (the Washington, DC area affiliate) took several significant actions in an attempt to regain the public's trust following a series of assertions and mistakes that dated back more than a year. This organization had been the subject of multiple audits arranged for by the organization, as well as investigations by government agencies, in response to allegations pertaining to a variety of acts, including:

- Withholding from local charities an extra $1.3 million of funds earmarked for those charities by donors
- Paying out the retirement of a former official two years before his retirement
- Questionable or undocumented expenditures in excess of $100,000

One of the actions taken by the organization, with the support of the national United Way of America, was to bring in an interim president to oversee the day-to-day activities. Another action was to form a special task force to address specific issues related to the assertions. This task force was comprised of ten members, none of whom sat on the organization's board of directors.

One of the results of the task force's work was a recommendation to remove all current board members and replace them with 21 new individuals. The outgoing board members had been subject to much criticism for poorly handling the allegations of wrongdoing. Thirteen of the replacements were selected by the task force, while the other eight were identified by local United Way volunteer committees.

Source: Salmon, Jacqueline L., "21 Picked to Run Charity," *The Washington Post*, November 27, 2002.

15

Financial Oversight and Analysis

Much goes into the financial oversight of any nonprofit organization. But in the fight against fraud, two financial management tools stand out as being particularly useful:

- Budget preparation and analysis
- Ratio and trend analysis

These two topics will be the focus of this final chapter. These topics are included in Part V, which deals with the role of management and the board of directors, because it is critical that there be significant management oversight and involvement in both of these areas.

THE BUDGET AS A FINANCIAL OVERSIGHT TOOL

Every nonprofit should prepare an annual budget. The budget serves as a vitally important management tool. It represents a projection of the income that the organization anticipates receiving and the costs of carrying out its program services and supporting activities. It is the financial plan for accomplishing the organization's mission. At the end of each fiscal year, the organization can assess how well it did in terms of achieving its financial targets, just as it should be doing with respect to programmatic and other goals.

For organizations that operate many different programs and have multiple supporting activities (fundraising, management and general, membership solicitation, etc.), an organization-wide budget actually represents the sum of many smaller budgets—one for each program or functional area and one for each supporting activity.

There are many aspects of and uses for budgets in nonprofit organizations. But a comprehensive discussion of budgeting is beyond the scope of this book (for an excellent book on budgeting, see *Budgeting for Not-for-Profit Organizations* by David Maddox, published by John Wiley & Sons). With respect to controlling fraud and abuse in nonprofit organizations, there are two primary uses of the budget:

- Utilizing zero-based budgeting techniques in developing a budget
- Using variance analysis to identify accounts whose actual balances differ materially from budgeted amounts

Zero-Based Budgeting

Many organizations prepare their annual budgets by starting with the prior year's budget or actual amounts, then adding or subtracting from them based on anticipated changes for the coming year. As Best Practices 15.1 illustrates, this approach can have the unintended effect of budgeting for fraud. This has happened in numerous organizations, much to the board's dismay, when it is discovered.

Zero-based budgeting refers to a method of preparing an annual budget as though the organization (or each program and department) were starting from scratch each year. With a zero-based budgeting approach, each budgetary unit (depart, program, etc.) presents a detailed plan of what it plans to accomplish for the next year, along with planned revenue and expenses. Justification for the planned utilization of resources (the costs) must be included. Programs and costs that cannot be justified will be omitted from the final budget.

Zero-based budgeting certainly doesn't prevent a fraud from taking place. But it can make it more difficult to conceal or escalate from year to year.

Variance Analysis

Variance analysis refers to the investigation of differences between actual revenues and expenses versus budgeted amounts. Variance analysis serves as both an operational procedure and as an extremely valuable fraud detection tool.

The operational purpose for performing variance analysis is to sound the alarm that something is not going as planned. Every organization should compare actual revenues and expenses with budgeted amounts at various stages during the year (at least quarterly, preferably every month). The earlier this is done, the greater the chance to take appropriate corrective action to get things back on track.

BEST PRACTICES 15.1

ZERO-BASED BUDGETING IN ACTION

Assume an organization utilized $80,000 of school supplies in an educational program last year. For the coming year, it anticipates a 10 percent increase in students and program revenue.

In many organizations, $88,000 would be assumed to be a reasonable budget figure for supplies for the coming year (a 10 percent increase over the prior year, consistent with the increase in students). What if the $80,000 figure included a $5,000 embezzlement that was concealed in the supplies account? Hasn't this organization just given a $500 raise to the embezzler?

Under a zero-based budgeting approach, the program director would be asked to explain how $88,000 of supplies would be needed and efficiently utilized. This approach requires that budget managers start from scratch each year to justify their planned expenditures.

Variances from budget in excess of an established threshold (expressed in both dollars and as a percentage of budget) should be investigated. In order to accurately compare actual amounts with budgets at interim points during an organization's fiscal year, the budget needs to be expressed in monthly or quarterly increments. Many organizations fail to do this. They simply calculate an annual budget. The result is that no alarms go off until the full year's budget for a cost item has been exceeded! What happens if this takes place just eight months into the year?

In allocating a budget by month or quarter, organizations also should take into consideration the effects of seasonal trends or activities. The costs associated with an annual conference are not likely to be incurred evenly (one-twelfth each month) throughout the year. Taking the time and care to do this properly results in a year-to-date variance analysis at each stage of the year, which is infinitely more valuable.

This analysis is useful not only as a management tool, but also as a method of detecting fraud. Which of the following organizations stands a better chance of minimizing its losses from an embezzlement scheme that is being concealed by charging the stolen amounts to office supplies?

1. The organization that will identify a budget variance only when the full year's budget for office supplies has been used up
2. The organization that establishes and monitors monthly and year-to-date (cumulative) budget variances

The second organization is in a much better position to detect the fraud at the earliest possible stages.

Once a budget variance has been identified, the person(s) accountable for meeting that budget item should be asked two questions:

1. Why has this variance occurred?
2. What revisions to the plans for the rest of the year need to be made? (Can the variance be made up for by year end so that the annual budget is still intact; is it impossible to meet the budget; should changes in the program or activity be planned?)

From a fraud detection perspective, we're only interested in the first question. But both questions are important from an operational standpoint. In order for variance analysis to have value as either an operational tool or a fraud detection mechanism, it must be both timely and thorough.

Timeliness refers to the value of performing variance analyses at various stages throughout the year, using year-to-date budget and actual results. The earlier a variance is detected, the earlier corrective action can be implemented or fraud can be detected.

Thoroughness refers to providing substantive explanations for variances. In other words, if an organization is 20 percent over budget on office supplies, don't explain it by saying, "we needed more office supplies than we thought." Justify the variance. The persons providing the responses to these questions should be able to substantiate their explanations. If an executive director is told by one of her department heads that departmental spending will be 10 percent over budget because of increased prices or needs, and that there is nothing that can be done about it, the executive director must consider whether this is a legitimate explanation. Part of that consideration may involve examining expenditures and supporting documentation to verify the department head's explanation.

As Maddox points out, there are many games played by budget managers in developing a budget. Many of these same games can be played in the variance analysis stage. Some of the games are not really intended to subvert the process. Someone may simply be inexperienced, doesn't have all the needed answers, or has other time constraints that prevent him or her from devoting enough time to the budget analysis.

But sometimes these games represent part of the concealment process involved with an ongoing fraud. Board members and management (as well as auditors) must exercise judgment in attempting to differentiate between the two. The only way of doing so is to:

- Make certain that explanations make sense in light of all other facts and circumstances. (A common mistake is to look at an explanation for a budget variance by itself, without considering changes and circumstances involving other account balances or aspects of the organization's operations.)

- Do a bit of investigating into the underlying documentation and evidence supporting an explanation. (Examine invoices, program activity reports, price lists, etc.)

FINANCIAL ANALYSIS

Analytical procedures can be one of the most effective tools for identifying fraud in any organization. Analytical procedures can also provide critical insight into the operations and trends of an organization, alerting management to inefficiencies or negative trends before a crisis emerges. Even with respect to problems that management is already aware of, analytical techniques can provide clues as to the causes of such problems and the directions an organization should take to improve operations. In the preceding section, analysis of an organization's operations against budget was explored. In this section, other analytical tools will be explained.

The application of analytical procedures is a four-step process that consists of:

1. The development of an expectation
2. The identification of fluctuations (how actual results differ from expected)
3. The investigation of material fluctuations (why has the variance occurred)
4. The evaluation of the likelihood of a misstatement in the amount (either caused by error or fraud)

A fifth step, taking corrective action in response to an identified variance, could also be involved. But that is a step that is operational in nature, as explained in the section on budgeting. Our focus is on fraud detection, so the remainder of this section will center on the first four steps.

Examples of analytical procedures include:

- Comparison of current year account balances and summary balances with prior year(s) balances
- Comparison of current year account and summary balances as a percentage of total assets or total support and revenue with prior year(s) ratios
- Comparison of revenue and expense account balances with budgeted amounts
- Comparison of recorded account balances with estimated balances calculated using other data (for example, multiplying the number of people appearing on an attendance roster times the registration fee and comparing the result with recorded revenue)

- Comparison of account balances, summary balances, and pertinent ratios with industry averages, if such averages are available

In each case, an expectation is established and compared with actual results. The level of precision of an expectation depends on several factors, including the reliability of the data used in formulating the expectation and the basis on which the expectation was developed.

Reliability of Data

The key to any of the analytical techniques explained here being of any value is to base expectations on reliable data. We may use financial data, nonfinancial data, or a combination of the two in order to develop an expectation. In any case, the nonprofit manager (and auditor) must consider the reliability of the data by considering its source and the conditions under which it was gathered. For example, if a manager is attempting to test conference revenue by multiplying the registration rate by the number of attendees, the source of the data pertaining to attendees must be a reliable one. Relying on a representation made by an individual responsible for collecting registration fees would be inappropriate, as this person is in a position to divert funds from the organization.

The following factors should be considered in determining the reliability of data used for analytical purposes:

- Was the data obtained from independent sources outside the organization or from sources within the organization?
- Were sources within the organization independent of those who are responsible for the amount being analyzed?
- Was the data developed under a reliable system with adequate controls?
- Was the data audited in the current or prior year?
- Were the expectations developed using data from a variety of sources?

Although the source of these factors is an auditing standard (the AICPA's Statement on Auditing Standards No. 56), these are considerations that are every bit as important for board members and managers of nonprofit organizations as they are for auditors.

TYPES OF ANALYTICAL PROCEDURES

For purposes of detecting fraud, three types of analytical procedures are of greatest value:

- Reasonableness testing
- Trend analysis
- Ratio analysis

The remainder of this chapter will be devoted to explaining and illustrating each of these techniques. As with budget variance analysis, reasonableness testing, trend analysis, and ratio analysis are worthless if differences between expected and actual results are not properly investigated and substantiated (see Best Practices 15.2). Board members, managers, and auditors alike must exercise an appropriate level of skepticism when analyzing variances, particularly when the source of an explanation for a variance is in a position to commit a fraud that could be concealed in the account or relationship being analyzed. (This is often the case, because the initial inquiry about a variance is almost always directed at the person responsible for a particular element of income or expense.)

For auditors, this expectation to substantiate explanations of variances is quite clear. SAS No. 56 states that when an auditor receives such explanations from management of an audit client, the explanations should be corroborated with other evidential matter. Board members and managers should take a similar approach—don't blindly accept explanations for variances. You may regret it later.

BEST PRACTICES 15.2

**HOW TO INVESTIGATE DIFFERENCES BETWEEN
ACTUAL AND EXPECTED RESULTS**

A manager may use analytical procedures to test the reasonableness of the balance in the payroll taxes expense account by multiplying recorded salaries by the applicable payroll tax rates. The calculated amount should represent the maximum expected account balance, as it is expected that some employees may have salaries that exceed the maximum amounts subject to certain payroll taxes. Accordingly, a recorded balance in excess of expectations should not occur and could indicate an error or fraud. A recorded balance substantially lower than expectations could indicate other problems (such as failing to report or pay payroll taxes on certain employees) or simply that there are some employees whose salaries are substantially over the payroll tax limit.

For instance, further investigation may result in a management representation that there are ten employees with very large salaries that significantly exceed payroll tax thresholds. Proper additional procedures to verify this representation may include a review of salary approvals by the board of directors, agreement with W-2's and other payroll reports, or testing of specific paychecks issued to such employees. Acceptance of the management representation without further audit work, even though the representation appears reasonable, would not be appropriate.

Reasonableness Testing

Reasonableness testing is the analysis of account balances or changes in account balances within an accounting period that involves the development of an expectation based on financial and/or nonfinancial data. Reasonableness tests rely on a manager's (auditor's) knowledge of the organization and the environment in which it operates to develop expectations of an account balance.

As discussed in Chapter 3, one aspect of fraud detection in nonprofit organizations where reasonableness testing can be especially useful is in the area of income (testing to make sure the organization has received all the income to which it is entitled). Because certain categories of a nonprofit's income are more susceptible to theft, particularly when preventive controls are not (or cannot) be in place, proper design of analytical procedures, particularly reasonableness tests, may be crucial to assuring that income has not been skimmed from the organization.

Some examples of reasonableness tests that may confirm the completeness of income are as follows:

- Calculate expected revenue from conferences, trade shows, seminars, or meetings by multiplying average registration rates determined from a review of registration forms and promotional materials by the expected number of attendees. Attendance can be determined from:
  - Hotel invoices indicating the number of meals served
  - Sign-up sheets used for continuing education purposes
  - Room setup capacities as described in hotel contracts and floor plans
  - Inventories of handout materials (books, manuals, etc.) taken to the site and returned from the site
- Estimate expected revenue from membership dues by multiplying average dues rates determined from membership applications and promotional materials by the expected number of members, determined from:
  - Mailing records associated with member benefits, such as a monthly journal
  - A membership database used for purposes of determining members' eligibility for programs or benefits of the organization
  - A published member directory
  - Printing invoices for materials sent to members, indicating the quantities printed
- Assess the completeness of recorded contribution income. Do this by:
  - Comparing the *quantity* of contributions recorded (i.e., the number of donors, not the dollar amounts) with the quantity of items

for which postage was charged on a business reply mail account, if the fundraising materials provided such envelopes

— Comparing quantities or amounts of contributions from published donor listings or acknowledgments (in program books or other publications of the organization) to recorded amounts and/or names

Some of these techniques have been referred to earlier while others have not. In each case however, data obtained from sources that are not in a position to skim revenue is used to back into what the anticipated amount of revenue should be. If the actual recorded, deposited income is substantially less than the expected amount, this could indicate a skimming fraud.

As mentioned in Chapter 3, developing reliable expectations for contribution income is especially difficult, and may be impossible in many instances. Use of industry statistics regarding response rates to fundraising materials or ratios of fundraising costs to income tend to be unreliable due to the significant standard deviations associated with these averages. Comparing contribution income results from year to year can be particularly dangerous, for the simple reason that you may be comparing bad apples to bad apples. (What if the perpetrator is skimming a similar amount each year, as has been the case in several charity frauds?) Accordingly, reliance on analytical techniques other than the two illustrated here is not recommended for contribution income. See Chapter 3 for a discussion of the preventive controls that are essential to protect against skimming of contribution income.

Reasonableness testing also can be used with respect to a variety of expense accounts. Expecting payroll tax expenses to be a consistent percentage of salaries from year to year may be a reasonable assumption. Depreciation, commissions, rent, and many other expense accounts also may lend themselves to reasonableness testing.

Trend Analysis

Trend analysis is the analysis of changes over time in any of the following statistics:

- Account balances (individual accounts)
- Groups of account balances (department totals, or subtotals by type of account)
- Ratios

Trend analysis is most valuable as an analytical tool when the account or relationship is expected to be fairly stable over time. It is less appropriate when the organization has experienced operating changes (or changes in accounting methods). It also does not take into consideration changes in the environment in which an organization operates.

Examples of trends that may, if tracked over time, provide useful information about an organization include:

- Individual income and expense account balances
- Income and expense by department, function, or program
- Income and expense by site
- Income and expense by region
- Gross margin or net operating results by department, function, program, site, or region

As with the analytical techniques discussed thus far, unexplained trends may be an indicator of several causes, such as:

- Inefficiencies (or efficiencies) in operations
- The impact of environmental changes
- Fraud

Trend analysis involving financial ratios can be one of the most valuable analytical tools for detecting fraud. Tracking changes in ratios from period to period can reveal the effects of numerous different causes. The remainder of this chapter will be devoted to ratio analysis.

RATIO ANALYSIS

Ratio analysis involves determining the relationship between two financial statement accounts or between financial data and nonfinancial data. When compared over time (or with averages of similar organizations), valuable insight into an organization's operations are revealed.

What makes ratio analysis particularly effective in detecting fraud is its exploration of relationships, not merely individual account balances. Concealing fraud becomes much more difficult when the perpetrator must also attempt to maintain the consistency in these relationships (instead of simply fabricating a reason why a particular account balance has changed).

Ratio analysis is most effective when the relationship between accounts is fairly predictable and stable. Like trend analysis, ratio analysis tends to be most accurate when performed on disaggregated data.

Though not all are applicable, many of the financial performance ratios computed for commercial entities have value for nonprofit organizations as well. A nonprofit organization's goal may not be to maximize shareholder wealth, but that does not mean that other goals and objectives measured by financial ratios should not be established and monitored. Some of the more common financial ratios that provide valuable insight into an organization's performance, and that can help to detect fraud, are identified and described at the end of this chapter.

The list of potentially useful ratios is lengthy. The key is to identify those ratios that focus on the unique operating characteristics of a particular organization. Sometimes, minor adjustments in how the ratios are calculated can convert a useless ratio into a valuable one. Removing or adding certain accounts from the numerator or denominator of a calculation can provide valuable insight into the trends or operations of an organization.

In addition, it may make more sense to calculate some ratios on an organization-wide basis. Others may provide more valuable information by calculating them on some other basis, such as by:

- Site
- Program or function
- Department
- Product line
- Employee

USEFUL RATIOS

There are many ratios and trends that provide valuable information about a nonprofit organization's operations. In this section, we'll list some of those ratios and trends that are frequently identified as being among the most useful to calculate and track over time. The ratios explained in this section fall into the following categories:

- Liquidity measures
- Funding ratios
- Operating ratios
- Ratios involving nonfinancial factors

The first two categories are primarily useful in terms of monitoring and evaluating an organization's performance. They may reveal signs of fraud, but only in terms of the fraud's effect on the big picture. The final two categories of ratios are the most useful for detecting individual fraud schemes. That is where most of our attention will be aimed.

Liquidity Measures

Maintaining an organization's liquidity is critical to its survival. Changes in liquidity ratios may indicate deterioration or improvement in an organization's ability to pay its bills and remain solvent. Negative trends also may be a sign that fraud is having an effect on the organization's ability to meet its current obligations. The following six measures each provide insight into a different aspect of an organization's liquidity:

1. *Cash ratio = cash and cash equivalents/current liabilities.* The cash ratio measures an organization's ability to cover its nearest-term financial obligations (accounts payable, accrued wages and payroll taxes, interest, and current loan payments) with available cash and investments that are easily converted to cash.

2. *Cash reserve ratio = cash and cash equivalents/total annual expenses.* The cash reserve ratio is similar to the cash ratio, but eliminates any existing seasonality of current liabilities by basing the calculation on total annual expenses. This ratio provides a measure of how long an organization could last without any additional inflow of revenue or cash from asset conversions. For instance, a cash reserve ratio of .50 indicates the organization could pay its bills for the next 6 months. One useful variation on this calculation utilizes total annual cash disbursements in place of expenses, which substitutes cash obligations, such as loan principal payments, in place of noncash expenses, such as depreciation and amortization. While the probability of having no future revenue may not be realistic, monitoring this ratio and setting goals is always appropriate.

3. *Current ratio = current assets/current liabilities.* The current ratio also measures an organization's ability to meet upcoming financial obligations, but utilizes a broader measure of the term "ability to meet" by including noncash current assets in the numerator.

4. *Net working capital = current assets – current liabilities.* Net working capital utilizes the same factors as the current ratio, but expresses the result as a single dollar amount rather than as a percentage or ratio. Generally, the ratio provides more useful data than the dollar amount, however, an organization should probably track both.

5. *Asset ratio = current assets/total assets.* The asset ratio measures an organization's asset mix. The higher the ratio, the more liquid an organization. Lower ratios indicate that an organization may have greater difficulty turning assets into cash if the need arises.

6. *Target liquidity level = cash and cash equivalents + short-term investments – short-term loans.* The target liquidity level is simply an amount, rather than a ratio, that organizations should establish as a target for liquidity. There are several variations on this calculation, such as eliminating short-term loans from the formula.

It's probably not necessary to track all six liquidity ratios. But it is a good idea to track at least two—one that monitors liquidity based on recorded liabilities and one that is based on an organization's expenses or operating budget. This provides two completely different types of insight into this important characteristic.

Funding Ratios

Funding ratios measure the extent to which an organization relies on a specific revenue source to fund its operations. Again, their primary goal is operational. Organizations should strive to avoid being overly dependent on one source or category of income. Examples of funding ratios include:

Contribution ratio = total contribution income/total revenue

Dues ratio = total member dues revenue/total revenue

Conferences ratio = total conference revenue/total revenue

Funding ratios should be calculated for each of an organization's sources of revenue. The higher any of these ratios, the more dependent the organization is on that particular source of revenue. A higher ratio indicates increased risk—an organization is putting all of its eggs in one basket. Diversification of revenue sources is an important part of establishing the long-term stability of an organization.

As a fraud detection tool, organizations should establish goals for their funding ratios and monitor progress toward those goals. Falling short of a particular goal could be a sign of a skimming fraud.

Operating Ratios

Operating ratios measure various aspects of an organization's operations. While their value as a management and goal-setting tool is obvious, they also have great value as a fraud detection tool. Some examples of useful operating ratios follow:

- *Program expense ratio = total program expenses/total expenses.* This ratio is important for most nonprofit organizations, but it also can be frequently overemphasized by many funding sources and regulators. The ratio measures what portion of an organization's operating budget is devoted to the pursuit of activities that directly accomplish its tax-exempt mission. Due to its broad nature, it may not be as valuable a fraud detection tool as some of the other ratios illustrated here. However, abrupt changes, particularly improvements in the ratio, could indicate that changes in accounting methods are being used to fraudulently inflate program expenses (see Chapter 9).
- *Support services expense ratio = total support services expenses/total expenses.* This ratio is directly related to the program expense ratio and measures the portion of an organization's operating budget spent on fundraising and administration, activities that do not directly accomplish the organization's tax-exempt mission. This ratio's value as a fraud detection tool is identical to that of the program expense ratio.

- *Return ratio = total support and revenue/total assets.* This measures the efficiency with which an organization utilizes its assets. Commercial businesses refer to this ratio as the asset turnover ratio because it measures the frequency with which the investment in total assets turns over into sales. While a nonprofit organization's objectives may be different, this ratio is of no less value. Declining ratios over time could indicate skimming (Chapter 3).
- *Net operating ratio = change in net assets/total support and revenue.* This measures the profit of the organization. The nonprofit goal may not be to maximize profit, but an organization must set aside funds for investment in the future, and this ratio measures how well the organization is doing at that. Declining ratios over time could indicate disbursements, payroll, or external frauds (Chapters 4 through 7), but could also be caused by skimming (Chapter 3).
- *Net asset reserve ratio = net assets/total expenses.* This ratio is similar to the cash reserve ratio described earlier, but measures it in terms of total net assets (not just cash) available to an organization. An alternative to this calculation considers only unrestricted net assets in the numerator and may exclude expenses funded with restricted net assets from the denominator. Declining ratios may indicate disbursements, payroll, or external frauds (Chapters 4 through 7), but could even be caused by skimming (Chapter 3).
- *Receivable turnover = net program revenue/average net accounts receivable.* This ratio measures the number of times accounts receivable is turned over during the year. It measures the time between on-account sales and collection of the funds. High ratios indicate prompt collections, low ratios indicate slower collection times. Declining ratios over time could indicate skimming frauds or lapping schemes (Chapter 3).
- *Collection ratio = 365/receivable turnover ratio.* This is another measure of the speed with which an organization collects on its accounts receivable. Increasing ratios over time indicate that an organization is collecting receivables more slowly. Increases also could indicate skimming or lapping schemes (Chapter 3).
- *Inventory turnover = cost of goods sold/average inventory.* This ratio measures the number of times inventory is sold during the year. Higher ratios are generally considered to be preferable than lower ratios. However, increasing ratios also could indicate that an inventory scheme is taking place (Chapter 6). If the potential exists for burying other expenditures in the cost of goods sold account, an increasing ratio could mean that some other form of disbursement or payroll fraud is occurring (Chapters 4 and 5).
- *Average days in inventory = 365/inventory turnover ratio.* This ratio restates the inventory turnover ratio in terms of days. Increasing ratios indicate

larger inventories and longer stays in inventory, which can increase an organization's storage and interest costs as well as increase exposure to inventory obsolescence and market fluctuations. Declining ratios, though preferable, also could be a sign of an inventory scheme (Chapter 6).

- *Employee productivity ratio = total support and revenue/total compensation.* This measure of productivity is similar to the asset utilization ratio, except it measures the utilization of employees instead of recorded assets. Declining ratios could reveal a skimming fraud (Chapter 3) or a payroll scheme (Chapter 5).

- *Fundraising efficiency = contribution income/fundraising expenses.* As its name implies, this ratio measures the effectiveness of individual fundraising campaigns or an entire fundraising function or department, based on how the ratio is calculated. Declining ratios could indicate skimming (Chapter 3), disbursement frauds concealed in the fundraising expense accounts (Chapter 4), or vendor frauds (Chapter 7). Increasing ratios could be the result of fraudulent financial reporting designed to understate fundraising expenses (Chapter 9).

- *Investment yield = investment income/average investment balance.* The ratio measures an organization's overall investment performance. When calculated separately for realized and unrealized gains and losses and for interest and dividends, these ratios may shed light on an organization's investment strategy and policies, as well as its individual investment manager. Deteriorating ratios also could indicate a vendor fraud in the form of an investment manager overcharging management or transaction fees (Chapter 7).

Ratios and Trends Involving Nonfinancial Factors

Some of the most useful ratios result from applying financial results to pertinent nonfinancial data. These ratios are sometimes the most useful of all as fraud detection tools. This is because a perpetrator must conceal their fraud not only in the accounting records, but in nonfinancial records as well. The odds of identifying frauds by analyzing these types of relationships improve substantially. A few examples of useful applications of this form of analysis include:

- *Unit revenue = total program revenue/total units sold.* Deteriorating ratios (for example, conference revenue divided by number of attendees) could indicate skimming frauds (Chapter 3) or inventory schemes (Chapter 6). Units sold could also refer to the total number of people served.

- *Employee efficiency = total support and revenue/total number of employees.* Declining ratios could be a sign of skimming (Chapter 3).

- *Average contribution = total contribution income/total number of donors.* Deteriorating ratios could be a warning sign of a skimming fraud (Chapter 3).

- *Fund-raising efficiency = fundraising expense/total number of donors.* Increasing ratios could signal a vendor fraud (Chapter 7) or a disbursement fraud concealed in the fundraising expense accounts (Chapter 4). Declining ratios could indicate a financial reporting fraud (Chapter 9). Another method of tracking this ratio is by using the total number of solicitations in the denominator in place of the total number of donors.

- *Unit costs = total program or activity costs/total units served.* This ratio correlates to the first ratio (unit revenue). Increasing ratios, indicating a rising cost of goods sold or cost per unit of service, could be a sign of disbursements or payroll fraud (Chapters 4 and 5), inventory schemes (Chapter 6), or vendor frauds (Chapter 7). It could also be a sign of fraudulent expense allocations to inflate the program expense ratio (Chapter 9).

- *Administrative efficiency = total administrative expenses/total number of employees.* Increasing ratios could indicate a variety of disbursements, payroll, or vendor schemes (Chapters 4, 5, and 7). Decreasing ratios could indicate a financial reporting fraud (Chapter 9).

Board members, managers, and auditors should consider whether there are any other nonfinancial statistics that would be expected to have a steady relationship with one or more financial or accounting statistics. Be creative and design ratios that are pertinent for your organization. You'll be amazed at the insight into your organization that is revealed and the value that these ratios can have in terms of analyzing an organization's operations. And you'll also (hopefully) sleep better knowing that you've taken another important step toward protecting the organization against fraud.

APPENDIXES

SAMPLE POLICIES, CHECKLISTS, AND OTHER RESOURCES

Appendix A: Sample Audit Committee Charter

Appendix B: Sample Code of Conduct

Appendix C: Sample Policy on Suspected Misconduct

Appendix D: Sample Conflict of Interest Policy

Appendix E: Standards for Charitable Accountability from the BBB Wise Giving Alliance

Appendix F: List of Useful Web Sites Relating to Controlling Fraud and Abuse

A

Sample Audit Committee Charter

PURPOSE

The primary responsibility for the Organization's financial reporting and internal controls rests with senior operating management, as overseen by the organization's Board of Directors (the "Board"). The purpose of the Audit Committee (the "Committee") is to assist the Board in fulfilling this responsibility.

AUTHORITY

In fulfilling its responsibilities, the Committee is empowered to investigate any matter brought to its attention with complete and unrestricted access to all books, records, documents, facilities, and personnel of the Organization. The Committee shall also have the power to retain outside counsel, auditors, investigators, or other experts in the fulfillment of its responsibilities. The Committee shall be provided with the resources necessary to discharge its responsibilities. The Board shall review the adequacy of this charter on an annual basis.

MEMBERSHIP

The Audit Committee shall be a standing committee of the Board of Directors, comprised of not less than three members of the Board. Members of the Committee shall:

- Have no relationship to the Organization that may interfere with the exercise of their independence from management and the Organization
- Be financially literate regarding the specialized matters of nonprofit organizations or shall acquire such financial literacy within a reasonable time period after appointment to the Committee

In addition, at least one member of the Committee shall have accounting or financial management expertise and experience.

RESPONSIBILITIES

The Committee's role is one of oversight, recognizing that the Organization's management is responsible for preparing the Organization's financial statements and that the external auditors are responsible for auditing those financial statements. The Committee recognizes that the Organization's internal financial management team, as well as the external auditors, have more time and detailed information about the Organization than do Committee members. Consequently, in discharging its oversight responsibilities, the Committee is not providing expert advice or any assurances as to the Organization's financial statements or any professional certification as to the external auditor's services.

The Committee shall have responsibilities in the areas of financial reporting, internal control, and organizational governance. In the areas of financial reporting and internal control, the Committee shall:

- Oversee the external audit process, including nomination of the external audit firm, auditor engagement letters and fees, timing and coordination of audit fieldwork visits, monitoring of audit results, review of auditor's performance, and review of nonaudit services provided by the external audit firm for compliance with professional independence standards.
- Review accounting policies.
- Review the organization's financial statements, including year end and interim financial statements, statements and reports required under the Single Audit Act and OMB Circular A-133 (if applicable), other reports requiring approval by the Board before submission to government agencies, and auditor opinions and management letters.
- Review annual information returns filed with the Internal Revenue Service and State government agencies.

- Determine that all required tax and information return filings with federal, state, and local government agencies are current.
- Receive and review any other communications from the external auditors that the external auditors are required to submit to the Board or Committee under currently applicable professional auditing standards.
- Review and discuss with management the findings and recommendations of the external auditor included in the management letter (and Schedule of Findings and Questioned Costs, if an OMB Circular A-133 audit is performed).
- Inquire about the existence and nature of significant audit adjustments proposed by the external auditors and significant estimates made by management.
- Meet privately with the external auditors to discuss the quality of management, financial, accounting, information technology, and internal audit personnel, and to determine whether any restrictions have been placed by management on the scope of their external audit or if there are any other matters that should be discussed with the Committee.
- Review the letter of management representations provided to the external auditors as part of the annual audit and inquire as to whether any difficulties were encountered in obtaining the representation letter.
- Prepare a report, signed by the chair of the Committee, for presentation to the full Board of Directors, describing the activities and responsibilities of the Committee.
- Direct special investigations into significant matters brought to its attention within the scope of its duties.
- Review this charter on an annual basis and propose any recommended changes to the Board.

In the area of organizational governance, the Committee shall:

- Review Organization policies regarding compliance with laws and regulations, ethics, employee conduct, conflicts of interest, and the investigation of misconduct or fraud.
- Review current and pending litigation or regulatory proceedings impacting organizational governance in which the Organization is a party.
- Review significant cases of employee or director conflict of interest, misconduct, or fraud.
- Review and approve the internal audit charter, which explains the framework for providing internal audit services to management and the Committee.
- Review and approve management's appointment and termination of the Organization's director of internal auditing.

- Review plans and budgets associated with the internal audit function to determine that audit objectives, plans, financial budgets, and schedules provide for adequate support of the Audit Committee's goals and objectives.
- Require the director of internal auditing to prepare a written report on an annual basis describing the scope and results of internal audit procedures.
- Discuss with the director of internal audit and the external audit firm the reliability of the Organization's information technology system and any specific security measures required to protect the Organization against fraud and abuse.
- Meet regularly with the Organization's general counsel to discuss legal matters that may have a significant impact on the Organization.

The Committee shall meet on a regular basis and call special meetings as deemed necessary in fulfilling the responsibilities described in this charter.

B

Sample Code of Conduct

This code of conduct requires that all officers, directors, employees, and volunteers of the organization must, in the course of carrying out the organization's activities:

- Behave honestly and with integrity.
- Act with care and diligence.
- Treat everyone with respect and courtesy, and without harassment.
- Comply with all applicable federal, state, and local laws and regulations.
- Comply with the organization's policies.
- Comply with all lawful and reasonable direction given by someone in the organization who has authority to give the direction.
- Never provide false, misleading, or incomplete information in response to a request for information that is made for official purposes.
- Use organization resources in a proper manner.
- Never make improper use of inside information or the employee's duties, status, power, or authority.
- Behave in a manner that upholds the organization's values and good reputation.
- Report all known or suspected violations of this code of conduct or other acts described in the organization's policy on suspected misconduct.

In the fulfillment of these requirements, every officer, director, employee, and volunteer of the organization should be able to unequivocally answer "yes" in response to each of the following questions with respect to all of their activities carried out as a representative of the organization:

- Is my action legal and in compliance with all applicable laws and regulations?
- Is my action ethical?
- Does my action comply with all organizational policies?
- Am I sure that my action does not in any way *appear* to be inappropriate to anyone who may observe my behavior?
- Am I certain that I would not be embarrassed or compromised if my action became known within the organization or publicly?
- Am I sure that my action meets my personal code of ethics and behavior?
- Would I feel comfortable defending my actions on the evening news?

In addition to being able to respond affirmatively to each of the preceding questions with respect to all your actions, you should strive to respond "yes" to one additional question with respect to as many activities as possible:

Does my action meet a standard of behavior that surpasses all enforceable laws, policies, and rules, to achieve an exemplary level of ethical behavior that the organization would be proud of?

Author's Note: This is an example of a broad organizational code of conduct that is short and to the point. Alternatively, many organizations craft more detailed codes of conduct that specifically identify each behavior that is prohibited (e.g., conflicts of interest, bribes, violations of laws, relationships with vendors, violence in the workplace, harassment, etc.). Either approach can be effective. If a shorter code of conduct like the one illustrated here is utilized, it should be supplemented with individual policies addressing specific prohibited behavior.

C

Sample Policy on Suspected Misconduct

INTRODUCTION

The purpose of this document is to communicate the policy of ABC Organization regarding actions to be taken with respect to suspected misconduct committed, encountered, or observed by employees and volunteers of ABC Organization.

Like all organizations, the ABC Organization faces many risks associated with fraud, abuse, and other forms of misconduct. The impact of these acts, collectively referred to as misconduct throughout this policy, may include, but not be limited to:

- financial losses and liabilities
- loss of current and future financial support
- negative publicity and damage to the organization's good public image
- loss of employees and volunteers and difficulty in attracting new personnel
- deterioration of employee and volunteer morale
- loss of program participants (or members, students, etc.)
- harm to the organization's relationships with funding sources, vendors, bankers, and subrecipients
- litigation and related costs of investigations

Our organization is committed to establishing and maintaining a work environment of the highest ethical standards. Achievement of this goal requires the cooperation and assistance of every employee and volunteer at all levels of the organization.

DEFINITIONS

For purposes of this policy, misconduct includes, but is not limited to:

- actions that violate the organization's Code of Conduct (and any underlying policies)
- fraud (see below)
- forgery or alteration of documents
- disclosure to any external party of proprietary information or confidential personal information obtained in connection with employment with or service to the organization
- unauthorized personal or other inappropriate (nonbusiness) use of the organization's equipment, assets, services, personnel, or other resources
- acts that violate federal, state, or local laws
- failure to report known instances of misconduct in accordance with the reporting responsibilities described herein (including tolerance by supervisory employees of misconduct of subordinates)

Fraud is further defined to include, but not limited to:

- theft, embezzlement, or other misappropriation of assets (including assets of or intended for the organization, as well as those of our donors, members, funding sources, subrecipients, vendors, contractors, suppliers, and others with whom the organization has a business relationship)
- intentional misstatements in the organization's records, including intentional misstatements of accounting records or financial statements, or of program accomplishments
- authorizing or receiving payment for goods not received or services not performed
- authorizing or receiving payments for hours not worked
- forgery or alteration of documents, including but not limited to checks, timesheets, contracts, purchase orders, receiving reports

It is the policy of ABC Organization to prohibit each of the preceding acts of misconduct on the part of organization employees, officers, executives, volunteers, and others responsible for carrying out the organization's activities.

REPORTING RESPONSIBILITIES

It is the responsibility of every employee, officer, and volunteer to immediately report suspected misconduct to their supervisor, Internal Audit, or the Audit Committee. Supervisors, when they have received a report of suspected misconduct, must immediately report such acts to their supervisor, Internal Audit, or the Audit Committee.

Any reprisal against a reporting individual because that individual, in good faith, reported a suspected act of misconduct, is prohibited and will, in turn, be considered a misconduct.

In order to facilitate the reporting of suspected misconduct, the organization has established a telephone hotline which can be accessed 24 hours a day by calling 1(800)XXX-XXXX. In addition, the chair of the Audit Committee can be contacted directly at (XXX)XXX-XXXX to report suspected misconduct at any level of the organization.

INVESTIGATIVE RESPONSIBILITIES

Proper handling of allegations is imperative. Due to the sensitive nature of suspected misconduct, supervisors and managers should not, under any circumstances, perform any investigative procedures.

The Internal Audit Department (or chief financial officer or other department/employee) has the primary responsibility for investigating suspected misconduct involving employees below the director (executive) level and all volunteers (other than board members and officers). A summary of all investigative work conducted by the Internal Audit Department shall be made available to the Audit Committee.

The Audit Committee has the primary responsibility for investigating suspected misconduct involving director (executive)-level positions, board members, and officers. The Audit Committee may request the assistance of the Internal Audit Department in any investigation.

Investigation into suspected misconduct will be performed without regard to the suspected individual's position, length of service, or relationship with the organization.

In fulfilling its investigative responsibilities, the Audit Committee shall have the authority to seek the advice and/or contract for the services of outside firms, including but not limited to law firms, CPA firms, forensic accountants and investigators, and so on.

Properly designated members of the investigative team (as authorized by the Audit Committee) shall have free and unrestricted access to all organization records and premises, whether owned or rented, at all times. They shall also have the authority to examine, copy, and remove all or any portion of the contents (in paper or electronic form) of filing cabinets, storage facilities, desks, credenzas, and computers without prior knowledge or consent of any individual who might use or have custody of any such items or facilities when it is within the scope of an investigation into suspected misconduct or related follow-up procedures.

Neither the existence nor the status or results of investigations into suspected misconduct shall be disclosed or discussed with any individual other than those with a legitimate need to know in order to perform their duties and fulfill their responsibilities effectively.

DISCIPLINARY ACTION

Based on the results of the investigations into allegations of misconduct, disciplinary action may be taken against violators. Disciplinary action will be coordinated with appropriate representatives from the Human Resources Department. The seriousness of the misconduct will be considered in determining appropriate disciplinary action, which may include:

- reprimand
- probation
- suspension
- demotion
- termination
- reimbursement of losses or damages
- referral for criminal prosecution or civil action

This listing of possible disciplinary actions is for information purposes only and does not bind the organization to follow any particular policy or procedure.

ACKNOWLEDGMENT

The undersigned, having read this policy on suspected misconduct, fully understand my responsibilities and agrees to carry out those responsibilities.

Signature:_____

Print Name:_____

Date:_____

Author's Note: This policy should be signed by all employees, officers, directors, and volunteers upon commencement of service and reaffirmed on an annual basis thereafter.

D

Sample Conflict of Interest Policy

INTRODUCTION

XYZ is a nonprofit organization led by the board of directors and with a duty to serve the public. In the course of business, situations may arise in which an XYZ decision-maker has a conflict of interest, or in which the process of making a decision may create an appearance of a conflict of interest.

All directors and employees have an obligation to:

1. Avoid conflicts of interest, or the appearance of conflicts, between their personal interests and those of the organization in dealing with outside entities or individuals.
2. Disclose real and apparent conflicts of interest to the board of directors.
3. Refrain from participation in any decisions on matters that involve a real conflict of interest or the appearance of a conflict.

WHAT CONSTITUTES A CONFLICT OF INTEREST

A conflict of interest arises when a director or employee involved in making a decision is in the position to benefit, directly or indirectly, from his or her dealings with the organization or person conducting business with the organization.

Examples of conflicts of interest include, but are not limited to, situations in which a director or employee of the organization:

- Negotiates or approves a contract, purchase, or lease on behalf of the organization and has a direct or indirect interest in, or receives personal benefit from, the company or individual providing the goods or services
- Negotiates or approves a contract, sale, or lease on behalf of the organization and has a direct or indirect interest in, or receives personal benefit from, the company or individual receiving the goods or services
- Employs or approves the employment of, on behalf of the organization, a person who is an immediate family member of the director or employee
- Approves or authorizes the organization to provide financial or other assistance to persons who are related to the employee or director
- Sells products or services offered by the organization in competition with the organization
- Uses the organization's facilities, other assets, employees, or other resources for personal gain
- Receives a substantial gift from a vendor, if the director or employee is responsible for initiating or approving purchases from that vendor

Interests are considered reportable as a possible conflict under this policy if they exceed 1 percent of the ownership or profits in a business or partnership.

DISCLOSURE REQUIREMENTS

The first step in addressing conflicts of interest is disclosure. A director or employee who believes that he or she may be perceived as having a conflict of interest in a discussion or decision must disclose that conflict to the group making the decision. Most concerns about conflicts of interest may be resolved and appropriately addressed through prompt and complete disclosure.

In furtherance of that objective, the organization has adopted the following requirements:

1. On an annual basis, all directors, the executive director, members of senior management, and employees with purchasing and/or hiring responsibilities or authority shall make a written disclosure to the executive director and the chair of the audit committee of all reportable conflicts.
2. Prior to the preparation of the disclosure statements, the accounting department shall distribute to the persons identified in the preceding step a list of all vendors with whom the organization has transacted business

at any time during the preceding year, along with a copy of the disclosure statement.

3. The executive director shall review all forms completed by employees, and the audit committee shall review all forms completed by directors and the executive director, and determine appropriate resolution in accordance with the next section of this policy.

RESOLUTION OF CONFLICTS OF INTEREST

All real or apparent conflicts of interest shall be disclosed to the audit committee and the executive director of the organization.

The audit committee shall be responsible for making all decisions concerning resolutions of conflicts involving directors or the executive director. Should the conflict involve a member of the audit committee other than the chair of the audit committee, the chair shall be responsible for making all decisions concerning resolutions of conflicts involving the audit committee member. Should the conflict involve the chair of the audit committee, the chair of the board shall be responsible for making all decisions concerning resolutions of the conflict.

The executive director shall be responsible for making all decisions concerning resolutions of conflicts involving employees, subject to the approval of the audit committee.

A director or employee may appeal a determination that an actual or apparent conflict of interest exists. The appeal must be directed to the chair of the board. Appeals must be made within 30 days of the initial determination. Resolution of the appeal shall be made by vote of the full board of directors. Board members who are the subject of the appeal, or who have a conflict of interest with respect to the subject of the appeal, shall abstain from participating in discussing or voting on the resolution, unless their discussion is requested by the remaining members of the board.

VIOLATIONS OF THIS POLICY

Given the importance of resolving conflicts of interest, violations of this policy, including failure to disclose conflicts of interest, may result in termination of a director, at the direction of the chair of the audit committee, or employee, at the direction of the executive director or chair of the audit committee.

E

Standards for Charitable Accountability from the BBB Wise Giving Alliance

GOVERNANCE AND OVERSIGHT

The governing board has the ultimate oversight authority for any charitable organization. This section of the standards seeks to ensure that the volunteer board is active, independent and free of self-dealing. To meet these standards, the organization shall have:

1. *A board of directors that provides adequate oversight of the charity's operations and its staff.* Indication of adequate oversight includes, but is not limited to, regularly scheduled appraisals of the CEO's performance, evidence of disbursement controls such as board approval of the budget, fund raising practices, establishment of a conflict of interest policy, and establishment of accounting procedures sufficient to safeguard charity finances.

2. *A board of directors with a minimum of five voting members.*

3. *A minimum of three evenly spaced meetings per year of the full governing body with a majority in attendance, with face-to-face participation.* A conference call of the full board can substitute for one of the three meetings of the governing body. For all meetings, alternative modes of participation are acceptable for those with physical disabilities.

4. *Not more than one or 10% (whichever is greater) directly or indirectly compensated person(s) serving as voting member(s) of the board. Compensated members shall not serve as the board's chair or treasurer.*

5. *No transaction(s) in which any board or staff members have* material *conflicting interests with the charity resulting from any relationship or business affiliation.* Factors that will be considered when concluding whether or not a related party transaction constitutes a conflict of interest and if such a conflict is material, include, but are not limited to: any arm's length procedures established by the charity; the size of the transaction relative to like expenses of the charity; whether the interested party participated in the board vote on the transaction; if competitive bids were sought and whether the transaction is one-time, recurring or ongoing.

MEASURING EFFECTIVENESS

An organization should regularly assess its effectiveness in achieving its mission. This section seeks to ensure that an organization has defined, measurable goals and objectives in place and a defined process in place to evaluate the success and impact of its program(s) in fulfilling the goals and objectives of the organization and that also identifies ways to address any deficiencies. To meet these standards, a charitable organization shall:

6. Have a board policy of assessing, no less than every two years, the organization's performance and effectiveness and of determining future actions required to achieve its mission.

7. Submit to the organization's governing body, for its approval, a written report that outlines the results of the aforementioned performance and effectiveness assessment and recommendations for future actions.

FINANCES

This section of the standards seeks to ensure that the charity spends its funds honestly, prudently and in accordance with statements made in fund raising appeals. To meet these standards, the charitable organization shall:

Please note that standards 8 and 9 have different *denominators.*

8. *Spend at least 65% of its total expenses on program activities.*

Formula for Standard 8:

$$\frac{\text{Total Program Service Expenses}}{\text{Total Expenses}} \text{ should be at least } 65\%$$

9. *Spend should be no more than 35% of* related *contributions on fund raising.* Related contributions include donations, legacies, and other gifts received as a result of fund raising efforts.

Formula for Standard 9:

Total Fund Raising Expenses
——————————————————— should be no more than 35%
Total Related Contributions

10. *Avoid accumulating funds that could be used for current program activities. To meet this standard, the charity's unrestricted net assets available for use should not be more than three times the size of the past year's expenses or three times the size of the current year's budget, whichever is higher.*

   An organization that does not meet Standards 8, 9 and/or 10 may provide evidence to demonstrate that its use of funds is reasonable. The higher fund raising and administrative costs of a newly created organization, donor restrictions on the use of funds, exceptional bequests, a stigma associated with a cause and environmental or political events beyond an organization's control are among factors which may result in expenditures that are reasonable although they do not meet the financial measures cited in these standards.

11. *Make available to all, on request, complete annual financial statements prepared in accordance with generally accepted accounting principles.* When total annual gross income exceeds $250,000, these statements should be audited in accordance with generally accepted auditing standards. For charities whose annual gross income is less than $250,000, a review by a certified public accountant is sufficient to meet this standard. For charities whose annual gross income is less than $100,000, an internally produced, complete financial statement is sufficient to meet this standard.

12. *Include in the financial statements a breakdown of expenses (e.g., salaries, travel, postage, etc.) that shows what portion of these expenses was allocated to program, fund raising, and administrative activities.* If the charity has more than one major program category, the schedule should provide a breakdown for each category.

13. *Accurately report the charity's expenses, including any joint cost allocations, in its financial statements.* For example, audited or unaudited statements which inaccurately claim zero fund raising expenses or otherwise understate the amount a charity spends on fund raising, and/or overstate the amount it spends on programs will not meet this standard.

14. *Have a board-approved annual budget for its current fiscal year, outlining projected expenses for major program activities, fund raising, and administration.*

FUND RAISING AND INFORMATIONAL MATERIALS

A fund raising appeal is often the only contact a donor has with a charity and may be the sole impetus for giving. This section of the standards seeks to ensure that a charity's representations to the public are accurate, complete and respectful. To meet these standards, the charitable organization shall:

15. *Have solicitations and informational materials, distributed by any means, that are accurate, truthful and not misleading, both in whole and in part.* Appeals that omit a clear description of program(s) for which contributions are sought will not meet this standard.

    A charity should also be able to substantiate that the timing and nature of its expenditures are in accordance with what is stated, expressed, or implied in the charity's solicitations.

16. *Have an annual report available to all, on request, that includes:*

    a.   *the organization's mission statement,*

    b.   *a summary of the past year's program service accomplishments,*

    c.   *a roster of the officers and members of the board of directors,*

    d.   *financial information that includes (i) total income in the past fiscal year, (ii) expenses in the same program, fund raising and administrative categories as in the financial statements, and (iii) ending net assets.*

17. *Include on any charity websites that solicit contributions, the same information that is recommended for annual reports, as well as the mailing address of the charity and electronic access to its most recent IRS Form 990.*

18. *Address privacy concerns of donors by:*

    a.   *providing in written appeals, at least annually, a means (e.g., such as a check off box) for both new and continuing donors to inform the charity if they do not want their name and address shared outside the organization, and*

    b.   *providing a clear, prominent and easily accessible privacy policy on any of its websites that tells visitors (i) what information, if any, is being collected about them by the charity and how this information will be used, (ii) how to contact the charity to review personal information collected and request corrections, (iii) how to inform the charity (e.g., a check off box) that the visitor does not wish his/her personal information to be shared outside the organization, and (iv) what security measures the charity has in place to protect personal information.*

19. *Clearly disclose how the charity benefits from the sale of products or services (i.e., cause-related marketing) that state or imply that a charity will benefit from a consumer sale or transaction. Such promotions should disclose, at the point of solicitation:*

a. the actual or anticipated portion of the purchase price that will benefit the charity (e.g., 5 cents will be contributed to abc charity for every xyz company product sold),

b   the duration of the campaign (e.g., the month of October),

c. any maximum or guaranteed minimum contribution amount (e.g., up to a maximum of $200,000).

20. Respond promptly to and act on complaints brought to its attention by the BBB Wise Giving Alliance and/or local Better Business Bureaus about fund raising practices, privacy policy violations and/or other issues.

Source: *Standards for Charitable Accountability* reprinted with permission. Copyright 2003. BBB Wise Giving Alliance, 4200 Wilson Blvd., Arlington, VA 22203, www.give.org.

F

List of Useful Web Sites Relating to Controlling Fraud and Abuse

The following Web sites either have information directly relating to prevention and detection of fraud and abuse or address issues that are vulnerable to fraud and abuse, as discussed elsewhere in this book:

Alliance of Nonprofit Mailers—www.nonprofitmailers.org

American Institute of Certified Public Accountants—www.aicpa.org

American Institute of Philanthropy—www.charitywatch.org

Association of Certified Fraud Examiners—www.cfenet.com

Association of Fundraising Professionals—www.afpnet.org

BBB Wise Giving Alliance—www.give.org
BoardSource—www.boardsource.org

Charity Navigator—www.charitynavigator.org

EthicsLine—www.ethicsline.com

Financial Accounting Standards Board—www.fasb.org
Financial Executives International—www.fei.org

FraudNet (e-mail at General Accounting Office)—fraudnet@gao.gov

General Accounting Office—www.gao.gov

GuideStar—www.guidestar.org

IGNet (Inspectors General)—www.ignet.gov

Independent Sector—www.independentsector.org

Information Systems Audit and Control Association—www.isaca.org

The Institute of Internal Auditors—www.theiia.org

Institute of Management Accountants—www.imanet.org

Internal Revenue Service—www.irs.gov

Management Assistance Program for Nonprofits—www.mapnp.org

Multistate Tax Commission—www.mtc.gov

National Association of College and University Business
    Officers—www.nacubo.org

National Association of Corporate Directors—www.nacdonline.org

National Association of State Charity Officials—www.nasconet.org

National White Collar Crime Center—www.nw3c.org

The Network—www.tnwinc.com

Nonprofit Risk Management Center—www.nonprofitrisk.org

Society for Human Resource Management—www.shrm.org

U.S. Office of Management and Budget—www.whitehouse.gov/OMB/

Wall Watchers' Ministry Watch—www.ministrywatch.com

Bibliography

American Institute of Certified Public Accountants. *AICPA Audit and Accounting Guide: Not-for-Profit Organizations*. New York: AICPA, 2002.

American Institute of Certified Public Accountants. *Statement of Position 98-2: Accounting for Costs of Activities of Not-for-Profit Organizations and State and Local Governmental Entities That Include Fund Raising*. New York: AICPA, March 11, 1998.

American Institute of Certified Public Accountants. *Statement on Auditing Standards No. 99, Consideration of Fraud in a Financial Statement Audit*. New York: AICPA, October 2002.

Association of Certified Fraud Examiners. *2002 Report to the Nation, Occupational Fraud and Abuse*. Austin, TX: ACFE, 2002.

Association of Certified Fraud Examiners. *Report to the Nation on Occupational Fraud and Abuse*. Austin, TX: ACFE, 1996.

Burke, Frank M., and Guy, Dan M. *Audit Committees: A Guide for Directors, Management, and Consultants*, Second Edition. New York: Aspen Publishers, Inc., 2002.

Duca, Diane J. *Nonprofit Boards: Roles, Responsibilities, and Performance*. New York: John Wiley & Sons, Inc., 1996.

Eisenberg, Bernie, and Johnson, Esq., Linda. "Being Honest about Being Dishonest." *SHRM White Paper*, Society for Human Resource Management, March 2001.

Elzey, Laura. "Criminal Background Checks: a Checklist of the Pros and Cons." *SHRM White Paper*, Society for Human Resource Management, April 2002.

Gamble, Richard H. "Short Circuiting Wire Transfer Fraud." *Controller Magazine*, August 1998.

General Accounting Office. *SEPTEMBER 11, Interim Report on the Response of Charities*. GAO, September 2002.

Independent Sector. *Obedience to the Unenforceable*. Washington, DC, Revised 2002.

KPMG. *KPMG 1998 Fraud Survey*. KPMG, 1998.

Kurtz, Daniel L. *Managing Conflicts of Interest*. Washington, DC: National Center for Nonprofit Boards (now BoardSource), 2001.

Maddox, David. *Budgeting for Not-for-Profit Organizations*. New York: John Wiley & Sons, Inc., 1999.

National Health Council, Inc. and National Assembly of National Voluntary Health and Welfare Organizations, Inc. *Standards of Accounting and Financial Reporting for Voluntary Health and Welfare Organizations, Fourth Edition*, Dubuque, IA: Kendall/Hunt Publishing Company, 1998.

Patterson, James, and Peter Kim. *The Day America Told the Truth*. New York: Prentice Hall Publishing, 1991.

Romney, Marshall B. *Fraud-Related Internal Controls*. Austin, TX: Association of Certified Fraud Examiners, 2001.

United States Postal Service. *Nonprofit Standard Mail Eligibility (Publication 417)*. U.S Postal Service, October 1996.

Wells, Joseph T. *Occupational Fraud and Abuse*. Austin, TX: Obsidian Publishing Company, 1997.

Zack, Gerard M. *Accounting & Audit Issues of Nonprofit Organizations*. Rockville, MD: Nonprofit Resource Center and Williams Young, LLC, 1992–2002.

Index

A

Accountability, 14–15, 289–292
Accounts receivable, 57–59
Agents (agency), 165, 170–171
Airfare schemes, 111–113
Alliance of Nonprofit Mailers, 221
Allowability of costs, 209–211
Altered payee schemes, 81–83
American Association of Fund
    Raising Counsel, 180
American Bar Foundation, 66
American Cancer Society, 85, 233
American Federation of Teachers,
    69
American Institute of Certified
    Public Accountants (AICPA),
    16, 191, 272, 304, 319
American Institute of Philanthropy,
    188
American Management Associa-
    tion, 120
American Red Cross, 13, 174
Analytical procedures, 318–324
Asset misappropriations, 6–7,
    115–118, 121–126
Association of Certified Fraud Ex-
    aminers (ACFE), xiii, 5–6,
    9–10, 261, 264, 265, 301, 307
Association of Fundraising Profes-
    sionals, 180

Association of Personnel Test Pub-
    lishers, 239
Audit committees, 298–301,
    305–307, 333–336
Auditors:
    External, 3-1-307
    Internal, 307–308

B

Bad debt write-offs, 59
Background checks, 227, 232–236
Bank reconciliations, 86
Baptist Foundation of Arizona, xiv
BBB Wise Giving Alliance, 14–15,
    187, 188, 292, 346, 350
Bid-rigging, 94–96
Billing schemes:
    External, 128–134
    Internal, 68–75
Board committees, 297–298
Board of directors, 293–313
Bribery, 92
Budgeting, 314–318

C

Capital Area United Way, 82
Catalog of Federal Domestic Assistance
    (CFDA), 149

Central Bering Sea Fishermen's As-
  sociation, 310–311
Charitable contributions:
  Skimming of, 43–49
Charity Navigator, 188
Check tampering, 81–85
Check washing, 81
Check-writing, 67
Children's Wish Foundation Inter-
  national, 200
Code of conduct, 337–338
Code of Federal Regulations, 207
Commission schemes, 105–106
Communication systems, 261–265
Compensation adjustments, 245
Concealment, 24
Conference revenue, 54
Conflicts of interest, 88–92, 308,
  343–345
Consumers Union, 93
Copyright Act, 225–227
Corruption, 7, 64
Cost allocation, 198
Credit card abuse, 69–71
Credit checks (reports), 69,70
Credits, 60
Criminal records checks, 232–236
Crisis management, 284–289,
  309–312

D
Data access controls, 254–255
Data input controls, 256–257
Data transmission controls,
  255–256
Desk reviews, 150
Detective controls, 18, 28–29
Disaster recovery, 260
Disbursement schemes, 64
Discounts, 60
Donated assets, valuation of,
  165–167
Donated merchandise theft,
  61–63

Donor Bill of Rights, 180–181
Donor control, 175
Donor restrictions, 172–176
Dual control, 44–46, 54, 62
Due diligence, 276–277
Duplicate payments, 72–73,
  110–111

E
Economic interest, 202
Electronic Communications Pri-
  vacy Act of 1986 (ECPA),
  120–121
Electronic funds transfer, 85–88
Employee dishonesty bonds,
  265–267
Employee orientation, 240–241
Encryption, 88, 256
Endorsements, 40, 73
Ernst & Young, LLP, xiii, 103, 115,
  262
Ethicsline, 264
Evidence preservation, 286
Excess benefit transactions, 290
Exit interviews, 247–248
Expense reporting schemes,
  107–114
External frauds, 7–8, 127–154

F
Fair Labor Standards Act (FLSA),
  223–225
False Billings, 95
False Claims Act, 211, 212–213
False Claims Amendment Act of
  1986, 213
False statements, 9
Family & Medical Leave Act, 241
Federal Credit Reporting Act
  (FCRA), 235
Federal Sentencing Guidelines,
  276–277
Fictitious expenditures, 109–110

Fictitious vendors, 73–75
Fidelity bonds, 265–267
Financial Accounting Standards
     Board (FASB), 16, 201
Financial aid (assistance) schemes,
     79–81, 153–155
Financial analysis, 318–329
Financial controls, 26–29, 195–197
Financial reporting fraud, 183–205
Fondest Wish Foundation, 163
Forgery, 81, 82
Form 990, 14, 188–189, 215, 246,
     290
Foundation for New Era Philan-
     thropy, xiv
FraudNet, 264
Funding ratios, 326
Fundraising activities:
     Deceptive, 162–179
     Ethics in, 179–181
     Expenses, 189–199, 210
     Use of proceeds from, 176–179

G
General Accounting Office (GAO),
     12–13, 154, 264
Generally accepted accounting
     principles, 302
Ghost employees, 99–102
Goodwill Industries of Santa Clara
     County, 61
Government Auditing Standards, 299,
     304
Government grants, 206–211
Grassley, Sen. Charles, 13–14,
     154
Grievance policies, 246–247
GuideStar, 188, 246

H
Hermandad Legal Center, 212
Hiring practices, 232–240
Honesty testing, 239

Hotlines, 261–265
Human resource systems, 231–248

I
Identity theft, 227, 237, 250, 251
Identity verification, 236–237
Independent Sector, 291, 351
Information technology systems,
     252–261
Insurance, 265–267
Intent, 19
Internal audit, 307–308
Internal controls, *see* financial con-
     trols
Internal frauds, 6–7, 37–126
Internal Revenue Code, 4
Internal Revenue Service (IRS),
     13–14, 166, 170, 289
Inventory schemes, 121–126

J
Joint costs, 191–198

K
Kelley Blue Book, 166
Kickbacks, 92–93, 95
KPMG, 10

L
Lapping schemes, 57–59
Late fees, 49
Leave policies, 241–243
Liquidity measures, 324–325
Lobbying, 210
Lockbox services, 44

M
Mail fraud, 9
Management oversight, 30
Materiality, 303

Maui Foodbank, 233
Meeting revenue, 54–55
Membership dues revenue,
    50–53
Mississippi College, 44
Monitoring:
    Employee communications,
        119–121
    Subrecipients, 146–153
Motive, 19–22, 158
Multiple Sclerosis Association of
    America, 165, 168, 196
Multistate Tax Commission, 220
Muncie Public Library, 49

N
New York Public Radio, 251
New York University, 79
Noncash contributions, 199–201
Nonprofit mailing rates, 220–221
Nonprofit Risk Management Cen-
    ter, 267

O
Occupational fraud, 6
Odyssey House, 95
Office of Management and Budget
    (OMB):
    Circular A-21, 209
    Circular A-87, 210
    Circular A-110, 145
    Circular A-122, 209–210
    Circular A-133, 12, 145, 207,
        299, 304, 306, 334
Ogden (UT) Chamber of Com-
    merce, 288
On-site registrations, 54
Operating ratios, 326–328
Opportunity, 22–23
Outsourcing, 134–145

Overstatement of hours worked,
    103–104
Overstatement of pay rates,
    104–105

P
Pass-through entity, 145–147
Passwords, 254–255
Payroll schemes, 97–107
Payroll withholding schemes,
    106–107
Pell grants, 209
Performance evaluations,
    244–245
Perpetual inventory, 123
Phony checks, 83–85
Phony identification, 155
Physical inventories, 124–125
Physical security, 249–250, 254
Pinkerton, 264
Positive pay, 83
Ponzi schemes, xiv
Preventive controls, 18, 28
Private benefit, 175
Program fraud, 215–217
Property and equipment schemes,
    115–118
Property tax exemption, 221–222
Public records searches, 236–238
Purchase orders, 73

Q
Qualifications fraud, 240

R
Ratio analysis, 323–329
Rationalization, 25
Reasonableness testing, 51, 52, 55,
    319, 322

Refund schemes, 77–79
Related party transactions,
    203–206
Requests for proposals, 96,
    129–132
Reportable conditions, 306
Reporting:
    Financial, 182–189
    Fraudulent, 182–213
Restrictions, 172–176
Retail sales, 56
Risk management, 25
Rotation of duties, 47, 58, 62

S
Sales tax exemption, 217–220
Sarbanes-Oxley Act of 2002, 9, 12,
    263, 283
School for Careers, 209
Segregation (separation) of duties,
    38–40, 65, 68, 78, 98, 104, 116,
    122, 208, 216, 253
Service organizations, 134–145
Sexual offender records, 236, 238
Shorting, 121–122
Single Audit Act, 12, 207, 299,
    334
Skimming, 41–57
Society for Human Resource Man-
    agement, 239
Softloading, 226
Software controls, 257–258
Software piracy, 226
Standards for Charitable Account-
    ability, 346–350
Statement of Financial Accounting
    Standards No. 57, 203–206
Statement of Financial Accounting
    Standards No. 136, 201–203
Statement of Position (SOP) 98–2,
    191–195

Statement on Auditing Standards
    No. 56, 319–320
Statement on Auditing Standards
    No. 99, 35, 272–273, 304–305
Subrecipients:
    Monitoring of, 146–153
    Fraud committed by, 145–146
    Risk assessments of, 147–148
Suspected misconduct, policy on,
    339–342

T
Taxpayer Bill of Rights 2 Act, 290
Telemarketers, 168
Third-party reviews, 142–143
Timesheets, 103–104, 119
Training, 243, 278–279
Transparency, 289–292
Travel schemes, 111–113
Trend analysis, 322–323

U
Uncollectible accounts, 59
United Way of America, 15
United Way of the National Capital
    Area, 13, 16, 312
University of Nevada Medical
    School, 82
Unrecorded sales, 60
Unrelated business income tax, 218
U.S. Postal Service, 220–221
U.S. Sentencing Commission, 277

V
Variance analysis, 315–318
Variance power, 202
Vendor fraud, 128–134
Voluntary health and welfare orga-
    nization, 184–185

W

Wall Watchers' Ministry Watch, 188

Washington Teachers' Union, 69

Wells, Joseph T., 276–277

Whistleblower protection, 263, 283

Wire fraud, 9

Wishing Well Foundation, 163

Z

Zero-based budgeting, 315–316